Legal Culture, Legality and the I
the Grounds of Judicial Review
Action in England and Australia

Voraphol Malsukhum

Legal Culture, Legality and the Determination of the Grounds of Judicial Review of Administrative Action in England and Australia

Springer

Voraphol Malsukhum
Faculty of Law
Chulalongkorn University
Bangkok, Thailand

ISBN 978-981-16-1269-5   ISBN 978-981-16-1267-1 (eBook)
https://doi.org/10.1007/978-981-16-1267-1

© The Editor(s) (if applicable) and The Author(s), under exclusive license to Springer Nature Singapore Pte Ltd. 2021

This work is subject to copyright. All rights are solely and exclusively licensed by the Publisher, whether the whole or part of the material is concerned, specifically the rights of translation, reprinting, reuse of illustrations, recitation, broadcasting, reproduction on microfilms or in any other physical way, and transmission or information storage and retrieval, electronic adaptation, computer software, or by similar or dissimilar methodology now known or hereafter developed.

The use of general descriptive names, registered names, trademarks, service marks, etc. in this publication does not imply, even in the absence of a specific statement, that such names are exempt from the relevant protective laws and regulations and therefore free for general use.

The publisher, the authors, and the editors are safe to assume that the advice and information in this book are believed to be true and accurate at the date of publication. Neither the publisher nor the authors or the editors give a warranty, expressed or implied, with respect to the material contained herein or for any errors or omissions that may have been made. The publisher remains neutral with regard to jurisdictional claims in published maps and institutional affiliations.

This Springer imprint is published by the registered company Springer Nature Singapore Pte Ltd.
The registered company address is: 152 Beach Road, #21-01/04 Gateway East, Singapore 189721, Singapore

For my Parents

Preface

This book presents a navigating framework of legal culture and legality to facilitate a comprehensive understanding of the English and Australian determination of the grounds of judicial review. It is demonstrated that the distinctive constitutional orders embedded in the legal cultures of England and Australia influence the courts' deep understanding of what legality means and covers, and whether the issue in a disputed administrative action is one in which they have a proper role to intervene or not. These different understandings result in the English and Australian courts adhering to different modes of doctrinal approach and legal reasoning when determining the grounds of judicial review, namely, error of law, jurisdictional error, jurisdictional fact, rationality, proportionality and substantive legitimate expectations.

On the one hand, the English courts have flexibility to apply various justifications, doctrines and applications in their determination of the mentioned grounds of judicial review. These are products of the English legal culture based on the absence of a written constitution, the balancing process between parliamentary sovereignty and the rule of law, and the fluid separation of powers between court and executive. On the other hand, the Australian courts apply a pattern of relatively fixed doctrinal approach and legal reasoning to determine these grounds under the central approach of jurisdictional error. This is because, whether empowered or limited, they rigidly follow the framework of separation of powers prescribed in the written constitution, discussed as distinctive element of the Australian legal culture.

While a number of works in this field compare the advantages and disadvantages of the approaches within and between the English and Australian laws and occasionally describe them with the labels of pragmatism and formalism, a tangible process is facilitated in this book of how and why jurisdictional error, jurisdictional fact, rationality, proportionality and substantive legitimate expectations fluctuate and are debatable in English law, whereas they are either completely rejected or firmly entrenched in Australian law. It is argued that these differences are not just random. Legality is not just a fig-leaf, but is profoundly rooted in legal systems' legal culture; hence, it dictates the way in which courts empower, justify, constrain or limit the scope of judicial review.

Bangkok, Thailand   Voraphol Malsukhum

Voraphol Malsukhum is currently a lecturer at Chulalongkorn University, Bangkok, Thailand, teaching an array of public law courses and conducting a variety of research in the field of Comparative Administrative Law.

Table of Cases

UK Cases

A v Secretary of State for the Home Department [2013] EWHC 1272	114
Anisminic Ltd v Foreign Compensation Commission [1969] 2 AC 147	12, 14, 24, 93–94, 103–106, 109–110, 112, 118–120, 123, 126, 129, 144, 149–150, 152, 173, 253
Arlidge v Local Government Board [1915] AC 120	55, 109
Associated Provincial Pictures Houses Ltd v Wednesbury Corporation [1948] 1 KB 223	58, 175, 178–180, 182, 185, 187, 200, 226, 253
Attorney General of Hong Kong v Ng Yuen Shiu [1983] 2 AC 629	216, 221, 224, 242
Bank Mellatt v HM Treasury (No 2) [2013] UKSC 38	183, 197
Belfast City Council v Miss Behavin' Ltd [2007] 1 WLR 1420	187
Boddington v British Transport Commission [1999] 2 AC 143	123
Bugdaycay v Secretary of State for the Home Department [1987] 1 AC 514	186, 191, 212
Bunbury v Fuller (1853) 9 Ex 111	105, 156
Chief Constable of the North Wales Police v Evans [1982] 1 WLR 1155	145
Council of Civil Service Unions v Minister for the Civil Service [1985] AC 374	2, 4, 176, 186, 191
Dowty Boulton Paul Ltd v Wolverhampton Corporation (No 2) [1976] Ch13	152
E v Secretary of State for the Home Department [2004] EWCA Civ 49	14, 141, 143, 152–154, 252
Finucane [2019] UKSC 7	231

(continued)

IBA Healthcare Ltd v Office of Fair Trading [2004] ICR 1364	193
re Findlay [1985] AC 318	222, 227
R (Guardian News and Media Ltd) v City of Westminster Magistrates' Court [2013] QB 618	190
R v Chief Constable of Sussex Ex parte International Trader's Ferry Ltd [1999] 2 AC 418	66
Kennedy v Charity Commission [2014] UKSC 20	11, 15, 175, 177, 182, 184, 188–197, 199, 204, 210, 253
Keyu v Secretary of State for Foreign and Commonwealth Affairs [2015] UKSC 69	197
Kruse v Johnson [1898] 2 QB 91	7, 180
Lumba v Secretary of State for the Home Department [2011] UKSC 12	123
Nadarajah Abdi v The Secretary of State for the Home Department [2005] EWCA Civ 1363	216–217, 230, 234, 253
O'Reilly v Mackman [1983] 2 AC 237	109–110, 123, 145
Pearlman v Keepers and Governors of Harrow School [1979] QB 56	109
Pham v Secretary of State for the Home Department [2015] UKSC 19	11, 15, 175, 177, 182, 184, 188, 194–197, 199, 210, 253
Phillips v Upper Tribunal (Tax and Chancery Chamber) [2013] EWHC 2934	114
Piglowska v Piglowski [1999] 1 WLR 1360	145
Privacy International v SSFCA [2016] UKIP Trib 14_85-CH	114
Privacy International v Investigatory Powers Tribunal [2017] EWHC 114 (Admin)	114
Privacy International v Investigatory Powers Tribunal [2017] EWCA Civ 1868	115
R (Privacy International) v Investigatory Powers Tribunal [2019] UKSC 22	14, 93–94, 96–97, 101–103, 110, 114–123, 131–133, 252
Puhlhofer v Hillingdon London Borough Council [1986] 1 AC 484	10, 141, 152
R (A) v Croydon LBC [2009] UKSC 8	14, 141, 149, 155–158, 165, 253
R (Alconbury Developments Ltd) v Secretary of State for the Environment [2001] 2 WLR 1389	186–187
R (A) v Director of Establishments of the Security Service [2009] EWCA Civ 24	116
R (Jackson) and Ors v HM Attorney General [2005] EWCA Civ 126	4
R (Jones) v First-tier Tribunal [2013] UKSC 19	11, 14, 19, 141–143, 149, 158–159, 161, 165, 174, 253
R (Moseley) v Haringey London Borough Council [2014] UKSC 56	10
R (Osborn) v Parole Board [2013] UKSC 61	67

(continued)

Table of Cases xi

R (Quila) v Secretary of State for the Home Department [2011] UKSC 45	186
R (Tran) v Secretary of State for the Home Department [2005] EWCA Civ 982	154
R (Ullah) v Special Adjudicator [2004] UKHL 26	67
R v Board of Education [1910] 2 KB 165	109, 180
R v Bolton (1841) 1 QB 66	105
R v Cambridge Health Authority, Ex parte B [1995] 2 All ER 129	179
R v Criminal Injuries Compensation Board, Ex parte A [1999] 2 AC 330	148, 153
R v Fulham, Hammersmith and Kensington Rent Tribunal, Ex parte Philippe [1950] 2 All ER 211	104
R v Fulham, Hammersmith and Kensington Rent Tribunal, Ex parte Zerek [1951] 2 KB 1	150
R v Higher Education Funding Council, Ex parte Institute of Dental Surgery [1994] 1 WLR 242	11
R v Home Secretary, Ex parte Khan [1984] 1 WLR 1337	216
R v Liverpool Corporation, Ex parte Liverpool Taxi Fleet Operators' Association [1972] 2 QB 299	221
R v Ministry of Defence, Ex parte Smith [1996] QB 517	185, 191
R v North and East Devon Health Authority, Ex parte Coughlan [2000] 3 All ER 850	2, 12, 15, 191, 215–217, 220–221, 225–232, 240, 243, 253
R v Northumberland Compensation Appeal Tribunal, Ex parte Shaw [1952] 1 KB 338	104–105
R v Roberts, Ex parte Scurr [1924] 1 KB 514	58
R v Secretary of State for the Home Department, Ex parte Fire Brigades Union [1995] 2 AC 513	59
R v Secretary for the Home Department, Ex parte Hargreaves [1997] 1 WLR 906	217, 225–227, 229, 253
R v Secretary for the Home Department, Ex parte Zamir [1980] AC 930	150
R v Secretary of State for Education and Employment, Ex parte Begbie [2000] 1 WLR 1115	176, 216–217, 229–230
R v Secretary of State for the Home Department, Ex parte Daly [2001] 2 AC 532	186
R v Secretary of State for the Home Department, Ex parte Ruddock (1987) 1 WLR 1482	238
R v Secretary of State for Transport, Ex parte Richmond-Upon-Thames London Borough Council [1994] 1 WLR 74	15, 215, 217, 221–225, 253
R v Ministry of Agriculture, Fisheries and Food, Ex parte Hamble Fisheries Ltd [1995] 2 All E R 714	15, 215–217, 223–226, 230–231, 246, 253
R v Monopolies and Mergers Commission, Ex parte South Yorkshire Transport Ltd [1993] 1 WLR 23	160

(continued)

R v Secretary of State for Foreign and Commonwealth Affairs, Ex parte World Development Movement Ltd [1995] 1 WLR 386	10
R v Secretary of State for the Home Department, Ex parte Brind [1991] 1 AC 696	183, 193
R v Secretary of State for the Home Department, Ex parte Khawaja [1984] AC 74	14, 141, 143, 149–152, 155–156, 158, 253
re Racal Communications Ltd [1981] AC 374	94, 109
R v Inland Revenue Commission, Ex parte Preston [1985] AC 835	222
R v Inland Revenue Comrs, Ex parte Unilever plc [1996] STC 681	230
R (Bibi) v Newham London Borough Council [2002] 1 WLR 237	217, 230
R (Cart) v Upper Tribunal [2009] EWHC 3052	14, 58, 96, 111–112, 116, 119
R (Cart) v Upper Tribunal [2010] EWCA Civ 859	14, 58, 96, 111
R (Cart) v Upper Tribunal [2011] UKSC 28	11–12, 14, 16, 18–19, 22, 58, 63, 93–97, 101–103, 110–116, 118, 120, 122–123, 126, 131–133, 153, 159, 189, 252–253
R (Miller) v Secretary of State for Exiting the European Union [2017] UKSC 5	66
R (Animal Defenders International) v Secretary of State for Culture, Media and Sport [2008] 1 AC 1312	186
R (Rogers) v Swindon NHS Primary Care Trust [2006] 1 WLR 2649	179
R v Lord President of the Privy Council, Ex parte Page [1993] AC 682	4, 93–94, 109, 122, 145, 150
Schmidt v Secretary of State for Home Affairs [1969] 2 WLR 337	221
Secretary of State for Education and Science v Tameside MBC [1977] AC 1014	153, 197
Sharp v Wakefield [1891] AC 173	7, 208
Short v Poole Corporation [1926] Ch 66	185
Terry v Huntington (1679) Hardr 480	147
Thoburn v Sunderland City Council [2002] EWHC 195	52, 65
United Policyholders Group v Attorney General of Trinidad and Tobago [2016] UKPC 17	15, 215–217, 225, 230–232
White and Collins v Minister of Health [1939] 2 KB 838	150
Williams v Giddy [1911] AC 381	180
X Ltd v Morgan-Grampian Ltd [1991] 1 AC 1	56

Australian Cases

Anor and Gedeon v Commissioner of the New South Wales Crime Commission (2008) 236 CLR 120	171
Anvil Hill Project Watch Association Inc v Minister for the Environment and Water Resources [2007] FCA 1480	14, 143, 168–169, 171–172, 254
Attorney-General (NSW) v Quin (1990) 170 CLR 1	15, 166, 179, 182, 215, 217, 223, 234, 236–238, 241, 243
Australian Broadcasting Tribunal v Bond (1990) 170 CLR 321	145, 147, 202
Australian Communist Party v Commonwealth (1951) 83 CLR 1	74
Australian Heritage Commission v Mount Isa Mines Ltd (1997) 187 CLR 297	162
Barrick Australian v Williams (2009) 74 NSWLR 733	12, 171
Caterpillar of Australian Pty Ltd v Industrial Court of New South Wales (2009) 78 NSWLR 43	171
Church of Scientology v Woodward 154 CLR 25	78
Corporation of the City of Enfield v Development Assessment Commission (2000) 199 CLR 135	14, 141, 143–144, 147, 154, 161, 165–169, 172–174, 200, 203, 206, 254
Craig v The State of South Australia (1995) 184 CLR 163	14, 93–95, 101–102, 121, 125–128, 132–133, 135, 138, 254
Dietrich v The Queen (1992) 177 CLR 292	126
FAI Insurances Ltd v Winneke (1982) 151 CLR 342	209
Fiorentino v Companies Auditors and Liquidators Disciplinary Board [2014] FCA 641	210
Griffiths v Rose (2011) 192 FCR 130	200
Hossain v Minister for Immigration and Border Protection [2018] HCA 34	14, 20, 97, 101–102, 121, 134–135, 137–138, 213
House v The King (1936) 55 CLR 499	27, 181
Jackson v Sterling Industries Ltd (1987) 162 CLR 612	84
Kaur v Minister for Immigration and Citizenship (2012) 290 ALR 616	217, 244
Khan v Minister for Immigration, Local Government and Ethnic Affairs (1987) 14 ALD 291	26
Kioa v West (1985) 159 CLR 550	15, 26, 215–216, 234–235, 241, 254
Kirk v Industrial Court (NSW) (2010) 239 CLR 531	12, 14, 16–18, 22, 70, 77, 93, 95–97, 100, 102, 121, 124–125, 127–135, 138, 207, 254
Kruger v Commonwealth (1997) 190 CLR 1	181
Lange v Australian Broadcasting Corporation (1997) 189 CLR 520	26

(continued)

Londish v Knox Grammar School (1997) 97 LGERA 1	162, 164
Maxcon Constructions Pty Ltd v Vadasz [2018] HCA 5	135
McWilliam v Civil Aviation Safety Authority [2004] FCA 1701	244
Minister for Aboriginal Affairs v Peko-Wallsend Ltd (1986) 162 CLR 24	179, 200
Minister for Immigration and Border Protection v Singh (2014) 139 ALD 50	181, 210
Minister for Immigration and Citizenship v SZMDs [2010] HCA 16	15, 175, 177, 182, 200, 203–210, 212–213, 254
Minister of State for Immigration & Ethnic Affairs v Ah Hin Teoh [1995] HCA 20	15, 89, 215, 217, 234, 239–242, 244, 254
Murrumbidgee Groundwater Preservation Association Inc v Minister for Natural Resources (2005) 138 LGERA 11	176
NAFF of 2002 v Minister for Immigration and Multicultural and Indigenous Affairs (2004) 221 CLR 1	244
NAIS v Minister for Immigration and Multicultural Affairs (2005) 228 CLR 470	180
Parisienne Basket Shoes Pty Ltd v Whyte (1938) 59 CLR 369	73, 162, 164
Plaintiff M70/2011 v Minister for Immigration and Citizenship [2011] HCA 32	168–172
Plaintiff S157/2002 v Commonwealth of Australia (2003) 211 CLR 476	74, 76, 79, 128–129, 205, 207
Probuild Constructions (Aust) Pty Ltd v Shade Systems Pty Ltd [2018] HCA 4	135
Project Blue Sky v Australian Broadcasting Authority (1998) 194 CLR 355	140
PT Garuda Indonesia v Australian Competition and Consumer Commission [2012] HCA 33	84
R v Anderson, Ex parte Ipec-Air Pty Ltd [1965] HCA 27	208
R v Hickman, Ex parte Fox and Clinton (1945) 70 CLR 598	85, 124
R v Kirby, Ex parte Boilermakers' Society of Australia (1956) 94 CLR 254	72, 76, 80, 84, 125
R v The District Court, Ex parte White (1966) 116 CLR 644	145
Re Minister for Immigration and Citizenship v Li [2013] HCA 18	7, 15, 175, 177, 208–210
Re Minister for Immigration and Multicultural Affairs, Ex parte Applicant S20/2002 (2003) 198 ALR 59	15, 133, 175–177, 182, 200–208, 210, 212, 254
Re Minister for Immigration and Multicultural Affairs, Ex parte Lam (2003) 214 CLR 1	2, 15, 201, 204, 215–217, 234–235, 239, 241–244, 254
Shrimpton v The Commonwealth [1945] HCA 4	208–210
The Queen v Australian Stevedoring Industry Board, Ex parte Melbourne Stevedoring Co Pty Ltd (1953) 88 CLR 100	148

(continued)

Table of Cases

Timbarra Protection Coalition Inc v Ross Mining NL & Ors (1999) 46 NSW LR 55	7, 14, 26, 141–143, 154, 156, 162–170, 172, 174, 203, 206
Waterford v The Commonwealth (1987) 163 CLR 54	145
Williams v City of Melbourne [1933] 49 CLR 142	85
Wilson v Minister for Aboriginal & Torres Strait Islander Affairs [1996] HCA 18	72
Wingfoot Australia Partners Pty Ltd v Kocak (2013) 252 CLR 480	140
Woolworths v Pallas Newco (2004) 61 NSWLR 707	171

Other Jurisdiction

Marbury v Madison 5 US 137	74, 166

Table of Legislation

English Law

British Nationality Act 1981	194
Charities Act 1993	189–190
Child Care Act 1980	157
Children Act 1948	157
Criminal Injuries Compensation Scheme 2001	158–159
European Communities Act 1972	65
Foreign Compensation Act 1950	118
Freedom of Information Act 2000	188–189
Human Rights Act 1998	65–69, 83, 186–189, 191, 200, 211, 228–229, 253, 257
Immigration Act 1971	150
Immigration and Asylum Act 1999	152
Inquiries Act 2005	188
Intelligence Services Act 1994	114
Person Act 1861	158–159
Regulation of Investigatory Powers Act 2000	96, 101, 115, 119, 133
Tribunals and Inquiries Act 1958	62
Tribunals, Courts and Enforcement Act 2007	62, 96, 101, 110, 112–113

Australian Law

Administrative Appeals Tribunal Act 1975	83, 97, 102
Administrative Decisions (Judicial Review) Act 1977	12, 83, 140, 168, 200, 205, 210, 214, 257
Environmental Planning and Assessment Act 1979 (NSW)	162, 164–165
Industrial Relations Act 1996 (NSW)	97
Justices Act 1902 (NSW)	236
Local Courts Act 1982 (NSW)	236
Migration Act 1958 (Cth)	200–201, 204, 207–208, 235
Threatened Species Conservation Act 1995 (NSW)	164

Acknowledgements

Feeling gratitude and not expressing it is like wrapping a present and not giving it(William Arthur Ward, 1921–1994)

I would like to take this opportunity to unwrap my gratitude to the people involved in the completion of this book.

Since it began life as a doctoral thesis, I would like to firstly thank Professor Elizabeth Fisher, my thesis supervisor, who gave me unfailing support throughout the five years of my study at Oxford, as well as during the process of adapting the thesis into this book. She never deserted me in the most difficult times and this work would not have been finished without her.

I am also thankful for the constructive comments of the examiners of the doctoral thesis, namely, Professor Rebecca Williams, Professor Alison Young, Professor Paul Craig and Professor John Bell, which helped to mature the contents of this book. Without their suggestions, I would not be as happy as I am with this work.

My grateful thanks must also go to all the teachers and staff at the Faculty of Law, University of Oxford and Corpus Christi College. Importantly, the administration processes of completing the thesis and programme would not have run smoothly without the input of great correspondence from Ms. Geraldine Malloy and Ms. Rachel Clifford.

I also owe thanks for the academic resources and generosity of the wonderful colleagues in my workplace, the Faculty of Law, Chulalongkorn University, as well as the full scholarship from the Government of Thailand to complete my master and doctoral studies.

Importantly, the opportunity given by Springer to publish this book is greatly appreciated. My thank must especially go to the editor, Ms. Lucie Bartonek, the project co-ordinators, Ms. Malini Arumugam, Ms. Mariëlle Klijn, Ms. Arulmurugan Pavitra, and all concerned for their guidance and cooperation in the publishing process. I would also like to express my thanks to the Springer readers for their helpful feedback, which enabled me to enrich this book to its very best.

Last, but never least, I would like to thank my family for being everything to me, especially my parents, who had a limited opportunity to attend higher education as a result of the hardship they endured during their childhood. Yet, they made it possible for me, their son, to graduate from a world-renowned university and have the opportunity to publish his work with a reputable publishing house. Therefore, if there is any merit in this book, I would like to dedicate it all to them. However, any errors are mine alone.

Contents

1	**Comparing the Determination of the Grounds of Judicial Review in the Light of Deep-Water Legality and Legal Culture: A Navigating Framework**	1	
	1.1 Arc of Arguments	1	
	1.1.1 Legal Culture and the Determination of the Grounds of Judicial Review	3	
	1.1.2 Surface and Deep-Water Legality	4	
	1.1.3 English and Australian Law as a Case Study	7	
	1.2 Structure of the Book	8	
	1.2.1 Comparative Analysis of English and Australian Legal Cultures	8	
	1.2.2 Comparative Analysis of the Grounds of Judicial Review in Case Law	9	
	1.2.3 Example of a Combination of the Two Parts	16	
	1.3 Main Contributions of the Book	18	
	1.3.1 Legal Culture Rather than Pragmatism and Formalism	19	
	1.3.2 Detailed Unpacking Process of Analysing the Determination of the Grounds of Judicial Review	21	
	1.3.3 Bigger Picture of English and Australian Judicial Review	22	
	1.3.4 Exploration Through the Eyes of an Outsider	23	
	1.4 Scope and Caveats	23	
	1.5 Conclusion	28	
2	**Differences Between the English and Australian Legal Cultures**	31	
	2.1 Introduction	31	
	2.2 Concept of Legal Culture: A Navigating Methodology	33	
	2.2.1 Variations in Using Legal Culture	35	
	2.2.2 Judicial Review Constitutionalism	37	
	2.2.3 Elements of Legal Culture	40	
	2.2.4 Legal Mentality	43	

		2.2.5	Proposed Approaches............................	45
		2.2.6	Summary	50
	2.3	Flexible Legal Mentality of English Judicial Review Constitutionalism..		51
		2.3.1	English Constitutional Frameworks and Values..........	52
		2.3.2	Justification for the English Courts to Conduct Judicial Review	57
		2.3.3	Fluid Separation of Powers Between Court and Executive...................................	59
		2.3.4	Integrating Influences from Interrelated Legal Cultures	65
		2.3.5	Substantive Conclusion	69
	2.4	Rigid Legal Mentality of Australian Judicial Review Constitutionalism.......................................		70
		2.4.1	Australian Constitutional Frameworks	70
		2.4.2	Australian Constitutional Values That Justify Judicial Review	74
		2.4.3	Australian Constitutional Values That Limit Judicial Review	79
		2.4.4	Rigidly Reading the Framework of Separation of Powers Prescribed in the Written Constitution	87
		2.4.5	Unwelcoming Influences from Interrelated Legal Cultures	89
		2.4.6	Substantive Conclusion	90
	2.5	Snapshots of English and Australian Rivers		91
3	**Influence of the Legal Cultures on Error of Law and Jurisdictional Error**.....................................			93
	3.1	Introduction		93
	3.2	Error of Law and Jurisdictional Error at Surface and Deep Levels..		97
		3.2.1	Two Complicated Factors Limiting Scope of Judicial Review	98
		3.2.2	The Adjudicative Monopoly of the Courts	99
		3.2.3	Understanding the Complications Through Legal Culture	100
	3.3	English Doctrinal Approaches...........................		103
		3.3.1	Prior to *Cart*......................................	103
		3.3.2	*Cart*	110
		3.3.3	*Privacy International*.............................	114
		3.3.4	Products of the English Legal Culture................	121
	3.4	Australian Doctrinal Approaches.........................		124
		3.4.1	Prior to *Kirk*....................................	124
		3.4.2	*Kirk*	128

		3.4.3	After *Kirk*..	134
		3.4.4	Products of the Australian Legal Culture...............	138
	3.5	Conclusion..		138

4 Influence of the Legal Cultures on Jurisdictional Fact............ 141
   4.1 Introduction 141
   4.2 Judicial Review of Factual Issues at Surface and Deep Levels 144
        4.2.1 Distinction Between Law and Fact 144
        4.2.2 Courts' Reviews of Some Kinds of Fact 147
        4.2.3 Understanding Jurisdictional Fact by Means
               of Deep-Water Legality 148
   4.3 English Doctrinal Approaches.................................. 149
        4.3.1 Prior to *E* 149
        4.3.2 E... 152
        4.3.3 After *E* 154
        4.3.4 Products of the English Legal Culture.................. 159
   4.4 Australian Doctrinal Approaches............................... 161
        4.4.1 Timbarra.. 162
        4.4.2 Enfield 165
        4.4.3 After *Timbarra* and *Enfield* 168
        4.4.4 Products of the Australian Legal Culture............... 172
   4.5 Conclusion... 173

**5 Influence of the Legal Cultures on the Grounds Relating
to Substantive Exercise of Discretion** 175
   5.1 Introduction 175
   5.2 Judicial Review of Administrative Discretion at Surface
       and Deep Levels... 177
        5.2.1 Discretion: Power to Choose 178
        5.2.2 Courts Review Some Exercises of Discretion 180
        5.2.3 Extent of Judicial Review of Administrative
               Discretion.. 181
   5.3 English Doctrinal Approaches.................................. 184
        5.3.1 Choices in English Law............................. 185
        5.3.2 Kennedy.. 188
        5.3.3 Pham 194
        5.3.4 Other Elements in the English Picture.................. 197
        5.3.5 Products of the English Legal Culture.................. 198
   5.4 Australian Doctrinal Approaches............................... 199
        5.4.1 S20/2002 201
        5.4.2 SZMDs... 204
        5.4.3 Li 208
        5.4.4 Other Elements in the Australian Picture............... 210
        5.4.5 Products of the Australian Legal Culture............... 212
   5.5 Conclusion... 213

6	**Influence of the Legal Cultures on Legitimate Expectations**	215
	6.1 Introduction	215
	6.2 Legitimate Expectations at Surface and Deep Levels	218
	6.2.1 General Concepts Supporting and Rejecting the Ground	218
	6.2.2 Understanding Legitimate Expectations Through Legal Culture	219
	6.3 English Doctrinal Approaches	221
	6.3.1 Prior to *Coughlan*	221
	6.3.2 Coughlan	226
	6.3.3 After *Coughlan*	229
	6.3.4 Products of the English Legal Culture	231
	6.4 Australian Doctrinal Approaches	234
	6.4.1 Prior to *Lam*	235
	6.4.2 Lam	241
	6.4.3 After *Lam*	244
	6.4.4 Products of the Australian Legal Culture	245
	6.5 Conclusion	246
7	**Conclusion**	249
	7.1 Mapping the Book in Administrative Law Scholarship	249
	7.2 English Law Standing on the Edge of Two Boats	252
	7.3 Australian Law's Choice of One Boat for a Journey	254
	7.4 Standing and Further Implications of Deep-Water Legality and Legal Culture	255
	7.5 Concluding Remarks	258
Bibliography		259

Abbreviations

AAT	Administrative Appeals Tribunal Act 1975
ADJR	Administrative Decisions (Judicial Review) Act 1977
BNA	British Nationality Act 1981
CRA	Charities Act 1993
CJ	Chief Justice
CCCA	Commonwealth Court of Conciliation and Arbitration
CA	Court of Appeal
CICS	Criminal Injuries Compensation Scheme 2001
DCSA	District Court of South Australia
EPA	Environmental Planning and Assessment Act 1979
ECHR	European Convention on Human Rights
EU	European Union
FTT	First Tier Tribunal
FOIA	Freedom of Information Act 2000
GCHQ	Government Communications Headquarters
HCA	High Court of Australia
HL	House of Lords
HRA	Human Rights Act 1998
IAA	Immigration and Asylum Act 1999
IAT	Immigration Appeal Tribunal
ICNSW	Industrial Court of New South Wales
IRA	Industrial Relations Act 1996 (NSW)
IPT	Investigatory Powers Tribunal
J	Justice
JJ	Justices
LJ	Lord Justice
MA	Migration Act 1958 (Cth)
MRT	Migration Review Tribunal
NSW	New South Wales
RRT	Refugee Review Tribunal
RIPA	Regulation of Investigatory Powers Act 2000

SIS	Species Impact Statement
TCEA	Tribunals, Courts and Enforcement Act 2007
UK	United Kingdom
UKSC	United Kingdom Supreme Court
US	United States
UT	Upper Tribunal

Chapter 1
Comparing the Determination of the Grounds of Judicial Review in the Light of Deep-Water Legality and Legal Culture: A Navigating Framework

Abstract The framework and substantial contributions of this book are comprehensively described in this chapter. These involve navigating a more in-depth understanding of English and Australian judicial review through legal culture, deep-water legality and the process of unpacking the doctrinal approach and legal reasoning applied by the courts in determining the grounds of judicial review in leading cases.

1.1 Arc of Arguments

In recent years, a number of works in comparative administrative law have become increasingly focused on the different doctrinal approaches applied between legal systems to determine the grounds of judicial review.[1] Among these works, Paul Craig argues that *'All systems of administrative law resolve similar issues. They elaborate tests for review of law, fact and discretion'*.[2] It is difficult to disagree with this simple, but powerful statement. It has become generally accepted that the courts in different countries take different approaches through various grounds of judicial

---

[1] E.g. John Bell, 'Administrative Law in a Comparative Perspective' in Örücü E and David Nelken (eds), *Comparative Law: A Handbook* (Hart Publishing 2007); Paul Craig, 'Judicial Review of Questions of Law: A Comparative Perspective' in Susan R Ackerman and Peter L Lindseth (eds), *Comparative Administrative Law* (2nd edn, Edward Elgar 2017); Mark Aronson, 'The Resurgence of Jurisdictional Facts' (2001) 12 Public Law Review 17; Mark Aronson, 'The Growth of Substantive Review' in John Bell, Mark Elliott, Jason Varuhas and Philip Murray (eds), *Public Law Adjudication in Common Law Systems: Process and Substance* (Hart Publishing 2016). Further examples of literature related to the study of each ground of judicial review are discussed throughout the subsequent chapters of this book.

[2] He makes it in the context of examining different doctrines for judicial review concerning error of law in the United States ('US'), English, Canadian and European Union ('EU') administrative law (Craig (n 1) 389).

© The Author(s), under exclusive license to Springer Nature Singapore Pte Ltd. 2021
V. Malsukhum, *Legal Culture, Legality and the Determination of the Grounds of Judicial Review of Administrative Action in England and Australia*,
https://doi.org/10.1007/978-981-16-1267-1_1

review in deciding whether a question in administrative action is reviewable or not.[3] For example, Lord Carnwath of the United Kingdom Supreme Court ('UKSC') refers to the adjustable degree of intensity in the English courts' determination of the scope of judicial review in the following statement;

> *In 19 years as a judge of administrative law cases,…my approach I suspect has been much closer to the characteristically pragmatic approach suggested by Lord Donaldson in 1988, by way of a rider to what Lord Diplock had said in CCSU: "The ultimate question would be whether something had gone wrong of a nature and degree which required the intervention of the court, and what form that intervention should take".*[4]

This is completely opposite to the approach taken by the Australian courts. For example, Justice Hayne of the High Court of Australia ('HCA') rejects the notion of deference, which would allow the courts to enhance or lessen the degree of their intervention.[5]

These different doctrinal approaches frequently lead to dissimilar results in similar situations in different legal systems.[6] One area that will be examined in a later chapter of this book is substantive legitimate expectations, which claimants can argue as a valid ground of judicial review in the English[7] and EU courts,[8] but not under Australian law.[9] In French Law, other grounds, namely equality and legal certainty, have a function equivalent to legitimate expectations in the English and EU law.[10]

---

[3] It is worth noting that there is a close relationship between the issues of the determination of the grounds of judicial review, scope of judicial review, intensity of judicial review and jurisdiction of the court. This point will be further exemplified in this and subsequent chapters.

[4] Lord Carnwath, 'From Judicial Outrage to Sliding Scales: Where Next for Wednesbury' (the ALBA Annual Lecture, 12 November 2013).

[5] Kenneth Hayne, 'Deference: An Australian Perspective' [2010] PL 75.

[6] It should be noted that there are also situations that end with a similar result in different legal systems. Despite this fact, the courts still apply the different patterns of doctrinal approach and legal reasoning in reaching such results, for example, in the case of error of law and jurisdictional error in the English and Australian law, which is discussed in detail in Chap. 3. It is also be explained below that the main theme of this book is to connect the different doctrinal approaches and legal reasoning applied by the English and Australian courts as products of their legal system's legal culture.

[7] See *R v North and East Devon Health Authority, Ex parte Coughlan* [2000] 3 All ER 850. This will be discussed in Chap. 6.

[8] See Paul Craig, *EU Administrative Law* (3rd edn, OUP 2018) Chapter 18.

[9] *Re Minister for Immigration and Multicultural Affairs, Ex parte Lam* (2003) 214 CLR 1. This will be discussed in comparison to *Coughlan* (n 7) in Chap. 6.

[10] Neville Brown and John Bell, *French Administrative Law* (5th edn, Clarendon Press 1998) 235–236.

1.1 Arc of Arguments

1.1.1 Legal Culture and the Determination of the Grounds of Judicial Review

Various explanations are provided in the literature to describe these doctrinal variations as products of the *'normative divergences'* between legal systems.[11] For example, Cane explores the particularities of the English, American and Australian legal systems through a comparative historical methodology called *'control regimes'* and points out their influence on various areas of administrative law doctrines, namely the scope of judicial review, interpretation of law, policy-making, rule-making and controlling information.[12] Otherwise, Krygier explains this through the *'socio-legal aspects of the rule of law'*.[13] Based on the differences within societies, histories, practices, traditions and institutions between legal systems, the pursuit of legality involves the practical work of developing institutions and systems.[14] Atiyah and Summers describe the difference between English and US legal reasoning and institutions in terms of *'legal theories'*.[15]

However, the differences between legal systems will be explored in this book based on the concept of legal culture, which is defined as the *'continuous patterns of legal actions and attitudes in each legal system'*.[16] Specifically, the 'legal mentality of judicial review constitutionalism', which connotes the ways of legal thinking of the judiciary about their proper role in conducting judicial review in the light of their legal system's distinctive constitutional orders, will be applied as an adapted form of legal culture to better explain the different doctrinal approaches between legal systems.[17] This proposed approach and its contributions will be discussed in detail in Chap. 2; however, it is important here to introduce the connection between legal culture, as a kind of descriptive explanation, and the determination of the scope of judicial review. The diverse ways in which courts in different legal systems determine the grounds of judicial review are influenced by the different understanding of their role in conducting judicial review based on the distinctive constitutional orders of their legal system.[18]

---

[11] A descriptive explanation applied by Craig, 'Judicial Review of Questions of Law: A Comparative Perspective' (n 1).

[12] Peter Cane, *Controlling Administrative Power: An Historical Comparison* (CUP 2016).

[13] Martin Krygier, 'The Hart-Fuller Debate: Transitional Societies and the Rule of Law' in Peter Cane (ed), *The Hart-Fuller Debate in the Twenty-first Century* (Hart Publishing 2010) 130–132.

[14] ibid.

[15] P S Atiyah and R S Summers, *Form and Substance in Anglo-Amercian Law: A Comparative Study of Legal Reasoning, Legal Theory, and Legal Institutions* (Clarendon Press 1996).

[16] David Nelken, 'Using the Concept of Legal Culture' (2004) 29 Austl J Leg Phil 1.

[17] This is further adapted from administrative constitutionalism (See Elizabeth Fisher, *Risk Regulation and Administrative Constitutionalism* (Hart Publishing 2007) 35).

[18] Different scholars define the term 'constitutional order' differently to serve their particular purpose. For example, Tushnet connotes constitutional order as *'a reasonably stable set of institutions through which a nation's fundamental decisions are made over a sustained period, and the principles that guide those decisions'*. He clearly indicates that this is his own definition to

1.1.2 Surface and Deep-Water Legality

It is then submitted in this book that 'the principle of legality' can be applied as a general approach to facilitate a comprehensive understanding of the connection between the determination of the grounds of judicial review and legal culture. In general, the term 'legality' has many uses in administrative law doctrine. For example, its antonym, illegality, was used by Lord Diplock in *Council of Civil Service Unions v Minister for the Civil Service* to describe one of the three main grounds for an English judicial review.[19] This ground contains two sub-grounds relating to the compatibility of administrative action with the statute, namely improper purpose and relevant and irrelevant considerations. Alternatively, it is used as a principle of non-abrogation requiring Parliament to act lawfully and prohibiting it from overriding fundamental rights and norms.[20] In addition, it is explained as a philosophical concept, discussing the rule of recognition, the making of a legal system or question like what is law.[21]

However, at the heart of administrative law, the principle of legality functions as the minimum requirement of the rule of law, namely that administrative actions must be lawful.[22] In the name of protecting legality, the courts play a constitutional role in dealing with legal questions in administrative actions in order to ensure this compliance and this underpins their conduct of judicial review. This requirement of legality is commonly accepted in the administrative law of most legal systems, particularly those committed to democracy. For example, Lady Hale of the UKSC mentions that *'Judicial review is a critical check on the power of the state, providing an effective mechanism for challenging the decisions, acts or omissions of public bodies to ensure that they are lawful'*.[23] Lord Browne-Wilkinson also asserts in *R v Lord President of the Privy Court, Ex parte Page* that *'The fundamental principle*

---

particularly contrast different sets of institutions and principles in the US (Mark Tushnet, *The New Constitutional Order* (Princeton University Press 2009) 9–10). This book also has its own particular understanding of what constitutional order refers to, which will be gradually explained through the concept of legal culture in the next chapter.

[19] [1985] AC 374, 410C-G.

[20] See *R (Jackson) and Ors v HM Attorney General* [2005] EWCA Civ 126 (Lord Reed); Michael Fordham, *Judicial Review Handbook* (6th edn, Hart Publishing 2012) [P35.1]; Mark Aronson, Matthew Groves and Greg Weeks, *Judicial Review of Administrative Action and Government Liability* (6th edn, Thomson Reuters Australia 2017) [3.380].

[21] E.g. Scott Shapiro, *Legality* (Belknap Press of Harvard University Press 2011); Ronald Dworkin, 'Hart's Postscript and the Character of Political Philosophical' (2004) 24 OJLS 23; David Dyzenhaus, *Legality and Legitimacy: Carl Schmitt, Hans Kelsen, and Hermann Heller in Weimar* (Clarendon Press 1997).

[22] It is generally treated as a primary requirement for a formal and substantive rule of law (see Paul Craig, 'Formal and Substantive Conceptions of the Rule of Law: An Analytical Framework' [1997] PL 467).

[23] Lady Hale, 'Who Guards the Guardians?' (Public Law Project Conference, 14 October 2013) by quoting the statement of Ministry of Justice, *Judicial Review: Proposals for further reform*, 2013, Cm 8703, para 1.

1.1 Arc of Arguments

[of judicial review] *is that the courts will intervene to ensure that the powers of public decision-making bodies are exercised lawfully'*.[24] In the same vein, Chief Justice French of the HCA states that *'...the law will require them* [the courts] *to set aside the decisions of Ministers of the Crown and other public officials when such decisions are beyond power'*.[25] This is similar to the following statement made by Chief Justice Gleeson of the HCA;

> All public power must be based on law...This is the essence of the principle of legality ...the establishment of overriding legal limitations upon the power governments and parliaments, declared and enforced if necessary by the judiciary...[26]

Apart from the judges, this requirement of the principle of legality is generally recognised by scholars in different countries. For example, Wade and Forsyth argue that the principle of legality, ensuring that the actions of public authorities remain within legal boundaries, is the court's main concern.[27] Aronson, Groves and Weeks also regard legality as the main ideal of judicial review.[28] In another example, US scholar, Jaffe argues that *'The primary role of judicial review is the protection of interests specially affected by allegedly illegal official action'*.[29] Sackville also states that *'...judicial review involves a vindication of the legality of the administrative decision-making process'*.[30] This concept of legality, which is commonly applied to underpin judicial review in all legal systems, is defined in this book as 'Surface-Water Legality', analogous to the fact that all rivers look the same on the surface.

Rather than stopping here, it is proposed that it is necessary to dive deeper into the underwater perspective of legality in order to better understand the unknown contours of what lies beneath the surface. It is pointed out that different determinations of the scope of judicial review in different legal systems are products of how the courts in those legal systems understand and perceive 'what legality should cover and whether the issue in a disputed administrative action is one of which they have a proper role in protecting it or not'.

This logic can be recognised from judges' perception of the way judicial review raises tensions in terms of whether the role to decide the issue should belong to the court or the executive. For example, Lord Phillips of the UKSC asserts that *'Perhaps the most important and most difficult role of the Supreme Court is to maintain a*

---

[24] [1993] AC 682, 701C-D.

[25] Chief Justice French, 'Courts in a Representative Democracy' (University of Southern Queensland, Toowoomba, 25 June 2010).

[26] Chief Justice Gleeson, 'Legality: Spirit and Principle' (The Second Magna Carta Lecture, New South Wales Parliament House, Sydney, 20 November 2003).

[27] William Wade and Christopher Forsyth, *Administrative Law* (11th edn, OUP 2014) 4–5, 15–16.

[28] Aronson, Groves and Weeks (n 20) [1.10]; See also Anthony J Connolly, *The Foundations of Australian Public Law: State, Power, Accountability* (CUP 2017) 275.

[29] Louis Leventhal Jaffe, *Judicial Control of Administrative Action* (Little Brown 1965) 459.

[30] Ronald Sackville, 'The Limits of Judicial Review of Executive Action – Some Comparisons between Australia and the US' (2000) 28 Federal Law Review 315, 321.

proper balance between executive and judicial decision making'.[31] Sir Brennan of the HCA also stated that *'The subjection of executive action to judicial review has given rise to some tension between these two branches of government'.*[32] In the same vein, Chief Justice Gleeson of the HCA made the following statement;

> ...both constitutional and common law cases have elaborated the scope for judicial review and the principles according to which it is undertaken. Inevitably, this has created tension between the executive and judicial branches....[33]

This tension about whether or not it is the role of the court to conduct judicial review is indeed a consideration of legality. If the issue is within the scope of legality, the court then has a role to conduct judicial review; if it is not, the authority to decide should be left to the executive. The point is that the determination of the question of legality is influenced by the distinctive constitutional orders between legal systems, represented in this book by the concept of legal culture. For instance, the particular understanding of the rule of law and separation of powers in a legal system influence the deep understanding of legality; hence, the role of the court in conducting judicial review in such a legal system is different from others. Bell provides the following example;

> *In many legal systems, there is no code or statute that authorises the courts to control the legality of administrative action or defines the grounds on which this is done. Accordingly, there is much debate in various countries about the constitutional foundation of judicial review of the administration. For some, it is simply a matter of enforcing the wishes of the legislature. For others, there are more fundamental values that justify a restrictive interpretation of the powers of the administration. The debate on the foundations of judicial review turns around concepts of the rule of law...*[34]

It is proposed in this book that this way of perceiving legality in depth, which is complicated by the different legal cultures between legal systems, is explained as 'Deep-Water Legality'. This is analogous to the fact that different rivers contain different underwater geographies. This deep-water concept of legality has been expressed by other scholars, but in different terms. For example, Poole points to the characteristic entanglement of local conditions, which functionally interacts with the framework of the legal system.[35] Chief Justice Gleeson of the HCA also adopts this logic, asserting that *'...legality involves courts in the exercise of a capacity to*

---

[31] Lord Phillips, 'Judicial Independence and Accountability: A View from the Supreme Court' (The Politics of Judicial Independence, 8 February 2011).

[32] Sir Brennan, 'The Parliament, the Executive and the Courts: Roles and Immunities' (School of Law, Bond University, 21 February 1998).

[33] Chief Justice Gleeson, 'The Role of a Judge in a Representative Democracy' (Judiciary of the Commonwealth of the Bahamas, 4 January 2008).

[34] John Bell, 'Comparative Administrative Law' in Mathias Reimann and Reinhard Zimmermann (eds), *The Oxford Handbook of Comparative Law* (2nd edn, OUP 2019) 1270.

[35] Thomas Poole, 'Between the Devil and the Deep Blue Sea' in Linda Pearson, Michael Taggart and Carol Harlow (eds), *Administrative Law in A Changing State: Essays in Honour of Mark Aronson* (Hart Publishing 2008) 22.

declare and enforce limits on governmental and legislative authority. The nature of that responsibility varies between common law jurisdictions'.[36]

Subsequently, this deep-water legality explains how the courts apply different doctrinal approaches in determining the grounds of judicial review, particularly whether they should regard those that have been understood to be controversial as legal questions or not. For example, as mentioned above, the English courts perceive an issue on the ground of substantive legitimate expectations as a legal question on which they can conduct judicial review of. However, the Australian court rejects its jurisdiction to intervene in such an issue, as they do not regard it as a jurisdictional error.

1.1.3 English and Australian Law as a Case Study

Although it is difficult to present the arc of arguments precisely here as it will emerge throughout the book, what important to appreciate is the framework that the courts in different legal systems take diverse ways to determine the scope of judicial review based on their deep understanding of legality, which is embedded in the legal culture of their legal system. This framework will be explored through a comparative study of English and Australian law.

It is generally known that Australia was once a British colony and its constitution was passed as part of an Act of the UK Parliament. Therefore, the Australian administrative law has been developed from an English background.[37] It has made much use of the English legal features, for example, placing ordinary courts at the centre of control of administrative power.[38] Also, the Australian courts constantly refer to the relevant English case law in their judgments. For example, cases like *Sharp v Wakefield*[39] and *Kruse v Johnson*,[40] and academic works such as Wade and Forsyth's Administrative Law textbook[41] were discussed in the judgments of *Minister for Immigration and Citizenship v Li*.[42] *Wednesbury* Unreasonableness has also become a starting approach in determining the scope of judicial review of the substantive exercise of administrative discretion in both the English and Australian law.[43]

---

[36] Gleeson, 'Legality: Spirit and Principle' (n 26).

[37] See Peter Cane, 'The Making of Australian Administrative Law' (2003) 24 Australian Bar Review 114; Gerard Brennan, 'Courts, Democracy and the Law' (1991) 17 Commonwealth Law Bulletin 696, 701.

[38] As a result of the general implication of the Diceyan concept of rule of law. This will be discussed in detail in Sect. 2.3.1 of Chap. 2.

[39] [1891] AC 173.

[40] [1898] 2 QB 91.

[41] William Wade and Christopher Forsyth, *Administrative Law* (10th edn, OUP 2009).

[42] [2013] HCA 18 [24], [65]–[67], [70], [106].

[43] This will be discussed in detail in Chap. 5.

However, the Australian legal system has become increasingly different from its English roots. For example, it has adopted some legal frameworks from the US, namely a federal state system and a written Constitution.[44] Therefore, it is interesting to examine how the Australian courts' deep understanding of deep-water legality and the determination of the grounds of judicial review have shifted from those in England based on these and other developments. In other words, the English and Australian legal systems are chosen for a comparison between the three aforementioned themes because they share some similarities and differences in relation to their legal culture,[45] as illustrated in the following statement made by Chief Justice French of the HCA;

> Australia and the United Kingdom, in many respects sharing similar legal cultures and methodologies and a common legal heritage, nevertheless differ in important areas of the common law, differences not directly explicable by reference to constitutional arrangements although they sometimes reflect a particular view of the extent to which the Court should go in changing the law.[46]

1.2 Structure of the Book

The three themes introduced above, namely legal culture, legality and the determination of the grounds of judicial review and the connection between them will be explored in detail throughout this book, divided into two main parts. The structure and methodologies applied in these two parts are discussed below.

1.2.1 Comparative Analysis of English and Australian Legal Cultures

The first part, which will be presented as Chap. 2 of the book, will contain an examination of the differences between the English and Australian legal cultures. This part will begin with the definition and general application of the concept of legal culture before narrowing the scope to the proposed approach of the legal mentality of judicial review constitutionalism as a particular form of legal culture

---

[44] Matthew Groves and H P Lee, 'Australian Administrative Law: The Constitutional and Legal Matrix' in Matthew Groves and H P Lee (eds), *Australian Administrative Law: Fundamentals, Principles and Doctrines* (CUP 2007) 4; Chief Justice French, 'Courts in a Representative Democracy' (University of Southern Queensland, Toowoomba, 25 June 2010).

[45] See Gerhard Dannemann, 'Comparative Law: Study of Similarities or Differences?' in Mathias Reimann and Reinhard Zimmermann (eds), *The Oxford Handbook of Comparative Law* (2nd edn, OUP 2019) 391.

[46] Chief Justice French, 'The Globalisation of Public Law: A Quilting of Legalities' (Public Law Conference, Cambridge, 12 September 2016).

applied in the book. For example, the constitutional frameworks, constitutional values and ways of justification and limitation the courts rely on when conducting judicial review will be regarded as elements of legal culture and identified through various materials such as judgments, speeches and judges' secondary works, considered as evidence of legal culture. The legal mentality of the judiciary, who play a leading role in determining the scope of judicial review of administrative action, will also be indicated as another subject of the analysis. It will be argued that this framework better reflects the depth and sophistication of judges' perception of their role in conducting judicial review based on their legal system's distinctive constitutional setting. Since these approaches contain a number of subjects and complexities, they will be fully expanded in the next chapter. The differences between the English and Australian legal cultures will subsequently be examined in detail based on those approaches.

According to the river metaphor, the legal cultures of English and Australian judicial review are equivalent to the geography of the rivers. The elements such as the constitutional framework, constitutional value and justification and limitation of judicial review are compared to natural underwater features such as stones. The chapter begins by describing the specific methodology used to examine such geography in the exploration, namely, what kinds of stones we are interested in. Then, this methodology is applied to reveal an overall underwater picture of English and Australian rivers, which will function as the navigating framework to understand different English and Australian deep-water legality and the determination of the grounds of judicial review in all subsequent chapters.

1.2.2 *Comparative Analysis of the Grounds of Judicial Review in Case Law*

The second part will be presented in Chaps. 3, 4, 5 and 6 of the book based on the various grounds of judicial review. This part will consist of an examination of how those differences between the English and Australian legal cultures lead to a different understanding of deep-water legality and determination of the grounds of judicial review by the English and Australian courts. While the approaches in the part related to legal culture will be examined in the next chapter, three important aspects in examining the determination of the grounds of judicial review are proposed below.

1.2.2.1 Selection of the Examined Grounds of Judicial Review

When considering the grounds of judicial review, three different areas of court intervention can be seen.[47] Grounds related to the provisions in the legislation, namely improper purpose, relevant and irrelevant considerations and procedural impropriety, can be seen on the left side of the spectrum, being more easily justified as a legal question than the other grounds.[48] This is not to argue that there is no disagreement or debate at all about the determination of these grounds of judicial review. For instance, various tests are applied by the courts to determine whether discretion was used for an improper purpose.[49] Among these tests, the court's approach in *R v Secretary of State for Foreign and Commonwealth Affairs, Ex parte World Development Movement Ltd*,[50] in which the ground was determined based on reading an additional requirement into the statute, was heavily criticised for depriving the executive of a *'considerable degree of autonomy'*, thereby blurring *'the boundary between appeal and review'* and *'undermining the constitutional foundations on which the courts' supervisory jurisdiction rests'*.[51] In the same vein, some cases like *R (Moseley) v Haringey London Borough Council* and *Puhlhofer v Hillingdon London Borough Council*, in which the grounds related to procedural impropriety were determined, are contestable and need to be understood through the framework of legal culture.[52]

However, it is argued that there are fewer contestable areas of the determination of these grounds of judicial review than other grounds, because the determination is more directly related to the law of the legislature. If the courts determine that there is a stipulation in the statute, they feel that they are playing 'their rightful role' in intervening in an administrative decision, since this intervention is compatible with their main function based on the separation of powers. According to the approach taken in this book, these grounds of judicial review are generally included in the meaning of legality, which the courts understand as their role to protect. Therefore, they are not the grounds selected for examination in this book.[53]

---

[47] As inspired by Jowell's analysis of different intensities of review for the grounds of judicial review in English law (See Jeffrey Jowell, 'Of Vires and Vacuums: The Constitutional Context of Judicial Review' in Christopher Forsyth (ed), *Judicial Review and the Constitution* (Hart Publishing 2000) 329–336).

[48] ibid 329–332.

[49] See Paul Craig, *Administrative Law* (8th edn, Sweet & Maxwell 2016) [19–011]–[19–014].

[50] [1995] 1 WLR 386.

[51] Derry Irvine, *Human Rights, Constitutional Law and the Development of the English Legal System* (Hart Publishing 2003) 164–165.

[52] [2014] UKSC 56; [1986] 1 AC 484.

[53] In fact, the framework of deep-water legality and legal culture can also be used to navigate a more comprehensive understanding of these grounds of judicial review. However, this examination needs to be conducted in the future as an extension of this book. See the note about the further implications of deep-water legality and legal culture in Chap. 7.

1.2 Structure of the Book

Conversely, the grounds on the right side of the spectrum are relatively technical and require administrative agents' expertise, such as grounds concerning intrinsic polycentric issues, such as the decision of the Education Funding Council to allocate research grants to universities.[54] Therefore, the courts usually 'hesitate' to intervene in decisions in the area of appreciation of administrative agents,[55] because they are not their main function; rather, they are the duties of executives who are experts in their field and whose power to manage the public administration is conferred on them by Parliament.[56]

The grounds on these left and right sides of the spectrum are relatively similar in English and Australian law. Since whether or not the courts have a role to conduct judicial review is not controversial, it is not the focus of this book.[57] Instead, the grounds located in the middle area of the spectrum are emphasised based on the controversy of whether they are legal questions or not. Those selected for inclusion in this book are jurisdictional error, jurisdictional fact, and the grounds relating to substantive exercise of discretion, namely rationality, proportionality and substantive legitimate expectations. These grounds are perceived to be a matter of law by the courts in some legal systems, but not in others, or there are different approaches in reaching a conclusion. The influence of their deep-water legality and legal culture on the courts' determination of these grounds will be demonstrated in Chaps. 3, 4, 5 and 6 of this book.

1.2.2.2 Legal Reasoning of Leading Cases

Secondly, while various materials, namely judgments, speeches and judges' secondary works, are examined in the discussion of English and Australian legal cultures in Chap. 2, the determination of the grounds of judicial review will focus in-depth on the legal reasoning given in the judgments and transcripts of legal arguments in English and Australian cases,[58] because this can best represent the practice of the determination of judicial review. Importantly, it will demonstrate the profundity of how such determinations are influenced by the legal culture. As Atiyah

---

[54] *R v Higher Education Funding Council, Ex parte Institute of Dental Surgery* [1994] 1 WLR 242.

[55] It should be noted that, although the courts leave this area to the discretion of the executive, they still conduct judicial review of it on procedural grounds, such as the duty to give reason.

[56] Jowell (n 47) 332.

[57] Except the ground of procedural legitimate expectations, which has some connection to deep-water legality, as discussed in Chap. 6.

[58] While transcripts of the HCA can be accessed from its website, the transcripts of the UKSC are unpublished. However, with the cooperation of Professor Elizabeth Fisher, I would like to thank Lord Carnwath and Mr. Ben Wilson of the UKSC for providing footage of the cases, namely *R (Cart) v Upper Tribunal* [2011] UKSC 28; *R (Jones) v First-tier Tribunal* [2013] UKSC 19; *Kennedy v Charity Commission* [2014] UKSC 20; *Pham v Secretary of State for the Home Department* [2015] UKSC 19 for the use of this book.

and Summers state, '*...reasoning reflects a deep difference in legal style, legal culture, and more generally, the visions of law which prevail in the countries*'.[59]

However, the legal reasoning in every case will not be examined in Chaps. 3, 4, 5 and 6 as it is in textbooks; instead, the focus will be on the leading cases on each ground, which are cited as precedent and authoritative by judges and scholars in subsequent cases, textbooks and articles. The main idea is to compare the judgments of the House of Lords ('HL') and the UKSC with those of the HCA in order to demonstrate the depth to which the doctrinal approaches and legal reasoning applied by the highest courts of the legal systems are influenced by the legal system's legal culture. However, it should be noted that the judgments of lower court are not absolutely excluded. Those that provide guidance of the operation of the court's determination of the grounds of judicial review, like the judgment of the Court of Appeal in *Coughlan*, will also be examined. Furthermore, the different doctrinal approaches delivered by the courts in the same case, but at different levels, namely *Cart*, will also be emphasised. In short, the cases chosen for the analysis in this book are mainly those that provide the clearest indication of the influence of the legal culture on the understanding of the doctrine. They are mainly the judgments of the highest courts, although the judgments of the lower courts are not omitted from the analysis.

For Australian law, the determination of the grounds of judicial review at federal level will be studied in this book rather than at state level,[60] because the book focuses on the overall picture rather than the small parts of it. In addition, although the contemporary law will be the primary focus, some important past cases will also be analysed at various points, in order to demonstrate the continuity of how legal culture of a legal system influences the determination of the grounds of judicial review.[61] It is also worth noting that this book will focus on a common law judicial review rather than cases related to specific statutes that govern judicial review. It will not focus on the codification of the grounds of judicial review in the statute, such as the Administrative Decisions (Judicial Review) Act 1977 ('ADJR') in Australian law, because there are no parallel factors in the two countries selected for this study.[62]

---

[59] Atiyah and Summers (n 15) 1.

[60] Although the analysis of *Kirk v Industrial Court (NSW)* (2010) 239 CLR 531 in Chap. 3 relates to the scope of judicial review at the state level, it connects to the federal level in the way that the HCA as having supervisory jurisdiction in conducting judicial review of the administrative actions and judgments of state courts. Additionally, the legal reasoning in some cases at the state level, for example, *Barrick Australian v Williams* (2009) 74 NSWLR 733, are also included in Chap. 4 in order to demonstrate the continuous adherence of jurisdictional fact as a ground of judicial review in Australia.

[61] For example, the choice between the collateral fact doctrine and the theory of limited review under the distinction between jurisdictional error and non-jurisdictional error, which the English courts applied as an approach before *Anisminic Ltd v Foreign Compensation Commission* [1969] 2 AC 147, will also be analysed as part of the flow of flexibility of English law in Chap. 3.

[62] See more about the approach of selecting what to compare in Dannemann (n 45) 411–415.

1.2 Structure of the Book

1.2.2.3 Doctrinal Approaches

Thirdly, there are many aspects of the determination of the grounds of judicial review that can be demonstrated as being influenced by the legal culture. In this book, they are called 'doctrinal approaches' used to determine the grounds of judicial review, and are categorised into five 'points', namely the status of the ground of judicial review (whether or not it is valid in the legal system), the justifications and doctrines the courts apply in determining whether or not they have the jurisdiction to conduct judicial review, the application in considering each doctrine, and the integration of international treaties in their consideration.[63]

It is acknowledged that these points overlap and contain some inconsistencies. For example, proportionality was introduced to the English law as a general 'principle' from EU law and the European Convention on Human Rights ('ECHR').[64] At the same time, it is recognised either as a 'doctrine' or a 'concept' applied to determine other grounds of judicial review, for example, substantive legitimate expectations.[65] Whether proportionality should be a general 'ground' for judicial review is also debatable. In the same way, jurisdictional error is a ground of judicial review in Australian law,[66] at the same time, it is a central approach that covers the overall common law grounds of judicial review. Additionally, the terms of doctrine, standard, approach or even outcome vary when referring to the rules the courts apply to determine whether they have the jurisdiction to conduct judicial review of the disputed administrative action or not.

In reality, these points of the determination of the grounds of judicial review merge and become a package of legal reasoning given in judgments. This book proposes a process to unpack them with the recognition that they are not fixed. Not all of these five points will be discussed in each subsequent chapter, but the only those that are obviously influenced by the different English and Australian legal cultures.

1.2.2.4 Grounds and Leading Cases Selected for Chapters 3 to 6

Up to this point, this book proposes an approach to 'unpack' different 'doctrinal approaches', namely the validity, justification, doctrines, application and integration of international treaties into the consideration, applied by the English and Australian courts in determining the grounds of judicial review, from the 'legal reasoning' in leading cases. These doctrinal approaches in the courts' determination of the grounds of judicial review, unpacked in Chaps. 3, 4, 5 and 6, will be connected to

---

[63] This approach will be considered based on specific terminology 'interrelated legal culture', which will be explained in the next chapter.
[64] See more in Chaps. 2 and 5.
[65] See more in Chap. 6.
[66] See more in Chap. 3.

legal mentality of the English and Australian judicial review constitutionalism analysed in Chap. 2. The grounds of judicial review and leading cases in Chaps. 3, 4, 5 and 6 are briefly outlined below.

Chapter 3 will contain an analysis of the influence of the English and Australian legal cultures on the grounds of error of law and jurisdictional error, particularly in judicial review of the decision of a tribunal or inferior court, a body with a restrictive clause according to the legislature. The section devoted to the English law will begin with an examination of the flexibility accorded to the courts in applying the jurisdictional fact doctrine, before turning to the contemporary approaches in *Anisminic Ltd v Foreign Compensation Commission*,[67] *R (Cart) v Upper Tribunal*,[68] and *R (Privacy International) v Investigatory Powers Tribunal*.[69] It will be shown that the courts in these cases determined the grounds of judicial review based on the flexible application of various justifications and doctrines. This was different from the doctrinal approach applied in *Craig v The State of South Australia*,[70] *Kirk v Industrial Court (NSW)*[71] and *Hossain v Minister for Immigration and Border Protection*,[72] in which the boundary of the court's power to conduct judicial review of the tribunal and inferior court was confined to jurisdictional error based on the framework of the separation of powers prescribed in the written Australian Constitution.

Although jurisdictional fact is a ground of judicial review in both England and Australia, the doctrinal approaches are different in these legal systems, as will be demonstrated in Chap. 4. In terms of the English law, the status and application of the ground have been shown to fluctuate in the legal reasoning of cases such as *R v Secretary of State for the Home Department, Ex parte Khawaja*,[73] *E v Secretary of State for the Home Department*,[74] *R (A) v Croydon LBC*[75] and *R (Jones) v First-tier Tribunal*.[76] Conversely, the ground is far more entrenched with a clear application in defining an issue as jurisdictional error in Australia. This was demonstrated by the legal reasoning in *Timbarra Protection Coalition Inc v Ross Mining NL & Ors*[77] and *Corporation of the City of Enfield v Development Assessment Commission*,[78] and continuously in some later cases, notably, *Anvil Hill Project Watch Association Inc*

---

[67] [1969] 2 AC 147.
[68] [2009] EWHC 3052; [2010] EWCA Civ 859; [2011] UKSC 28.
[69] [2019] UKSC 22.
[70] (1995) 184 CLR 163.
[71] (2010) 239 CLR 531.
[72] [2018] HCA 34.
[73] [1984] AC 74.
[74] [2004] EWCA Civ 49.
[75] [2009] UKSC 8.
[76] [2013] UKSC 19.
[77] (1999) 46 NSW LR 55.
[78] (2000) 199 CLR 135.

v *Minister for the Environment and Water Resources*[79] and *Plaintiff M 70/2011 v Minister for Immigration and Citizenship*.[80]

As will be illustrated in Chap. 5, the English and Australian legal systems initially adopted a similar approach in reviewing the substantive exercise of discretion of public administrators, namely, the *Wednesbury* doctrine, but the doctrinal approaches in this area have been developed differently in both countries. The legal reasoning in *Kennedy v Charity Commission*[81] and *Pham v Secretary of State for the Home Department*[82] demonstrates the flexibility of the English courts in developing new doctrinal approaches like anxious scrutiny and modified rationality, and adopting grounds from EU law and the ECHR like proportionality in determining their scope of judicial review. Conversely, the constitutional orders in the Australian legal culture reduce the speed of development in this area. For example, new ground of illogicality and irrationality has not been flexibly accepted in Australia and proportionality has been firmly rejected. This is evident from analysing cases like *Re Minister for Immigration and Multicultural Affairs, Ex parte Applicant S20/2002*,[83] *Re Minister for Immigration and Citizenship v SZMDs*[84] and *Re Minister for Immigration and Citizenship v Li*.[85]

Chapter 6 will contain a comparative analysis of the legal reasoning of English cases in the area of legitimate expectations; for example, *R v Secretary of State for Transport, Ex parte Richmond-Upon-Thames London Borough Council*,[86] *R v Ministry of Agriculture, Fisheries and Food, Ex parte Hamble Fisheries Ltd*,[87] *R v North and East Devon Health Authority, Ex parte Coughlan*[88] and *The United Policyholders Group v The Attorney General of Trinidad and Tobago*[89] and Australian cases namely, *Kioa v West*,[90] *Attorney-General (NSW) v Quin*,[91] *Minister of State for Immigration & Ethnic Affairs v Ah Hin Teoh*[92] and *Re Minister for Immigration and Multicultural Affairs, Ex parte Lam*.[93] While the English courts flexibly regard substantive legitimate expectations as a ground of judicial review, the Australian courts firmly reject it.

---

[79] [2007] FCA 1480.
[80] [2011] HCA 32.
[81] [2014] UKSC 20.
[82] [2015] UKSC 19.
[83] (2003) 198 ALR 59.
[84] [2010] HCA 16.
[85] [2013] HCA 18.
[86] [1994] 1 WLR 74.
[87] [1995] 2 All ER 714.
[88] [2000] 3 All ER 850.
[89] [2016] UKPC 17.
[90] (1985) 159 CLR 550.
[91] (1990) 170 CLR 1.
[92] [1995] HCA 20.
[93] (2003) 214 CLR 1.

Apart from these doctrinal approaches and legal reasoning, discussions and debates on academic concepts related to the scope of judicial review, will be examined in Chaps. 3, 4, 5 and 6 as an 'additional indicator' of the influence of English and Australian legal culture. For example, deference is an academic concept, which runs throughout the determination of the grounds of judicial review analysed in Chaps. 3, 4, 5 and 6. Generally, it connotes an idea that the courts would necessarily defer to the decision-maker's view in some particular areas of decision-making.[94] However, the concept of deference is referred to and applied diversely in different legal systems. For example, it is variously debated in English law, but has been firmly rejected in Australian law. Although not a main focus of this book, this difference is also a product of the different legal cultures.

1.2.3 Example of a Combination of the Two Parts

It should be clarified that the methodologies of the aforementioned two parts and the connection between them are newly proposed in this book. Therefore, this section will contain an example to make sense of how they work in the following chapters. As mentioned, the doctrinal approaches in the legal reasoning of *Cart* of English law will be compared with that in *Kirk* of Australian law in Chap. 3. On the one hand, the courts in *Kirk* rigidly applied jurisdictional error as a ground of judicial review and central approach in determining whether or not they had the jurisdiction to conduct judicial review of the Industrial Court's decision. On the other hand, the courts in *Cart* flexibly applied various doctrinal approaches to decide if they had jurisdiction to conduct judicial review of the decision of the Upper Tribunal ('UT').[95] Many authors have emphasised that the differences in *Kirk* and *Cart* are based on the different constitutional orders of the English and Australian legal systems.[96] The question that immediately follows is, what kind of different 'constitutional order' does this statement refer to?

The comparison between the discussion of the rule of law by the UKSC and HCA judges serves as perfect introductory example. For the former, Lady Hale, a UKSC judge in *Cart*, concluded in a speech that Dicey's concept regarding the English courts' conduct of judicial review contained two major strands as follows;

---

[94] See Mark Elliott and Jason Varuhas, *Administrative Law: Text and Materials* (5th edn, OUP 2017) 284–288.

[95] The UKSC eventually held that judicial review of permission-refusal decisions is to be constrained by the second appeals criteria. The legal reasoning of the judgment in *Cart* will be analysed in detail in Chap. 3.

[96] For example, Janina Boughey and Lisa Crawford, 'Jurisdictional Error: Do We Really Need It?' in Mark Elliott, Jason Varuhas and Shona Stark (eds), *The Unity of Public Law?: Doctrinal, Theoretical and Comparative Perspectives* (Hart Publishing 2018). The contributions of the analysis in this book that are further from the other literature in the field are pointed out in Sect. 1.3 below and emphasised in each subsequent chapter.

> *(1) that Parliamentary is sovereign and can make or unmake any law, and*
> *(2) that everyone is subject to the same rule of law; this includes the Government and public officials, who must act within the powers which the law has given them.*[97]

It will be demonstrated in Chap. 2 that these two concepts are intertwined as the foundation of the English courts in conducting judicial review. On the one hand, the courts have a role to protect the rule of law by conducting judicial review of administrative action. On the other hand, they must respect the decision because the powers of administrative agents are conferred by Parliament, which has supreme power. Lady Hale further demonstrated her thinking that these concepts generally influence current English administrative law in that *'Dicey is the better known to [English] law students today... In many respects, the Constitution which we have today would be easily recognisable as the same constitution which...Dicey knew'*.[98]

On the other hand, the following oral pleading of Mr. Gageler, an Australian barrister,[99] to the HCA judges in *Kirk* illustrates a different understanding of the rule of law;

> *Mr Gageler: ... the sense being that within our constitutional system, any repository of governmental power is constrained by legal limits on that power and that the processes of the courts must be available to discern and enforce those legal limits on power.*
> *Justice Heydon: A Diceyan idea?*
> *Mr Gageler: A Diceyan idea, yes. Of course, not confined to him, but it does seem to be, your Honour, just really – – –*
> *Justice Heydon: No, it is a classical integer according to A.V. Dicey of the rule of law...*
> *Mr Gageler: ...What we are concerned about is a constitutional principle, which says that the rule of law as embodied in the Constitution means that a duty imposed by law must always be practically capable of compliance...*[100]

In the conversation, Gageler attempts to claim that the court has jurisdiction to conduct judicial review in this case because it has the role to enforce the legal limits on executive power. This is a reference to the surface-water of legality, requiring administrative action to be lawful. A discussion of deep-water legality begins when Justice Heydon asks if whether Gageler is referring to Dicey's idea. Gageler answers that he is, but his comments are not confined to Dicey. This means that the Australian law starts with Dicey's concept, placing the courts as the main institution to protect the rule of law by conducting judicial review. However, the concept to explain the courts' role in conducting judicial review is not limited, but further adapted in the Australian legal system. Gageler mentions that the courts shall consider constitutional principles, which in this case is the rule of law that *'is embodied in* [the written]

---

[97] Lady Hale, 'The Supreme Court in the United Kingdom Constitution' (The Bryce Lecture 2015, Oxford, 5 February 2015).

[98] ibid. It should be noted that the content of the rule of law in England is subject to widespread disagreement. However, as will be exemplified in Sect. 2.3.1 of Chap. 2, a 'general form' of Diceyan concept of the rule of law was influential in shaping the development of the English administrative law.

[99] This was before Stephen John Gageler was appointed to the HCA in October 2012.

[100] The Transcript of legal argument in *Kirk v Industrial Court (NSW)* (2010) 239 CLR 531.

Constitution'. The implication of this sentence is that the consideration of whether the court has role to conduct judicial review in a particular case needs to be concerned with the rule of law as the constitutional value that operates with the written Constitution.

This way of thinking about the role of the courts in conducting judicial review based on the particular understanding of the rule of law is an example of the constitutional order this book attempts to examine based on the concept of legal culture in Chap. 2. The doctrinal approaches of jurisdictional error are then unpacked in Chap. 3 from the legal reasoning in *Kirk*, and are demonstrated to be influenced by the mentioned understanding of the rule of law being operated with the written Constitution. Conversely, the flexibility of the doctrines applied by the English courts in *Cart* is an example of how the rule of law cooperates with parliamentary sovereignty.

Since the aim of this book is to simplify the comprehensive understanding of the determination of the scope of judicial review, the structure of Chaps. 3, 4, 5 and 6 will be similar. Each chapter will start with an explanation of how the role of the courts in conducting judicial review through the ground is controversial; hence deep-water legality and legal culture are needed to understand them. After that, the English and Australian doctrinal approaches will be comparatively unpacked from the legal reasoning in the mentioned leading cases, and then connected to the English and Australian legal cultures.

All the analyses will eventually be concluded in the final chapter to reflect the overall picture of the English and Australian determination of the scope of judicial review. Additionally, further implications of the deep-water concept of legality and legal culture as useful navigating approaches to understand other administrative law doctrines and grounds of judicial review in legal systems apart from England and Australia, will also be briefly pointed out.

1.3 Main Contributions of the Book

As described above, it may appear that the main areas of inquiry in this book, namely the connection between doctrinal approaches in conducting judicial review and the distinctive constitutional orders of the legal system, are obvious to administrative law scholars. It should be noted that the aim of this book is not to change the world, but to simply propose a new way to better understand it. Inspired by Feldman,[101] it desires to illuminate the fact that the determination of the grounds of judicial review in England and Australia can be comprehensively understood based on the approaches of legal culture, deep-water legality and unpacking process of the legal reasoning in leading cases. This substantial contribution will gradually

---

[101] *'Scholarship is...guided by certain ideals,...include: the desire to publish the work for the illumination of students, fellow scholars or the general public...'* (David Feldman, 'The Nature of Legal Scholarship' (1989) 52 MLR 498, 503).

1.3.1 Legal Culture Rather than Pragmatism and Formalism

Firstly, some scholars describe the English and Australian judicial review processes using the labels of pragmatism and formalism respectively. On the one hand, pragmatism is primarily used to refer to the flexibility of an English judicial review. For example, Craig states that *'...it is... possible to interpret the law/fact distinction in a more pragmatic, functional or policy-oriented way...'*.[102] Elliott and Thomas describe the approach of the court in *Cart* to decide its jurisdiction as pragmatic[103] and in *Jones*, Lord Hope clearly stated that,

> A pragmatic approach should be taken to the dividing line between law and fact, so that the expertise of tribunals at the first tier and that of the Upper Tribunal can be used to best effect. An appeal court should not venture too readily into this area by classifying issues as issues of law which are really best left for determination by the specialist appellate tribunals.[104]

Furthermore, some scholars use pragmatism as an emblem for criticising the excessive flexibility of the determination of judicial review, thereby leading to issues of uncertainty, confusion and illegitimacy. Forsyth, who suggests that the courts' determination should be more *'deeply rooted in orthodox doctrine'* rather than depending on *'pragmatic discretion'*, is one of the most prominent.[105]

On the other hand, Fisher describes formalism in regard to Australia as a tautological term that refers to *'a style of legal reasoning that gives authority to formal legal concepts'*.[106] In the context of administrative law, the idea is that *'public administration is capable of operating within clearly identifiable legal boundaries'*.[107] Furthermore, she mentions three of the five features of formalistic reasoning referred to by Poole, namely, *'an emphasis of rules and the avoidance of principles, de-contextualising decisions under review*, and *adherence to strict canons of*

---

[102] Craig, *Administrative Law* (n 49) [16–039].

[103] Mark Elliott and Robert Thomas, 'Tribunal Justice and Proportionate Dispute Resolution' (2012) 71 CLJ 297, 309.

[104] n 76 [16].

[105] Christopher Forsyth, '"Blasphemy Against Basics': Doctrine, Conceptual Reasoning and Certain Decisions of the UK Supreme Court' in John Bell, Mark Elliott, Jason Varuhas and Philip Murray (eds), *Public Law Adjudication in Common Law Systems: Process and Substance* (Hart Publishing 2016) 154.

[106] Elizabeth Fisher, '"Jurisdictional" Facts and "Hot" Facts: Legal Formalism, Legal Pluralism, and the Nature of Australian Administrative Law' (2015) 38 Melbourne University Law Review 968, 971–972.

[107] ibid 976.

statutory construction,[108] as a result of the approach of the court to adhere to certain legal boundaries.[109]

However, it is argued in this book that these terms should neither be applied to refer to the entire distinction between English and Australian judicial review because they are merely labels without any deep substance; in other words, their supporting elements and evidence have not been fully discussed. Additionally, both systems lead to a similar result in practice, namely, that the court is the final arbitrator to decide if the decision of the public administrator is reviewable or not. It could be said of this aspect that the Australian system also contains an element of pragmatism. Apart from this, Australian scholars have pointed to other aspects of pragmatism in the legal system. For example, while Aronson comments on the pragmatic distinction between the duty of tribunals and courts to review the substance of administrative action,[110] Raad criticises the Australian court's approach in *Hossain* for endorsing a pragmatic approach to jurisdictional error.[111] On the flip side, there is a suggestion to apply formalistic categorisation to the distinction between an error of law and fact in English law.[112] Therefore, since both legal systems contain elements of pragmatism and formalism, it should not be concluded that they use either of these terms.

Instead, the difference between English and Australian judicial review will be unpacked in this book with a framework of legal mentality of English and Australian judicial review constitutionalism, which is a further comprehensive, detailed and substantive concept to represent the entire geography of English and Australian judicial review. As will be fully discussed in Chap. 2, this particular form of legal culture is not just about conclusory constitutional differences, but the aggregation of judges' shared legal thinking about their role in conducting judicial review. Therefore, this novel way to explore differences between English and Australian judicial review is claimed to be the first contribution of this book.

---

[108] Poole (n 35) 25.

[109] Fisher (n 17) 4–5; See also Michael Taggart, 'Australian Exceptionalism in Judicial Review' (2008) 36 Federal Law Review 1, 6–7.

[110] For example, Mark Aronson, 'The Growth of Substantive Review' in John Bell, Mark Elliott, Jason Varuhas and Philip Murray (eds), *Public Law Adjudication in Common Law Systems: Process and Substance* (Hart Publishing 2016).

[111] Courtney Raad, '*Hossain v Minister for Immigration and Border Protection*: A Material Change to the Fabric of Jurisdictional Error?' (2019) 41(2) Sydney Law Review 265.

[112] Rebecca Williams, 'When is an Error not an Error? Reform of Jurisdictional Review of Error of Law and Fact' [2007] PL 793.

1.3.2 Detailed Unpacking Process of Analysing the Determination of the Grounds of Judicial Review

A second contribution is claimed in terms of the determination of the grounds of judicial review on a similar approach as that of the first point. Rather than concluding that the courts' approach is pragmatic or formalistic without substance, or only focusing on the outcomes of the English and Australian legal systems' acceptance or rejection of the grounds, Chaps. 3, 4, 5 and 6 will contain a deeper examination by unpacking a full detailed analysis of the doctrinal approaches used to determine the grounds of judicial review based on the legal reasoning of leading cases.

It may be questionable that an examination of English and Australian judicial review should only be conducted by analysing 'a few' cases. It is argued on this point that the main purpose of this book, which is to illustrate the depth of influence of legal culture on the judgment's engagement with the principle of legality in determining the grounds of judicial review, will not be achieved without a detailed examination of the legal reasoning of the cases. However, it is not possible to provide this kind of detailed analysis of a number of cases in a book of this length. Therefore, rather than touching on the reasoning given in the judgments of many cases or subjecting them to a general discussion, as in textbooks,[113] the English and Australian judicial review are mapped by analysing some 'leading cases' that have had an essential impact on the law and which judges and scholars have described as being authoritative.[114]

Discussed as the next contribution below, this detailed unpacking process will more clearly demonstrate how the determination of the grounds of judicial review is influenced by the distinctive understanding of legality and legal culture of the legal system. Furthermore, the examination will become obvious from a comparison of the English and Australian law, especially when recognising the different patterns shared across the determination of the grounds of judicial review in England and Australia. This kind of analysis, in which the legal mentality involved in the legal reasoning of judgments is demonstrated, has never been applied before as a catalyst to develop an understanding of the determination of the scope of judicial review.

---

[113] Also, the task fulfilled by this book is different from Nason's work, in which she develops a method of constructive interpretation by combining the tools of legal theory with empirical legal research with an examination of 482 administrative judgments (Sarah Nason, *Reconstructing Judicial Review* (Hart Publishing 2015)).

[114] Juss and Sunkin term these kinds of cases as 'landmark cases' (see Satvinder Juss and Maurice Sunkin, *Landmark Cases in Public Law* (Hart Publishing 2017)).

1.3.3 Bigger Picture of English and Australian Judicial Review

The third contribution is based on the way in which the parts of legal culture and the determination of the grounds of judicial review in English and Australian law are combined. Apart from the example of *Cart* and *Kirk* demonstrated in the Sect. 1.2.3 above, another illustration of the working of the framework of this book is Taggart's statement, which reads as follows;

> ...with some of the Australian responses to substantive legitimate expectations...is the claim of exceptionalism...there is something about the Australian Constitution or separation of powers that answers the question without more.[115]

As will be shown throughout the book, a number of academic works in the field of comparative administrative law focus on the outcome when comparing the different doctrinal approaches between legal systems; for example, the question of whether to accept or reject substantive legitimate expectations as a valid ground of judicial review.[116] Instead, the aim of this book is to explore 'the bigger picture' by understanding the determination of the grounds of English and Australian judicial review in the light of their legal culture.

According to the statement above, the *'Australian response to substantive legitimate expectations'*, which involved rejecting the notion that the ground gives rise to a jurisdictional error, will be unpacked in this book based on a detailed examination of the legal reasoning given in some leading Australian cases. It will be then demonstrated as being deeply embedded in the Australian legal culture, particularly in terms of the Australian courts' rigid adherence to the framework of separation of powers prescribed in the written constitution. The term *'exceptionalism'* will also be unpacked by comparing Australia's firm rejection of substantive legitimate expectations with various doctrinal approaches the English courts can flexibly use to determine the ground based on the legal mentality of English judicial review constitutionalism.

Rather than chastising the flexibility of the English law or the rigidity of the Australian law as problematic in this book, they are regarded as being different but valid ways to determine the scope of judicial review based on their diverse contexts.[117] In other words, an attempt is made in this book to facilitate a tangible process of how and why proportionality and substantive legitimate expectations are debatable in English law, whereas they are completely rejected in Australia, based on the framework of deep-water legality and legal culture. This proposed approach

---

[115] n 109.

[116] Examples from the literature will be provided and discussed in Chap. 6.

[117] See examples of literature that are also aimed to make the same kind of contribution, but based on examining different subject matters and legal systems, namely, Paul Craig, *The Hamlyn Lectures: UK, EU and Global Administrative Law* (CUP 2015) and Janina Boughey, *Human Rights and Judicial Review in Australia and Canada: The Newest Despotism?* (Hart Publishing 2017).

underpins a holistic understanding of the influence of normative settings on particular areas of law; therefore, it is a significant means of navigation for any research of the development of the administrative law doctrine in the legal system.

1.3.4 Exploration Through the Eyes of an Outsider

Next, an additional contribution in comparing English and Australian law comes from my starting position as an outsider of these legal systems. It will be discussed in the next chapter that some lawyers may be too familiar with some of the concepts in their legal system and feel uncomfortable with other concepts in other legal systems. For example, an English administrative law scholar may be familiar with the theme that various constitutional values can underpin a body of legal doctrine. Variance across cases may be an indication that judges prioritise different values in the same context.[118] This may be uncomfortable for Australian lawyers, who refer the question of jurisdiction of the courts to the rigid framework of separation of powers, rather than diverse values. Conversely, it may sound strange when English scholars hear Australian judges saying that Australia does not have the concept of deference.[119] The benefit of this book is claimed to be that I have fresh eyes in comparing the differences between English and Australian legal cultures and the determination of judicial review.

1.4 Scope and Caveats

Since a number of new methodological aspects are applied in this book, its scope and caveats need to be clarified. Six main points are introduced here and others will follow with each chapter.

Firstly, it was revealed in the discussion of the two-part structure of this book that the relationship between legal culture and the determination of the grounds of judicial review is similar to the 'chicken and egg' dilemma. The overall argument will be incomplete without considering both parts in unity. Therefore, English and Australian judicial review constitutionalism, as analysed in Chap. 2, will be frequently referred to in Chaps. 3, 4, 5 and 6.

The second caveat is that the categorisation of the grounds of judicial review is inconsistent, both within and between these legal systems. It is acknowledged that the grounds analysed in Chaps. 3, 4, 5 and 6 overlap. The division of these grounds into different chapters is not fixed. For example, the ground of jurisdictional fact in

---

[118] E.g. Rebecca Williams, 'The Multiple Doctrines of Legitimate Expectations' (2016) 132 LQR 639.

[119] E.g. Hayne (n 5).

Chap. 4 and the ground of substantive legitimate expectations in Chap. 6 can be regarded as a subset of the grounds for substantive control of discretion in Chap. 5. Alternatively, error of law and error of fact are usually discussed in the same chapter in textbooks, especially in English law, in which the terminologies of jurisdictional error and jurisdictional fact have fluctuated from the origin of judicial review in the seventeenth century to the abandonment in *Anisminic* in the 1970s and the exception of the courts to intervene in factual issue in contemporary cases.[120] This is why Gellhorn and Robinson describe the scope of judicial review as a seedless grape.

However, it is still necessary for this book to separate them because this facilitates an insight into the in-depth legal reasoning between the different grounds of judicial review. The subsequent chapters will demonstrate that the relationship between the grounds will reflect some different themes between the legal systems, which will be regarded as another product of the different legal cultures. For example, the argument of Gellhorn and Robinson that the scope of judicial review resembles a seedless grape may be carry less weight in Australia, where the grounds of judicial review including jurisdictional fact, *Wednesbury* Unreasonableness, illogicality and irrationality and legitimate expectations, are systematically categorised under the approach of jurisdictional error.

The third caveat concerns the scope of application of legal culture. There are two important points to be introduced here before being exemplified in the next chapter. Firstly, since the focus of this book is the contemporary legal mentality of judges in England and Australia pertaining to their role in conducting judicial review, legal history is not the main research methodology. Where some historical context is described, it is only to demonstrate the growth of the legal thinking in the different legal systems.[121] Therefore, the purpose of the book is different from the work of Cane, who conducted a historical analysis of the different architectural development of government systems in the UK, US and Australia.[122] Secondly, it is important to point out here that legal culture is non-monolithic in nature. Variations can be found in many aspects, namely, how legal culture is formed and identified. Additionally, there are usually disagreements on the elements of legal culture between lawyers within the same legal culture. For example, there are many different ways to explain the rule of law within one legal culture, as well as a choice between ultra vires and common law models to justify judicial review in English law.[123] The role of legal culture as a concept to express disagreement and uniformity in and between legal system(s) will be exemplified in the next chapter.

Another caveat pointed out here is that there are various terminologies in this book both across and between the legal systems. For example, various terms have been applied by English and Australian judges to imply what the courts do according

---

[120] This will be examined in Chaps. 3 and 4.

[121] This will be exemplified in Sect. 2.2.4 of Chap. 2.

[122] Cane, *Controlling Administrative Power: An Historical Comparison* (n 12).

[123] Chief Justice French, 'The Rule of Law as a Many Coloured Dream Coat' (20th Annual Lecture Singapore Academy of Law, 18 September 2013, Singapore). This will be discussed in Chap. 2.

1.4 Scope and Caveats

to the principle of legality, namely function,[124] role,[125] job,[126] and duty. It should be noted that this book sticks with the term 'role' because it refers to what the courts do in the sense of how they see themselves, which is compatible to the methodology of legal mentality, explained in the next chapter. Also, it will be seen that some terminologies are applied in England and Australia, such as ultra vires, deference, jurisdictional error and jurisdictional fact, but they refer to different meanings. These differences can also be understood in the light of the deep-water concept of legality and legal culture, as will be demonstrated in the following chapters. Apart from these, other terminologies will be clarified alongside the arguments in the following chapters.

Fifthly, it should be noted here that the river metaphor is not aimed to play a central role in the argument in this book; rather, it is applied for two reasons. Firstly, it is believed to be functional in illustrating the general statement of the book, particularly in terms of comparing legality as a general concept (surface-water) and as substantive concept (deep-water) in different legal systems. Secondly, the analogy of elements of legal culture to the geography and depth under water is compatible to metaphors applied by other scholars when normatively describing its influence on the administrative law doctrine. For example, Taggart raises a question to point out the exceptionalism of the Australian administrative law, namely, '...*what are the distinctive features of the Australian public law landscape that might be thought singly or collectively to be distinctive or exceptional?*'[127] In addition, Poole analogously describes the UK jurisprudence of rights, related to judicial review as '*the deep blue sea*'.[128] Furthermore, legality is discussed by Harlow as an example of a shallow theory, which is affected by a deep theory, which entails an explanation of the function of law in general, namely the rule of law.[129] These Harlow's shallow and deep theories match the metaphor of the surface and deep-water concepts of legality applied in this book.

The sixth caveat is to clarify that judicial review in a broad sense can refer to both a review of administrative action and legislature, which is called a constitutional review or constitutional adjudication. Although the general methodological approaches of legal culture may be able to be applied to the area of constitutional

---

[124] Cameron Stewart, 'The Doctrine of Substantive Unfairness and the Review of Substantive Legitimate Expectations' in Matthew Groves and HP Lee (eds), *Australian Administrative Law: Fundamentals, Principles and Doctrines* (CUP 2007) 281.

[125] Justice McHugh, 'Tensions between the Executive and the Judiciary' (Australian Bar Association Conference, Paris, 10 July 2002).

[126] Stephen Sedley, *Ashes and Sparks: Essays on Law and Justice* (CUP 2011) 261.

[127] Taggart (n 109).

[128] Poole (n 35).

[129] Carol Harlow, 'Changing the Mindset: The Place of Theory in English Administrative Law' (1994) 14 OJLS 419, 421–424.

review,[130] it should be clear that the focus of this book is only judicial review of administrative action, as demonstrated in its title.

Last, but perhaps most importantly, since it will be concluded in the book that the Australian courts' determination of the grounds of judicial review is relatively rigid compared to the English courts', some points need to be introduced here before being gradually established throughout the book. Firstly, this argument does not apply to the entire English and Australian public law. It is surely incorrect to claim that either the English public law is always flexible or the Australian public law is fundamentally rigid. For example, it is debatable if the Australian courts should limit the interpretation of the freedom of political communication by only referring to the Constitutional text and structure, or if they should apply the proportionality test, which enables some values external to the Constitution to be considered to facilitate stricter scrutiny, and thereby promote transparency and flexibility in some cases.[131] This area is not examined in this book, but only the flexibility of the English courts' determination of the grounds of judicial review and the rigidity of the Australian courts' determination, as embedded in their deep understanding of legality and legal culture.

Next, it is not claimed in this book that an English judicial review is flexible and diametrically opposed to the Australian law, which is necessarily rigid. In the same vein as the point of pragmatism and formalism noted above, there is clearly a degree of flexibility in the determination of the grounds of judicial review in both legal systems. The Australian courts are able to adapt the scope of judicial review depending on the particular circumstances of the case. For example, it was explained in *Kioa v West* that the courts have to determine what the duty to act fairly in the way of procedural fairness means in the specific context.[132] In the same vein, as will be unpacked in Chap. 4, the judges in *Timbarra* also needed to make a general assessment of the statutory scheme in order to reach the conclusion that the disputed factual reference was a jurisdictional fact.[133] Whether the Australian approach should be more flexible in terms of giving '*proper, genuine and realistic consideration to the merits of the case*' is deliberated by judges and scholars.[134] Undoubtedly, flexible judicial discretion and incremental change are common features of a

---

[130] There are some shared elements of legal culture that influence both judicial review and constitutional review, for example the balance between parliamentary sovereignty in England (See Lady Hale, 'The Supreme Court in the United Kingdom Constitution' (n 97)) and the written constitution and federal system in Australia (See Chief Justice French, 'The Courts and the Parliament' (Queensland Supreme Court Seminar, Brisbane, 4 August 2012)).

[131] See more in *Lange v Australian Broadcasting Corporation* (1997) 189 CLR 520; Adrienne Stone, 'The Limits of Constitutional Text and Structure: Standards of Review and the Freedom of Political Communication' (1999) 23 Melb U L Rev. 668; Bonina Challenor, 'The Balancing Act: A Case for Structured Proportionality under the Second Limb of the Lange Test' (2015) 40 UW Austl L Rev. 267.

[132] *Kioa v West* (1985) 159 CLR 550, 613.

[133] n 77 [44]–[94].

[134] See *Khan v Minister for Immigration, Local Government and Ethnic Affairs* (1987) 14 ALD 291 in Aronson, Groves and Weeks (n 20) [5.150]

common law system. In short, the Australian courts also have a way to flexibly stretch the boundary of their function to conduct judicial review of the factual and discretionary issues of an administrative action they consider to be unlawful.[135]

However, what is found to be interesting and as demonstrated throughout the chapters of this book, is that the Australian courts apply a 'relatively rigid' mode of doctrinal approaches and legal reasoning to determine the grounds of judicial review compared to the English courts. For example, it is revealed in the analysis in Chap. 3 that, while individual judges in the English law have flexibly adopted the determination of error of law, the status of the tribunal and interpretation of restrictive clauses based on various justifications and doctrines, the determinations of Australian judges have rigidly followed the framework of the separation of powers. Likewise, it is unpacked in Chap. 4 that, while jurisdictional fact is determined as an entrenched ground of judicial review in Australian law, it is fluctuating in English law. Also, Chap. 5 unpacks the various choices, namely, *Wednesbury* unreasonableness, modified rationality, anxious scrutiny, proportionality and deference available for the English courts to apply flexibly in determining the scope of judicial review of administrative discretion. Conversely, the Australian courts have relatively limited grounds on which to apply judicial review under the approach of jurisdictional error. And Chap. 6 demonstrates the flexibility the English courts have in determining substantive legitimate expectations as a ground of judicial review. This is compared to the Australian courts' firm rejection of it. The main task in this book is to demonstrate that these different modes of doctrinal approaches and legal reasoning are not rambling, but deeply dominated by the legal system's legal culture.

Additionally, it should be noted that it is the doctrinal approaches and the legal reasoning applied by the courts in Australia to determine the grounds of judicial review that are claimed to be relatively rigid, not the outcomes of the cases. To be specific, it is not claimed in this book that Australian cases will always be fixed in terms of permitting or rejecting claimants' request for judicial review. It is recognised that many times the two legal systems have applied different approaches, but reached a similar outcome. For example, although substantive legitimate expectations is accepted as a valid ground of judicial review in England, Thomas points out that, not only do the courts rarely intervene in administrative action based on this ground, but they also apply a light-touch review when they do.[136] On the flip side, the Australian courts are definitely able to review cases that involve what would be substantive legitimate expectations in England under different grounds, such as illogicality and irrationality.

---

[135] For example, the majority in *Li* refers to *House v The King* (1936) 55 CLR 499 in claiming that, even without the identification of a specific legal error, the courts can still invalidate an administrative decision based on failure to exercise discretion and the fact that the result is unreasonable, plainly unjust, or lacks justification (see n 85 at [76]).

[136] Robert Thomas, 'Legitimate Expectations and the Separation of Powers in English and Welsh Administrative Law' in Matthew Groves and Greg Weeks (eds), *Legitimate Expectations in the Common Law World* (Hart Publishing 2017).

Nevertheless, it will be demonstrated by the in-depth examination in this book that there are still some differences in detail between these dissimilar approaches. For example, as a product of the English legal culture, the application of substantive legitimate expectations by the English courts is complicated by other grounds of judicial review, like proportionality.[137] Therefore, the court's determination of judicial review can be conducted based on a series of questions to consider proportionality, namely Necessity, Sufficiency and a Narrow Sense of Proportionality. Therefore, the claimed benefits of applying proportionality, for example, that it has a more structured analysis that requires the courts to give specific detailed reasoning when striking down an administrative decision,[138] are also included in the determination of substantive legitimate expectations in England. Although this book is not aimed to assess the advantages and disadvantages of these different doctrinal approaches between legal systems, it should be well-read in terms of how they are influenced by their legal system's legal culture. In fact, whether or not these differences grow to become essential to cases in reality, it is an academic task that we, as comparative lawyers, should dive deeply into.

1.5 Conclusion

The test of the review of law, fact and discretion, entwined with the courts' jurisdiction and the scope of judicial review of administrative action,[139] are important questions to be discussed in the administrative law of most legal systems. It is postulated in this chapter that they are all asking whether the disputed administrative action is within the scope of legality or not. Beyond the surface-water concept of legality, it is proposed in this book that the deep-water legality, which is distinctive between legal systems, is complicated by their particular legal culture. Therefore, this different in-depth understanding of legality influences the different determinations of the grounds of judicial review between legal systems, particularly the controversial grounds, namely jurisdictional error, error of law, jurisdictional fact, rationality, proportionality and substantive legitimate expectations.

The connections between these three themes of legal culture, legality and the determination of the grounds of judicial review are the core of this book. The legal mentality of English and Australian judicial review constitutionalism will be explored in Chap. 2 and treated as a reference to navigate the different determinations of the grounds of judicial review in Chaps. 3, 4, 5 and 6. In these chapters, the doctrinal approaches that involve the validity of the grounds, justification, doctrine, application and integration of international obligation into consideration will be

---

[137] This will be unpacked in detail in Chap. 6.

[138] See more in Sect. 5.3.1 of Chap. 5.

[139] Leeming connotes general meaning of jurisdiction as *'authority to decide'* (Mark Leeming, *Authority to Decide: the Law of Jurisdiction in Australia* (2nd edn, The Federation Press 2020)).

1.5 Conclusion

unpacked from the legal reasoning of leading English and Australian cases. It will be demonstrated that all these doctrinal approaches are the products of the legal mentality of English and Australian judicial review constitutionalism. The final chapter will be concluded with a reflection of some notions of the comparison of English and Australian law and some further implications of the general methodology of deep-water legality to other administrative law doctrines and other legal systems. The navigating approaches of legal mentality of judicial review constitutionalism and the process of unpacking the legal reasoning in leading cases applied for a more in-depth understanding of English and Australian judicial review are proposed to be substantial contributions of this book.

Chapter 2
Differences Between the English and Australian Legal Cultures

Abstract The legal mentality of judicial review constitutionalism, as a particular form of legal culture, exploring individual judges' understanding of their role in conducting judicial review based on the distinctive constitutional orders of the legal system is presented in this chapter. This is followed by an examination of the differences between the legal mentality of English and Australian judicial review constitutionalism. As for the English law, the courts understand their role as flexible due to certain elements, namely the absence of a written Constitution, a balancing process between the twin concepts of parliamentary sovereignty and the rule of law and a fluid relationship between the court and the executive. Conversely, the rule of law, the rigid separation of powers, the distinction between legality and merits and the concept of jurisdiction are distinctively understood to both entrench and limit the courts' scope of judicial review in Australia. Hence, the courts understand their role as having to rigidly follow the framework of separation of powers prescribed in the written constitution and statutory construction. These connotations of English and Australian legal cultures will navigate an inclusive understanding of different determinations of the grounds of judicial review in England and Australia in the following chapters.

2.1 Introduction

> *Change in the laws of any country can be a complex function of history, culture, economy, social conditions and the nature and distribution of public and private power within the society...*
>
> *...It is necessary to focus on the reality of legal diversity generally, and particularly in the area of public law given its intimate connection with domestic constitutional frameworks, statutory regimes and local legal cultures.*[1]

The core of this book examines how the distinctive constitutional orders of England and Australia influence the courts' deep understanding of legality, and therefore the

---
[1] Chief Justice French, 'The Globalisation of Public Law: A Quilting of Legalities' (Public Law Conference, Cambridge, 12 September 2016).

different doctrinal approaches applied in the determination of the grounds of judicial review. Full details of the differences between English and Australian legal cultures will be provided in this chapter. The above quotation of Chief Justice French of the HCA demonstrates the chapter's spirit that it is 'necessary' to unpack 'what's really going on' in the English and Australian courts' deep understanding of their role in conducting judicial review according to 'the distinctive constitutional orders' of their legal systems. The results of the exploration in this chapter will 'navigate' a 'comprehensive understanding' of how the doctrinal approaches in the determination of the grounds of judicial review have been applied and developed by the English and Australian courts, discussed in the following chapters.

In terms of structure, the general definitions and benefits of the concept of legal culture in representing the differences between English and Australian constitutional orders will be described in the next section. It will discuss the 'slippery' nature of legal culture, which leads to a variation in its use. Then, legal mentality of judicial review constitutionalism will be introduced as a particular form of legal culture applied to explore the differences between English and Australian judicial review.[2] Following, Sects. 2.3 and 2.4 will be a comprehensive exploration on the differences between legal mentality of English and Australian judicial review constitutionalism, according to the proposed methodologies. Apart from the different substantive views on the rule of law,[3] how the English and Australian courts explain their role in conducting judicial review according to distinctive constitutional frameworks and other constitutional values will also be discussed. For example, Sect. 2.3 will contain a discussion of how the English courts particularly understand their role and scope of judicial review as being flexible based on the absence of a written constitution, the nature of the balancing process between the rule of law and parliamentary sovereignty, as well as the fluid relationship between the court and the executive. This is to compare with Sect. 2.4, deliberating how the federal system and written Constitution influence the Australian courts' understanding of the rule of law, the separation of powers, the concept of jurisdiction and thereby their role in conducting judicial review as relatively rigid. Eventually, snapshots[4] of the geography[5] of English and Australian legal cultures will be concluded in the final section.[6]

---

[2] Noteworthy, constitutional law scholars give various meanings to 'constitutionalism'. In the same way with 'constitutional order' (See n 18 of Chap. 1), this book has a specific connotation and methodology in referring constitutionalism, which will be exemplified in Sects. 2.2.2 and 2.2.3 below.

[3] Mentioned as example in Sect. 1.2.3 of Chap. 1.

[4] The use of this methodology will be described in Sect. 2.2.4 below.

[5] See the metaphor how English and Australian legal cultures are analogous to geographical features under deep-water in Chap. 1.

[6] I have acknowledged and considered many times about whether or not this chapter is too long. However, I have reached this conclusion based on the reason that the task of exploring and comparing the geography of the English and Australian legal cultures should be structured in the same chapter.

2.2 Concept of Legal Culture: A Navigating Methodology

The concept of legal culture has been increasingly applied in a number of works in the field of comparative law.[7] The most basic way to consider its definition is to divide the words into 'legal' and 'culture'. While the former simply refers to law, the later connotes particular patterns of behaviour, opinions, thinking or ideas.[8] Therefore, in the most general sense, legal culture is a way to describe *'relatively stable patterns of legally oriented social behaviour and attitudes'*.[9] Nelken asserts that this way of considering *'law as a cultural artefact'* can bring together aspects of socio-legal studies and comparative law by requiring studies on surrounding elements such as history, international relations, political science, psychology and economics.[10] In other words, it comparatively studies the way laws are applied and developed with wider social elements,[11] reflecting that law is embedded in larger frameworks of different social contexts.[12]

The general benefits in using the concept of legal culture for exploring the laws are discussed and divided into three main points. First, the nature of legal culture considering *'law inside culture'*[13] helps us *'line up relevant phenomena concerning the relationship between law and culture'*.[14] Thereby it allows us *'to gather more substance in particular about public attitudes towards the law and legal institutions'*.[15] The use of legal culture therefore can aggregate interrelated

---

[7] See Lawrence Friedman, 'The Place of Legal Culture in the Sociology of Law' in M Freeman (ed), *Law and Sociology* (OUP 2006); Roger Cotterrell, 'Comparative Law and Legal Culture' in Mathias Reimann and Reinhard Zimmermann (eds), *The Oxford Handbook of Comparative Law* (2nd edn, OUP 2019).

[8] David Nelken, 'Defining and Using the Concept of Legal Culture' in Örücü Esin and David Nelken (eds), *Comparative Law: A Handbook* (Hart Publishing 2007) 111.

[9] David Nelken, 'Using the Concept of Legal Culture' (2004) 29 Austl J Leg Phil 1. Friedman also provides various definitions of legal culture, but they all contain the same components. For example, he refers to it *'attitudes and behaviour patterns toward the legal system'* (See Lawrence Friedman, *The Legal System: A Social Science Perspective* (Russell Sage Foundation 1975) 193. Alternatively, it connotes *'ideas, attitudes, expectations and opinions about law, held by people in some given society'* (Lawrence Friedman, 'Is there a Modern Legal Culture?' (1994) 7 Ratio Juris 117, 118).

[10] Nelken 'Defining and Using the Concept of Legal Culture' (n 8) 109, 111; See also David Nelken, 'Disclosing/ Invoking Legal Culture: An Introduction' (1995) 4 Social & Legal Studies 435, 445; Roger Cotterrell, 'The Concept of Legal Culture' in David Nelken (ed), *Comparing Legal Cultures* (Dartmouth 1997) 13.

[11] David Nelken, 'Comparative Sociology of Law' in Reza Benakar and Max Travers (eds), *Introduction to Law and Social Theory* (Hart Publishing 2002) 342.

[12] ibid 343–345; See also Cotterrell, 'The Concept of Legal Culture' (n 10) 13.

[13] Cotterrell, 'Comparative Law and Legal Culture' (n 7) 711–713.

[14] Lawrence Friedman, 'The Concept of Legal Culture: A Reply' in David Nelken (ed), *Comparing Legal Cultures* (Dartmouth 1997) 33.

[15] ibid.

phenomena into a whole picture of legal life rather than in isolation.[16] Webber called such aggregation as *'webs of interaction'*, representing overall content of law.[17] Apart from that, legal culture also reflects deepness and sophistication of the examined account.[18] Webber discusses that *'As a lens through which the elements are recognised and formulated...legal culture offers a richer and ultimately more accurate account of the content of legal principle'*.[19] Legal culture is not a categorisation or collection of doctrines, rules, legislations, jurisprudence, static ideal or legal order described in textbooks.[20] Instead, it is a way to *'look more deeply the commonsense assumptions and shared understandings that do not need to be expressed in legal rules but colour all understanding of them'*.[21] In essence, thinking about legal culture adds thickness to the issues referring to *'substantive, complex and dynamic nature'* of the account at the point of *'contact between sociological description and normative assessment'*.[22] The third benefit in using the concept of legal culture is that it *'thinks about law in the breath as culture'*.[23] This methodology alerts us to recognise similarities and differences, particularly disagreements, in the way law is conceived and lived.[24] It stresses that different cultural settings can influence similar rules to be understood differently.[25] Such differences are very important for the comparatists to detect, understand, value, and cherish.[26]

In summary, the concept of legal culture can reflect thickness of what really happens in a legal community, by aggregating elements from the larger social frameworks and forming an overall picture, which express differences within and among the legal system(s). As discussed in Chap. 1, this is compatible to the aim of this book, exploring the overall deep and substantive pictures of differences between English and Australian constitutional orders, and demonstrate their connections with the different determinations of the scope of judicial review in the legal systems. This is the reason for selecting the concept of legal culture over other normative frameworks to discuss the differences between English and Australian judicial review. These benefits in using legal culture will become more obvious in relation

---

[16] Cotterrell, 'The Concept of Legal Culture' (n 10) 28; See also Nelken, 'Disclosing/ Invoking Legal Culture: An Introduction' (n 10) 444.

[17] Jeremy Webber, 'Culture, Legal Culture, and Legal Reasoning: A Comment on Nelken' (2004) 29 Austl J Leg Phil 27, 28, 32, 36.

[18] Culture is regarded as a reflexive phenomenon (John Bell, *French Legal Cultures* (2nd edn, CUP 2008) 4–5); See also Nelken, 'Comparative Sociology of Law' (n 11) 350.

[19] Webber (n 17) 31, 35.

[20] Bell (n 18) 1, 14; Elizabeth Fisher, *Risk Regulation and Administrative Constitutionalism* (Hart Publishing 2007) 36.

[21] Cotterrell, 'Comparative Law and Legal Culture' (n 7) 724.

[22] Fisher (n 20) 36.

[23] Nelken, 'Defining and Using the Concept of Legal Culture' (n 8) 127.

[24] Nelken, 'Using the Concept of Legal Culture' (n 9) 2.

[25] Cotterrell, 'Comparative Law and Legal Culture' (n 7) 713.

[26] ibid.

to the discussion of legal mentality of judicial review constitutionalism as a particular form of legal culture below.

2.2.1 Variations in Using Legal Culture

Like other overarching social science concepts,[27] there are unsolved questions about how to use the concept of legal culture.[28] Nelken states clearly that the meaning and using of legal culture is far from settled.[29] This is because of its abstract and slippery nature of both the terms 'legal' and 'culture'.[30] In talking about law, we can refer to either rule, doctrine, legal practice, legislation, jurisprudence or institution.[31] As Nelken notes, law is a word *'whose interpretation and definition have illocutionary effects'*.[32] Likewise, culture can mean various things namely historical memory, tradition, practice, attitude, expectation or way of thinking.[33] According to Nelken, culture is *'particularly difficult to define and easy to abuse'*.[34] When these words are combined, legal culture therefore covers a variety of examinations on social influences towards legal subjects. This leads Friedman to conclude that *'one can speak of legal culture at many levels of abstraction'*.[35]

There are two main ways, in which scholars respond to this unsettlement. First, some scholars argue against the use of the concept of legal culture, requesting for changing its definition and application into other terms. For example, Cotterrell

---

[27] Similar to most of the basic conceptual building-blocks of social science, legal culture is *'general or hard to define or delimit'* (Friedman, 'The Concept of Legal Culture: A Reply' (n 14) 33).

[28] David Nelken, 'Towards a Sociology of Legal Adaption' in David Nelken and Johannes Feest (eds), *Adapting Legal Cultures* (Hart Publishing 2001) 26.

[29] Nelken, 'Disclosing/ Invoking Legal Culture: An Introduction' (n 10) 437.

[30] Friedman, 'The Place of Legal Culture in the Sociology of Law' (n 7) 191.

[31] Cotterrell, 'Comparative Law and Legal Culture' (n 7) 710–711.

[32] Nelken, 'Defining and Using the Concept of Legal Culture' (n 8) 111. Pennisi also asserts that *'the clarity of the concept depends on the criterion chosen to define what counts as legal'* (Carlo Pennisi, 'Sociological Uses of the Concept of Legal Culture' in David Nelken (ed), *Comparing Legal Cultures* (Dartmouth 1997) 106).

[33] Nelken, 'Defining and Using the Concept of Legal Culture' (n 8) 120. It can be regarded as praxis connoting a pattern of behaviour or set of ideas and values towards the activity (See Zygmunt Bauman, *Culture as Praxis* (Sage 1999); Clifford Geertz, *The Interpretation of Cultures* (2nd edn, Basic Books 1993) 5).

[34] Nelken, 'Using the Concept of Legal Culture' (n 9) 6. Critiques of legal culture on the inconsistent or misleading referents often come with a wide variety of meanings of the term 'culture'. (See Nelken, 'Defining and Using the Concept of Legal Culture' (n 8) 114–115); By referring to Clifford Geertz, *The Intepretation of Cultures: Selected Essays* (Basic Books 1973), Cotterrell also asserts that *'the variety of meanings of legal culture here is strikingly reminiscent of the variety of meanings of the term "culture" itself'* (Cotterrell, 'The Concept of Legal Culture' (n 10) 16). Friedman refers this to *'the idea of a plurality of legal cultures'* (Lawrence Friedman, *The Republic of Choice: Law, Authority and Culture* (Harvard University Press 1990), 213).

[35] Friedman, *The Legal System: A Social Science Perspective* (n 9) 204.

suggests *'legal ideology'* instead of legal culture as a concept focusing on *'the ideas of legal professionals and jurists and their influence over popular consciousness'*.[36] The examples of other terms do the same job with legal culture are living law, law in action, legal consciousness,[37] law and its environment,[38] legal traditions[39] and legal styles.[40] Alternatively, some scholars attempt to integrate the various aspects of legal culture into one. For example, Blankenburg and Bruinsma argue that legal culture should be treated as

> ...*a multi-layered concept which includes legal norms, salient features of legal institutions and their infrastructure, social behaviour in creating, using and not using law, as well as legal consciousness in the legal professions and amongst the public.*[41]

The second way to solve the abstract nature of legal culture is to conclude that the variation on the use of legal culture are valid for the different purposes of works. As Nelken points out, legal culture is considered as having various meanings, according to its use in a variety of ways.[42] It opens to all of those mentioned subjects namely professional practice, thinking, wish, idea, mentality, attitude, consciousness, tradition, opinion, expectation, ideology of legal doctrine, principle, legislation, jurisprudence and concept.[43] All different definitions and subjects of study are dependent on the purpose of the analysis,[44] which the concept of legal culture is

---

[36] Cotterrell, 'The Concept of Legal Culture' (n 10) 21–22; See also Roger Cotterell, *Law's Community: Legal Theory in Sociological Perspective* (OUP 1995) 7–14; Nelken, 'Defining and Using the Concept of Legal Culture' (n 8) 116; Nelken, 'Disclosing/ Invoking Legal Culture: An Introduction' (n 10) 446.

[37] As Blankenburg and Bruinsma describe, *'Legal culture is defined to include four components: law in the books, law in action as challenged by the institutional infrastructure, patterns of legally relevant behaviour and legal consciousness, particularly, a distinctive attitude toward the law among legal professionals'* (E Blankenburg and F Bruinsma, *Dutch Legal Culture* (2nd edn, Kluwer Law International 1995).

[38] According to the description given by King, *'The environment for law is a world, which can only be understood in terms of, first whether it is amenable or not to law, second the legality or illegality of events. Law exists within this legal environment* (Michael King, 'Comparing Legal Cultures in the Quest for Law's Identity' in David Nelken (ed), *Comparing Legal Cultures* (Dartmouth 1997) 127).

[39] Tradition is an important part of culture, and especially within the law. It connects norms, practices and people (Bell (n 18) 6).

[40] Zweigert and Kötz refers legal style as *'predominant and characteristic mode of thought in legal matters, its particularly distinctive concepts or institutions, which legal sources it uses and how it handles them, and its ideology'* (ibid preface vi).

[41] Blankenburg and Bruinsma (n 37) in Nelken, 'Disclosing/Invoking Legal Culture: An Introduction' (n 10) 438. Cotterrell also mentions this kind of concept that *'legal culture does not appear as a unitary concept but indicates an immense, multitextured overlay of levels and regions of culture'* (Cotterrell, 'The Concept of Legal Culture' (n 10) 16–17).

[42] Nelken, 'Using the Concept of Legal Culture' (n 9) 2; See also Friedman, 'Is there a Modern Legal Culture?' (n 9) 118–119; Friedman, 'The Concept of Legal Culture: A Reply' (n 14) 38.

[43] See Friedman, 'The Concept of Legal Culture: A Reply' (n 14) 35–38.

[44] For example, in applying the concept to European legal culture, while Gessner focuses on the degree of legalisation of state activities and the frequency of corrupt behaviour of public officials

particularly intended to serve.[45] Therefore, a preliminary question to be asked in the use of the concept of legal culture is *'what we mean by...term* [legal culture] *we adopt, and why we think that it could best serve the purpose of our particular enquiry'*.[46]

This book reaches an agreement with the second solution. Although the generality of the concept of legal culture covers a wide range of phenomena, the particular purpose, subject and scope have to be clarified in the work. As discussed in Chap. 1, the subject of study in this book is the 'legal mentality of judicial review constitutionalism', which connotes the way judges in England and Australia think about the distinctive constitutional orders of their legal systems, which they rely on in perceiving their role in conducting judicial review. The next sub-sections will discuss this form into 'legal mentality' and 'judicial review constitutionalism', before combining them into one.

2.2.2 Judicial Review Constitutionalism

A wide range of literature shows that the concept of legal culture can be applied to understand law inside a culture in various fields. For example, Lazarus applies the concept to contrast the impact of legal culture on prisoners' rights between the English and German legal systems,[47] Buxbaum uses it in the area of competition law[48] and Johnson utilises it to understand the Japanese way of prosecution.[49] The first clarification of the subject of legal culture in this book is that it applies legal culture in the area of public law. The work mentioned as example here is Bell's examination of French legal culture. He discusses legal culture in the core activities,

---

to illustrate the impact on legal preferences and practices between legal systems, Gibson and Caldeira emphasise a survey of popular attitudes toward law of European citizens to compare the implementation of EU law in each member state. Meanwhile, Selznick refers to an understanding of value, like the rule of law culture founded in Western legal tradition with the aim of demonstrating the impact on the application of the rule of law to spheres in which power is exercised (See nn 15–17, 26 in Cotterrell, 'Comparative Law and Legal Culture' (n 7)).

[45] Bell (n 18) 1–2; Nelken, 'Comparative Sociology of Law' (n 11) 346.

[46] Nelken, 'Defining and Using the Concept of Legal Culture' (n 8) 116. Noteworthy, within this openness, a boundary in the use of the concept of legal culture is still needed to be set distinctively from other concepts. For example, legal culture does not focus on empirical aspect as the way sociology of law does. As Nelken points out, *'sociology of law has not been in the forefront of those seeking to understand differences between legal cultures or the possible implications of these various trends'* (Nelken, 'Disclosing/ Invoking Legal Culture: An Introduction' (n 10) 435). See also Friedman, 'The Place of Legal Culture in the Sociology of Law' (n 7) 185, 189.

[47] Liora Lazarus, *Contrasting Prisoners' Rights: A Comparative Examination of Germany and England* (OUP 2004).

[48] Hannah L Buxbaum, 'German Legal Culture and the Globalisation of Competition Law: A Historical Perspective on the Expansion of Private Antitrust Enforcement' (2005) 23 Berkeley Journal of International Law 474.

[49] David Johnson, *The Japanese Way of Justice: Prosecuting Crime in Japan* (OUP 2002) 161–165.

institutional setting, norms, concepts, legal reasoning and legal personnel of French administrative law.[50] In another section of the same book, Bell examines legal culture in constitution making, interpretation, institutional setting, procedure and method and consequence in French constitutional law.[51]

Instead of analysing legal culture in administrative law and legal culture in constitutional law separately, this chapter focuses on public law legal culture in the aspect that constitutional law and administrative law have influences on each other. This is obviously discussed by a number of works in general. For example, Poole argues that *'administrative law is entwined with constitutional law'*.[52] Metzger asserts that *'constitutional law and ordinary administrative law are inextricably linked'*.[53] The administrative agencies need to take constitutional concerns seriously in their decision-making because they underlie administrative law doctrines.[54] Some literature regard this relationship as a specific form of public law legal culture called *'Administrative Constitutionalism'*, connoting a way to display *'how ideas, aspirations and mentalities in constitutional order shape understandings of the administrative world'*.[55]

According to the nature of legal culture described above, there are variations of purposes and subjects in applying administrative constitutionalism.[56] Merztger points out that *'understanding administrative world'* can mean either *'how agencies make decisions, the substance of those decisions, or judicial review of agency decision-making'*.[57] In one paper, she applied administrative constitutionalism to examine how well-established constitutional requirements in the US are engaged in the administrative state and actions of administrative agencies.[58] In another article, she applied it to argue that administrative law has important task in reinforcing and securing federalism.[59] Alternatively, Sunstein and Vermeule can be seen to apply administrative constitutionalism in discussing multiple goals of administrative law, which the court's approach promises to honour, according to the US constitutional

---

[50] Bell (n 18) 153.

[51] ibid 199.

[52] Thomas Poole, 'Between the Devil and the Deep Blue Sea' in Linda Pearson, Michael Taggart and Carol Harlow (eds), *Administrative Law in A Changing State: Essays in Honour of Mark Aronson* (Hart Publishing 2008) 22.

[53] Gillian Metzger, 'Administrative Law as the New Federalism' [2008] Duke Law Journal 2023, 2026.

[54] ibid.

[55] Fisher (n 20) 35–37.

[56] Gillian Metzger, 'Administrative Constitutionalism' (2012) 91 Texas Law Review 1897, 1903; Metzger categories three main modes which constitutional law manifests in administrative contexts; Ordinary Administrative Law as Constitutionally Mandated, Ordinary Administrative Law as Constitutionally Inspired and Encouraging Administrative Constitutionalism (See Metzger, 'Administrative Law as the New Federalism' (n 53) 2028).

[57] Metzger, 'Administrative Law as the New Federalism' (n 53) 2027, 2061.

[58] Metzger, 'Administrative Constitutionalism' (n 56).

[59] Metzger, 'Administrative Law as the New Federalism' (n 53).

law, reflected in the Administrative Procedure Act and the Constitution.[60] Otherwise, Fisher applies administrative constitutionalism as a lens in order to understand the different models of explaining the legitimacy of public administration in the area of risk regulation.[61] She begins by explaining that there is a deficit of legitimacy in public administration because of its unelectable nature.[62] In this situation, there are diverse ways to explain the justification of public administration in different legal cultures.[63] For example, the concept of an administrative state in the US is highly legalised, while the substantive context of public law in the UK is a result of the blurring of law, policy, political theory, ideology and convention. On the other hand, the Australian constitutional order is analysed as having a rule-bound nature, holding administration to account on merits review.[64] These differences between legal concepts influence how public administration, in particular in the area of risk regulation, is constituted and limited in the legal systems.[65]

While Fisher mainly focuses on public administration, the flip side is the question of how the courts control public administrators.[66] This is adapted into the subject of this book and regarded as 'judicial review constitutionalism', focusing on 'the courts' roles in conducting judicial review, as being constituted or limited, in the line of distinctive constitutional orders in the legal system'.

It should be noted that the term 'constitutionalism' has been widely recognised in constitutional law referring to the use of society's basic laws to establish and form a framework for organising the government, namely procedures, institutions and rights, as well as legally limited government' powers.[67] The term has been adapted by a number of works to discuss the subject matter by considering its bigger framework. For example, Chief Justice French of the HCA applies *'Common Law Constitutionalism'* as *'the authority of the courts in their relationship with the other branches of government and the extent to which it can be defined by the courts*

---

[60] Cass R Sunstein and Adrian Vermeule, 'The New Coke: On the Plural Aims of Administrative Law' (2016) 2015.1 The Supreme Court Review 41.

[61] Fisher (n 20) 35–39, 51–52.

[62] Elizabeth Fisher, 'Food Safety Crises as Crises in Administrative Constitutionalism' (2010) 20 Health Matrix 55, 60–61; See also Sidney Shapiro, Elizabeth Fisher and Wendy Wagner, 'The Enlightenment of Administrative Law: Looking inside the Agency for Legitimacy' (2012) 47 Wake Forest Law Review 463, 466.

[63] Fisher, *Risk Regulation and Administrative Constitutionalism* (n 20) 39.

[64] ibid 52–55.

[65] ibid 57–58.

[66] Indeed, Fisher also touches on the courts' duty to review administrative action. However, the focuses are still on the side of public administration (Fisher, 'Food Safety Crises as Crises in Administrative Constitutionalism' (n 62) 65–88).

[67] Wil Waluchow, 'Constitutionalism' The Stanford Encyclopedia of Philosophy <https://plato.stanford.edu/archives/spr2014/entries/constitutionalism/> accessed 2 March 2018.

themselves'.[68] Metzger also calls the explanation on judicial legitimacy and authority as *'judicial constitutionalism'*.[69]

This book's proposal of judicial review constitutionalism shares a similar logic with these connotations. The word *'-ism'* in constitutionalism, as a suffix connoting *'the system of'*,[70] upholds this methodology exploring the courts' role in conducting judicial review in the light of 'the system of constitutional orders' of the legal systems. Particularly, Chief Justice French refers to similar set of constitutional orders namely the written Constitution, the separation of powers and the federal system as influencing the function of the courts in Australia.[71] However, while French emphasises on the legitimacy of the courts in conducting constitutional review over legislature, this book specifically studies the role of the courts in conducting judicial review of administrative action.

2.2.3 Elements of Legal Culture

As legal culture can be formed from diffused sources,[72] a further step is to point out what the important elements are in relation to the subject of judicial review constitutionalism.[73] This section proposes three main ones.

2.2.3.1 Constitutional Framework

The first of which is a 'constitutional framework' in the law. One needs to appreciate that this term is relatively slippery, and can refer to various things according to different purposes.[74] However, this book particularly refers to a constitutional framework as a construction of each legal system, such as the existence of a written constitution or the governmental arrangement of a unitary or federal state. Some

---

[68] Chief Justice French, 'Common Law Constitutionalism' (Robin Cooke Lecture, Wellington, New Zealand, 27 November 2014).

[69] See Metzger, 'Administrative Constitutionalism' (n 56) 1902.

[70] *Oxford Advance Learner's Dictionary* (9th edn, OUP 2015).

[71] French, 'Common Law Constitutionalism' (n 68).

[72] They can range from *'facts about institutions such as the number and role of lawyers or the ways judges are appointed and controlled, to various forms of behaviour such as litigation or prison rates...'* (Nelken, 'Using the Concept of Legal Culture' (n 9) 1); *'Culture becomes the vision of the whole, which includes all these elements as parts'* (Webber (n 17) 2).

[73] This can be regarded in other various terms namely, component (Cotterrell, 'Comparative Law and Legal Culture' (n 7) 715), boundary, parameter (ibid 717–718) and indicators (Bell (n 18) 17). However, for consistency, this book will stick with the term 'element of legal culture'.

[74] In the same way with 'constitutional order' (see n 18 of Chap. 1) and 'constitutionalism' above.

constitutional frameworks are the result of the historical contexts in a legal system.[75] For example, it will be pointed out in a later section that the federal system and written constitution of Australia are constructed based on its huge expanse of territory and its history as a range of different colonies. Apart from these national constitutional frameworks, the influences of some international treaties will also be categorised in this point, since they are also a construction, which reflects a distinctive understanding of the role of the courts in conducting judicial review.[76] For example, it will be demonstrated in the next section that EU law and the ECHR are significant to English judicial review because they have gradually become part of the English legal culture since the 1970s and do have influence on the courts' legal reasoning in the determination of the scope of judicial review.[77]

2.2.3.2 Constitutional Value

The constitutional frameworks described above are focusing on the first element because they ground influences on the next element, which is the view of the courts on constitutional values. Once again, it is notable that the definition of 'constitutional value' is unclear and can refer to various meanings. Additionally, it frequently overlaps and is confused with other terms namely theory,[78] morality[79] or principle. This book will stick with the term 'value', considered to be more substantial than others because it contains the dimension of legal mentality, discussed below, in its connotation.

It should be clarified that this book does not regard constitutional value in the philosophical sense,[80] but as value that is commonly accepted by the courts in each legal system and held as a starting point when they conduct judicial review. For example, as mentioned in Chap. 1, each legal system has its own particular understanding of the rule of law. As Bell states, *'Although the term rule of law is frequently used to express a fundamental value of any liberal political system, there*

---

[75] Chief Justice French also applies the terminology of 'framework' in this sense (See Chief Justice French, 'Australia's Constitutional Evolution' (John Fordham Law School Constitutional Law Master Class, 20 January 2010).

[76] This will be perceived based on the approach of 'interrelated legal cultures' and exemplified in Sect. 2.2.5 below.

[77] This will be deliberated in more detail in Sect. 2.3.4 below.

[78] See Harlow's categorisation of the theory of public law into shallow and deep, and foreground and background in Chap. 1.

[79] For example, Connolly applies the term morality to refer to '...*individuality, equality, liberty, the rule of law, legality, democracy, accountability, legitimacy and others'* in Australian public law (Anthony J Connolly, *The Foundations of Australian Public Law: State, Power, Accountability* (CUP 2017) Chapter 4).

[80] E.g. Joseph Raz, 'The Rule of Law and its Viture' (1977) 93 LQR 195; Ronald Dworkin, *Taking Rights Seriously* (Bloomsbury Academic 2013).

are different understandings of this idea among different legal systems'.[81] Literature refers to these differences as a substantive meaning of the rule of law.[82] This is the example of constitutional value emphasised in this book because the courts rely on it when perceiving their role in conducting judicial review to protect legality. Apart from the rule of law, other distinctive constitutional values in a legal system, such as parliamentary sovereignty, the separation of powers and the concept of jurisdiction are also important elements in the formation of judicial review constitutionalism. The particular understanding of these constitutional values in England and Australia will be unpacked and regarded as the back-drop of the contrast between the English and Australian legal cultures.

2.2.3.3 Way of Justification and Limitation of Judicial Review

The third element focused on is the way of justification and limitation, in which the scholars and judges explain the constitutional values to support or confine their role in conducting judicial review. For example, while the Australian courts mainly justify and limit their jurisdiction by referring to the separation of powers and the written Constitution, the English courts understand their role as related to Parliament through the theorists' models called Ultra Vires and Common Law theory. The next sections will demonstrate that these ways of justification and limitation of judicial review are also important elements of the snapshots of how the English and Australian courts understand their role in conducting judicial review.

It is important to note here before exemplifying in Sect. 2.2.5 below that this set of three elements of legal culture is flexible. Other scholars may have the other ways in setting them. For example, apart from the existence of a written constitution and type of reasoning of the courts, Fisher also regards the geography and economics of England and Australia as element of legal culture in understanding three narratives concerning objectors' rights to bring legal actions in challenging land use decisions in the countries.[83] In general discussion of English constitutional orders, much literature merges constitutional frameworks and values and explains them together.[84]

---

[81] John Bell, 'Comparative Administrative Law' in Mathias Reimann and Reinhard Zimmermann (eds), *The Oxford Handbook of Comparative Law* (2nd edn, OUP 2019) 1262; See also Preston Brian, 'The Enduring Importance of the Rule of Law in Times of Change' (2012) 86 Australian Law Journal 175, 175–176; Chief Justice Gleeson, 'Courts and the Rule of Law' (The Rule of Law Series, Melbourne University, 7 November 2001).

[82] Paul Craig, 'Formal and Substantive Conceptions of the Rule of Law: An Analytical Framework' [1997] PL 467.

[83] Elizabeth Fisher, 'Challenging Land Use Decisions in the UK and Australia: Three Overlapping Narratives' (Cityscapes: A Conference on Comparative Land Use Law, Yale Law School, 1–2 April 2016).

[84] E.g. *'The Character of the United Kingdom Constitution'* (Eric Barendt, *An Introduction to Constitutional Law* (OUP 1998) 32–34)). The next sections will do so in case of English judicial review, but will separate them in examining Australian judicial review constitutionalism.

This book unpacks English and Australian constitutional orders into the three aforementioned elements, because it considers them to be important aspects representing the overall pictures of differences between English and Australian judicial review. Additionally, it aims to demonstrate the connection and flow between such elements. For example, it is shown in Sect. 2.4 below that the Australian constitutional frameworks, such as the federal system and the written constitution, directly shape the particular understanding of the rule of law, the separation of powers and other constitutional values in the legal culture. On the other hand, the merger of the constitutional framework and constitutional value in the English system triggers flexibility for the courts in conducting judicial review. In short, elements of legal culture are designed upon the subject matter and purpose of the particular work. This set of three elements is merely a particular device of this book to describe the courts' mentality of their role in conducting judicial review more tangibly.

2.2.4 Legal Mentality

Another important aspect of the subject of legal culture of this book is 'legal mentality'. According to the Sect. 2.2.1 above, judicial review constitutionalism can be examined in various aspects, for example, focusing on patterns of practices of the lawyers or institutional design in process of judicial review according to distinctive constitutional orders of the legal system.[85] However, this book focuses on legal mentality (of judicial review constitutionalism), which Legrand describes as *'an entire distinctive way of thinking about law'*.[86] It is a collective mental programme, which contains the assumptions, attitudes, aspirations and antipathies that provide the deep structures of legal rationality.[87] Bell refers it as a pre-logical set of core perspectives that shape action.[88]

Three points about this methodology of legal mentality needed to be clarified. Firstly, Friedman conceptualises legal culture into two types; internal and external. While the former means *'the ideas and practices of legal professionals'*, the latter refers to *'the demands on law brought to bear by those in the wider society'*.[89] It should be clear that this book is focused on the former, particularly on the legal

---

[85] According to various connotations of legal culture (See Sect. 2.2.1 above).

[86] Pierre Legrand, 'What "Legal Transplants"?' in David Nelken and Johannes Feets (eds), *Adapting Legal Cultures* (Hart Publishing 2001) 55, 65; Zweigert and Kötz also consider legal mentality as significant mode of legal thinking in a legal system (See Bell, *French Legal Cultures* (n 18) 15).

[87] Legrand (n 86) in Bell, *French Legal Cultures* (n 18) 15.

[88] ibid 14–15.

[89] Friedman, *The Legal System: A Social Science Perspective* (n 9) 193–267. These definitions are flexible among scholars (see Nelken, 'Defining and Using the Concept of Legal Culture' (n 8) 112). Also, it should be noted that this is different issue from the methodology of internal and external in terms of unit of legal culture, which will be described below.

mentality of the English and Australian judiciary, rather than lawyers in general. This is because it is the court that plays the leading role in determining the scope of judicial review in each case in reality, as well as deliberating the issue in relation to the entire administrative law system. According to Groves and Lee,

> Administrative law is all about what the agencies of the executive government...can and cannot do. More particularly, administrative law encompasses the different mechanisms and principles that enable people to question or challenge the decisions of these agencies of government
> ...the courts play a significant role in these processes.[90]

Therefore, an examination of courts' particular understanding of their role in conducting judicial review in a legal system, needs to focus on the legal thinking of the judges in that legal system. In other words, the judiciary is a specific legal institution or actor, on which the determination of the grounds of judicial review is operated and shaped.[91] The point is that the English and Australian courts determine such questions differently because of their legal thinking within their legal systems' judicial review constitutionalism.

Secondly, legal mentality can be overlapping with other subjects of legal culture namely consciousness, experience of law, traditions, feeling and legal style. For example, Lloyd asserts that the approach to mentality still talks of style of inquiry and reasoning.[92] This book argues that it is impossible and unnecessary to set clear distinction between these diffused terms. The different works might refer to similar things with diverse terms. What this book does instead is demonstrating an example of legal mentality of judicial review constitutionalism, which this book is interested in. The obvious one is the quotation put at Sect. 1.2.3 of Chap. 1, displaying different 'ways of the judges' thinking' on the rule of law in England and Australia, which influence different perceptions of the English and Australian courts on their constitutional role in conducting judicial review.

Thirdly, as introduced in Sect. 1.4 of Chap. 1, although this chapter is focused on an examination of the current legal thinking in judicial review constitutionalism in these legal systems, a context is needed to better explain and understand the dynamic nature of judicial review.[93] As Webber asserts, the fit and normalisation of the past in the present in the process of continual change is required.[94] For example, some contexts of English history since the seventeenth century in which individuals were fighting against the Monarchy are mentioned as a ground for describing the distinctive features of English law, such as the mentality in upholding parliament as

---

[90] Matthew Groves and H P Lee, 'Australian Administrative Law: The Constitutional and Legal Matrix' in Matthew Groves and H P Lee (eds), *Australian Administrative Law: Fundamentals, Principles and Doctrines* (CUP 2007) 1.

[91] According to the methodology of 'Practices of Legal Institutions' proposed by Sally Engle Merry, 'What is Legal Culture' in David Nelken (eds), *Using of Legal Culture* (Wildy, Simmonds & Hill Publishing 2012) 62–63.

[92] G E R Lloyd, *Demystifying Mentalities* (CUP 1990) in Bell, *French Legal Cultures* (n 18) 14–17.

[93] Bell, *French Legal Cultures* (n 18) 256.

[94] Webber (n 17) 36.

the sovereign power in the legal system.[95] Additionally, how the relationship between the court, the executive and tribunals has been discussed malleably in some significant English governmental committee reports since the beginning of the twentieth century to the present will be explained in the next section.[96] All of these will be aggregated as part of the flow of the legal mentality of English judicial review constitutionalism. In the same vein, some discussions related to the role of the Australian courts in conducting judicial review in the past, namely the proposal of Dixon's Legalism in the 1950s and the Kerr Report in the 1970s, will also be demonstrated as significant elements in the formation of the contemporary mentality of Australian judicial review constitutionalism.[97]

Up to this point, the section discusses legal mentality of judicial review constitutionalism as the subject of legal culture applied in this book. It connotes a structure for pattern of legal thinking or mental map of the English and Australian judiciary about their role in conducting judicial review,[98] which are embedded in the distinctive explanation of elements of constitutional orders such as constitutional frameworks, constitutional values and way of justification in their legal systems. This particular form of legal culture emphasises the contributions of the concept of legal culture discussed above. Rather than a dry categorisation of constitutional law, legal mentality of judicial review constitutionalism aggregates all elements of the judges' perspectives and conceptualised explanations into one whole picture, representing deep account of the differences between English and Australian judicial review.

2.2.5 Proposed Approaches

Apart from the above, there are other methodological approaches regarding the scope of the use of legal culture in this book. Five of the most important are described in detail below.

---

[95] This will be exemplified in the next section.
[96] Namely, Committee on Ministers' Powers, *Report 1932* (so called 'the Donoughmore Committee'), Committee on Administrative Tribunals and Enquiries, *Report 1957* ('the Franks Committee') and Review of Tribunals by Sir Andrew Leggatt, *Tribunals for users: One system, One service 2001* ('the Leggatt Committee'). See more in Sect. 2.3 below.
[97] See description and references of these elements in detail in Sect. 2.4 below.
[98] Bell, *French Legal Cultures* (n 18) preface vi.

2.2.5.1 Evidence of Legal Culture

Firstly, as a state of mind, we cannot look inside the individual judges' brains to learn about their legal thinking. On this point, Nelken argues that what judges do and say can be regarded as evidence of legal culture.[99] Since judges will only present the reasoning they perceive to be legitimate, these legal materials can be treated as their acceptable beliefs.[100] Therefore, legal thinking expressed by the judges in the pages of judgments, transcripts of legal argument, speeches and secondary literature are used to identify legal mentality of judicial review constitutionalism in this book.[101] Additionally, some leading textbooks and articles by scholars describing and commenting the judges' thinking are also examined in this chapter. Since the next sections are focused on *'the fundamental structures of thinking...which lie behind what is expressed'*,[102] these materials, which are regarded as 'supporting elements', will facilitate to growth of the depth of judges' legal mentality of judicial review constitutionalism.

It is also important to note that a study of legal culture needs a boundary.[103] Rather than a 'too big' picture of differences between English and Australian judicial review, this book applies the method of a 'snapshot', examining only the important aspects in such differences. Among diffused and massive source of evidence of legal culture, this book focuses only on significant 'official culture' such as the judgments and transcripts of legal argument of leading cases and speeches of the upper courts namely the HL, UKSC and HCA, and a few important ones from the lower courts. According to the metaphor of this book, rather than considering every single stone at the bottom of the rivers, the main purpose of the next sections is to point out that the overall pictures of English and Australian geographies are different.[104]

2.2.5.2 Unit of Legal Culture

Secondly, Nelken demonstrates that there are many levels of legal culture that can be examined, ranging from the culture of the local institution like a courthouse or prosecutor's office, called the micro level, to the culture of the nation, state and wider entity such as culture in Latin law, modern law or common law, called

---

[99] Nelken, 'Comparative Law and Comparative Legal Studies' in Örücü Esin and David Nelken (eds), *Comparative Law: A Handbook* (Hart Publishing 2007) 32.
[100] Fisher, *Risk Regulation and Administrative Constitutionalism* (n 20) 61.
[101] A good example is Stephen Sedley, *Lions Under the Throne: Essays on the History of English Public Law* (CUP 2015) since it is written with a mind-set that judges are part of legal culture.
[102] Bell, *French Legal Cultures* (n 18) 20.
[103] ibid 2.
[104] This is similar to Fisher using this methodology of snapshot to present the overall picture of how public administration is influenced by the constitutional orders of the legal systems (Fisher, *Risk Regulation and Administrative Constitutionalism* (n 20) 52).

macro-level.[105] Nelken regards this as *'unit of legal culture'*. He calls *'legal attitudes and behaviour within a given society or unit'* as internal legal culture, and *'societies or other units of legal culture'* as external legal culture.[106] As stated in Chap. 1, the English and Australian laws have been chosen as the units of legal culture. It should be noted that although this book is focused on a comparison of these national legal cultures, it will also touch on the influence of international treaties on English and Australian judicial review. As mentioned above, there have been a spillover of EU law and the ECHR into ordinary English judicial review constitutionalism since the 1970s. Therefore, the adaptation of the methodology from 'external legal culture' into 'interrelated legal culture' is proposed in this book based on this closely integrated relationship. It will be demonstrated in Sect. 2.3 below that the English legal mentality is flexible to adopt this and other interrelated legal cultures in perceiving the roles of the courts in conducting judicial review. Conversely, the integration of the international influence into the Australian judicial review constitutionalism is not flexible, but relatively limited.[107] This different mentality of interrelated cultures is another significant difference between the English and Australian legal cultures, and this will be connected to the different determination of the grounds of judicial review in subsequent chapters.[108]

2.2.5.3 An Outsider Perspective

Thirdly, legal culture can be examined by researchers of different perspectives. For example, it can be considered by an insider who is educated originally from the studied legal system. By this approach, the works are trying to understand and appreciate the views, processes and experience of participants within the culture.[109] Alternatively, it might be examined by an outsider of the legal system. Sometimes elements of legal culture might be close to lawyers' everyday uses of legal rules and ideas in their own legal system.[110] Therefore, perspectives of an outsider provide the benefit that the observation is conducted with fresh eyes. As stated in Sect. 1.3 of Chap. 1, my starting point in studying English and Australian legal culture was as

---

[105] Nelken, 'Using the Concept of Legal Culture' (n 9) 3–7; Nelken, 'Comparative Law and Comparative Legal Studies' (n 99) 28–29; Nelken, 'Comparative Sociology of Law' (n 11) 350–355; Cotterrell, 'The Concept of Legal Culture' (n 10) 29.

[106] Nelken, 'Towards a Sociology of Legal Adaption' (n 28) 27.

[107] Despite this fact, the influence of international treaties will still be regarded as the interrelated legal culture of Australian law, rather than external legal culture, because it can become domestic law if it is stipulated in a statute.

[108] For example, they will facilitate a more comprehensive understanding of why the Australian law is confined to the conceptual structure of jurisdictional error and traditional grounds related to the substantive exercise of discretion, while the English law develops various doctrinal approaches to determine the grounds of judicial review including some from the ECHR.

[109] Nelken, 'Comparative Sociology of Law' (n 11) 348–349.

[110] ibid.

an outsider. Therefore, I am neither too familiar nor uncomfortable about carrying out research on them.

2.2.5.4 Descriptive Approach

Fourthly, Webber points out that the two main approaches to narrate the accounts of examining legal culture are explanatory (or descriptive) and interpretive.[111] The former regards culture as *'an aggregating concept, capturing everything relevant to the operation of law in a specific social field'*.[112] The latter describes legal culture as *'the mode to understand how aspects of legal culture resonate and fit together'*.[113] It should be clear that the use of legal culture in this book is to narrate the thick descriptions of the English and Australian judicial review, rather than interpreting them. As discussed in Sect. 1.4 of Chap. 1, this book does not compare whether English or Australian judicial review constitutionalism is a preferable way of thinking about the courts' roles in protecting legality. As Webber stated, legal culture can be applied in the sense of standing in the position of an observer, not participant, speaking *'the language of tendency, not of right and wrong'*.[114]

2.2.5.5 Non-monolithic Nature

Most importantly, it shall be emphasised that all the above-proposed methodologies of legal culture are non-monolithic. As mentioned, the set of three elements in the formation of judicial review constitutionalism, consists of constitutional framework, constitutional value and the way of justification and limitation of judicial review, is this book's particular design in order to demonstrate the pictures of legal culture. In the same vein, different works might see different materials as evidence of legal culture. Likewise, the accounts of legal culture can be narrated in various ways, dependent upon the author's style of describing.

Apart from the non-monolithic nature in designing a particular application of legal culture, the result of examination on legal mentality of each element of legal culture also contain variations of thought. It is acknowledged that individual judges could have different thinking about their role in conducting judicial review.[115] This could be because of the different ways the rule of law is explained, not only in different legal cultures, but also within one legal culture. Alternatively, the ultra

---

[111] Webber (n 17) 1; See also Nelken, 'Using the Concept of Legal Culture' (n 9) 1, 8.
[112] ibid.
[113] ibid.
[114] Webber (n 17) 35.
[115] ibid 30. In the same way, Bell described that *'individuals develop their attitudes within a particular context'* ((n 18) 10–11).

2.2 Concept of Legal Culture: A Navigating Methodology

vires and common law models of the justification for judicial review have different ways of interpreting the rule of law and parliamentary sovereignty.

According to the nature of legal culture, these variations are not unpredictable. The debates related to the legitimacy and scope of the court to conduct judicial review is ongoing in most legal cultures. Nevertheless, there is always a shared theme and pattern in the distribution of these ideas and values in the legal system.[116] As Bell explains, *'The concept of culture identifies the shared beliefs, interests and ideologies which people have with regard to their activity within an institution or organization. Such beliefs help to legitimate their activity and give it purpose'*.[117] Therefore, the focus of the examination in subsequent sections will be shared themes of legal mentality in English and Australian judicial review constitutionalism.

An example that can be given here before examining others below is that, despite some Australian judges being said to be more conservative[118] or activist[119] than others, they share an overall position of legal thinking that the courts' role in conducting judicial review is relatively rigid in their constitutional structures.[120] This kind of shared theme in a legal culture frequently appears as a package and needs to be unpacked, as will be conducted in subsequent sections. For example, Justice McHugh asserted that the common law's function in developing the law relied on a judge making legal rules and principles. However, he acknowledged that this creation of rules and principles had to be combined with constitutional structures to *'maintain its continuity and preserving its coherence'*.[121] This is compatible with what was expressed by Chief Justice Gleeson, namely, that the common law developed by the courts must conform to the Constitution. Therefore, the ultimate limitation of judicial review is the constitution.[122] However, sometimes it is directly expressed; for instance, when Chief Justice Mason of the HCA explained that;

> *I employ the expression "attitudinal basis" to signify the judicial perspective that there exists, or should exist, a relationship of mutual respect between the courts and the other*

---

[116] Friedman, 'The Concept of Legal Culture: A Reply' (n 14) 34.

[117] Bell, *French Legal Cultures* (n 18) 11. This approach is similar to others, but with a slightly different explanation, namely the metaphor of *'common intention'* of a group of individuals drinking at a cocktail party (J R Searle, *The Social Construction of Reality* (London 1995) 26 cited in ibid 4–5), the recognition of culture as a *'collective phenomenon'* (ibid), and the concepts of *'organisational culture'* and *'typical or representative culture'* (ibid 10–12).

[118] Justice Heydon is usually commented as a judge who rejected the judicial activism, as it leads to the destruction of the rule of law in Australian legal culture (Dyson Heydon, 'Judicial Activism and the Death of the Rule of Law' 10 Otago L Rev 493). See more in Sect. 2.4.4 below.

[119] E.g. Justice Kirby cautions the dangers of a *'mind-lock of strict textualism and the futility of media and political bullying of judges who simply do their duty'*, and suggests *'the necessities and justifications of some judicial creativity'* (Michael Kirby, 'Judicial Activism: Power without Responsibility-No, Appropriate Activism Conforming to Duty' (2006) 30 Melb UL Rev 576).

[120] This will be exemplified in detail in Sect. 2.4 below.

[121] Justice McHugh, 'The Judicial Method' (Democracy and the Law, the Australian Bar Association Conference, London, 5 July 1998).

[122] Gleeson (n 81).

arms of government. This perspective entails that the courts will avoid, so far as it is legitimately possible to do so, trespassing upon administrative decision-making, thereby generating public controversy leading to criticism of the courts and possible loss of respect for, and public confidence in, the courts. It was probably such an attitude of mind that lay behind Sir Owen Dixon's conception of judicial power...

I do not suggest that this attitude of mind is confined to judges. Far from it. It is an attitude that may well be shared by the Australian legal community or a large section of it and perhaps by the wider community. In essence, it conceives of judges as appearing to have a limited role....[123]

This approach, which was applied to find uniformity of a legal culture will also be applied to English law; however, the result of the examination will be different from the Australian law. It will be demonstrated in the next section that the various discussions on the role of the English courts in conducting judicial review reflect the shared flexible legal mentality of the English legal culture.

2.2.6 Summary

This section proposes legal mentality of judicial review constitutionalism, as a particular form of legal culture, and its methodological approaches examining the ways of legal thinking of the judiciary about their proper role in conducting judicial review in the light of their distinctive constitutional orders. These subjects will be identified through the snapshot methodology on official documents such as important judgments, speeches and secondary literature of the judges. The English and Australian laws are selected as the units of legal culture to be examined and the narration will be based on a descriptive approach in an attempt to understand its connection to the determination of the grounds of judicial review, rather than using an interpretative approach and trying to compare and prefer one over the other. In addition, the results of the examination contain many disagreements but some shared themes of legal thinking can be drawn from them. This proposed form of legal mentality of judicial review constitutionalism is designed aiming to aggregate all important aspects into the whole pictures, containing a thick description of legal thinking, which will uphold comprehensive understanding of the courts' determination of the grounds of judicial review.

---

[123] Mason A, 'Mike Taggart and Australian Exceptionalism' in David Dyzenhaus, Murray Hunt and Grant Huscroft (eds), *A Simple Common Lawyer: Essays in Honour of Michael Taggart* (Hart Publishing 2009) 180.

2.3 Flexible Legal Mentality of English Judicial Review Constitutionalism

The legal mentality of English and Australian judicial review constitutionalism will be examined in line with the above proposed methodologies in this and the next sections. At some points, the description has to be divided into the parts of 'legal mentality' and 'judicial review constitutionalism'. The analysis begins with the latter, describing each element of judicial review constitutionalism, and then promptly follows with a demonstration of the judges' ways of thinking, recognising, accepting or limiting their role in conducting judicial review based on this element. This is similar to Bell's template in proposing distinctive features of French legal culture, for example, starting with content of the loi and the droit ecrit, before pointing out their importance in French lawyers' perspective, indicated by the term 'primacy'.[124] However, legal mentality and judicial review constitutionalism are not completely separated as the sections aim to conclude them as overall pictures of differences between English and Australian judicial review. Therefore, by 'promptly following' this book means that the relationship between them will be revealed in the analysis.

As described by Craig, English administrative law has been developed for more than 400 years since the establishment of administrative institutions to deal with facing situations during the fifteenth century,[125] but there was no general rationale for allocating these local authorities or defining the concept of the court to conduct judicial review until the seventeenth century.[126] In the first edition of his administrative textbook, De Smith states that '...*it was not until the seventeenth century that the modern conception of judicial review took shape.*[127] Subsequently, the English administrative law was gradually established related to remedies during the eighteenth century and grew considerably in 19th and 20th.[128] During this time, the courts have engendered some distinctive ways when thinking about their role in conducting judicial review by relying on some distinctive constitutional orders. This section runs through legal mentality of each element of English judicial review constitutionalism from the seventeenth century to the present. As mentioned earlier, the methodology of legal history is not applied to this examination; however, some historical contexts are significant for demonstrating the continuity of the English legal culture. The conclusion of contemporary legal mentality will be reached that the English courts perceive that they have flexibility in protecting legality of administrative actions. This is different from the legal mentality of Australian judicial review constitutionalism, described in the next section, that the judges understand their role in conducting judicial review as relatively rigid based on the framework of separation of powers prescribed in the written constitution.

---

[124] Bell, *French Legal Cultures* (n 18) Preface.
[125] Paul Craig, *Administrative Law* (8th edn, Sweet & Maxwell 2016) [1-002], [2-001].
[126] ibid [2-002].
[127] De Smith, *Judicial Review of Administrative Action* (1st edn, Stevens & Sons Limited 1958) 65.
[128] Craig, *Administrative Law* (n 125) [1-004], [2-001]-[2-002].

2.3.1 English Constitutional Frameworks and Values

Although this chapter proposes the methodology of unpacking the elements in order to see the depth of legal mentality within them, constitutional frameworks and constitutional values will be considered together in the case of English law because they are closely related. It is generally acknowledged that there is no written constitution in the UK. Therefore, constitutional values have become recognised as significant in explaining English administrative law.[129] As Lord Justice Laws states in *Thoburn v Sunderland City Council* that, although without a written constitution, the UK has a number of constitutional instruments, namely Magna Carta, the Petition of Right 1628, the Bill of Rights 1689, the Act of Settlement 1701 and the Act of Union 1707. The common law itself also recognises certain principles as fundamental to the rule of law.[130]

In other words, the common law, statutes and constitutional values or general principles of law have become the main sources of the UK constitution.[131] Among them, the rule of law and parliamentary sovereignty are the constitutional values that have much influence on the courts' mentality in conducting judicial review. How these values have become integrated into the UK's unwritten constitution and have formed the background of English judges' mentality is a result of the context, described as follows.

Instead of a sudden and painful constitutional changes to recognise the importance of individuals' rights like the revolution in France,[132] the English process has been gradually developed through the qualification of powers between the Monarchy and individuals throughout its history; for example, the Magna Carta and the Glorious Revolution.[133] Two features were generated as result of this context. First, rather than the need for a canonical constitution to instantly guarantee individuals' rights after a revolution, the system gradually gave importance to the value that the governed had to be respected by the governors. Second, instead of a robust concept of the state as having authority and autonomy vis-à-vis the individuals, as explained in the French system, English legal thought is mainly based on the fluidity between the state and society.[134]

These features, namely unnecessity of a canonical constitution and a concept of the state, have thereby generated two significant themes in achieving a liberal

---

[129] John Gardner, 'Can there be a Written Constitution?' <http://papers.ssrn.com/sol3/papers.cfm?abstract_id=1401244> accessed 2 March 2018.

[130] [2002] EWHC 195.

[131] Colin Turpin and Adam Tomkins, *British Government and the Constitution* (7th edn, CUP 2012) 160–198.

[132] Leslie Scott, 'Evolution of Public Law' 14 J Comp Legis & Int'l L 163, 168–171.

[133] See Peter Leyland, *The Constitution of the United Kingdom: A Contextual Analysis* (3rd edn, Hart Publishing 2016) 14–17.

[134] Cécile Laborde, 'The Concept of the State in British and French Political Thought' (2000) 48 Political Studies 540; Janet McLean, *Searching for the State in British Legal Thought: Competing Conceptions of the Public Sphere* (CUP 2012) 39–40.

2.3 Flexible Legal Mentality of English Judicial Review Constitutionalism

democracy in the UK. Firstly, the legal system sees parliament as the main governing institution that reduces the arbitrary prerogative of the Crown.[135] Secondly, it applies the common law tradition, through the exercise of prerogative writs, believing that judges should control public administrators.[136] Modern UK public law has been developed based on these two main themes,[137] which can be explained by various legal concepts.[138] The two themes of parliamentary sovereignty and the courts' control of public administration have also shaped the English administrative law since the seventeenth century.[139] However, the most prominent explanation was A V Dicey's provision of a framework of an unwritten constitution in a discussion of parliamentary sovereignty in relation to the three limbs of the rule of law.[140]

In relation to parliamentary sovereignty, Dicey explains the Westminster Parliament as having apparently unrestricted power;

> Parliament has, under the English constitution, the right to make or unmake any law whatever; and, further, that no person or body is recognised by the law of England as having a right to override or set aside the legislation of Parliament.'[141]

This principle is explained together with the three limbs of the rule of law, the first of which is that *'no man is punishable... except for a distinct breach of the law established in the ordinary legal manner before the ordinary courts of the land'*.[142] The second limb focuses on the principle of equality, so that *'every man, whatever be his rank or condition, is subject to the ordinary law of the realm and amenable to the jurisdiction of the ordinary tribunals'*.[143] Finally, the third limb is what distinguishes the English understanding of the rule of law from that of other states;

> The (unwritten) constitution is pervaded by the rule of law on the ground that the general principles of the constitution are with us the result of judicial decisions determining the rights of private persons in particular cases brought before the courts.[144]

---

[135] Scott (n 132) 163.

[136] Dicey later called this mentality the *'august dignity of the judges'* (A V Dicey, *Introduction to the Study of the Law of the Constitution* (7th edn, Macmillan 1908) 389).

[137] McLean (n 134) 12–18.

[138] E.g. William Blackstone, *An Analysis of the Laws of England*, vol 1 (The Clarendon Press 1771); Walter Bagehot, *The Collected Works of Walter Bagehot*, vol 5 (Norman St John-Stevas ed, The Economist 1974).

[139] Peter Cane, *Administrative Tribunals and Adjudication* (Hart Publishing 2010) 26–31; Louis Leventhal Jaffe and Edith Henderson, 'Judicial Review and the Rule of Law: Historical Origins' (1956) 72 Quarterly Review.

[140] Christopher Knight, 'The Rule of law, Parliamentary Sovereignty and the Ministerial Veto' (2015) 131 The Law Quarterly Review 547; Peter Cane, 'Understanding Administrative Adjudication' in Linda Pearson, Carol Harlow and Michael Taggart (eds), *Administrative Law in a Changing State: Essays in Honour of Mark Aronson* (Hart Publishing 2008) 276–277.

[141] A V Dicey, *Introduction to the Study of the Law of the Constitution* (10th edn, Macmillan 1959) 39–40.

[142] ibid 188.

[143] ibid 193.

[144] ibid 195.

Although this Diceyan concept was subjected to considerable criticism,[145] its 'general form' was extremely influential on legal mentality and shaped the development of English administrative law.[146] This is because it matched the duty of Parliament and the court in controlling the administrative actions with the two themes in achieving a liberal democracy described above. First, Parliamentary sovereignty upholds the will of the nation as supreme according to its elected nature;[147] therefore, the exercise of public power has to be channelled through Parliament.[148] Second, the three limbs rule of law reinforce the courts' role in protecting legality of administrative actions. In the first and second limbs, there is an emphasis on the function of the *'ordinary courts'* to equally chastise any individual for any breach of the law. Most importantly, the third limb directly points out that the court's main role is to engage in the protection of individuals' rights. Drawing on the historical context, Dicey clearly argues that common law without a written constitution was a more effective technique in protecting the rights of individuals than that used on the continent. For him, constitutional documents could be easily revoked, while it was more difficult for governors to be arbitrary under the common law, where there are numerous judicial decisions to speak for individuals' rights.[149]

In short, the Diceyan concept not only describes a unitary democracy in which all public power is channelled through Parliament, but it is also for the court to conduct judicial review to ensure that the tasks of public administrators are legally performed. This cooperative function between the principle of parliamentary sovereignty and the rule of law is accepted and embedded as the widespread foundation of the English courts' mentality in perceiving their role in conducting judicial review. Jowell regarded it as *'perhaps the most enduring contribution of our common law'*, supplying the foundation of a new model of democracy in Britain.[150] Apart from Lady Hale's speech mentioned in Sect. 1.2.3 of Chap. 1, a number of

---

[145] E.g. Paul Craig, *Public Law and Democracy in the United Kingdom and the United States of America* (Clarendon Press 1990) 12–13; Harry W Arthurs, 'Rethinking Administrative Law: A Slightly Dicey Business' (1979) 17 Osgoode Hall LJ 1.

[146] Craig, *Public Law and Democracy in the United Kingdom and the United States of America* (n 145) 12); Loughlin also argues that *'the predominant approach to the subject in the 20th century has absorbed far too much of Dicey's method and underlying values'* (Martin Loughlin, 'Why the History of English Administrative Law is not Written' in David Dyzenhaus, Murray Hunt and Grant Huscroft (eds), *A Simple Common Lawyer: Essays in Honour of Michael Taggart* (Hart Publishing 2009)).

[147] Craig, *Public Law and Democracy in the United Kingdom and the United States of America* (n 145) 16.

[148] Craig, *Administrative Law* (n 125) [1-002].

[149] A V Dicey, *Introduction to the Study of the Law of the Constitution* (n 141) 200–202.

[150] Jeffrey Jowell, 'The Rule of Law' in Jowell J and O'Cinneide C (eds), *The Changing Constitution* (9th edn, OUP 2019). Cane also argues that *'Judicial attitudes to Parliament were strongly influenced by Dicey's espousal of Parliamentary supremacy as the fundamental principle of the English constitution'* (Peter Cane, *Controlling Administrative Power: An Historical Comparison* (CUP 2016) 44).

2.3 Flexible Legal Mentality of English Judicial Review Constitutionalism

judges also accept these constitutional values in understanding their role in conducting judicial review, which can be categorised into two sides of mentality.[151]

Firstly, the courts regard their role as protecting the rule of law by conducting judicial review. For example, Lord Neuberger argues that *'...the role of the courts is therefore crucial in a democracy which is run in accordance with the rule of law'*.[152] Lord Phillips also states that *'The rule of law requires that the courts have jurisdiction to scrutinise the actions of government to ensure that they are lawful'*.[153] Lord Justice Sedley displays this mentality by describing judges as sleeping lions, who *'woke to scrutinise all public law adjudications and decisions for both legality and fairness'*.[154] Scholars like Robson supports this through a concept that *'judicial habits of mind'* enforce the ordinary courts to supervise the decisions of the inferior courts and bureaucracy.[155]

However, this is to be balanced with another side of legal thinking that the courts should not always intervene in any administrative action, because they still need to be aware of the legitimate limits of the exercise of their judicial power in the light of parliamentary sovereignty. This mentality was demonstrated in *Arlidge v Local Government Board*, where the court did not intervene into the order of the local government board because judicial standards should not be applied to administrative decision-making.[156] By way of contrast to the last paragraph, Lord Justice Sedley also mentions that *'the judges... were also required to respect and maintain the ring-fences erected by Parliament around newly created administrative bodies'*.[157] Galligan asserts that, although the function of the courts is to maintain the standard of legality, the scope of judicial review is limited by the doctrine of parliamentary sovereignty.[158]

These two important constitutional values in English judicial review namely the rule of law and parliamentary sovereignty, are commented on as 'generally' standing on different sides of the scale. While the former mainly supports and constitutes the role of the courts to conduct judicial review, the latter limits the courts' authority in this context.[159] This nature is recognised and described by scholars in various ways,

---

[151] Jeffrey Jowell, 'Administrative Law' in Vernon Bogdanor (ed), *The British Constitution in the Twentieth Century* (OUP 2003) 374–384.

[152] Lord Neuberger, 'The UK Constitutional Settlement and the Role of the UK Supreme Court' (The Legal Wales Conference, 10 October 2014).

[153] Lord Phillips, 'Judicial Independence and Accountability: A View from the Supreme Court' (The Politics of Judicial Independence, 8 February 2011).

[154] Sedley (n 101) 39–40.

[155] William A Robson, *Justice and Administrative law: A Study of the British Constitution* (3rd edn, Stevens & Amp 1951) xi–xviii, 28–34, 40–42, 360–363, 409–418.

[156] [1915] AC 120.

[157] Sedley (n 101) 59–60.

[158] Denis Galligan, 'Judicial Review and the Textbook Writers' (1982) 2 OJLS 257, 260.

[159] Parliamentary sovereignty is considered generally to limit their role in conducting judicial review, as it requires the courts to respect the power of public administrator, conferred from parliament as the supreme power. However, it will be shown below that ultra vires and common law

for example, Craig's *twin concepts*[160] and Lord Justice Sedley's concept of *'Bi-polar sovereignty of the Crown in Parliament and the Crown in its courts'*.[161] In the same vein, Allan states that parliamentary sovereignty is constrained by legality, and qualified by the courts.[162] This is recognised by judges namely Lord Bridge stating in *X Ltd v Morgan-Grampian Ltd* that *'In our society the rule of law rests upon twin foundations: the sovereignty of the Queen in Parliament in making the law and the sovereignty of the Queen's courts in interpreting and applying the law'*.[163] Lord Woolf also asserts two principles upon which the rule of law depended in a secondary work as the supremacy of parliament and the function of the courts as final arbiters in the application of the law.[164]

All the mentioned works indicate that the courts have a role to 'strike a balance' between these two sides of constitutional values and find the most appropriate solution, whether they have jurisdiction to conduct judicial review in a particular case or not. Importantly, the nature of a balancing process is that the two values can be struck in different ways. Combining the absence of a written constitution to prescribe the boundary of the courts' scope of judicial review with this balancing process between the rule of law and parliamentary sovereignty, the English courts therefore understand their role in conducting judicial review to protect legality as flexible. They can malleably decide whether to give weight to the rule of law, and say that the case is within its scope of judicial review, or to emphasise on parliamentary sovereignty, and hold that they do not have the jurisdiction to intervene into the administrative action in another case. This merger between an unwritten constitution and the balancing process between the twin concepts is the first important constitutional order, generating flexible mentality of the English courts according to their judicial review geography.[165]

---

theories particularly blend the explanation of parliamentary sovereignty as also supporting the courts' role in conducting judicial review.

[160] Craig, *Public Law and Democracy in the United Kingdom and the United States of America* (n 145) 19–20.

[161] Stephen Sedley, 'Human Rights: a Twenty-First Century Agenda' [1995] PL 386, 389.

[162] T R S Allan, 'Questions of Legality and Legitimacy: Form and Substance in British Constitutionalism' (2011) 9 International Journal of Constitutional Law 155, 156–157.

[163] [1991] 1 AC 1, 48.

[164] Lord Woolf, 'Droit Public- English Style' [1995] PL 57.

[165] The term *'twin concepts'* is borrowed from Craig, *Public Law and Democracy in the United Kingdom and the United States of America* (n 145), and will be used throughout the book referring to the rule of law and parliamentary sovereignty in English law.

2.3.2 Justification for the English Courts to Conduct Judicial Review

Apart from the collaboration between an unwritten constitution and the twin concepts, there are further explanations in regard to the role of the English courts in conducting judicial review. The point debated among academics is whether the courts have to justify their powers to conduct judicial review by relying on Parliament, or whether they can do so by their own powers independently of Parliament. While the ultra vires model represents the role of the courts on the former basis, the common law model holds on the latter one.[166]

Initially, the (traditional) ultra vires model was proposed in the way that a court is justified in striking down actions that are *'beyond or exceed the scope of power'* of the administrative body transferred from Parliament through legislation.[167] According to this model, the court is an agent of Parliament, charged with policing the boundaries of administrative powers stipulated by Parliament. However, several aspects of this traditional ultra vires model were severely criticised. For example, in some cases public authority is provided by prerogative, not statutory power.[168] Therefore, another camp of the justification for judicial review was introduced in the form of the common law model. Apart from explicit Parliamentary intention, the courts can also overturn administrative acts that are contrary to the principles of common law, such as the rule of law. Judicial review is the creation of the common law by the court, which is the institution of judicial review per se. The ultra vires model, which was conceived in terms of legislative intent, could not provide the heads of review and their particular meanings.[169] Instead, according to the common law model, the proposition of the courts therefore has inherent powers to control administrative actions.

In response to the common law model, the ultra vires camp firstly defended the critique by confirming that under the ultra vires model, the sovereignty of Parliament should remain a fundamental element of the constitutional order.[170] Secondly, they developed a modified ultra vires model. Although Parliamentary intention does not explicitly appear in the wording of the statutes, the courts can overturn administrative acts that are contrary to the implied intentions of Parliament. Therefore, the grounds of judicial review, applied by the courts, are part of Parliamentary

---

[166] This chapter narrates these models, in order to demonstrate the different ways to interpret the role of the courts relating to parliament. It does not explain them in a chronological order.

[167] William Wade and Christopher Forsyth, *Administrative Law* (11th edn, OUP 2014) 27–28.

[168] Dawn Oliver, 'Is the 'Ultra Vires' Rule the Basis of Judicial Review?' [1987] PL 543.

[169] John Laws, 'Illegality: The Problem of Jurisdiction' in Christopher Forsyth (ed), *Judicial Review and the Constitution* (Hart Publishing 2000).

[170] Christopher Forsyth, 'Of Fig Leaves and Fairy Tales: the Ultra Vires Doctrine, the Sovereignty of Parliament and Judicial Review' (1996) 55 CLJ 122.

intention.[171] Thirdly, it criticises the common law model as abolishing the sovereignty of Parliament and leading to judicial supremacy.[172]

There are various debates about these models in academic circles. Apart from those that involve the preference between them, Allan points out that these models are based on a similar set of values, and have similar implications in reality.[173] Firstly, whether they are called implied intention or common law, they apply to the same long-standing principles, such as the rule of law. Secondly, in practice, it is the courts that decide what are implied intentions and common law principles.[174]

This book does not intend to argue one model in preference over the other, or find solutions for the debates. However, it points out that the choices between these models are 'options' for the English courts in perceiving their position relating to Parliament when conducting judicial review. Judges heterogeneously rely on either of these models in actual cases. For example, although the model came later, the judgment in *R v Roberts, Ex parte Scurr* implicitly applied the ultra vires approach to find that the payment was unlawful because it was excessive and went beyond the limits of legality.[175] Another example is that of Lord Greene, who applied the model in *Associated Provincial Pictures Houses Ltd v Wednesbury Corporation* and declared that the judicial role was primarily to ensure that the local authority remained *'within the four corners of the matters which it ought to consider'*.[176] However, judges in *R (Cart) v Upper Tribunal* applied the common law model to justify that the court has inherent powers to protect the rule of law because common law is another limb of the development of a standard judicial review.[177] On the other hand, Lord Carnwath argues in a secondary work that there is no need to have a single foundation for judicial review;

> While the ultra vires is a valid and useful tool, in those parts of the law which depend on a statutory or other constitutional foundation, the other important principles can be derived from the common law in the areas of law that the ultra vires principle cannot be readily applied.[178]

---

[171] Mark Elliott, 'The Ultra Vires Doctrine in a Constitutional Setting: Still the Central Principle of Administrative Law' (1999) 58 CLJ 129.

[172] There was a debate between Craig and Allan about the meaning of legislative intent on this point (See their arguments in Christopher Forsyth (ed), *Judicial Review and the Constitution* (Hart Publishing 2000)).

[173] T R S Allan, 'The Constitutional Foundations of Judicial Review: Conceptual Conundrum or Interpretative Inquiry?' (2002) 61 CLJ 87, 101–102.

[174] T R S Allan, 'The Rule of Law as the Foundation of Judicial Review' in Christopher Forsyth (ed), Judicial Review and the Constitution (Hart Publishing 2000).

[175] [1924] 1 KB 514.

[176] [1948] 1 KB 223, 228 and 234.

[177] [2009] EWHC 3052; [2010] EWCA Civ 859; [2011] UKSC 28. Legal reasoning in the case will be unpacked in detail in the next chapter.

[178] Robert Carnwath, 'No Need for a single Foundation' in Christopher Forsyth (ed), *Judicial Review and the Constitution* (Hart Publishing 2000) 243.

The flexibility that different judges in particular cases can malleably apply either ultra vires, common law model or none of them in their legal reasoning to justify their judicial review flowed from the previous elements. Jowell points out that it is the absence of a written constitution to set clear boundary for the courts' authority to conduct judicial review, which allow such variation to exist.[179] This book adds that these models are generated from the gap in the balancing process between the twin concepts of parliamentary sovereignty and the rule of law. The courts use these models to make a firm justification for their position relating to parliament when they conduct judicial review.

Consequently, the choice between ultra vires and common law models is regarded as another distinctive element in English judicial review constitutionalism, demonstrating the overall position that the English courts have flexibility in justifying their role to conduct judicial review. By ultra vires theory, the courts consider their roles to conduct judicial review as relying on Parliament. By common law theory, the courts regard themselves as having inherent and independent power to develop their own principles to control public authorities. Alternatively, some judges and scholars analyse these models as similar, and unnecessary to be chosen in practice. The next section will demonstrate that this flexibility is a distinctive feature of the English law. The Australian courts do not need these models to justify their scope of judicial review, as they have the framework of power prescribed in the written constitution to do so.

2.3.3 Fluid Separation of Powers Between Court and Executive

It is a feature of the peculiarly British conception of the separation of powers that Parliament, the executive and the courts have each their distinct and largely exclusive domain (Lord Mustill in *R v Secretary of State for the Home Department, Ex parte Fire Brigades Union*)[180]

It has been demonstrated in the analysis up to this point that the court and the parliament in England have a distinctive relationship, in which the English courts need to balance the rule of law and parliamentary sovereignty to identify their proper role in conducting judicial review in a particular case. This sub-section will complete Lord Mustill's '*peculiarity of the British concept of the separation of powers*' by unpacking the particular understanding on the relationship between court and executive in the English legal culture.

As mentioned earlier, although the contemporary form of English administrative law has its roots in the seventeenth century, it was extensively developed during the

---

[179] Jeffrey Jowell, 'Of Vires and Vacuums: The Constitutional Context of Judicial Review' in Christopher Forsyth (ed), *Judicial Review and the Constitution* (Hart Publishing 2000) 339–340.
[180] [1995] 2 AC 513, 567.

19th and 20th centuries. This was the result of significant social changes based on the Industrial Revolution and the birth of the concept of welfare state.[181] This led to a considerable growth in public administration and the number of tribunals throughout this period, and the role of the courts to maintain these organs within their scope of power was widely discussed.[182] This led to the place of the court and these organs being included in some significant reports of governmental committees during the twentieth century, namely the Donoughmore Committee, the Franks Committee and the Leggatt Committee, which will be discussed below.[183] It will be seen that the discussions contained varied and flexible understandings of the relationship between the court and the executive and the proposition of tribunals. This will be regarded as another landscape of the English legal culture.

The first example is 'The New Despotism', which was written in 1929 by Gordon Hewart, the Lord Chief Justice of England.[184] Among various proposals,[185] he expressed his concern about the *'increasing tendency to assign judicial powers to specialist tribunals'*.[186] This opinion corresponded with Dicey's concept that the ordinary courts should be the only proper constitutional forum for resolving disputes.[187] The proposition of tribunal being a kind of executive holding adjudicative power should be rejected because it *'would pose a threat to the rule of law'*.[188] This meant that the boundary of authority between the court and the executive would remain firm. The adjudicative role should be dominated by the ordinary courts rather than the executive or tribunal. This was also related to the reluctance to the validity of administrative law at that time.[189]

As a result, the Donoughmore Committee was established to consider Hewart's critique of the proliferation of tribunals and administrative law.[190] In the report in 1932, the committee generally insisted on the allocation between the judicial and the executive. The principles by which legal questions should be decided by the court and policy questions should primarily be the province of the executive were

---

[181] Craig, *Administrative Law* (n 125) [2-002], [2-011]; Cane, *Administrative Tribunals and Adjudication* (n 139) 23–31; See also Gavin Drewry, 'The Judicialisation of "Administrative" Tribunals in the UK: From Hewart to Leggatt' (2009) 28 TRAS <http://rtsa.ro/tras/index.php/tras/article/view/27> accessed 5 November 2018; Chantal Stebbings, *Legal Foundations of Tribunals in Nineteenth Century England* (CUP 2006).

[182] Craig, *Administrative Law* (n 125) [2-017].

[183] n 96.

[184] Lord Hewart, *The New Despotism* (London Ernest Benn Ltd. 1928).

[185] For example, the abolition of the Office of Lord Chancellor (see Cane, *Administrative Tribunals and Adjudication* (n 139) 33–34; Drewry (n 181)).

[186] Drewry (n 181).

[187] ibid.

[188] ibid.

[189] Arthurs (n 145).

[190] n 96.

2.3 Flexible Legal Mentality of English Judicial Review Constitutionalism

underlying.[191] However, the application of this concept of the separation of powers was not fixed, as clarified in the report with the following statement;

> Our conclusion on the whole matter is that there is nothing radically wrong about the existing practice of Parliament in permitting the exercise of judicial and quasi-judicial powers by Ministers [a reference to public enquiries] and of judicial powers by Ministerial tribunals[192]

Apart from this quotation, the relationship between the court and tribunal was unclear; hence some scholars may have said that the report had *'little or no impact'* on this constitutional issue.[193] It was just designed *'to take the heat out of a rather synthetic controversy without unduly offending a top judge* [Hewart]*'*.[194] However, it is considered in this section to have been a demonstration of the flexible legal mentality in terms of how the relationship between the court and the executive could be understood. This can be seen from the following example of the wording of the report;

> *In the British Constitution there is no such thing as the absolute separation of legislative, executive, and judicial powers; in practice it is inevitable that they should overlap...*
> *One of the main problems of a modern democratic state is how to preserve the distinction, whilst avoiding too rigid an insistence on it...*[195]

Interestingly, Leslie Scott, the chairman of the Donoughmore Committee affirmed and connected this flexible mentality to other distinctive constitutional orders, namely, the absence of a written constitution, in an article published in the same year in which he made the following statement;

> *In the British Empire the process of constitutional change is less painful than it would have been in most other States because our Constitution is not written. Our constitutional usage...and our rules are flexible, not rigid as are the paragraphs of enactments.*[196]

Some scholars also emphasise this flexible mentality in Donoughmore; for example, Cane, who states that

> *Perhaps in response to the distinction between judicial and quasi-judicial decisions, the Committee itself threw separation of powers into the mix, saying that although it was impossible absolutely to separate legislative, executive and judicial powers, the distinction between them "is none the less real, and for our purposes significant"*[197]

Based on the non-fixed position in allocating powers between the court and the executive and in recognising that status of tribunal in Donoughmore, it was open for further discussion in the later reports.

---

[191] Cane, 'Understanding Administrative Adjudication' (n 140) 285.
[192] Donoughmore (n 96) 115.
[193] Drewry (n 181).
[194] ibid.
[195] Donoughmore (n 96) 4.
[196] Scott (n 132) 170.
[197] Cane, *Administrative Tribunals and Adjudication* (n 139) 35.

The next report to consider is that of the Franks Committee in 1957. Apart from creating a common framework for a number of ad hoc tribunals and articulating their operational principles of openness, fairness and impartiality,[198] the status of tribunal was also elaborated as *'not ordinary courts, but neither are they appendages of Government Departments'*.[199] It was *'machinery provided by Parliament for adjudication rather than as part of the machinery of administration'*.[200] This identification was *'the clear and unmistakable intention of Parliament'* to enable tribunals to operate independently from the government.[201]

Many scholars have commented on the huge shift from Donoughmore by Franks. For example, Harlow and Rawlings consider that *'tribunals were pushed increasingly towards a court-substitute function'* in the report.[202] This is similar to Drewry, who described the report as *'the road of increased legal formality and judicialisation* [to the tribunals]' and *'something of a watershed'* from Donoughmore.[203] Instead, this move of the proposal of tribunal from *'not radically wrong'* in Donoughmore to *'more formally part of adjudication'* in Franks will be considered in this section to be the continuous manifestation of flexible legal mentality by which the relationship between the court and the executive can be understood. Neither Donoughmore nor Franks provided a clear cut or fixed distinction between them.

This flexible legal mentality has continued to flow. Another significant discussion comes from the Leggatt Committee,[204] whose report began with a comment on the development of tribunals as *'wide variations of practice and approach, and almost no coherence....'*[205] A more coherent framework was required to meet *'the needs of the user'*.[206] Hence, a new structure of two-tier tribunals, namely the First Tier Tribunal ('FTT') and the UT, was proposed. While all the ad hoc specialist tribunals were collected and described as the former, the latter was established as an appellant institution on the questions of law. This recommendation led to the implementation of the Tribunals, Courts and Enforcement Act ('TCEA').[207] The report and the Act were commented in the way embedding tribunals *'even more solidly into the fabric of the judicial system'* for at least three reasons.[208] Firstly, the status of the UT is stipulated in Section 3 (5) of the TCEA as *'a superior court of the record'*. Therefore, whether a UT's decision is excluded from judicial review or not

---

[198] n 96 [41]-[42].

[199] ibid [40].

[200] ibid.

[201] ibid. All these recommendations were accepted and resulted in the Tribunals and Inquiries Act 1958.

[202] Carol Harlow and Richard Rawlings, *Law and Administration* (2nd edn, Butterworths 1987) 393.

[203] Drewry (n 181); See Cane, who also regards Franks as *'a judicialised model of non-judicial administrative adjudication'* (Cane, *Administrative Tribunals and Adjudication* (n 139) 43).

[204] Leggatt (n 96).

[205] ibid [1.3].

[206] ibid [1.4].

[207] The structure of two-tier tribunals has been enacted in s 3 of the TCEA.

[208] Drewry (n 181).

2.3 Flexible Legal Mentality of English Judicial Review Constitutionalism

is questionable. Secondly, some of the legally-qualified members of tribunals are called 'judges', even though they do not hold judicial office in the traditional sense. Thirdly, Section 3 of the Constitutional Reform Act 2005, in which *'judicial independence'* is guaranteed, also applies to the UT in the same way as it does to the traditional judiciary.[209]

In the next chapter, various doctrinal approaches the courts at different levels in *Cart* apply in determine the status of the UT according to Section 3 (5) will be unpacked. However, what can be concluded here is that the relationship between court, executive and tribunal in England has not been as fixed, but various in the committee's reports since the early of twentieth century to the present. After Leggatt, the flow of flexible approaches has continued. For example, the Law Commission's report about the Housing: Proportionate Dispute Resolution ('PDR') in 2004 stated that

> *In practice the distinction between the two* [courts and tribunals] *is by no means clear cut, and is arguably becoming less clear and less important...*
> *We find it difficult to accept the rigid distinction drawn between courts and tribunals*[210]

Drewry comments that this reflects *'the same flexible and holistic objective ...courts and tribunals have become and are becoming both more similar and more closely integrated in all kinds of ways'.*[211]

Rather than finding out which report provides the best answer for the proposition between court, executive and tribunal, it is considered in this section that the variation between them illustrates a shared theme of flexibility of the English legal culture. Some scholars point to this flexible mentality;[212] but the most interesting proposal is from Cane, since it involves the application of a process to balance this non-fixed relationship between the court, the executive and tribunals, as follows;

> *Tracing the long history of the English system has shown not only that a system of government may contain concentrating and diffusing elements at one and the same time, but also that the mixture of such elements and the balance between them may vary over time.*[213]

This is clearly compatible with the analysed balancing process between the rule of law and parliamentary sovereignty when perceiving the relationship between the court and Parliament. The peculiarity of the English separation of powers can be concluded as being relatively fluid when these two lines are combined, and it becomes another significant landscape in the English legal culture. This will become

---

[209] Cane, 'Understanding Administrative Adjudication' (n 140) 286.

[210] The Law Commission, *A Consultation Paper No. 180 on Housing: Proportionate Dispute Resolution – The Role of Tribunals* [2.107].

[211] Drewry (n 181); See also Review of Administrative Law in the United Kingdom, *Discussion Paper April 1981* (so called *'The Justice-All Souls Review'*), which discusses the limitations of the scope and approach of tribunals on some particular topics (see more in Craig, *Administrative Law* (n 125) [2-020]).

[212] Drewry (n 181).

[213] Cane, *Controlling Administrative Power: An Historical Comparison* (n 150) 57.

key to understanding the flexibility of the English courts have in applying various doctrinal approaches in their determination of the grounds of judicial review, which will be demonstrated in subsequent chapters.

Conversely, although the rule of law and separation of powers are included in the Australian legal system, its deep understanding of them is different from that of the English system. For example, it will be demonstrated in the next section that the distinction between the court and other governmental organs is discussed in a relatively rigid way, particularly in the Kerr Report. This and other elements of the Australian legal culture result in the application of relatively fixed and confined doctrinal approaches applied in determining the grounds of judicial review, which will also be unpacked in subsequent chapters.

Apart from the discussion in the report of the governmental committee, the fluid relationship between the court and the executive in English legal culture is also endorsed by academic work. Scholars have proposed a number of different approaches to find a solution to this relationship. For example, Loughlin clearly accepts fluidity in understanding the concept of the separation of powers.[214] Particularly, he mentions Maitland's work to describe how '...*the two* [court and executive] *have been inextricably blended for ages*'.[215] Loughlin regards this as an '*unbalanced working of the doctrine of a separation of powers*',[216] and proposes a solution, which he calls '*The New Separation of Powers*'.[217] In short, rather than making tribunals closer to courts, Loughlin emphasises that the executive is '*the primary interpreter of statutes in the modern state*'.[218] He confines the role of the courts to conducting judicial review as follows;

> *Most of these interpretations are never reviewed by the judiciary...*
> *All governmental action should be reviewable in the light of a means-end rationality, the precise specification of which is determined by the institutional remit and competence of the particular official agency.*[219]

Judicial review is conducted '*under the ground that all agencies should have taken on the task of promoting or coordinating the 'public interest' – in the light of the rationality, reasonableness, and proportionality of their action*'.[220] Apart from Loughlin, Harlow and Rawlings also show a variation of how the relationship between the court and the executive can be perceived in English law based on the Red-Light/Green Light models.[221] In the former, courts are considered as 'brakes' that prevent the public authorities from abusing their powers. Therefore, the

---

[214] Martin Loughlin, *Foundations of Public Law* (OUP 2012) 445–447.

[215] Williams Maitland, 'The Shallows and Silences of Real Life' in H A L Fisher (ed), *Collected Papers* (CUP 1911) 467–479 cited in ibid 446.

[216] Loughlin, *Foundation of Public Law* (n 214) 453.

[217] ibid 447–453.

[218] ibid 456.

[219] ibid.

[220] ibid 460.

[221] Carol Harlow and Richard Rawlings, *Law and Administration* (3rd edn, CUP 2009) Chapter 1.

boundary between the court and the executive standing on the different sides should be firm. Conversely, based on the latter, the courts and decision-makers need to cooperate to produce a framework of coordinated administration. Despite there are various possibilities, the courts 'generally' facilitate the administrative bodies to perform their public functions rather than stopping them from doing so. Therefore, the boundary between them could be loose in some cases.

Similar to the above debate between ultra vires and common law theories, the aim of this section is not to find the best answer for the relationship between the court and the executive among these academic works. Instead, they are all considered to be 'acceptable distinct approaches', which can be deliberated flexibly based on English legal culture. In short, flexibility is the over-riding theme of the relationship between the court and the executive in English law.

2.3.4 Integrating Influences from Interrelated Legal Cultures

At this juncture, the particular understandings of the twin concepts of parliamentary sovereignty and the rule of law, the debate between ultra vires and common law theories of justification of judicial review and the fluid separation of powers between the court, the executive and tribunals in England have been deliberated. These are the detailed examination of Lady Hale's speech, quoted in Sect. 1.2.3 of Chap. 1, which recognises the influence of Dicey's concepts on English administrative law.

However, this is not the end of the story. Lady Hale further describes that

> But in many respects, the Constitution which we have today would have been unrecognisable to...Dicey. Some may think that this is the great virtue of an unwritten constitution – that it can change and develop with changing times...
>
> In particular...where stands the sovereignty of Parliament, given the ceding of legislative competence both downwards – to the devolved Parliaments in Scotland, Wales and Northern Ireland – and upwards – to the law-making powers of the European Union?[222]

This addition is in the same vein with the further notice of Lord Justice Laws stated in *Thoburn* that the UK have a number of constitutional instruments. By this, the European Communities Act 1972 and the Human Rights Act 1998 ('HRA') may now be added to this list.[223] Therefore, the influence of EU law and the convention, namely the ECHR, is recognised by the English courts as being significant to understand the analysed constitutional values and the mentality of their role in conducing judicial review. As Brandy regarded, the HRA is *'one of the most significant developments ever to occur in British public law'*.[224]

---

[222] Lady Hale, 'The Supreme Court in the United Kingdom Constitution' (The Bryce Lecture 2015, Oxford, 5 February 2015).

[223] n 130.

[224] Alan Brandy, *Proportionality and Deference under the UK Human Rights Act: An Institutionally Sensitive Approach* (CUP 2012) 1.

First and foremost, it shall be clarified that EU law mainly relates to constitutional law issues, which is the relationship between the supranational nature of the EU and English parliamentary sovereignty. Despite this is not directly to the influences of constitutional orders on judicial review doctrine, as the subject of legal culture explored in this chapter, it reinforces the idea of flexible mentality of English public law. The majority in the *R (Miller) v Secretary of State for Exiting the European Union* demonstrates this clearly that;

> Unlike most countries, the UK does not have a constitution in the sense of a single code of fundamental law which prevails over all other sources of law. Our constitutional arrangements have developed over time in a pragmatic as much as in a principled way, through a combination of statues, events, conventions, academic writings and judicial decisions. Reflecting its development and its contents, the UK constitution was described by the constitutional scholar, Professor AV Dicey, as "the most flexible polity in existence"...[225]

This is similar to what has been analysed above, that without written constitution, it is flexible to integrate constitutional values, statues and common law as parts of development of English public law. The judgment relies on this mentality demonstrating the development of how EU law as flexibly integrated with parliamentary sovereignty, since 1971 to 2016, and thereby answers the steps required from the domestic law in the process of leaving the European Union.[226]

Instead, the only direct relation of EU law to judicial review doctrine is that the English courts are obliged to apply EU legal principles such as proportionality to domestic cases.[227] However, these are applied merely in cases when the decision-makers are acting within the scope of EU law. For example, in *R v Chief Constable of Sussex Ex parte International Trader's Ferry Ltd*, the court held that the Chief Constable's decision to limit the free movement of goods in the interest of public security or public health was not disproportionate.[228]

In contrast to EU law, the ECHR is more related to English judicial review constitutionalism since it has direct influence on legal mentality of the courts in conducting judicial review in general. The ECHR was not formally adopted into national law, until the HRA entered into force in 2000.[229] Mainly, the HRA added two mechanisms assigning the courts to protect individuals' rights according to the ECHR. First, Section 6 incorporates listed rights (contained in ECHR) to be actioned in the UK as domestic law. Second, Section 2 brings the principles and jurisprudence of the European Court of Human Rights into the domestic law; for example, proportionality has been imported into English legal culture.[230]

According to the proposed methodology, what this chapter focuses is how these provisions in the HRA as the results of the interrelated legal culture (the ECHR)

---

[225] [2017] UKSC 5 [40] (Majority).
[226] ibid [2].
[227] Craig, *Administrative Law* (n 125) [21-014].
[228] [1999] 2 AC 418.
[229] Craig, *Administrative Law* (n 125) [20-001].
[230] ibid [20-033].

2.3 Flexible Legal Mentality of English Judicial Review Constitutionalism

change, adapt, or integrate with the existing legal mentality of the courts perceiving their role in conducting judicial review. For example, it is questioned how the courts recognise the convention rights relating to the common law rights as a source of their role in conducting judicial review.[231] Various explanations of their relationship are given. For example, Lady Hale perceives European instruments

> ...as the source of rights, remedies and obligations, emerge a renewed emphasis on the common law and distinctively UK constitutional principles as a source of legal inspiration...
> ...the natural starting point in any dispute should be domestic law, albeit not always unanimously. The Convention may then be used as a check to see if any further development of the common law may be required.[232]

Alternatively, Lord Bingham in *R (Ullah) v Special Adjudicator* states that '*the duty of national courts is to keep pace with the Strasbourg jurisprudence as it evolves over time: no more, but certainly no less*'.[233]

The bottom line of this variation in thinking about the interrelationship between Common law rights and Convention rights, is that the ECHR (through the HRA) increases the options for the English courts in protecting individuals' rights by that executive decisions being challenged in court. Whether as a source of inspiration or being a ceiling, a shared pattern recognised is flexibility and willingness for the English courts in adapting such options into their conducting of judicial review. Lord Neuberger describes that

> ...the introduction of the Convention into UK law has been a breath of fresh air...[which] has spurred the UK judiciary into fresh thinking about the law, because we now have new ideas to grapple with and to apply to our domestic law...
> ...the exercise carried out by the court can be characterised as far more intrusive or far less technical than under traditional judicial review.[234]

Lady Hale also asserts that

> The future of the Human Rights Act...is another example of the interesting ways in which the relationship between the courts and Parliament is developing. It has always been the role of a constitutional court to protect fundamental rights, within the framework of the law and the constitution, and that is what an independent judiciary will continue to do to the best of its ability.[235]

There are two notable points regarding this aspect of flexible mentality of the English courts in integrating interrelated influences into the perception of the role in

---

[231] E.g. Lady Hale stated raises the issue about '*the relationship between the protection offered by the HRA 1998 and the protection offered by these common law principles*' (Lady Hale, 'UK Constitutionalism on the March?' (The Constitutional and Administrative Law Bar Association Conference, 12 July 2014).

[232] ibid; See also *R (Osborn) v Parole Board* [2013] UKSC 61.

[233] [2004] UKHL 26 [20].

[234] Lord Neuberger, 'The Role of Judges in Human Rights Jurisprudence: A Comparison of the Australian and UK experience' (Conference at the Supreme Court of Victoria, Melbourne, 8 August 2014); See also Lord Neuberger, 'The Supreme Court and the Rule of Law' (The Conkerton Lecture, 9 October 2014).

[235] Hale, 'The Supreme Court in the United Kingdom Constitution' (n 222).

conducting judicial review. Firstly, the courts retain the process of balancing the twin concepts of parliamentary sovereignty and the rule of law and the fluid separation of powers, in perceiving their role to conduct judicial review in particular cases. This can be seen from Lord Neuberger's assertion that,

> The role of the court when balancing the reasons against the interference is quite sensitive, and the extent to which the court will have regard to the view of the executive decision maker will depend very much on this nature of the issues.[236]

Secondly, this flexibility in English judicial review constitutionalism flows from the constitutional framework namely the absence of written constitution. Lady Hale mentions this that *'Some may think that this is the great virtue of an unwritten constitution, that it can change and develop with changing times'*.[237] Lord Neuberger also asserts that *'the absence of a constitution means that UK judges cannot easily refuse to follow a Strasbourg court decision on the ground that it would involve infringing our constitution'*.[238] He confirms this by reiterating in another speech that,

> While the UK has no constitution, in a typically understated and almost half-hearted we are now developing a sort of quasi-constitution...through signing up to the ECHR and then incorporating it in our domestic law in the HRA 1998. That means that judges in the UK can now give effect to many of the fundamental rights which are enshrined in most constitutions. So, if a decision of the executive infringes someone's human rights, the courts can quash it, and the common law, that it the law developed by the judges, has to be adjusted to accommodate such rights. So, new life has been breathed into the law, with proper recognition for the first time to fundamental rights...[239]

In summary, the openness and variation of thoughts in integrating the influences of interrelated legal cultures, particularly the ECHR (via the HRA) is another element that indicates the flexible mentality of the English courts in understanding their role in conducting judicial review. It will be shown in the next chapters, particularly Chaps. 5 and 6, that this mentality permeates the English courts so that they malleably adopt various doctrinal approaches from interrelated legal cultures, such as proportionality, in their determination of the scope of judicial review. On the other hand, it will be demonstrated in the next section that the Australian courts have a different mentality whereby they firmly reject the integration of influence from international treaties into their framework of the separation of powers.

---

[236] Neuberger, 'The Role of Judges in Human Rights Jurisprudence: A Comparison of the Australian and UK experience' (n 234)

[237] Hale, 'The Supreme Court in the United Kingdom Constitution' (n 222).

[238] Neuberger, 'The Role of Judges in Human Rights Jurisprudence: A Comparison of the Australian and UK experience' (n 234).

[239] Neuberger, 'The UK Constitutional Settlement and the Role of the UK Supreme Court' (n 152).

2.3.5 Substantive Conclusion

All the analyses above demonstrate the flow of legal mentality of English judicial review constitutionalism. In essence, the constitutional framework of an unwritten constitution influences the courts to rely on the constitutional values when explaining their role in conducting judicial review. This generates the first milestone of flexible thinking when they operate legality. The important constitutional values the English courts apply as their foundation of judicial review are the rule of law and parliamentary sovereignty, which are explained as the concepts needed to be balanced. On the one hand, the courts refer to the rule of law to claim their jurisdiction of judicial review. On the other hand, they do not intervene into administrative action because they are concerned with parliamentary sovereignty. The nature of the balancing process between the twin concepts adds further flexibility to the mentality of the courts in understanding their role in conducting judicial review. The debate between two models of justification for judicial review, namely, ultra vires and common law also demonstrates malleability for English courts in interpreting the constitutional values to claim their scope of judicial review according to Parliament. Additionally, the flexible legal thinking in understanding relationship between the court, the executive and tribunals discussed in significant governmental reports and academic works is another distinction of English legal culture. The last distinguishing feature is flexibility in integrating the influences from interrelated legal cultures, particularly the ECHR (via the HRA) into the English courts' understanding of their role to conduct judicial review. With these elements, this section concludes that the English courts have a flexible mentality in understanding their role in conducting judicial review to protect legality. Lord Mance's statement fits with this conclusion;

> *Britain is peculiar in having no written constitutional backdrop. The 17th century left us with Parliamentary sovereignty, qualified now by Parliament's acceptance of the European Treaties and Human Rights Convention. But absolute sovereignty is only acceptable when tempered by give and take. Fundamental common law principles do exist central to the rule of law; and what courts might do if any legislator, national or supranational, ever acted directly contrary to the rule of law is best left unanswered.*[240]

This flexible mentality of English judicial review constitutionalism will become more obvious and understandable, when comparing with the Australian courts' mentality considering their role in conducting judicial review as relatively rigid.

---

[240] Lord Mance, 'The Rule of Law – Common Traditions and Common Issues' (175th Anniversary of Founding of Hoge Raad, the Netherlands, 1 October 2013).

2.4 Rigid Legal Mentality of Australian Judicial Review Constitutionalism

The particular way in which the English courts flexibly understand their role in conducting judicial review according to the distinctive understanding of some constitutional orders, namely, the rule of law, parliamentary sovereignty and the separation of powers, was unpacked in the previous section. The general forms of these constitutional values have been adopted into the Australian system based on its former colonial status. For example, the rule of law, which places the courts at the centre of the system for controlling administrative power, was also a starting constitutional value in Australia. Chief Justice French clarifies that *'Australia's Constitution which is rooted in the history of its British colonisers... has delivered a system of democratic government, and structures to protect the rule of law'*.[241] Particularly, Sir Brennan states that *'The Constitution substantially followed the Westminster practice described by Dicey'*.[242]

However, the Australian law has gradually developed its own distinctive ways to understand these constitutional orders apart from the English one.[243] For example, as shown in the transcript of the legal argument of *Kirk*, quoted in Sect. 1.2.3 of Chap. 1, the understanding of rule of law is not confined to Dicey, but operates within the written constitution. This section runs through this kind of legal mentality of each distinctive element of Australian judicial review constitutionalism. Apart from the rule of law, the particular understanding of the separation of powers, the concept of jurisdiction, the distinctions between legality and merits and between courts and tribunals in Australia will be unpacked. All of these will be demonstrated as sources of the greater rigid legal mentality by which the Australian courts understand their role in conducting judicial review.

2.4.1 Australian Constitutional Frameworks

Due to Australia's huge expanse of territory, the centralisation of power through a unitary state system could not function well. Therefore, the US model of a federal state system with a written constitution was introduced to the system as a workable constitutional setting.[244] This model was considered to reduce the tension between

---

[241] French, 'Australia's Constitutional Evolution' (n 75).

[242] Sir Brennan, 'The Parliament, the Executive and the Courts: Roles and Immunities' (School of Law, Bond University, 21 February 1998).

[243] Matthew Groves and Janina Boughey, 'Administrative Law in the Australian Environment' in Matthew Groves (ed), *Modern Administrative Law in Australia: Concepts and Context* (CUP 2014) 4; Groves and Lee (n 90) 2.

[244] Peter Cane, 'The Making of Australian Administrative Law' (2003) 24 Australian Bar Review 114; Groves and Lee (n 90) 4.

2.4 Rigid Legal Mentality of Australian Judicial Review Constitutionalism

the colonies, in both the aspect of diverse cultures and the allocation of governmental powers.[245] The framework of a federal system prescribed in the convention between the states was then enacted as the Commonwealth Constitution, which came into existence on the 1st January 1901.[246]

It is acknowledged that the Constitution does not contain a provision that is directly related to the role of the courts in conducting judicial review of administrative action. However, it is still the starting point of the difference between the English and Australian legal cultures because the three main governmental powers, namely, legislative, executive and judicial, were initially setup under a framework of federal system in the first three chapters of the constitution. The Australian courts then gradually developed a distinctive understanding of constitutional values and hence, their role in conducting judicial review through the reading of this framework of federal separation of powers prescribed in the written constitution. In other words, the written constitution and the federal system became the ground of the Australian river, which has since been thickened by other geographical features. Groves and Lee point out this logic in the following statement;

> *The Commonwealth Constitution is another important influence upon Australian administrative law. The adoption of a written constitution marked a crucial point of difference between Australia and England. The Constitution introduced a division or separation of powers that underpins the role of the courts and many other consequences that flow from that separation, such as the constitutional limitations on judicial review...*[247]

> *The Commonwealth Constitution does not expressly spell out the existence of a separation of powers doctrine, but the High Court held that the compartmentalisation of the legislative, executive and judicial powers into Chapters I, II and III of the Constitution respectively led inevitably to the proposition that Australia's constitutional framework dictated a separation of powers*[248]

Not only in academic works, but also Justice Kirby stated in a case that

> *The doctrine of the separation of powers in Australia rests on the construction of the Constitution. The separation of the judicial power of the Commonwealth is inferred from*

---

[245] A federalism is considered as a solution to combine *'different political communities in a national polity'*, and answer to the colonial states' concern about their states' affairs namely foreign affairs, defence, and trade at that time. It was the decentralisation of penal colonies and launch of the white Australia policy. (See Patrick Parkinson, *Tradition and Change in Australian Law* (5th edn, Thomson Reuters 2013) 155–159; Helen Irving, *To Constitute a Nation: A Cultural History of Australia's Constitution* (CUP 1997)).

[246] See Cheryl Saunders, *The Constitution of Australia: A Contextual Analysis* (Hart Publishing 2011) 9–13; Gabrielle Appleby, Alexander Reilly and Laura Grenfell, *Australian Public Law* (3rd edn, OUP 2019) 56–62. Noteworthy, it does not mean that Australia had yet become independent nation by such creation of the Commonwealth on 1st January 1901. The position in 1900 was that the Constitution was legally binding because of the status accorded to British States as an original source of the law (Owen Dixon, 'The Law and the Constitution' (1935) 51 LQR 590).

[247] Groves and Lee (n 90) 2.

[248] ibid 6. See also Peter Cane and Leighton McDonald, *Principles of Administrative Law: Legal Regulation of Governance* (3rd edn, OUP 2018) 13 and Saunders (n 246) 16, 186.

the structure and language of the Constitution, rather than spelt out expressly in it (Wilson v Minister for Aboriginal & Torres Strait Islander Affairs)[249]

Therefore, the written constitution and the federal system should be regarded as the founding constitutional frameworks of the Australian judicial review. However, the key to understanding the rigid legal mentality has not only been given by them, but by the relatively rigid way the Australian courts read the framework of federal separation of powers prescribed in the written constitution, which can be perceived through the particular understanding of some significant constitutional values, namely the rule of law and separation of powers. According to Aroney,

> *Combining the sematic and syntactical meaning and strictly logical implications of the relevant sections in Chapter I and III, the Constitution does not of itself generate the 'rule of law', federalism' and 'judicial review'. It is our reading of these provisions in the light of our shared cultural understandings that leads us to discern these larger concepts*[250]

'The rule of law, federalism and judicial review' influenced by *'the reading of the constitution in the light of* [Australian] *shared cultures understandings'* will be examined in depth in the next subsections but first, it should be noted that the Australian legal mentality not developed with the existence of the constitution, but continuously throughout the twentieth century to the present day. Some notes about the timeframe of the exploration should be briefly clarified here.

After 1901,[251] the discussion of public law did not emphasise the role of the courts in conducting judicial review of administrative action; rather, it was focused on constitutional issues, namely the interpretation of the constitution and the constitutional review of legislation.[252] Despite this fact, two events that occurred during the 1950s-1960s are argued to have influenced the contemporary Australian legal culture. The first was the proposal of a judicial method called *'Strict and Complete Legalism'* by Dixon (so-called *'Dixon Legalism'*), when he became Chief Justice in 1955.[253] The second was an establishment of the concept of separation of judicial power in 1956 in a case of *R v Kirby, Ex parte Boilermakers' Society of*

---

[249] [1996] HCA 18 [30].

[250] Nicholas Aroney, 'The Justification of Judicial Review: Text, Structure, History and Principle', in Rosalind Dixon (ed) *Australian Constitutional Values* (Hart Publishing 2018) 37. This logic has also been recognised by other judges and scholars, for example, Hayne stated that '*...the Constitution must be the starting point for any examination of the rule of law in Australia. The Constitution provides the essential framework of government within which the rule of law takes its place in Australia*' (Kenneth Hayne, 'Rule of Law' in Cheryl Saunders and Adrienne Stone (eds) *The Oxford Handbook of the Australian Constitution* (OUP 2018) 171).

[251] An exploration of the Australian legal culture cannot begin in the seventeenth century like the English one, but only from the existence of the Constitution in 1901. This is because the Australian administrative law still followed the English one before the 1900s; hence, there is no need for a comparison.

[252] See Jeffrey Goldsworthy, *Australia: Devotion to Legalism in Interpreting Constitutions: A Comparative Study* (Oxford Constitutions of the World 2007).

[253] Owen Dixon, 'Judicial Method' [1956] 29 ALJ 468.

2.4 Rigid Legal Mentality of Australian Judicial Review Constitutionalism

Australia.[254] These two are explored below. However, at this stage, it is clear that the Australian legal culture neither existed at any point of time, nor did it grow overnight; rather it gradually developed from the past to the present.

The determination of the scope of judicial review of administrative action was not explicitly discussed in detail until the 1970s. The earliest scheme of Australian administrative law was complex due to the combination of English and US heritage.[255] Therefore, the Commonwealth Administrative Review Committee (the so-called 'Kerr Committee') was established to reform and create the *'New Administrative Law'*. In the 1971 report,[256] the Kerr Committee proposed the introduction of some mechanisms related to legal thinking about the courts' role in conducting judicial review.[257] For example, as illustrated below, there was some deliberation about how the framework of federal separation of powers prescribed in the written constitution had been integrated with constitutional values. The Kerr report was later recognised as an important source of the mentality of judicial review in Australia. Groves and Lee repeatedly stated that

> *The growth of administrative law in Australia has continued in an unabated form since the introduction of innovative reforms in the mid-1970s...*
> *...the 'New Administrative Law'...signalled the birth of a uniquely Australian system of administrative law that continues to evolve*
> *...these developments have constituted the corpus of administrative law in Australian today...*[258]

In summary, the back-drop of the greater rigidity of Australian judicial review will be unpacked in the following analysis, not only from the existence of the written constitution, but also from the distinctively rigid way in which the framework of federal separation of powers prescribed in the written constitution has been read by judges and scholars. This will be demonstrated through a particular understanding of significant constitutional values, namely the rule of law and the separation of powers, which were not directly pre-ordained by the Constitution, but have continuously and distinctively grown from the English one since 1901 through 1950s and 1970s until today.

---

[254] (1956) 94 CLR 254.

[255] This resulted in some complex cases such as *Parisienne Basket Shoes Pty Ltd v Whyte* (1938) 59 CLR 369 (See Groves and Boughey (n 243) 6).

[256] Australian Commonwealth Administrative Review Committee, *Kerr Report* (Parliamentary Paper no 144/1972, August 1971).

[257] Groves and Boughey (n 243) 5–12.

[258] Groves and Lee (n 90) Preface, 2, 14; See also Robin Creyke, John McMillan and Mark Smyth, *Control of Government Action; Text, Cases and Commentary* (5th edn, LexisNexis Butterworths 2019) [1.4.1] and Groves and Boughey (n 243) 4–5.

2.4.2 Australian Constitutional Values That Justify Judicial Review

As explained above, the legal mentality of Australian judicial review constitutionalism is more rigid than the English one. However, this does not mean that the courts will always have either a broad or narrow scope of judicial review in all cases; in fact, the Australian constitutional values can be said to provide both 'entrenched justification'[259] and 'firm limitation' of the courts' role in conducting judicial review. With this strong justification and limitation, the Australian courts must rigidly adhere to the framework of separation of powers prescribed in the written constitution and statutory construction to determine if their jurisdiction to conduct judicial review in a particular case is conferred or confined. They do not engage in a balancing process like their English counterparts. These two sides of the understanding of constitutional values, namely justifying and limiting judicial review, will be unpacked in this and the next subsections before moving to the following subsection to demonstrate that the rigid legal mentality of Australian judicial review constitutionalism is the result of these two sides of constitutional values.

Starting from the constitutional values that justify judicial review, similar to the English analysis, the first concept to be examined is the rule of law. With regard to the role of the courts in conducting judicial review, there are two main features of the Australian understanding of the rule of law. Firstly, rather than the interrelationship between the rule of law and parliamentary sovereignty, the Australian rule of law relies on the operation of a written constitution.[260] Under the principle of Supremacy of the Constitution,[261] individuals' rights are protected by the courts, whose powers are certified by the Constitution, which is the supreme law of the land. A number of examples affirm this distinctive understanding of the rule of law. For example, Chief Justice Gleeson mentions that *'The existence of a written constitution as the basic law of a federal democratic society has a specific implication for the substantive content of the rule of law'.*[262] In *Australian Communist Party v Commonwealth*, Justice Dixon stated that *'The rule of law is an assumption*

---

[259] This terminology is borrowed from the judgment of *Plaintiff s157/2002 v Commonwealth* (2003) 211 CLR 476, in which Section 75 (v) of the constitution was described as providing the *'minimum entrenched provision of judicial review'* (See more below).

[260] Chief Justice French, 'Administrative Law in Australia: Themes and Values Revisited' in Matthew Groves (ed), *Modern Administrative Law in Australia: Concepts and Context* (CUP 2014) 28; Saunders (n 246) 216.

[261] Although this principle has not been explicitly cited in Australian judgments, it can be extracted from the frequent quoting of the US case of *Marbury v Madison* 5 US 137 by the Australian lawyers (see Stephan Gageler, 'The Constitutional Dimension' in Matthew Groves (ed), *Modern Administrative Law in Australia: Concepts and Context* (CUP 2014) 171). This also has been expressed in the judge's mentality that the '*Supreme Court... bowing to no power but the supremacy of law*' (Gleeson (n 81)).

[262] Gleeson (n 81).

2.4 Rigid Legal Mentality of Australian Judicial Review Constitutionalism

of the Australian Constitution'.[263] This simply means that the rule of law is the starting value and the main purpose of any operation of the Constitution. On the flip side, this statement also confirms that the Australian form of the rule of law is operated through the written Constitution. Spencer argues that this Australian form of the rule of law surpasses the sovereignty of Parliament in English law.[264] Justice Dixon asserts that the doctrine of parliamentary sovereignty was inconsistent with the requirements of federalism and contrary to Australia's legal history.[265]

Directly relating to the first feature, the Australian rule of law is not implemented through the Bill of Rights,[266] but emphasises the separation of powers as a dominant requirement. However, this principle does not operate in the same way as it does in the analysed English law, in which the courts rely their power to conduct judicial review on parliamentary sovereignty and the authority of the executives has a fluid boundary. Instead, the framework of the separation of powers between the three branches of government prescribed in the written constitution must be rigidly protected. In term of justifying judicial review, the power of the legislative and the executive must be controlled and determined in a final and binding manner by the exercise of judicial power.[267] Justice Hayne confirms this mentality by stating that.

> *The whole system of Government in Australia is constructed upon the recognition that the ultimate responsibility for the final definition, maintenance and enforcement of the boundaries within which governmental power may be exercised rest upon the judicature.*[268]

Sir Brennan also states that *'Under...the Australian Constitution, the political branches of government are kept separate from the judicial branch'.*[269] Therefore, a particular power needs to be clearly identified, whether judicial or non-judicial. If it is a non-judicial power, it must be controlled by judicial power.[270] The keystone of this particular understanding of the separation of powers, the so-called 'Separation of Judicial Power', can be traced to a number of Australian cases, particularly the

---

[263] (1951) 83 CLR 1. Justice Brennan exemplified this in the speech that *'Our Constitution, rooted in the common law...express the proposition that the nation is under the rule of law and that the Courts are the organ of government responsible ultimately for the enforcing of the rule of law'* (Brennan (n 242)).

[264] Tom Spencer, 'An Australian Rule of Law' (2014) 21 Australian Journal of Administrative Law 98.

[265] Michael Wait, 'The Slumbering Sovereign: Sir Owen Dixon's Common Law Constitution Revisited' (2001) 29 Federal Law Review 57.

[266] Chief Justice French asserts that *'there was probably a variety of reasons behind the absence in Australia's Constitution of a Bill of Rights, some related to the desire to maintain the capacity to discriminate against particular racial groups* [following the Australian white policy] *and others reflecting a loftier version of the nascent Australian constitutionalism'* (Chief Justice French, 'Courts in a Representative Democracy' (University of Southern Queensland, Toowoomba, 25 June 2010)).

[267] French, 'Administrative Law in Australia: Themes and Values Revisited' (n 260) 28; Saunders (n 246) 185; Connolly (n 79) 136–137.

[268] Kenneth Hayne, 'Deference: An Australian Perspective' [2010] PL 75, 76.

[269] Brennan (n 242).

[270] Groves and Lee (n 90) 7; Brennan (n 242).

Boilermakers' case, in which the conferral of judicial powers on non-judicial bodies was prohibited.[271]

This requirement of the separation of powers, as a part of the rule of law, is connected to the federal system and written Constitution. For the former, the separation of powers contains the legal framework and the establishment of institutions for the federal sphere of government by prescribing the continuance, powers and functions of the HCA.[272] For the latter, such framework is prescribed as provisions in the written constitution. As Chief Justice French stated, '*A sharp separation of the judicial from the legislative and executive powers is established under the Constitution of the Commonwealth*.[273]

Apart from Chapter III of the Constitution, which defines and separates judicial powers from legislative and executive powers,[274] the courts also justify their jurisdiction of judicial review of administrative action by interpreting particular provisions in the written Constitution. In *Plaintiff S157/2002 v Commonwealth of Australia*,[275] the judgment states that privative clauses must be interpreted in the light of the '*minimum entrenched provision of judicial review*' introduced by Section 75(v) of the Constitution.[276] Chief Justice Gleeson ties this interpretation of the provision to the rule of law by saying that '*Section 75(v) secures a basic element of the rule of law… it cannot deprive this Court of its constitutional jurisdiction to enforce the law so enacted*'.[277] This thereby enables the HCA to have jurisdiction to conduct judicial review in all matters and to contribute to the evolution of the grounds of judicial review.[278] Furthermore, Gleeson described section 75 (v) as '*a basic guarantee of the rule of law*' in his secondary work.[279] Additionally, although

---

[271] n 254; Groves and Boughey (n 243) 16–17.

[272] Saunders (n 246) 39; Michael Taggart, 'Australian Exceptionalism in Judicial Review' (2008) 36 Federal Law Review 1, 4–5; Connolly (n 79) 35.

[273] French, 'Courts in a Representative Democracy' (n 266).

[274] French, 'Administrative Law in Australia: Themes and Values Revisited' (n 260) 28. It shall be noted that, apart from judicial review of administrative action, the powers of the HCA and other Federal courts on judicial review of legislation are also valid under the Commonwealth Constitution (French, 'Australia's Constitutional Evolution' (n 75)). However, this chapter studies particularly on the aspect of judicial review of administrative action.

[275] n 259.

[276] Section 71 of the Constitution stipulates that '*The judicial power of the Commonwealth shall be vested in a Federal Supreme Court, to be called the High Court of Australia, and in such other federal courts as the Parliament creates, and in such other courts as it invests with federal jurisdiction*'. Section 75(v) stipulates that '*In all matters: (v) in which a writ of Mandamus or prohibition or an injunction is sought against an officer of the Commonwealth; the High Court shall have original jurisdiction*'.

[277] n 259, 482–483.

[278] Groves and Lee (n 90) 11–12; Mark Aronson, Matthew Groves and Greg Weeks, *Judicial Review of Administrative Action and Government Liability* (6th edn, Thomson Reuters Australia 2017) [1.50]; Gageler (n 261) 172–173; Chief Justice French, 'Statutory Interpretation and Rationality in Administrative Law' (National Administrative Law Lecture, Canberra, 23 July 2015).

[279] Murray Gleeson, *The Rule of Law and the Constitution* (ABC Books 2000) 67; See also Creyke, McMillan and Smyth (n 258) [5.1.1].

2.4 Rigid Legal Mentality of Australian Judicial Review Constitutionalism

this book focuses on judicial review at a federal level, it shall be shown that this interpretation of the provision in written constitution to entrench jurisdiction of the courts was also adopted at the level of the State Supreme Courts. This was Section 73 of the Constitution, which was interpreted in *Kirk*. This will be exemplified in detail in the next chapter.

All of these constitutional values, which read the framework of separation of powers prescribed in the written constitution in a way that justified the role of the courts to conduct judicial review were affirmed in the Kerr Report. For example, relating to the federal system, the report stated that *'The normal way in which judicial review of Commonwealth administrative decisions may be sought is by proceedings in the High Court'*.[280] This means that if the individual is affected by a government official exercising discretionary functions, he or she could seek judicial review from the HCA.[281] This suggestion highlights the role of the HCA to act as the final appellate court having supervisory jurisdiction of all administrative actions, whether committed by executive or state court.[282] It is an integration of the federal system into Australian judicial review constitutionalism. As the original purpose in importing federal system into the legal system, the HCA has duty to protect the boundary of power between the federation and states and between states. Regarding the engagement with the written Constitution, the Kerr Report mentions clearly that *'...under the Constitution...the High Court shall have original jurisdiction'*.[283] This displays that the written Constitution becomes important reference for the courts in perceiving their role in conducting judicial review. As Connolly regarded, the constitution is the *'ultimate source'* of the judicial power in Australia.[284]

So far, the analysis has demonstrated the distinctive way the rule of law in Australian law has been understood according to the constitutional frameworks. In essence, it emphasises rigid separation of powers between the Governments, particularly that the judicial powers need to review non-judicial powers, in order to respond and maintain the allocation of powers according to the federal system. This leads another concept, called the concept of jurisdiction, to be important in Australian judicial review constitutionalism. Generally, the concept of jurisdiction premises the notion that *'All powers have limits'*.[285] It is described in different ways. For example, Sir Brennan asserts that *'The supervision of the judicial power in order to ensure conformity with the Constitution and the laws made under it'*.[286] Justice Spigelman defines this duty of the courts to be the *'Integrity Branch of*

---

[280] Kerr (n 256) [20].

[281] Groves and Boughey (n 243).

[282] Chief Justice French, 'The Courts and the Parliament' (Queensland Supreme Court Seminar, Brisbane, 4 August 2012).

[283] Kerr (n 256) [23].

[284] Connolly (n 79) 241, 284.

[285] Aronson, Groves and Weeks (n 278) [3.20].

[286] Brennan (n 242).

Government'.[287] Some scholars regard this concept as a part of the Australian substantive rule of law[288] and the principle of legality.[289] However, in terms of justification, they all have similar content, namely that the courts have a role to conduct judicial review in order to police, enforce and ensure that the exercise of power is supported by constitutional authority and remains within the scope of that authority.[290]

In summary, further details have been added to the deep understanding of the constitutional values that justify the scope of judicial review in Australia. The rule of law emphasises the rigid separation of powers between government organs, particularly in terms of judicial power requiring to review non-judicial power, in order to respond to and maintain the allocation of powers according to the federal system. This subsection points out that, rather than the ultra vires and common law models introduced by academic, the Australian judges straightforwardly refer to these constitutional frameworks and constitutional values as their justification to conduct judicial review. For example, Gageler asserts that

> *Within a constitutional system which establishes and secures such a separation of powers, it is the province and duty of the judicial power to declare and enforce the law that constrains and limits the powers of the other branches of government.*[291]

He also mentions the judgment in *Church of Scientology v Woodward* stating that *'judicial review is neither more nor less than the enforcement of the rule of law over executive action'*.[292] Chief Justice Gleeson also asserts in his speech that *'judicial review of administrative action is a familiar example of the application of the rule of law'*.[293] The concept of jurisdiction also endorses that the courts have to conduct judicial review because they have to police the boundaries of executive and judicial powers. This functions to demarcate the limits of administrative powers and the reach of a supervisory review.[294] Chief Justice French clearly asserts this mentality that

---

[287] James Spigelman, 'The Integrity Branch of Government' 78 Australian Law Journal 724; James Spigelman, 'The Centrality of Jurisdictional Error' 21 Public Law Review 77.

[288] Gleeson, 'Courts and the Rule of Law' (n 81); Chief Justice French, 'The Rule of Law as a Many Coloured Dream Coat' (20th Annual Lecture Singapore Academy of Law, 18 September 2013, Singapore).

[289] Chief Justice Gleeson, 'Legality: Spirit and Principle' (The Second Magna Carta Lecture, New South Wales Parliament House, Sydney, 20 November 2003).

[290] See Mark Leeming, *Authority to Decide: the Law of Jurisdiction in Australia* (2nd edn, The Federation Press 2020) Chapter 2; Groves and Lee (n 90) 2–3; French, 'The Rule of Law as a Many Coloured Dream Coat' (n 288).

[291] Stephan Gageler, 'The Underpinnings of Judicial Review of Administrative Action' (2000) 28 Federal Law Review 303, 309.

[292] 154 CLR 25, 70 (See Gageler, 'The Constitutional Dimension' (n 261) 171).

[293] Gleeson, 'Courts and the Rule of Law' (n 81).

[294] Groves and Boughey (n 243) 20.

We can then consider the role of the court, essential to the rule of law, in the protection of rights and freedoms and policing the exercise of official power when it exceeds its legal limit.[295]

Apart from that, the justification also comes from the described provision in the written constitution, particularly Chapter III and section 75(v). For example, Justices Gaudron, McHugh, Gummow, Kirby and Hayne connect the interpretation to the concept of jurisdiction in *Plaintiff s157/2002* that *'Section 75(v)... means of assuring to all people affected that officers of the Commonwealth obey the law and neither exceed nor neglect any jurisdiction which law confers on them.*[296]

It should be noted that, as observed by Aronson, Groves and Weeks, the term 'ultra vires' used to be applied in the early development of Australian administrative law. However, it was applied in a simple way as 'outside' the scope of power for others apart from judicial bodies.[297] It did not contain the substantive content of the ultra vires model relating the position of the court to Parliament as applied in England. At present, the concept of jurisdiction (and the approach of jurisdictional error) has become the dominant conclusory term in Australian law, rather than ultra vires.[298] As a result, the justification for judicial review is more entrenched in Australian law than in English law because it is tied to the constitutional order in the Australian legal system. The ultra vires and common law models, as the result of flexibility in explaining the role of the courts, do not have relevance in Australian legal culture.

2.4.3 *Australian Constitutional Values That Limit Judicial Review*

The way in which the Australian courts read the framework of separation of powers prescribed in the written constitution in order to justify their role in conducting judicial review was illustrated in the previous subsection by a particular understanding of the rule of law, the separation of powers and the concept of jurisdiction. However, this entrenched justification of judicial review does not completely explain the rigidity of the Australian legal culture. The other side of the mentality which the Australian courts read the constitution in a way that limits their role to conduct judicial review, will be illustrated in this subsection through the same set of constitutional values but diverse ways of deliberation.

To begin with, the relatively rigid separation of powers is still a significant requirement of the rule of law in Australia. However, not only are the legislative and executive required to stay within the boundary of their power, but also the judiciary.

---

[295] French, 'Courts in a Representative Democracy' (n 266).
[296] n 259, 513.
[297] Aronson, Groves and Weeks (n 278) [1.100]-[1.110].
[298] ibid.

As Foster points out, *'Boilermakers solidified the two limbs of the separation of judicial power doctrine'*.[299] The first limb prohibits *'the executive and legislative branches from exercising judicial power'*, while the second restricts the courts from *'carrying out the executive function of administration or the legislative function of determining policy'*.[300] This limitation of judicial review has been widely regarded by judges and scholars as a significant aspect of the rule of law and the separation of powers in Australia. For example, according to Chief Justice Gleeson, *'The rule of law is not just a principle that…is enforced by courts. It controls the operation of courts themselves…'*.[301] Crawford repeatedly states in her analysis of the Australian rule of law that *'…the HCA also derives its powers from the Constitution. It cannot exceed those powers, when reviewing the legality of executive action, or performing any other of its functions'*.[302] In the same vein, Saunders argues that *'…the separation of judicial power can be used not only to protect the authority of courts but also to constrain it'*.[303] Creyke, McMillan and Smyth also clearly articulate that *'…the separation of powers doctrine entrenches the tripartite distribution of legislative, executive and judicial functions between the three branches of government. This doctrine permeates Australian administrative law and has constrained the scope of judicial review'*.[304]

In the same way as it is justified, this particular understanding of the rule of law and separation of powers that rigidly limit of judicial review is operated with the written constitution. As deliberated by Chief Justice Gleeson,

> The principle that courts are bound by the Constitution, and all other laws, defines the relationship between judges and the other arms of government, and between judges and the community.[305]

This opinion is shared by Chief Justice French when he compares it to the English law; *'In Australia, unlike the United Kingdom and New Zealand, written Commonwealth and State Constitutions, read together, constrain official power, be it legislative, executive or judicial'*.[306] Not only judges, but also scholars perceive this connection between the rule of law, separation of powers and the constitution to limit the courts to conduct judicial review. For example, Crawford states that

---

[299] Michelle Foster, 'The Separation of Judicial Power' in Cheryl Saunders and Adrienne Stone (eds), *The Oxford Handbook of the Australian Constitution* (OUP 2018) 678–679.

[300] ibid.

[301] Gleeson, 'Courts and the Rule of Law' (n 81).

[302] Lisa Crawford, *The Rule of Law and the Australian Constitution* (The Federation Press 2017) 132.

[303] Saunders (n 246) 207.

[304] Creyke, McMillan and Smyth (n 258) [7.3.12].

[305] Gleeson, 'Courts and the Rule of Law' (n 81).

[306] French, 'Statutory Interpretation and Rationality in Administrative Law' (n 278).

2.4 Rigid Legal Mentality of Australian Judicial Review Constitutionalism

...the nature and scope of the legislative power of the Commonwealth, the judicial power of the Commonwealth, and the executive power of the Commonwealth, all of which are conferred and constrained by the Australian Constitution.[307]

Taggart provides a prominent example;

The Constitution is generally construed as establishing a firm separation of powers between the three branches of government...

...when it comes to administrative law the price to be paid for that strength on the constitutional side is considerable restraint; limiting the courts to enforcing the law...[308]

Apart from the rule of law and separation of powers, the position that the role of the courts to conduct judicial review should be clearly and rigidly limited is also deliberated through other constitutional values, the most significant of which is the distinction between legality and merits.[309] While the courts' role is to determine legality, merits of the cases is for the executives. Judges and scholars in Australia share this rigid mentality based on the premise that the courts' jurisdiction to intervene in the merits should be limited. For example, Chief Justice Mason stated that *'...it would be a serious mistake to think that judicial review...comprehends review on the merits'*.[310] Indeed, this rigid distinction between legality and merits is rooted in the rule of law, the separation of powers and the constitution. For example, Saunders draws the connection that *'the separation of powers understood as...limiting courts to questions of law, ruling out considerations equated with merits'*,[311] is a *'characteristic features of Australian administrative law that are not shared with other Commonwealth countries'*.[312] In the same vein, Cane and McDonald state that

...in Australian law the legality/merits distinction is increasingly thought to be an outworking of complex ideas about the separation of powers...

This is central to the court's understanding of how the rule of law is secured within Australia's constitutional arrangements.[313]

A particular comparison to the English law on this point was made by Elias, as follows,

In Australia, the separation of powers provided by the Constitution has been used by the High Court to protect its constitutional responsibility to say what the law is. That has had

---

[307] Crawford (n 302) 6.

[308] Taggart (n 272).

[309] See Debra Mortimer, 'The Constitutionalisation of Administrative Law', in Cheryl Saunders and Adrienne Stone (eds) *The Oxford Handbook of the Australian Constitution* (OUP 2018).

[310] Anthony Mason, 'Administrative Review – The Experience of the First Twelve Years' (1989) 18 Federal Law Review 122, 125.

[311] Cheryl Saunders, 'Constitution as Catalyst: Different Paths within Australian Administrative Law' (2012) 10 NZJPIL 154.

[312] ibid 147.

[313] Cane and McDonald (n 248) 23; See also Groves and Lee (n 90) 10–11; Creyke, McMillan and Smyth (n 258) [5.1.2], [5.3.45], [7.2.2]; French, 'Administrative Law in Australia: Themes and Values Revisited' (n 260) 35.

implications for the development of Australian administrative law. It has been taken to emphasise a distinction between legality and merits which in other jurisdictions is less sharp. In Australia, the strict line observed between legality and merits means it is difficult to develop standards for judicial intervention from values obtained from the common law, international conventions ... Reference to such values is seen to give rise to 'merits review', a line the courts will not pass.

In the UK..., where executive dominance of Parliament and parliamentary sovereignty is untrammelled by a constitutional text which distributes powers, judicial review is less secure.[314]

Correspondingly, the analysed constitutional values that limit the conduct of judicial review results in another distinctive element of the Australian legal culture. The relationship between the court and the executive and the proposition of tribunals in England was demonstrated as being flexible in the previous section. However, this is not the same in Australia, since the boundary of powers is relatively fixed. The most explicit source of rigidity on this point is the Kerr Report. Although the report accepted the fact that judicial review could not be the sole mechanism to provide adequately review administrative actions, it was clearly stated that the role of the courts and other governmental organs need to be rigidly distinct.[315] Additionally, the rigid distinction between legality and merits are clearly the reason for this position. For example, the report repeatedly deliberates that *'...we are of opinion that review on the merits should not and indeed...cannot be undertaken by the courts...'*.[316] Unlike the analysed English law, these distinctions between legality and merits and between court and executive are systematically linked to the framework of separation of judicial powers. For instance, concept of separation of judicial power was expressly stated in the report.[317] Importantly, all of these constitutional values are operated by the written constitution. This is not only *'to prevent the exercise of the judicial power of the Commonwealth by bodies other than the courts mentioned in Chapter III'*,[318] but *'the Commonwealth Constitution'* also *'impose[s] significant qualifications on the exercise of the judicial power of the Commonwealth'*.[319]

The discussion in Kerr resulted in the creation of another two mechanisms of the Australian administrative law. Firstly, it proposed the enactment of legislation to simplify, codify and expand common law judicial review. This subsequently resulted

---

[314] Dame Sian Elias, 'The Unity of Public Law?', in Mark Elliott, Jason Varuhas and Shona Stark (eds), *The Unity of Public Law?: Doctrinal, Theoretical and Comparative Perspectives* (Hart Publishing 2018) 25–26.

[315] The Kerr Report (n 256) [5]-[7]. Interestingly, some significant English reports, namely Donoughmore, Franks, Leggatt and Law Commission were discussed in the report ([113]-[116], [124], [136], [138]-139]).

[316] ibid [21]; See also [227], [228], [239], [247], [354] and [390] (2).

[317] ibid [6], [65].

[318] ibid [61].

[319] ibid [59].

2.4 Rigid Legal Mentality of Australian Judicial Review Constitutionalism

in the ADJR,[320] an act stipulating template for federal judicial review.[321] Secondly, the report proposed a new general administrative review tribunal to replace the inefficient proliferation of specialist tribunals, and this led to the establishment of the Administrative Appeals Tribunal by the Administrative Appeals Tribunal Act 1975 ('AAT').[322] Based on the same methodology as was used to analyse the relationship between EU law and English law above, although the systems of ADJR and AAT are not the scope of analysis in this book,[323] they reinforce the idea of the rigid mentality of Australian judicial review constitutionalism. For the ADJR, it demonstrates the mentality of the legal system to categorise the grounds of judicial review, and prescribe them as the written provisions.[324] In the same vein, the AAT's main purpose is that the courts cannot infringe on the merits of administrative actions, since this is not within their remit, but that of executives.[325] These emphasise the distinctive mentality that the Australian court has to rigidly consider, follow and refer to a framework of powers, prescribed in the form of a written document in considering their scope of judicial review. This position does not exist in the English law. The influence of this difference between the legal cultures on the determination of the grounds of judicial review, particularly one related to administrative discretion, will be demonstrated in the following chapters. For instance, while there are overlaps and flexibility in recognising the status of common law judicial review and the HRA, the Australian law has a clearer and more systematic distinction between judicial review by the ADJR and the common law judicial review. These are also products of the legal cultures.

Apart from the Kerr report, academic works in Australia also share this overall position of a rigid relationship between the court and other governmental organs. For Cane, it is *'a constitutional requirement'* that *'the rigidity of the Australian approach to separation of powers makes it impossible for the federal Parliament to*

---

[320] For example, that the grounds of review should be clarified and set out explicitly by statute (ibid [248]).

[321] Creyke McMillan and Smyth (n 258) [2.2.8].

[322] We have recommended that a new Administrative Court be created to exercise a general supervisory jurisdiction over administrative action (Kerr (n 256) [251]).

[323] See Sect. 1.4 of Chap. 1.

[324] Section 5 of the ADJR systematically sets out the grounds of judicial review namely, breach of the rules of natural justice, error of law, no evidence, fraud, contrary to law, improper purpose, relevant consideration, bad faith, unreasonable and abuse of power.

[325] It is recognised that there are many occasions in which judges hear merits appeal cases when they are members of the AAT (see statistical data at <https://www.aat.gov.au/about-the-aat/who-we-are> accessed 13th June 2020). As noted in Chap. 1, although the outcomes of the English and Australian law may not be too different in reality, it is still important to point out the distinctively rigid legal mentality caused by this attempt to clarify the structure between the executive and the judiciary. This and other aspects of the legal culture will be demonstrated in subsequent chapters as reinforcing the rigidity of the doctrinal approaches and legal reasoning applied in Australia to determine the grounds of judicial review, which is different from their English counterparts.

establish multi-functional agencies...'.[326] This *'unique and rigidifying significance'* of the Australian legal culture leads to the courts *'discouraging aggressive judicial review'* and *'stressing the proper limits of the judicial ...'*[327] Once again, the reasons for them are steadily linked to the other analysed constitutional values. The most prominent linkage is drawn by Owen, as follows;

> State tribunals may, but Commonwealth tribunals may not, be vested with judicial power. The reason for that restriction is, of course, the separation of powers inherent in Chapter III, as identified in R v Kirby; Ex parte Boilermakers' Society of Australian[328]

Crawford also clarifies that,

> All this suggests that there is some clear distinction between legality and merits...These divisions and distinctions are said to be required by the Constitution. It should also be noted that the merits of executive decision-making are not, by reason of these distinctions, completely impervious to review within the Australian legal framework. Rather, it has become the clear province of Australia's administrative review tribunals, which are not courts for the purposes of Ch III[329]

Besides the rule of law, the separation of judicial powers, the rigid distinctions between legality and merits and between court and executive, the concept of jurisdiction is another significant constitutional value that strengthens this overall position. As described above, the key requirement of the concept of jurisdiction is that court has the duty to police the boundary of governmental powers. Based on the same logic as the separation of judicial power, not only do the executive and the legislative need to be policed, but also the boundary of the courts' authority. As Leeming deliberates, *'There are no courts of "unlimited jurisdiction" in Australia'*.[330] This particular understanding of the concept of jurisdiction can be found in the judgment of some cases, for example, *Jackson v Sterling Industries Ltd*[331] and *PT Garuda Indonesia v Australian Competition and Consumer Commission*.[332] Once again, this is compatible with the other analysed constitutional orders. For example, as Groves and Lee describe, *'it is fundamental to the rule of law in the Australian Constitution that there is no such thing as an unfettered discretion'*.[333] Therefore, the particular understanding of the concept of jurisdiction not only warrants judicial

---

[326] Cane, 'Understanding Administrative Adjudication' (n 140) 282, 292–293; See also Cane, *Controlling Administrative Power: An Historical Comparison* (n 150) 501.

[327] Cane, 'The Making of Australian Administrative Law' (n 244); See also Saunders, *The Constitution of Australia: A Contextual Analysis* (n 246) 201.

[328] Nicholas Owens, 'The Judicature', in Cheryl Saunders and Adrienne Stone (eds) *The Oxford Handbook of the Australian Constitution* (OUP 2018) 661.

[329] Crawford (n 302) 124.

[330] Leeming (n 290) 4.

[331] (1987) 162 CLR 612, 630.

[332] [2012] HCA 33 [16].

[333] French, 'Administrative Law in Australia: Themes and Values Revisited' (n 260) 18; See also Crawford (n 302) 132.

2.4 Rigid Legal Mentality of Australian Judicial Review Constitutionalism

intervention, but also limits their judicial review to within the scope of power prescribed in the written constitution and statutory construction.

The last constitutional value unpacked in this section is the Concept of Legalism expounded by Dixon in 1955. In essence, this concept deliberates the role of the courts to *'determine the substance of the law'*, because they *'conform with ascertained legal principles'*.[334] Rather than *'a freedom of choice'*, *'the inherited system must be given a rigidity and statute must become the only source of law'*.[335] Josev provides the following example of the application of legalism;

> If a legalistic judge was required to find the meaning of particular words in a statute, they...required reference to be made exclusively to authoritative legal materials in the search for meaning...the legalist therefore eschewed any decision-making on the basis of social factors or policy considerations...[336]

Despite being commented on various ways,[337] the uniformity of Australian thinking has resulted in Dixon's Legalism meaning that the role of the courts should be rigidly confined to the determination of the law without considering the policy or consequences. For example, although the courts are free to reach a new conclusion, they must *'maintain its continuity and preserve its coherence'*.[338] Conversely, Justice Kirby described four limitations, namely, opportunity, needs, inclination and methodology, which he regarded as *'guideposts'* to *'keep in the judicial mind as limits of judicial activism'*.[339] It was emphasised that *'...the judge is not a completely free agent. A measure of creativity is allowed. But it is a limited one whose parameters are fixed by the very nature of the judicial function'*.[340]

Similar to the status of Dicey's concept analysed in the previous section, this 'general form' of Dixon's Legalism had a profound influence on the legal mentality of Australian courts' understanding of their constitutional role. For example, Saunders mentioned that *'legalism is widely accepted as the orthodox methodology*

---

[334] Dixon, 'Judicial Method' (n 253); Tanya Josev, *The Campaign against the Courts: A History of the Judicial Activism Debate* (The Federation Press 2017) 6.

[335] ibid.

[336] Josev (n 334) 93.

[337] It is arguable that Dixon was not the strict legalist he claimed to be in practice, because he applied other sources and tools outside the statute to the consideration of his judgment in many cases. For example, he stated in *Williams v City of Melbourne* [1933] 49 CLR 142 [155] that '...The true nature and purpose of the power must be determined, and it must often be necessary to examine the operation of the by-law in the local circumstances to which it is intended to apply'. Similarly, as will be seen in the next chapter, his approach in *R v Hickman, Ex parte Fox and Clinton* (1945) 70 CLR 598 mainly relies on judicial discretion to determine if the disputed decision breached a fundamental jurisdictional requirement or not.

[338] Dixon, 'Judicial Method' (n 253); See also Heydon (n 118); Justice Hayne, '"Concerning Judicial Method"- Fifty Years on' (The Fourteenth Lucinda Lecture, Monash University, 17 October 2006).

[339] Justice Kirby, 'Judicial Activism' (The Bar Association of India Lecture, New Delhi, 6 January 1997).

[340] ibid.

for constitutional adjudication in Australia',[341] and Justice Gageler considers it to be *'the dominant theme of the judicial style of the Court for much of the 20th century'*.[342]

As explained above, at the time it existed, Dixon's Legalism was related to the role of the courts in interpreting the constitution. However, it will be argued in this section that it applies to judicial methods in general rather than a specific area. This can be recognised from Dixon's assertion that

> It [Legalism] *goes deep in legal thinking. The influence is far-reaching that has been exerted upon the judicial and juridical thought of this country by the functions which the courts must fulfil under those great constitutional guarantees.*[343]

Consequently, Dixon's Legalism also influenced the legal mentality of Australian judicial review constitutionalism. Most clearly, Justice Heydon stated that *'Sir Owen Dixon thought that non-constitutional cases should be decided by recourse to legalism as well'*.[344] Importantly, he regarded it as a part of *'mentalite, which I interpret as mindset'*.[345] Therefore, Dixon's Legalism is represented another requirement for the role of the courts to be limited to the determination of law, not policy. It is further connected in this section, that this limitation can be perceived from the framework of separation of powers prescribed in the written constitution. This is supported by some scholars; for instance, in an analysis of legalism, Goldsworthy states that

> ...*the Court has often been guided by broad principles that it regards as underlying parts of the Constitution...The most important are federalism, the separation of powers, responsible government, representative government, nationhood, and the rule of law...*
> [By these values] ...*the Court...look no further than the terms of the law in question....*[346]

In the same vein, Saunders asserts that '...*it* [legalism] *revealed ways in which those parts of the Constitution that distribute functions between the institutions of Commonwealth government might also operate as a constraint on power...*'[347] Stellios describes Dixon's concept as a *'conception of the role of the judiciary within the constitutional system'*.[348]

In summary, the particular understanding of constitutional values in Australia, namely the rule of law, the separation of judicial power, the rigid distinctions between legality and merits and between court and other governmental organs, the concept of jurisdiction and Dixon's Legalism were unpacked in this subsection to

---

[341] Saunders, *The Constitution of Australia: A Contextual Analysis* (n 246) 90.

[342] Stephen Gageler, 'Legalism' in Tony Blackshield, Michael Coper and George Williams (eds), *The Oxford Companion to the High Court of Australian* (OUP 2001) 429.

[343] Dixon, 'Judicial Method' (n 253).

[344] Heydon (n 118).

[345] ibid.

[346] Goldsworthy (n 252).

[347] Saunders, *The Constitution of Australia: A Contextual Analysis* (n 246) 94.

[348] James Stellios, 'Concepts of Judicial Review: Commentary on Dixon' (2015) 43 Federal Law Review 511.

2.4 Rigid Legal Mentality of Australian Judicial Review Constitutionalism

demonstrate the distinctive way in which the framework of separation of powers prescribed in the written constitution is read in order to rigidly limit the role of the courts in conducting judicial review.

As an additional indicator, a number of academics propose various approaches to deliberate the role of the courts in conducting judicial review in Australia; for example, Justice Spigelman's concept of the Integrity Branch of Government,[349] Justice Gleeson's concept of Judicial Legitimacy[350] or the distinctive way of common law by Selway,[351] but they uniformly agree that judicial review must adhere to the clear and rigid constitutional limitations. The various thoughts discussed in governmental committees' reports and academic works in the English legal culture do not exist in Australia. All of these analysed elements are the detailed examination of Justice Mason's recognition of *'judges...appearing to have a limited role'* as *'attitude of mind...shared by the Australian legal community'*,[352] as well as of Cane and McDonald's statement that ...[This] *separation of powers sensibility that runs much deeper in the Australian judicial psyche than in the English'*.[353]

2.4.4 Rigidly Reading the Framework of Separation of Powers Prescribed in the Written Constitution

> *Perhaps the most important was an acceptance that the role of the courts in judicial review is a mixture of constitutional duty and limits.*[354]

Consistent with the above statement by Groves and Boughey, it was demonstrated in the previous subsections that the constitutional values can be understood in a distinctive way to both justify and limit the Australian courts' conduct of judicial review. Rather than a balancing process, the entrenched justification and firm limitation result in a legal mentality the Australian courts have to rigidly follow the framework of separation of powers in determining the scope of judicial review in a particular case. This can be determined from the written constitution and statutory construction. This rigid mentality and approach are embedded in the Australian law, as exemplified in the Kerr Report as follows;

> ...it is necessary to decide what is the scope of review to be entrusted to the courts...The courts have steadfastly refused to adopt the attitude that they will review administrative

---

[349] James Spigelman, 'The Integrity Branch of Government' (n 287).

[350] Chief Justice Gleeson, 'Judicial Legitimacy' (Australian Bar Association Conference, New York, 2 July 2000).

[351] Bradley Selway, 'The Principle behind Common Law Judicial Review of Administrative Action – The Search Continues' (2002) 30 Federal Law Review 217.

[352] As quoted in n 123 above.

[353] Cane and McDonald (n 248) 24.

[354] Groves and Boughey (n 243) 17.

decisions on the merits, except in so far as a particular statutory provision gives them that jurisdiction, and enables them to substitute their decision for that of the administrator.[355]

This is also deliberated through the concept of jurisdiction that *'The validity of executive action must be decided by reference to the statute by which the power is conferred....'*,[356] and the concept of Integrity Branches of Government that *'...intervention by a court is...depend on the statutory scheme under consideration'*.[357] Chief Justice French similarly asserts that *'Typically, the courts look to text, context and purpose'*.[358] According to Justice Hayne,

> *...judges make the common law... [However]...attention must focus upon that text. It matters not whether the text is the Constitution, a statute, a contract, or some other written instrument. The text must be both the starting point and the finishing point for the application of that standard of reasoning...*[359]

It should be noted that the English courts also consider the statute when determining the scope of judicial review. However, the Australian mentality is more rigid because of the analysed distinctive judicial review constitutionalism. Justice Gummow compared the two legal cultures on this point when he made the following statement;

> *In this distinctive position of the English judges may be seen the origin both of the separation of the judicial power from that of the executive and the legislature, and the attribution to the judicial branch of the authority to construe first statue law and, thereafter, written and rigid constitutions...in Australia*
>
> *The latter judicial function was contrary to what in England became the "unadorned Diceyan percept of parliamentary sovereignty"*[360]

Cane further clarified it by stating that

> *... the judicial review jurisdiction of the English High Court is inherent in the sense that it is not dependent on or derived from a statutory grant of power. In the English system, judicial power is autonomous rather than conferred, and the common law is an independent source of law rather than a gloss on the Constitution and statutes...*[361]

> *[In Australia] ...the Constitution and statutes are...the only sources of governmental power...*[362]

All of these constitutional structures are gathered into a cluster of the rigid legal mentality of Australian judicial review constitutionalism. If the issue concerns a legal question (legality), the courts' justification to conduct judicial review is

---

[355] Kerr (n 256) [88].

[356] Crawford (n 302) 126.

[357] James Spigelman, 'Jurisdictional Integrity' (2nd Lecture National Lecture Series for the Australian Institute of Administrative Law, 5 August 2004).

[358] French, 'Statutory Interpretation and Rationality in Administrative Law' (n 278).

[359] Hayne, '"Concerning Judicial Method"- Fifty Years on' (n 338).

[360] William Gummow, 'Common Law' in Cheryl Saunders and Adrienne Stone (eds), *The Oxford Handbook of the Australian Constitution* (2018 OUP) 191.

[361] Peter Cane, *Controlling Administrative Power: An Historical Comparison* (n 150) 495.

[362] ibid 497.

entrenched, but their ability to conduct judicial review is firmly limited if it is a question of merits. They must *'rigorously'* follow the *'boundary of powers' prescribed in the written constitution and statutory construction'* because *'To do more would be to abdicate the judicial function... To do less would be to blur the legality/merits distinction...'*.[363] This *'strict approach of the separation of judicial power'*[364] and other analysed constitutional values are the source of the rigidity of the Australian legal culture, which have a consequential impact on the confined doctrinal approaches in the development of the grounds of judicial review clearly different from the English law.

2.4.5 Unwelcoming Influences from Interrelated Legal Cultures

The last contrast between the English and Australian legal cultures is influence of international treaties. As seen in the last section, the English law is flexible for the courts to adopt interrelated legal cultures, namely EU law and the ECHR, to perceive their role in conducting judicial review. Conversely, this element is not included in the geography of Australian judicial review constitutionalism. The simple explanation for this is that Australia is not a member of a supranational organisation like the EU. Additionally, it is not in the same context of English law that needs to integrate provisions from the ECHR into the domestic law. However, this section argues that the rigid legal mentality of the Australian courts is the key to understanding this position. For example, although the Australian courts can take the international conventions signed by the executive into the determination of their judicial review, they cannot integrate them flexibly in the same way as English law. Taggart recognises this situation by saying that

> [In England]...*This has opened the door to the use in relation to exercises of discretionary power of reinvigorated interpretative principles favouring compliance with common law rights and compliance with international legal obligations. This trend has been hastened ...an increasing number of challenges to the exercise of discretionary power as inconsistent with domestic, regional and international human rights instruments. The judges in these countries, as well as in Australia, have affirmed the "principle of legality" and the centrality of the "rule of law" ...*
>
> *...there are formidable doctrinal and practical difficulties in using the doctrine of legitimate expectation to achieve the desirable end of giving greater effect to unincorporated international human rights treaties in domestic law.*[365]

Taggart is answered in this section by explaining that the difficulty involved in adopting a doctrine from an international treaty is the product of the different way

---

[363] Spigelman, 'Jurisdictional Integrity' (n 357).

[364] In Cane and McDonald's words (n 248) 23.

[365] Taggart (n 272) 12, 15. Legal reasoning in *Minister of State for Immigration & Ethnic Affairs v Ah Hin Teoh* [1995] HCA 20 will be discussed in detail in Chap. 6.

in which the Australian courts understand 'the rule of law' and 'legality'. Rather than being flexible like the English one, the Australian judicial review constitutionalism emphasises the rigidity of separation of federal powers prescribed in the written constitution as a key mechanism in protecting the rule of law. Therefore, the courts avoid any influence, which might affect the entrenchment of such framework of powers. This rigid mentality leads them not to adopt the doctrines of proportionality and substantive legitimate expectations into their determination of judicial review. The connection between these doctrinal approaches and this aspect of legal culture will be compared to the English law in further detail in Chaps. 5 and 6.

2.4.6 Substantive Conclusion

> *The Constitution and its implications are now the dominant force shaping Australian administrative law at the federal and state levels* (Spigelman)[366]

The Australian written constitution is the starting point for examining the differences between the English and Australian legal cultures, especially the framework of the federal separation of powers prescribed in its first three chapters. However, the key to understanding the rigidity of the Australian legal culture is not only the constitution and its provisions, but the distinctive way in which the courts read the constitution, which is demonstrated by a particular understanding of the constitutional values. On the one hand, the courts have entrenched the justification to conduct judicial review according to the rule of law, the separation of judicial power, the concept of jurisdiction and the interpretation of Article 75(v) of the constitution. On the other hand, the limitations of judicial review are also firmly limited by the rule of law, the separation of judicial powers, the rigid distinction between legality and merits and between the court and the executive, the concept of jurisdiction and Dixon's Legalism. These two sides of mentality lead to the Australian courts having to rigidly consider, refer to, or follow the framework of separation of powers prescribed in the written constitution and statutory construction to determine the scope of judicial review. They also result in rejecting the integration of interrelated legal cultures in Australian courts' consideration, because they may affect this rigid framework of power. As stated by Justice Spigelman above, it is not only *'the constitution'*, but also *'its implications'*, that provide a back-drop for the rigid legal mentality of Australian judicial review constitutionalism, which becomes the *'dominant force'* in shaping the greater rigidity in the determination of the grounds of judicial review demonstrated in the following chapters.

---

[366] James Spigelman, 'The Centrality of Jurisdictional Error' (n 287).

2.5 Snapshots of English and Australian Rivers

> *English law turns to judicial discretion to determine the scope of judicial review... Australian* [approach] *stands at the rule end of the rule-to-discretion spectrum.*[367]

This quotation by Aronson, Groves and Weeks functions in the same way, as the labels of pragmatism and formalism and pragmatic and formalistic approaches referring to complex accounts by simplistic terms or sentences. This chapter goes deeper by demonstrating more detailed pictures of differences between English and Australian judicial review through legal mentality of judicial review constitutionalism, as a particular form of legal culture, exploring legal thinking of the individual judges in understanding their role in conducting judicial review according to distinctive constitutional orders. As for the English law, the courts understand that their role in conducting judicial review is flexible based on certain elements, namely the absence of a written Constitution, a balancing process between the twin concepts of parliamentary sovereignty and the rule of law, the choice between ultra vires and common law models of justification for judicial review, the fluid relationship between the court, the executive and tribunals, as well as the ability to integrate norms from interrelated legal cultures, like EU law and the ECHR into the consideration. Conversely, the legal mentality of Australian judicial review constitutionalism is concluded as being relatively rigid.[368] The constitutional values, namely the rule of law, the separation of powers, the distinction between legality and merits, the rigid relationship between the court and the executive and the concept of jurisdiction are distinctively understood to both entrench and limit the courts' scope of judicial review. Hence, the courts have to rigidly follow the federal framework of power prescribed in the written constitution and statutory construction in determining their scope of judicial review.

Through the metaphor of this book comparing English and Australian legal culture as the geography of rivers, this chapter concludes with the overall picture of an English river as having sandstone, where the water can flow flexibly through the spaces between them. On the other hand, the stones in an Australian river are a kind of granite, which create the certain ways and force water to flow around them.

These connotations of legal mentality of English and Australian judicial review constitutionalism will be referred to in the next chapters as a detailed examination of differences between English and Australian constitutional orders. The contrast between them is the central conceptual claim of the book, which will navigate a comprehensive understanding of deep-water legality and different determinations of the grounds of judicial review in England and Australia in the following chapters.

---

[367] Aronson, Groves and Weeks (n 278) [1.120]-[1.130].

[368] As noted in Chap. 1, this argument is not based on the entire Australian public law, but specifically on the courts' deep understanding of their role in conducting judicial review as embedded in the Australian legal culture.

Chapter 3
Influence of the Legal Cultures on Error of Law and Jurisdictional Error

Abstract This chapter contains an analysis of the influence of the English and Australian legal cultures on error of law and jurisdictional error, particularly in a judicial review of the decision of a tribunal or inferior court, a body with a restrictive clause according to the legislature. The section devoted to the English law begins with an examination of the flexibility accorded to the courts when applying the jurisdictional fact doctrine before turning to the contemporary approaches in *Anisminic Ltd v Foreign Compensation Commission* [1969] 2 AC 147 (HL), *Regina (Cart) v Upper Tribunal* [2011] UKSC 28 and *R (Privacy International) v Investigatory Powers Tribunal* [2019] UKSC 22. It is demonstrated that the English courts determined the grounds of judicial review based on various justifications and doctrines. This was different from *Craig v The State of South Australia* (1995) 184 CLR 163 and *Kirk v Industrial Court (NSW)* (2010) 239 CLR 531, in which the determination of the scope of judicial review was confined to jurisdictional error based on the framework of separation of powers prescribed in the written Constitution and statutory construction. It is pointed out that these different doctrinal approaches were driven by the different English and Australian legal cultures.

3.1 Introduction

The English approach;

> *The common law now, we could say that ... it is ridiculous to give any more* [emphasis] *on Pre-Anisminic.* (Lord Brown, *R (Cart) v Upper Tribunal*)[1]
> *...any error of law made by an administrative tribunal or inferior court in reaching its decision can be quashed for error of law.* (Lord Browne-Wilkinson, *R v Lord President of the Privy Council, Ex parte Page*)[2]

In comparison with the Australian one;

---

[1] The oral pleading of *R (Cart) v Upper Tribunal* [2011] UKSC 28, proceeded on 14th March 2011.
[2] [1993] AC 682, 702.

Your first proposition cannot be supported, can it, that Their Honours could not look at it? If Their Honours were inquiring whether or not there was a jurisdictional error, they were perfectly entitled to look at it. (Justice Brennan, *Craig v State of South Australia*)[3]

In the previous chapter, differences between English and Australian constitutional orders were examined through the framework of legal mentality of judicial review constitutionalism. While the legal mentality of English judicial review constitutionalism is flexible, the Australian one is relatively rigid. As structured in Chap. 1, these different legal cultures drive a comprehensive understanding of the courts' determination of the grounds of judicial review discussed in Chaps. 3, 4, 5 and 6. Like most Administrative Law textbooks, the discussion in this chapter begins with the influence of legal cultures on error of law and jurisdictional error.[4]

Superficially, these grounds of judicial review seem to be simple and conclusory. The English courts used to apply the distinction between jurisdictional and non-jurisdictional error in their determination of the scope of judicial review,[5] before moving to the approach that all error of laws are reviewable by a court of law in *Anisminic Ltd v Foreign Compensation Commission*.[6] The two first quotes above stated by Lord Brown in oral pleading of *Cart* and Lord Browne-Wilkinson in judgment of *Page* clearly assert this position.[7] On the other hand, jurisdictional error has not been obsolete in Australian law. Instead, it has become a central approach for the courts' determination of judicial review. Apart from the quote of Sir Brennan stated above, this position has been widely recognised by Australian judges and scholars.[8]

---

[3] The Transcript of legal argument in *Craig v The State of South Australia* (1995) 184 CLR 163.

[4] E.g. Paul Craig, *Administrative Law* (8th edn, Sweet & Maxwell 2016) Chapter 16; Peter Cane, *Administrative Law* (5th edn, OUP 2011) Chapter 7.1; Mark Aronson, Matthew Groves and Greg Weeks, *Judicial Review of Administrative Action and Government Liability* (6th edn, Thomson Reuters Australia 2017) Chapter 4; William Wade and Christopher Forsyth, *Administrative Law* (11th edn, OUP 2014) Chapter 8; Mark Elliott and Jason Varuhas, *Administrative Law: Text and Materials* (5th edn, OUP 2017) Chapter 2.

[5] This will be exemplified in Sect. 3.3.1 below.

[6] [1969] 2 AC 147.

[7] It should be noted that, at a deeper level, the interpretation of *Anisminic* was debated in many later cases. For example, in his judgment in *R (Privacy International) v Investigatory Powers Tribunal* [2019] UKSC 22 [155]–[158], Lord Lloyd-Jones discussed Lord Diplock's judgment in *re Racal Communications Ltd* [1981] AC 374 as reflecting the possibility that *'the distinction between jurisdictional and non-jurisdictional errors of law may survive in the case of decisions by judicial bodies...'*. The variation and complexity of some leading English cases are unpacked and connected to the English legal culture in Sect. 3.3 below.

[8] Mark Aronson, 'Jurisdictional Error and Beyond' in Matthew Groves (ed), *Modern Administrative Law in Australia* (CUP 2014); Mark Aronson, 'Jurisdictional Error without the tears' in Matthew Groves and H P Lee (eds), *Australian Administrative Law: Fundamentals, Principles and Doctrines* (CUP 2007); Robin Creyke, John McMillan and Mark Smyth, *Control of Government Action; Text, Cases and Commentary* (5th edn, LexisNexis Butterworths 2019) [13.4.8]–[13.4.9]; Lisa Crawford and Janina Boughey, 'The Centrality of Jurisdictional Error: Rationale and Consequences' (2019) 30 PLR 18; Janina Boughey and Lisa Crawford, 'Jurisdictional Error: Do We Really Need It?' in Mark Elliott, Jason Varuhas and Shona Stark (eds), *The Unity of Public*

3.1 Introduction

However, this chapter argues that error of law and jurisdictional error are one of the most complicated areas in English and Australian administrative law. Apart from entitling an article *'Jurisdictional Error without the Tears'* to imply that administrative law students normally cry when dealing with this area,[9] Aronson also states that

> *But a sizeable proportion of any administrative law class will start to get seriously edgy when they are introduced to the doctrinal distinction between errors of law that are jurisdictional and those that are not, and most of those students will not confine themselves to that particular distinction. They will start asking harder questions.*[10]

This chapter points out that the determination of error of law and jurisdictional error are complicated because they are mixed with two main factors, which the courts have to consider in the question of scope of judicial review. These factors will be discussed in detail in Sect. 3.2 below, but introduced here as follow.

First, the courts have to deliberate 'what type of institution' they are reviewing. As Leeming stated, *'the truth that whether there is jurisdictional error depends upon the body said to have made it…'*[11] The role of the courts to quash administrative decision becomes controversial when the institutions they review are not 'regular' executive agencies, but tribunals and inferior courts, which have adjudicative authority aiming for efficiency, expertise and neutrality in some areas of public administration. As expressed in the transcript of legal argument of *Kirk*, Mr. Hatcher, a barrister stated that

> *The fact is that the lines in Craig v The State of South Australia are hardly well drawn. They do not sort of put a very clear border around what will constitute jurisdictional error and what will not, particularly in a circumstance where one is dealing with a statutory tribunal…*[12]

Lady Hale of the UKSC also considers this nature of institution as an important factor in the determination of judicial review by stating in an oral pleading of *Cart* that *'there are members of the UT, who are not lawyers, and who sit alone and have jurisdiction to decide points of law? That's to me a highly relevant consideration…'*.[13]

Law?: Doctrinal, Theoretical and Comparative Perspectives (Hart Publishing 2018). It is worth noting that, although most of the scholars in the literature acknowledge the essentiality of jurisdictional error in Australian law, they have slightly different views of the status of the ground. The prominent example is Leighton McDonald, 'Jurisdictional Error as Conceptual Totem' (2019) 42 UNSW Law Journal 1019, in which he regards jurisdictional error as being pivotal rather than central. The determination of jurisdictional error and these relevant scholars in the literature will be navigated in Sect. 3.4 below based on a framework of legality and legal culture.

[9] Aronson, 'Jurisdictional Error without the tears' (n 8).
[10] Aronson, 'Jurisdictional Error and Beyond' (n 8) 249.
[11] Mark Leeming, *Authority to Decide: the Law of Jurisdiction in Australia* (2nd edn, The Federation Press 2020) 53.
[12] The Transcript of legal argument in *Kirk v Industrial Court (NSW)* (2010) 239 CLR 531.
[13] n 1.

Secondly, such tribunals and inferior courts usually come with legislative restrictions to exclude the courts from conducting judicial review of their decision. For example, a clause in legislation mentions status of tribunal and inferior court as 'superior court of record', or regards its decision as 'final and conclusive' or 'shall not be subject to appeal or be liable to be questioned in any court'. Therefore, the second factor relating is 'to what extent a legislative restriction can be effective'.

These two factors fit into the determination of error of law and jurisdictional error. To be specific, if the court considers that the tribunal or its decision has a special status or that a restrictive clause is effective according to the legislature, it can be argued that judicial review of its decision is limited. On the surface level, the English and Australian courts reach a similar kind of overall outcome that their jurisdiction in conducting judicial review in this area is limited.

However, at the deep level, the English and Australian courts apply different doctrinal approaches under the grounds of error of law and jurisdictional error in determining 'the extent to which they limit their jurisdiction in conducting judicial review of decisions of this kind of quasi-judicial institutions with legislative restriction'. Some scholars have pointed out the connection between the doctrines and the constitutional backdrop of the legal systems. For example, Lewans points out that the incoherence of the determination of jurisdictional error was a product of the *'Diceyan Dialectic'* or *'Diceyan constitutionalism'*.[14] A recent one is Boughey and Crawford's considering jurisdictional error as a doctrine in pursuing the *'Australian constitutional purpose'*, particularly in upholding the framework of separation of powers.[15]

These different doctrinal approaches and the legal culture of legal systems will be further unpacked, connected and compared in this chapter with a detailed examination of the legal reasoning given in leading cases. In terms of English law, Sect. 3.3 below will contain a discussion of *R (Cart) v Upper Tribunal*, in which the claimants sought judicial review of the decision of the UT, given a superior court of the record status by Section 3(5) of the TCEA,[16] as well as an analysis of the determination of the scope of judicial review of the decision of the Investigatory Powers Tribunal ('IPT'), which, as stipulated in Section 67(8) of the Regulation of Investigatory Powers Act 2000 ('RIPA') *'shall not be subject to appeal or be liable to be questioned in any court'*, as discussed in *R (Privacy International) v Investigatory Powers Tribunal*.[17]

This will be compared to Sect. 3.4, examining *Kirk v Industrial Court (NSW)*, a significant Australian case heard during the same period with *Cart*, discussing

---

[14] Matthew Lewans, *Administrative Law and Judicial Deference* (Hart Publishing 2016) 44–58.

[15] Janina Boughey and Lisa Crawford, 'Reconsidering *R (on the application of Cart) v Upper Tribunal* and the Rationale for Jurisdictional Error' (2017) PL 592; See also Crawford and Boughey, 'The Centrality of Jurisdictional Error: Rationale and Consequences' (n 8); Aronson, 'Jurisdictional Error and Beyond' (n 8) 264–267; Aronson, 'Jurisdictional Error without the tears' (n 8) 344–345; James Spigelman, 'The Centrality of Jurisdictional Error' 21 Public Law Review 77.

[16] [2009] EWHC 3052; [2010] EWCA Civ 859; [2011] UKSC 28.

[17] n 7.

whether the court has a role to conduct judicial review of the decision of the Industrial Court of New South Wales ('ICNSW'), which is given the status of a superior court of the record by Section 152 of the Industrial Relations Act 1996 of NSW ('IRA').[18] The analysis will continue with an examination of some later cases, such as *Hossain v Minister for Immigration and Border Protection*, in which the scope of judicial review of the decision of the AAT was determined by the HCA.[19]

Four points, namely the validity of error of law and jurisdictional error as grounds of judicial review, the justifications, doctrines and application, applied by the English and Australian courts to determine their jurisdiction in conducting a judicial review of the decision of the UT, the IPT, the ICNSW and the AAT will be unpacked from the legal reasoning in the mentioned cases. As noted in Chap. 1, it is an indisputable fact that both the English and Australian courts can determine the scope of judicial review flexibly based on the changing circumstances and the statutory context. However, what is highlighted in this chapter is firstly that the English and Australian courts apply different patterns of doctrinal approach and legal reasoning in determining the scope of judicial review. While the determination of error of law, the status of the tribunals and the interpretation of the restrictive clauses was flexibly adopted by individual judges in *Cart* and *Privacy International* with various justifications and doctrines, the consideration of jurisdictional error was rigidly determined based on following the framework of the separation of powers in *Kirk* and *Hossain*. Secondly, these different approaches are proof of the flexible legal mentality of English judicial review constitutionalism and the rigidity of the Australian one. In short, the approaches of deep-water legality, legal culture and the unpacking process of legal reasoning are presented in this chapter to draw a more holistic picture of this area of the law in England and Australia.

3.2 Error of Law and Jurisdictional Error at Surface and Deep Levels

As introduced above, this section exemplifies how the determination of error of law in English law and jurisdictional error in Australian law are complicated by the nature of institution and legislative restriction. At a surface level, these two factors are premised in a similar way in England and Australia supported by general principles regarded as institutional and democratic reasons for creating tribunals and inferior courts. These lead to controversy whether courts have to limit jurisdiction in conducting judicial review of their decisions. However, at a deep-water level, the different ways of considering the determination of the grounds of judicial review of the English and Australian courts are complicated by these factors.

---

[18] (2010) 239 CLR 531.
[19] [2018] HCA 34.

3.2.1 Two Complicated Factors Limiting Scope of Judicial Review

As Justice McHugh of the HCA described that '*In carrying out judicial review, the Judiciary often undermines Executive power*',[20] scope of judicial review is therefore a question of, to what extent the court should intervene into the executive's action. Then, the first complication is that tribunals and inferior courts are the institutions at the centre of the tension between the court and the executive, because they perform an adjudicative function but are not courts in the traditional sense.[21] As described in the previous chapter, this kind of institution was first established in England when the Industrial Revolution led to the extremely rapid and complex growth of public administration, which resulted in a significant shift in the setting of the role of government. Mainly, authority in deciding various social and economic administrations was centralised from local authorities to specialised executive agencies.[22] With names like 'board' and 'commission', such institutions were delegated an admixture of administrative and judicial functions from statutory schemes.[23] They were regarded as 'quasi-judicial' institutions, and called by various terms such as 'administrative tribunals'.[24]

This nature of tribunals having an adjudicative function is claimed as advantageous in tackling the complexity of social and economic administration.[25] Three main points can be conceptualised as reasons to prefer tribunals over courts in adjudicating disputes between citizen and government.[26] First, tribunals offer speedier, cheaper and more accessible processes than the courts' procedure, which are considered as too formal, elaborate, slow, costly, and unduly disruptive to some areas of public administration requiring prompt decisions namely welfare, industrial, financial, social security and revenue matters. This point of efficiency is advanced by the second advantage that specialised tribunals have more expertise than courts to resolve disputes in the mentioned areas of complex public administration. The third reason in preferring tribunals over court is regarding their mentalities of being neutral in considering the disputes. It is claimed that the courts might not be sympathetic in advancing substantive interests of the individuals, according to the intention

---

[20] Justice McHugh, 'Tensions between the Executive and the Judiciary' (Australian Bar Association Conference, Paris, 10 July 2002).

[21] Peter Cane, 'Understanding Administrative Adjudication' in Linda Pearson, Carol Harlow and Michael Taggart (eds), *Administrative Law in a Changing State: Essays in Honour of Mark Aronson* (Hart Publishing 2008) 273–274.

[22] ibid.

[23] Some of them were also delegated legislative function (Chantal Stebbings, *Legal Foundations of Tribunals in Nineteenth Century England* (CUP 2006) 8).

[24] The first tribunal was an income tax commissioner created at the very end of the eighteenth century (see Peter Cane, *Administrative Tribunals and Adjudication* (Hart Publishing 2010) 13–14).

[25] ibid 31; Craig (n 4) [2–017]–[2–019].

[26] Wade and Forsyth (n 4) 765–766; Anthony J Connolly, *The Foundations of Australian Public Law: State, Power, Accountability* (CUP 2017) 312–313.

of legislation particularly one relating to the foundation of the welfare state or migration at the time of operation.[27]

These three reasons that support the tribunal as having 'institutional competence' for adjudicative functions, have been widely discussed by scholars.[28] For example, Stebbings argues that *'the flexibility, continuity and relative political neutrality of non-departmental agencies made them* [tribunals] *ideally constituted for specialised purposes of dispute-resolution'*.[29] They lead to the issue that the courts should limit or should not be able to conduct judicial review of the decisions taken by a tribunal, unless the aforementioned reasons for creating tribunals would be undermined.[30]

Apart from such institutional reasons, the jurisdiction of the courts in conducting judicial review of tribunals and inferior courts is argued to be limited according to 'democratic reason'.[31] This is because the authority of tribunals and inferior courts to adjudicate disputes between citizens and the government is legitimatised by Parliament, as the representative of the people in the legal system. Additionally, their decisions are usually excluded from judicial review due to a clause in the legislature, for example, stipulating that the decision is 'final', 'authoritative', 'conclusive' or 'shall not be subject to appeal or liable to be questioned in any court'.[32] This kind of legislative restriction is variously termed as a 'privative clause' or an 'ouster clause', which has the aim of according a degree of certainty and finality to tribunals' decisions. It would be disruptive in running public administration, if it were to be uncertain whether the tribunal's decision would be overturned by the court or not.

3.2.2 The Adjudicative Monopoly of the Courts

So far, this section discusses the two factors namely the nature of being quasi-judicial institution and legislative restriction, which lead to the argument of limiting the role of the court in conducting judicial review of the decisions of tribunals and inferior courts. However, the other side of argument is that courts are still understood as having an adjudicative monopoly in providing final answers over disputes

---

[27] McHugh (n 20).

[28] This is compatible to the reasons in discussing the concept of deference. However, the definition and application of concept of deference varies between scholars and legal systems. As discussed in Sect. 1.4 of Chap. 1, it is not focus of this book, but only additional indicator of influences of legal culture, which will become more obvious in the analyses in Chaps. 4 and 5.

[29] Stebbings (n 23) 63.

[30] Cane, *Administrative Law* (n 4) 181–183; See also William A Robson, *Justice and Administrative law: A Study of the British Constitution* (3rd edn, Stevens & Amp 1951) 35–36, 91, 236–237, 282, 319, 321.

[31] This is another limb in the discussion of the concept of deference (see n 28).

[32] Another way to do this is to give an institution a special status, such as 'a superior court of record' or 'a special tribunal' to the quasi-judicial institution.

between citizens and government in order to protect legality of the actions.[33] This is justified generally by the rule of law and separation of powers. Although tribunals have an adjudicative function, they are not a court in the traditional sense.[34] Their review of original administrative actions is not regarded as 'judicial review', but an 'internal review' within the executive branch[35] but by different officials.[36] Cane refers to Fuller's concept of adjudication explaining that such internal review comes from a party in the dispute itself.[37] Conversely, judicial review provides the opportunity for parties that their cases be heard before a neutral third party.[38] In the same vein, Wade argues that tribunals are less desirable than courts on the ground of independence that *'the whole object of the tribunals was to provide a cheaper and speedier source of justice…You cannot reduce the price of an article and speed up production without lowering quality'*.[39]

These two sides of the argument, limiting and supporting the court's role in conducting judicial review of tribunals and inferior courts' decisions, float at the surface level of both the English and Australian legal systems, and fit into the determination of the grounds of judicial review. The judgment in *Kirk* refers to the logic of tension between court and executive by mentioning Sawer's work that

> *Those two purposes* [of keeping tribunal within the scope of judicial review and reasons for their expertise] *pull in opposite directions. There being this tension between them, it is unsurprising that the course of judicial decision-making in this area has not yielded principles that are always easily applied.*[40]

3.2.3 Understanding the Complications Through Legal Culture

As mentioned above, the determination of the scope of judicial review complicated with the two factors have been answered differently in England and Australia. It will be demonstrated in the next sections that this difference can be better navigated based on a framework of legal culture. The rule of law and separation of powers may appear as shared constitutional values behind the distinction between

---

[33] Cane, *Administrative Tribunals and Adjudication* (n 24) 39.

[34] ibid foreword.

[35] By this, judicial review is an external review as it takes place by court which is a different institution from executive (ibid 7).

[36] ibid 7–8; See also Peter Cane, 'Judicial Review in the Age of Tribunals' [2009] PL 479.

[37] Lon L Fuller, 'The Forms and Limits of Adjudication' (1978) 92 Harvard Law Review 353 in Cane, *Administrative Tribunals and Adjudication* (n 24) 10–11.

[38] Cane, *Administrative Tribunals and Adjudication* (n 24) 10–11.

[39] H W R Wade, *Towards Administrative Justice* (University of Michigan Press 1963) 88.

[40] Geoffrey Sawer, 'Error of Law on the Face of an Administrative Record' (1956) 3 University of Western Australia Annual Law Review 24, 34–35 in n 18 [57].

3.2 Error of Law and Jurisdictional Error at Surface and Deep Levels

reviewable and non-reviewable tribunal's decision in England and Australia.[41] However, the English and Australian courts have different deep understandings of such constitutional values, and thereby differently perceive their role and apply different doctrinal approaches in determining their scope of judicial review in this area. These notions reside in the legal reasoning of leading cases, namely *Cart*, *Privacy International*, *Craig*, *Kirk* and *Hossain*, but a brief background information of the tribunal system and restrictive clause in England and Australia will be provided before discussing these cases.[42]

As described in Sect. 2.3.3 of Chap. 2, the status of tribunals in England has been discussed flexibly from Donoughmore to Franks, Leggatt, and other later reports of governmental committees. This flexibility has led to various doctrinal approaches being applied to determine the scope of judicial review of tribunal's decision. The doctrines applied in the past, namely the jurisdictional fact doctrine and the error on the face of the record, will be connected in this section as a part of the continuity of the legal mentality of English judicial review. However, the focus starts with *Cart*, which is regarded as the leading case in the contemporary law. As introduced in the previous chapter, the current framework of a two-tier tribunal, namely the FFT and the UT, was established under the TCEA. The UT is the appellant institution of the FFT on questions of law. If the UT allows and determines the appeal, the claimant can further appeal to the Court of Appeal ('CA').[43] However, if the UT refuses permission, it is then questionable whether such refusal is subjected to judicial review by the court or not. The TCEA does not give a clear answer on this, but the status of the UT is stipulated in Section 3(5) where it is described as a superior court of the record. This was the situation in *Cart*, in which the courts included the consideration of the nature of the UT and interpretation of Section 3(5) of the TCEA in their determination of the scope of judicial review. The flexibility of the different levels of courts in *Cart* in applying various justifications, doctrines and legal reasoning to decide these questions will be unpacked in the next section. Apart from this two-tier tribunal system, there are also tribunals that are established by other statutes to adjudicate specific areas of administrative activity. For example, the IPT was established and given jurisdiction by the RIPA to examine the conduct of the intelligence services, including the Security Service, the Secret Intelligence Service and the Government Communications Headquarters ('GCHQ').[44] This jurisdiction is accompanied by an obvious ouster clause in Section 67(8) of the RIPA, that *'its decisions (including ones as to whether they have jurisdiction) shall not be subject to appeal or be liable to be questioned in any court'*. The question of the reviewability of judicial review of the IPT's decision in the light of the statutory ouster

---

[41] Cane, *Administrative Tribunals and Adjudication* (n 24) 32.

[42] It should be noted that the structure and system of tribunals and restrictive clauses vary in England and Australia, but since they are not the focus of this chapter, they will only be described in terms of being the necessary background to examine the different determinations of the scope of judicial review in the English and Australian laws.

[43] TCEA, s 3, 9, 11.

[44] RIPA, paras 3–4, s 65(2), 67(8).

clause was disputed in *Privacy International*. The pattern of flexible doctrinal approaches and legal reasoning of the individual judges in the case in determining the scope of judicial review of the IPT's decision will also be unpacked in the next section.

This is completely different from the Australian law, where tribunals and inferior courts were established with different frameworks. At the federal level, there are two types of review, namely judicial review and merits review. The former is generally a judicial function of the courts, which is operated by common law. The latter is a judicial function of tribunals operated by the AAT, a general system of administrative review tribunals. This is a separate mechanism from judicial review by the courts to supplement a merits review, which was the result of a suggestion by the Kerr Committee in 1971. At state level, a number of specialist tribunals and inferior courts such as industrial and environmental courts have been established.[45]

The scope of judicial review of the decisions of institutions at state level has been significantly discussed in common law cases, particularly *Craig*[46] and *Kirk*.[47] The doctrinal approaches applied by the courts in these cases will be unpacked in Sect. 3.4 below. It will be demonstrated that the courts rigidly determined the scope of judicial review based on the framework of the separation of powers prescribed in the written constitution and statutes, analysed as the main elements of Australian judicial review constitutionalism. On the other hand, as described in Sect. 2.4 of Chap. 2, the scope of common law judicial review in Australian law is generally distinctive from merits review by the AAT. However, an individual can still claim that an AAT's decision contains a jurisdictional error and therefore is subject to judicial review, as was the case in *Hossain*. Although the judgment contained an aspect of flexibility,[48] it will be demonstrated that the application of jurisdictional error has remained entrenched in determining the scope of judicial review. In essence, there is a pattern of a relatively rigid doctrinal approach and legal reasoning, embedded in the analysed Australian legal culture, shared between the judgments in *Craig*, *Kirk* and *Hossain*.

A caveat before the main analysis is that the comparison of these cases may be complex, since they have different subjects and contexts. While the discussion in *Cart* was related to the scope of judicial review of the UT, which is a tribunal, *Craig* and *Kirk* involved the jurisdiction of the HCA and State Supreme Court over the District Court and ICNSW. On the other hand, *Hossain* involved determining the jurisdiction of the court over the AAT at the federal state level. Also, the UT is a tribunal under the different statutory framework from the IPT. Additionally, it can be argued that there are different types of restrictive clauses among these cases. As Lord Sumption mentioned in *Privacy International* in particular, '…[*Cart*] *is not*

---

[45] Cane, 'Understanding Administrative Adjudication' (n 21) 57–67.
[46] (1995) 184 CLR 163.
[47] n 18.
[48] Expressed in the form of the doctrine of gravity of the error and threshold of materiality (n 19). This point is exemplified in Sect. 3.4 below.

3.3 English Doctrinal Approaches   103

direct authority on the question before us because it was not a case about ouster clauses. There was no ouster clause in the relevant statutes'.[49]

It should be clarified that the focus of this chapter is not the different structures of tribunal systems and privative clauses of the English and Australian law, but the different determinations of the scope of judicial review of 'this kind of quasi-judicial institution with legislative restriction', whether they are called tribunals or inferior courts. It will be pointed out that there are distinctive patterns of doctrinal approaches and legal reasoning shared across the determination of the scope of judicial review of this kind of institution in England and Australia. For instance, even though Lord Sumption noted the different contexts between *Cart* and *Privacy International*, he accepted and applied the approach of Laws LJ in *Cart*, namely to determine whether or not the quasi-judicial institution has already satisfied the material principle of the rule of law, to the determination in *Privacy International*.[50] These shared patterns will be unpacked and connected to the analysed English and Australian legal cultures in the next sections.

3.3 English Doctrinal Approaches

The various justifications and doctrines flexibly applied by English judges to determine the scope of judicial review of the tribunals' decision will be examined in this section, ranging from the distinction between jurisdictional and non-jurisdictional error applied from the seventeenth century to the turning point in *Anisminic* in the 1970s and the variations of the law in *Cart* and *Privacy International*. Such flexibility is influenced from the flexible legal mentality of English judicial review constitutionalism.

3.3.1 Prior to Cart

As unpacked in the previous chapter, the flexible legal mentality of English judicial review has gradually been developed since the seventeenth century based on the inter-relationship between parliamentary sovereignty and the rule of law. Therefore, the influence of this flexible mentality on the determination of the scope of judicial review should also be seen to have flowed from the seventeenth century to modern cases as well, in order to sustain the argument that the English law is more flexible than its Australian counterpart. As Craig points out,

---
[49] n 7 [189].
[50] ibid [198].

The present attitude of the courts towards judicial review cannot be adequately understood without some idea of 18th and 19th century case law. This history reveals the differing judicial views as to how far they should be reviewing tribunals and other inferior bodies.[51]

The English courts determined the extent of control of administrative action from the origin of judicial review by the distinction between jurisdictional error and non-jurisdictional error approach.[52] The court could conduct judicial review of the administrative decision if the issue was jurisdictional error, but it could not do so if it was a non-jurisdictional error. The English law deployed this approach for more than 300 years before abandoning in *Anisminic* in the 1970s. This may cast a doubt on the argument in this section that the English approaches have been flexible since the seventeenth century.

It is contended that there were at least two aspects of flexibility in English courts' determination of the scope of judicial review based on the dichotomy of jurisdictional error. Firstly, they could use either the collateral (preliminary) fact doctrine or the theory of limited review to determine the extent of control of administrative action.[53] Although these two main theories were based on a similar approach of the distinction between jurisdictional and non-jurisdictional errors,[54] their different explanations demonstrated flexibility in terms of the justification the court could provide to claim the scope of judicial review.[55] According to the collateral fact doctrine,

A public body is given power on the existence of certain conditions. There are certain preliminary questions that it must decide before it can proceed to the merits. These include matters such as whether the public body was properly constituted and whether the case was of a kind referred to the statute.[56]

On the other hand, Gordon proposed a later theory, as follows;

If a public body is given jurisdiction over a certain topic, the question is whether the facts relating to that topic exist in the opinion of the public body... The public body's jurisdiction was limited, but that limit was determined not by the truth or falsehood of its findings, but by their scope or nature.[57]

---

[51] Craig, *Administrative Law* (n 4) [16–017].

[52] ibid [16–001].

[53] ibid [16–001], [16–003].

[54] ibid [16–001]; See also Wade and Forsyth (n 4) 234; *R v Northumberland Compensation Appeal Tribunal, Ex parte Shaw* [1952] 1 KB 338, 346 and *R v Fulham, Hammersmith and Kensington Rent Tribunal, Ex parte Philippe* [1950] 2 All ER 211.

[55] There were also other theories apart from these two (See Craig, *Administrative Law* (n 4) [16–008]–[16–011]).

[56] ibid [16–004]. It was also later explained by Lord Diplock in *Anisminic* (n 6) 887–905; hence Endicott calls it as *'Lord Diplock's presumption'* (Timothy Endicott, *Administrative Law* (4th edn, OUP 2018) 326.

[57] Craig, *Administrative Law* (n 4) [16–006]; Scott Gordon, 'The Relation of Facts to Jurisdiction' (1929) 45 QLR 458.

3.3 English Doctrinal Approaches

The courts malleably applied either of these to determine the scope of judicial review before the 1970s. For example, Justice Coleridge applied the collateral fact doctrine in *Bunbury v Fuller*, when he stated that

> Now it is a general rule, that no Court of limited jurisdiction can give itself jurisdiction by a wrong decision on a point collateral to the merits of the case upon which the limit to its jurisdiction depends...[Thus the question] *whether some collateral matter be or be not within the limits...must always be open to inquiry in the superior Court.*[58]

On the other hand, *R v Bolton* was a prominent example of a case that relied on the theory of limited review to justify the courts' jurisdiction in conducting judicial review.[59]

Secondly and more importantly, there are 'real difficulties' in both the collateral fact doctrine and the theory of limited review in terms of certainty in determining the dichotomy between jurisdictional error and non-jurisdictional error.[60] Craig provides some concrete examples of this. In terms of collateral fact,

> *The distinction between kind and type on the one hand, and truth or detail or situation on the other, proved illusory. There was no predictability as to how a case would be categorized before the court pronounced on the matter. There was also no ex post facto rationality that could be achieved by juxtaposing cases and asking why one case went one way and another was decided differently.*[61]

Gordon's theory also contained this kind of indetermination in terms of the '*difficulties in distincting scope and truth*'.[62] This led to the overall position that '*the scope of jurisdictional review is not self-defining*'.[63] Another factor that added complexity to the distinction between jurisdictional error and non-jurisdictional error was the error on the face of the record. As shown by Lord Justice Denning in *Shaw*, the court was able to quash any error of law on the face of the record of the proceedings regardless of whether it was a jurisdictional error or not.[64]

Most scholars regard the difficulty in finding certainty when considering the question of jurisdiction as a kind of problem, which was later solved by *Anisminic*. For example, Elliott and Varuhas describe that the '*diversity in legal meaning* [determined from the statute] *might be considered inimical to the rule of law requirement of legal certainty*'.[65] The first edition of De Smith's textbook also mentions that '*No satisfactory test has ever been formulated for distinguishing matters which go to*

---

[58] (1853) 9 Ex 111, 140; See also *Nichols. V Walker* (1632–1633) Cro. Car. 394 and other examples in Wade and Forsyth (n 4) 208–209.

[59] (1841) 1 QB 66. See other examples in nn 23–24, 32 of Craig (n 4) [16–018]; Elliott and Varuhas (n 4) 35–37.

[60] Craig, *Administrative Law* (n 4) [16–001]; See also Paul Craig, *The Hamlyn Lectures: UK, EU and Global Administrative Law* (CUP 2015) 30–35.

[61] Craig, *Administrative Law* (n 4) [16–005].

[62] ibid [16–007].

[63] ibid [16–016].

[64] See n 52; Wade and Forsyth (n 4) 224.

[65] Elliott and Varuhas (n 4) 38.

jurisdiction from matters which go to the merits'.[66] Henderson described this as a *'lack of theoretical clarity'* or *'theoretical vagueness'*.[67] All of this led to a negative impression that *'the courts manipulated the distinction for instrumental purpose, choosing to find that a particular issue was jurisdictional if they wanted to intervene, and non-jurisdictional if they did not'*.[68]

Rather than regarding this approach as problematic, this section considers that the distinction between jurisdictional error and non-jurisdictional error provided flexibility for the English courts in determining the scope of judicial review. Importantly, it was not depended on judicial desire but embedded in English legal culture. Firstly, as Craig stated,

> The answer resides not in a logic which compels, for example, that all questions of law must always be for the courts or the tribunal. Such logic is flawed. A response must always be based on a value judgment, the precise content of which will not necessarily always be the same.[69]

This reflects that the rigid distinction between legality and merits and between court and tribunal did not exist in England through the distinction between jurisdictional error and non-jurisdictional error. Instead, it was the implication of the flexible understanding of the role of the courts to conduct judicial review according to the fluid relationship between them and tribunals.

Most importantly, the flexibility in distinguishing jurisdictional error from non-jurisdictional error reflects the logic of the balancing process between parliamentary sovereignty and the rule of law. On the one hand, Craig regards the collateral fact doctrine and the limited theory of review as *'tools used to preserve judicial control'*.[70] Endicott also discusses the collateral fact doctrine,[71] as being justified by the rule of law.[72] This is done through a discussion of the nature of the institutions. The judges who are independent and have a better understanding of the standards of the law, should impose their views rather than the misguided views of the law expressed by the public authorities, otherwise the rule of law will fail.

On the other hand, the courts have to *'give some leeway to agency autonomy'*, as *'this would emasculate autonomy over issues that had been assigned to the body by Parliament'*.[73] As Craig asserts, *'The courts did not believe that they should be substituting judgment on every issue of law....'*[74] They had to respect the administrative

---

[66] De Smith, *Judicial Review of Administrative Action* (1st edn, Stevens & Sons Limited 1958) 69–70.

[67] E G Henderson, *Foundations of English Administrative Law: Certiorari and Mandamus in the Seventeenth Century* (Harvard University Press 1963) 158–159.

[68] Elliott and Varuhas (n 4) 39; See also Lewans (n 14) 4–5.

[69] Craig, *Administrative Law* (n 4) [16–016].

[70] ibid [16–038].

[71] Referred to Lord Diplock's doctrine in *Anisminic* (n 6).

[72] Endicott (n 56) 328–329.

[73] Craig, *Administrative Law* (n 4) [16–038].

[74] ibid.

authority conferred by parliament, which is a sovereign power. Furthermore, the logic of balancing these two sides of mentality was clear. As Craig recognised, *'the courts adopted with the collateral fact doctrine and limited review [for so long]... because they believed that these best captured the appropriate balance between judicial control and agency autonomy'*.[75] This logic was also supported by Murray, who stated that jurisdictional fact doctrine *'represented a compromise between judicial control of the administrative process and judicial restraint'*.[76]

This reflection of the twin concepts of parliamentary sovereignty and the rule of law through the dichotomy of jurisdictional and non-jurisdictional error can also be demonstrated through the writ system. Ever since the origin of English judicial review, the court's jurisdiction had been *'interwoven with the intricacies of the prerogative writs'*.[77] The snapshot of this is whether the court would give a writ or not was also the result of the balancing process between the rule of law and parliamentary sovereignty. On the one hand, the role of the courts to give remedy to an illegal administrative action was supported by the principle of legality and the rule of law. According to Craig,

> ...the motivation behind early judicial review resided principally in the desire to ensure the predominance of the HC over "inferior jurisdictions", and to provide remedies to those whom the established judiciary felt had been unjustly or illegally treated by such authorities.[78]

Henderson also regards a writ as *'a means by which a citizen could demand legality from his government'* and *'new modes of proceeding in the courts...which gave the aggrieved subject quicker and easier relief from illegal action by officials'*.[79] On the other hand, *'In striving to attain these objectives, the court could indeed often come into direct conflict with the legislative will'*.[80] Hence, the English courts had the flexibility to balance *'the necessity of general rules of law'* and *'the necessity of specialised knowledge, flexibility, and creativeness in the administration of government, setup from the legislature'*.[81]

This balancing process led to another connection to the English legal culture, namely, that the English courts' determination of the scope of judicial review paid relatively less attention to statutory construction. According to Henderson, *'...in the early days of judicial review, the courts inclined to the view that every question of statutory construction was jurisdictional, quite aside from the meaning of the*

---

[75] ibid.; Paul Craig, 'Jurisdiction, Judicial Control and Agency Autonomy, A Special Relationship' in Ian Loveland (ed), *American Influences on Public Law in the UK* (OUP 1995).

[76] Philip Murray, 'Process, Substance and the History of Error of Law Review' (Cambridge Public Law Conference, September 2014).

[77] Craig, *Administrative Law* (n 4) [1–003]; See also Peter Cane, *Controlling Administrative Power: An Historical Comparison* (CUP 2016) 249–251; Craig, *The Hamlyn Lectures: UK, EU and Global Administrative Law* (n 60) 51.

[78] Craig, *Administrative Law* (n 4) [1–003].

[79] Henderson (n 67) 1, 158–159.

[80] Craig, *Administrative Law* (n 4) [1–003].

[81] Henderson (n 67) 3.

word....[82] As will be seen below, this is different from the Australian law, which rigidly relies on the framework of separation of powers prescribed in the written constitution and statutory construction.

Although English judicial review had been based on the jurisdictional fact doctrine for a long time, it did not lead to the conclusion that the English approach was rigid. In reality, the courts manipulated the determination of the scope of judicial review through the jurisdictional error approach. While most scholars consider this to be problematic, it is regarded in this section as another product of the flowing flexible legal mentality of the English judicial review constitutionalism. The courts could apply various approaches such as the collateral fact doctrine, the theory of limited review and the error on the face of the record, integrated with the complex writ system, to determine the scope of judicial review. The determination was embedded in the balancing process between parliamentary sovereignty and the rule of law. Craig connects this to the logic of legality, as follows;

> *The discussion thus far focused on the judicial creativity evident in development of direct challenge though the prerogative writs. This operated in tandem with collateral attack, which constituted the early method of challenging decisions... The legality of the contested decision would be the central issue in the success or failure of such claims.*[83]

In short, the jurisdictional fact doctrine had already captured 'the best balance' for the determination of the role of the courts to conduct judicial review at that time. Based on its nature, '*We do not have to accept the balance between judicial control and agency autonomy adopted by earlier courts, but we should not forget that there is an issue here at all*'.[84] Therefore, a move to other doctrinal approaches was not made for a long time because flexibility had already been provided by the jurisdictional fact doctrine.

However, the English law did not remain there permanently. The door to move to other doctrinal approaches was always open. Craig endorsed this part of English legal mentality, as follows;

> *It is clear from a reading of the case law that the courts did not feel that they were bound by some a priori logic to employ either of the now discredited theories. They acknowledged the possibilities open to them when devising the tests for jurisdictional control.*[85]

Hence, the English courts changed without hesitation when it was time to do so.[86] This change was precipitated by the considerable social changes in England during the twentieth century. As described in Sect. 2.3 of Chap. 2, the Industrial Revolution and the concept of Welfare State led to the establishment of central institutions to perform functions that had previously been performed locally. A number of tribunals

---

[82] ibid 7.

[83] Craig, *The Hamlyn Lectures: UK, EU and Global Administrative Law* (n 60) 59.

[84] Craig, *Administrative Law* (n 4) [16–038].

[85] Craig, *The Hamlyn Lectures: UK, EU and Global Administrative Law* (n 60) 34.

[86] As mentioned, the jurisdictional error dichotomy was considered to be problematic. Therefore 'the demise of the collateral fact doctrine is to be welcomed' (Craig, *Administrative Law* (n 4) [16–037]).

3.3 English Doctrinal Approaches

were created to make decision in public administration. Based on this *'volume of public administrative decision-making'*, the courts *'started looking for ways to provide greater protection for citizens by extending their control over the executive and bureaucracy'*.[87] The distinction between jurisdictional and non-jurisdictional error that provided 'too intangible' flexibility for determining the scope of judicial review, was regarded as producing uncertainty in public administration. There was no magic line of division between the old and new centuries.[88] However, the most important step among cases[89] was the rebuilding of the approach to determine the court's jurisdiction in conducting judicial review in 1969 in *Anisminic*.[90]

This case was an important step for two main reasons.[91] Firstly, the court in *Anisminic* answered the question about the scope of judicial review through the discussion that the legislative restriction needs to be interpreted strictly. This increased the opportunities for judicial supervision of tribunals by the full range of judicial review grounds.[92] Secondly, it expanded the scope of judicial review by broadening the concept so that all errors of law would go to jurisdiction. These left behind the problem of unclear distinctions between jurisdictional and non-jurisdictional errors of law, as well as what was error on the face of the record.[93] This approach in *Anisminic* was expanded in later cases, one of the most important of which was Lord Browne-Wilkinson in *Page*, as stated at the beginning of this chapter.[94] It becomes the basis for the discussion of scope of judicial review in this area and in general that the courts are responsible and have a role to conduct judicial review of error of law; however, they would leave factual and discretionary issues to the executive to decide.[95]

While some scholars argue that *'administrative law was just invented in the second half of the twentieth century* [by the move in *Anisminic*]*'*,[96] in this section, it is

---

[87] Cane, *Controlling Administrative Power: An Historical Comparison* (n 77) 250.

[88] Craig, *Administrative Law* (n 4) [16–021].

[89] For example, *Arlidge v Local Government Board* [1915] AC 120 and *R v Board of Education* [1910] 2 KB 165.

[90] n 6; See B Gould, 'Anisminic and Jurisdictional Review' [1970] PL 358.

[91] This significance of *Anisminic* was generally recognised by literature, for example, David Feldman, '*Anisminic Ltd v Foreign Compensation Commission* [1968]: In Perspective' in Satvinder Juss and Maurice Sunkin (eds), *Landmark Cases in Public Law* (Hart Publishing 2017) 92.

[92] Aronson, Groves and Weeks (n 4) [1.100].

[93] Craig, *Administrative Law* (n 4) [16–034].

[94] See also *O'Reilly v Mackman* [1983] 2 AC 237; *re Racal Communications Ltd* [1981] AC 374; *Pearlman v Keepers and Governors of Harrow School* [1979] QB 56, even though with different kinds of explanation (See Craig, *Administrative Law* (n 4) [16–023]–[16–026]; Elliott and Varuhas (n 4) 46–50; Wade and Forsyth (n 4) 220–222).

[95] This premise leads to a discussion in the next chapters that the court regards some decisive factual and discretionary issues in administrative action as legal issues. However, the line in determining whether the factual and discretionary issue is decisive or not is set differently between the legal systems, according to their different legal cultures. This will be clearer when the discussion runs into the conclusion of this chapter.

[96] See Endicott (n 56) 61.

considered to be another wave in the continuous fluidity of the English law. The approach in *Anisminic* was an alternative way to provide flexibility for the courts to determine the scope of judicial review. Cane supports the view that it was a change of the *'form of action'* from *'procedure'* (related to the writ system) to *'substance'* (related to ground of judicial review), in *'a very different juridical environment'*.[97]

Despite this variation, the shared theme of English law that the courts have the flexibility to determine the scope of judicial review of quasi-judicial institutions can be captured. As Craig argues, *'the difference between then* [before 1970s] *and now is exaggerated*.[98] Rather than the contrast between the rigidity to the jurisdictional fact doctrine and the courts' ability to intervene in all errors of law, it was merely *'unsystematic'* in moving from one form of flexibility to another.[99] In this section, it was simplified by illustrating that they were all running in the light of the English legal culture. This will be further clarified in the analysis of *Cart* below, where the judgments of different levels of courts can either create a new doctrine in addition to *Anisminic* or articulate it differently in their determination of the scope of judicial review of the UT. In any doctrine, the determination is still based on the balancing process between the rule of law and parliamentary sovereignty.

3.3.2 Cart

After *Anisminic*, as described above, a significant milestone in discussing scope of judicial review of tribunal's decision was the reformation of the organisation of tribunals into two-tier institutions; FTT and UT, by the TCEA.[100] The courts in *Cart* had to determine whether they had a role to conduct judicial review of the refusal of appeal of the UT, which is an appellant tribunal with delegated adjudicative power and the status of a superior court of the record from parliament. The connection between the doctrinal approaches applied by the courts at different levels in *Cart* in considering the status of the UT, interpreting Section 3(5) of the TCEA and determining the scope of judicial review and English legal culture, is discussed in this section. Three main points of doctrinal approaches can be unpacked below.

First, all the judgments of different levels of court in *Cart* refer to the elements of English judicial review constitutionalism, namely the twin concepts of parliamentary sovereignty and the rule of law and the common law theory as their

---

[97] Peter Cane, 'The Making of Australian Administrative Law' (2003) 24 Australian Bar Review 114.

[98] Craig, *The Hamlyn Lectures: UK, EU and Global Administrative Law* (n 60) 25.

[99] ibid.

[100] This does not mean that the other cases between *Anisminic* and *Cart*, for example, *Racal* and *O'Reilly v Mackman* are beside the point. However, according to the approach in this book to unpack the legal reasoning of leading cases, *Cart* and *Privacy International* are selected as a 'bigger wave' to demonstrate the connection between the court's doctrinal approaches and the legal system's legal culture.

3.3 English Doctrinal Approaches

justifications in conducting judicial review of the UT's decision. To begin with, Lord Justice Laws of the Queen's Bench Division explained that it is the court's constitutional duty to protect the rule of law by judicial review.[101] He described the rule of law as related to the principle of parliamentary sovereignty, which requires all public bodies to remain within the scope of powers prescribed by parliamentary statutes.[102] However, since this principle alone cannot account for the entire rule of law because the texts produced by parliament cannot speak, an institution is needed to interpret the statutes. Lord Justice Laws claimed that this task must not be performed by the legislature, executive, or the public body itself, because they are not neutral and this may lead to arbitrary government; rather, it should be performed by the court because it is impartial and independent.[103] However, since the administrative powers are authorised by Parliament, which is sovereign, the courts, which have no connection to individuals, need to justify their intervention in administrative action. In this respect, Lord Justice Laws implies that this function of the courts can be explained through the common law theory of the justification for judicial review. It is the inherent power of the court (at common law) to determine whether or not an administrative action is lawful.[104] He further explained that the judicial review mechanism is not a refusal of legislative sovereignty; rather, it is a confirmation of the rule of law,[105] because mediation is required between parliamentary sovereignty and an independent judicial power to protect the legality of actions.[106]

Subsequently, judgments by the CA and the UKSC also describe their justification for judicial review in relations to these constitutional values. According to Lord Justice Sedley, the court has a constitutional duty to protect legality and due process to preserve the integrity of the rule of law.[107] Similarly, Baroness Hale explained that the purpose of judicial review is to maintain the rule of law and to protect the principle of legality by ensuring that decisions are taken in accordance with the law, especially the laws enacted by Parliament.[108] Lord Phillips of the UKSC also agreed that the rule of law requires those enacted by Parliament, together with the principles of common law, to be enforced by a judiciary that is independent of the legislature and the executive.[109] All the other judgments by Lord Brown, Lord Clarke and Lord Dyson also implicitly refer to the twin concepts of parliamentary sovereignty and the rule of law, together with common law theory, as justification for the court's

---

[101] *Cart* 2009 (n 16) [34].
[102] ibid [38].
[103] ibid [37].
[104] ibid [34].
[105] ibid [38].
[106] ibid [39].
[107] *Cart* 2010 (n 16) [28], [37].
[108] *Cart* 2011 (n 16) [37].
[109] ibid [89].

claim to its authority to decide its jurisdiction in judicial review of the UT's decision.[110]

All of this legal reasoning indicates compatibility with how the rule of law and parliamentary sovereignty are understood in English judicial review constitutionalism, as analysed in the previous chapter. They are the implications of the mentality that the courts have to solve the balance between the twin concepts of the rule of law and parliamentary sovereignty in particular cases. On the one hand, the courts respect the decision of the UT in adjudicating the dispute between the claimant and the FTT because its authority is delegated from Parliament through the TCEA and reinforced by the restrictive clause. On the other hand, they have to protect legality of administrative action according to the rule of law. The common law theory was implicitly added to strengthen the justification for the courts to conduct judicial review of the UT's decision.

Additionally, influence of English legal culture can be seen from the point that the courts can flexibly arrange the distinctive explanation of these constitutional values to justify or limit their scope of judicial review in the way they consider as appropriate to the cases. This flexibility relates to the nature of the balancing process of the twin concepts and the point that there is no written constitution to provide clear jurisdiction and justification for the courts in conducting judicial review. The next section will demonstrate that this is different from the Australian approach, where the way to explain these constitutional values as justification for the courts to conduct judicial review are relatively fixed, namely by emphasising the federal separation of powers.

Secondly, not only do the judgments of the courts at different levels in *Cart* have different explanations of constitutional values in justifying their scope of judicial review, but they also flexibly adapt or create various doctrines to determine their scope of judicial review of the UT's decision. According to the two described factors, it shall be clarified that all the judgments similarly held that judicial review will be excluded only when legislature expresses clear intention. However, they have different doctrines in considering the nature of the UT, leading to different determinations of the scope of judicial review.

According to Lord Justice Laws, the scope of judicial review is determined through the approach of 'jurisdictional error'. However, this is not the same concept of jurisdictional error applied before *Anisminic*. The judgment explained that the role of the UT established by the TCEA is a decisive factor in determining if the requirement of the principle of legality has been fulfilled.[111] For Lord Justice Laws, according to the TCEA, the UT is an alter ego of the High Court because it has some judicial qualifications. Firstly, it has the power to exercise a 'judicial review', and can grant forms of relief.[112] Secondly, its members, who consist of Lords Justices,

---

[110] ibid [100] (Lord Brown), [102] (Lord Clarke), [127] (Lord Dyson).
[111] *Cart* 2009 (n 16) [78].
[112] ibid [14], [88].

3.3 English Doctrinal Approaches

High Court judges, circuit judges and district judges, are ex officio judges.[113] Thirdly, the UT is part of a comprehensive judicial structure, which is regarded as a rationalised court.[114] Therefore, it is the final judge of the law and thus is unable to make a legal error. Since the nature of the UT is an institution which already satisfies the requirement of the principle of legality, the court has no duty to intervene in its decisions. There was no jurisdictional error committed by the UT.[115]

In contrast, Lord Justice Sedley applied different doctrine in determining the scope of judicial review over the UT. Although the TCEA invests the UT with powers akin to those of the High Court, it is not an 'avatar' of the court; it stands in the shoes of a tribunal rather than in those of the High Court.[116] It would be against the rule of law if there was an error in its decision and the court could correct it; therefore, it is still the function of the court to protect legality. However, apart from the duty to protect legality, the new coherent tribunal system invested by Parliament was another factor to consider when seeking to apply a proper 'judicial policy'.[117] Therefore, the court will only intervene in cases of a serious error of law.[118] In this case, it chose to limit its scope of judicial review because of the consideration of Parliament's intention to establish a new structure of tribunals.[119]

In terms of the UKSC, all the judgments led by Baroness Hale also relied on the discussion about the nature of the UT in deciding the court's jurisdiction to conduct judicial review of the UT, but solved by different doctrines from the lower courts'. Particularly, the judgments focus on the consistency of the role of the UT according to the TCEA. They applied the second-tier appeal from civil procedure as a rational and proportionate approach to determine the availability of a judicial review.[120] There were two main reasons for supporting this approach. Firstly, the court had to consider Parliament's intention to restructure the tribunal system expressed in the TCEA. Since the UT plays three roles,[121] it would be inconsistent to distinguish the scope of judicial review among these various roles.[122] There should only be one approach for all three of the UT's roles, namely, a second-tier appeal approach. Secondly, Parliament's intention in the TCEA was to create tribunals to adjudicate on disputes in specialised areas of expertise. Therefore, this approach, which only focuses on important errors or other legally compelling issues, is an appropriate

---

[113] ibid [16].
[114] ibid [87].
[115] ibid [94].
[116] ibid [19].
[117] ibid [35]–[37].
[118] ibid [30], [45].
[119] ibid [30], [31], [42].
[120] *Cart* 2011 (n 16) [38]–[39].
[121] Firstly, it acts as the tribunal of first instance. Secondly, the UT may exercise a statutory jurisdiction equivalent to the judicial review of the High Court. Thirdly, there is a right of appeal to the UT (ibid [24]–[26]).
[122] ibid [37].

level of independent scrutiny outside the tribunal structure.[123] Other judgments (Lord Phillips,[124] Lord Clarke[125] and Lord Dyson[126]) in the UKSC followed this approach, leaving the court to consider whether or not an error was sufficiently important to lead to an infringement of the rule of law.

Although the outcomes of these doctrines were similar, that the court shall not intervene into the decision of the UT in this case, they were determined by different doctrines and lines of reasoning. This variation reflects the flexible legal mentality of English judicial review constitutionalism. Without the written constitution to prescribe the courts' boundary of jurisdiction and the nature of balancing process of the twin concepts, different judges can flexibly apply different doctrines they consider as appropriate to determine the scope of judicial review of the UT's decision in this case. It will be demonstrated below that, rather than variation, jurisdictional error has been applied as an entrenched doctrine in this area in Australia.

3.3.3 Privacy International

It has been demonstrated by the analysis so far that the justifications and doctrines applied by the courts at different levels in *Cart* were due to the flexible legal mentality of English judicial review constitutionalism. It will be illustrated in this section how this pattern of flexible doctrinal approaches and legal reasoning continued in *Privacy International*.[127] The appellants in the case argued that the hacking of their computer by the GCHQ was unlawful because the warrants authorised by the Secretary of State included a thematic one instead of specified acts in respect of specified property; hence, they were incompatible to Section 5 of the Intelligence Services Act 1994. The appellants then claimed their issue before the IPT; but it was dismissed on the ground that the warrant was *'as specific as possible in relation to the property to be covered by the warrant'*.[128] Subsequently, a judicial review was sought and the issue became whether the High Court had the jurisdiction to determine the substantive issue of the IPT's decision or not. While the Divisional Court dismissed the case, mainly on the ground that the IPT had already exercised the power of judicial review on the GCHQ's action,[129] and the CA did so based on considering the statutory language and context, indicating Parliament's intention to

---

[123] ibid [51].

[124] ibid [61].

[125] ibid [103]–[105].

[126] ibid [128], [130–132].

[127] The doctrinal approaches and legal reasoning in the cases after *Cart*, namely *Phillips v Upper Tribunal (Tax and Chancery Chamber)* [2013] EWHC 2934 and *A v Secretary of State for the Home Department* [2013] EWHC 1272 were also various and flexible. However, the main approach remains similar to the one in *Cart*.

[128] *Privacy International v SSFCA* [2016] UKIP Trib 14_85-CH [47].

[129] *Privacy International v Investigatory Powers Tribunal* [2017] EWHC 114 (Admin).

3.3 English Doctrinal Approaches

accord the IPT with very high-quality expertise and independence, as well as provide effectiveness to Section 67(8) of the RIPA.[130] The case came to the UKSC on the issues of whether or not the ouster clause could exclude the supervisory jurisdiction of the High Court and, if it could, what justification would be for ousting judicial review.[131]

As noted above, it is acknowledged that the context in *Privacy International* was different from that of *Cart* in some respects. However, the judgments in *Privacy International* possessed a similar conceptual question as *Cart* as to how the court should determine its scope of judicial review over the decision of a quasi-judicial institution with legislative restriction.[132] This is indeed a question of the extent to which the IPT's decision should be determined as being covered by the court's (deep) understanding of legality. Although the outcome of *Cart* and *Privacy International* could be different, there would still be a shared pattern of flexible doctrinal approaches and legal reasoning in deciding this question. There are two prominent connections between this pattern and the English legal culture, as detailed below.

Firstly, in parallel to the above analysis of *Cart*, the judgments in *Privacy International* reflected two sides of reasoning, both supporting and rejecting the court's jurisdiction to conduct judicial review of the IPT's decision. On the one hand, the institutional competence and democratic reasoning of the IPT were claimed to limit the High Court's judicial review. This was drawn from the respondent's argument,[133] namely that the RIPA established the particular framework, rules, procedures and features of the IPT to work as a bespoke, expert and independent adjudicator of the national security service's activities, particularly in respect of breaches of human rights and complaints about the interception of communications.[134] On the other hand, the courts' jurisdiction to conduct judicial of the IPT's decision was reinforced, since keeping the inferior courts and tribunals within their boundary of power has been a long-established common law principle.[135] It was explained that '*…a statute should not be interpreted as ousting judicial review of a*

---

[130] *Privacy International v Investigatory Powers Tribunal* [2017] EWCA Civ 1868.

[131] See the fact of the case in detail in n 7 [1]–[21], [146]–[149], [169]–[172], [213].

[132] As described above, the determination of the scope of judicial review is complicated by the two factors of the nature of the institution and the interpretation of the restrictive clause. This is reflected in the judgment in *Privacy International*, which was determined by analysing the issues of the authorities, roles and judicial supervision of the High Court over inferior courts and tribunals (see n 7 [30]–[33], [59]–[61]), specialist tribunal ([75]–[78], [193]–[198]), ouster clauses ([34]–[37], [173]–[175]), errors of law ([38]–[40], [79]–[84], [182]–[192]) and ultra vires ([79]).

[133] Also, approved by Sales LJ's decision in the CA (see n 130 [38], [42] in n 7 [17]–[19]).

[134] For example, the features to deal with sensitive matters through closed material procedures, the placing of the IPT on an equal footing with the High Court in respect of judicial review, etc. (see n 7 [27], [106], [138], [167]).

[135] Drawn from the appellants' argument (see ibid [22]–[23], [105], [120], [208]–[209]).

statutory tribunal of limited jurisdiction if there is a tenable construction which would preserve the supervisory jurisdiction of the High Court'.[136]

This reasoning was relatively on the surface level, available in any legal system, including the Australian law. However, it became distinctive in English law, since it was connected to the twin concepts of parliamentary sovereignty and the rule of law. The legal reasoning in judgments has reflected this connection on many occasions. For example, Lord Carnwath noted of the appellant's claim that *'It is...objectionable in principle, and inimical to the rule of law, that a body with such broad jurisdiction should be entirely immune from challenge...'.*[137] It is fundamental to our constitution that *'the independent arbiter must...be a court of unlimited jurisdiction, such as the High Court...'.*[138] On the other hand, he also connected the respondent's argument with parliamentary sovereignty when he said that

> *...there was nothing constitutionally offensive about legislative arrangements whereby Parliament reallocates the High Court's judicial review jurisdiction to a judicial body that is both independent of the Executive and capable of providing an authoritative interpretation of the law.*[139]

Additionally, the two sides of justification of the rule of law and parliamentary sovereignty given by Laws LJ in *Cart* were referred to.[140] On the one hand, there was *'the need under the rule of law for statute law to be "mediated by an authoritative source", the "paradigm" being the High Court as "the principal constitutional guardian of the rule of law"'.*[141] It was confirmed that *'This is not a denial of legislative sovereignty, but an affirmation of it...'.*[142] On the other hand, it was explained that *'there is no constitutional principle to preclude such legislative choices about which such judicial body is to have the power to make final decisions...'.*[143]

Importantly, the process of balancing was a way to give results to these two sides of justification at all levels, since the parties' argument, the judgments of the lower courts and the UKSC. For example, the respondent argued that *'The balance between the correction of judicial error and the policy considerations in favour of finality is a judgement properly for the legislature'.*[144] In the CA, Sales LJ referred to Dyson LJ in *R(A) v Director of Establishments of the Security Service* in stating that *'the rules were carefully drafted to achieve "a balance between fairness to a complainant and the need to safeguard the relevant security interests"'.*[145] On the

---

[136] ibid [22].
[137] ibid [26].
[138] ibid [114].
[139] ibid [29]; See also [115].
[140] ibid [116]–[117].
[141] ibid [116].
[142] ibid [116] by citing Laws LJ's judgment in *Cart* 2009 (n 16) [38].
[143] ibid [117].
[144] ibid [115].
[145] [2009] EWCA Civ 24 [48] in n 7 [19].

3.3 English Doctrinal Approaches

other hand, Lord Carnwath explicitly determined the rule of law over parliament's intention by holding that,

> ...there are certain fundamental requirements of the rule of law which no form of ouster clause (however "clear and explicit") could exclude from the supervision of the courts...[146]
> ...To deny the effectiveness of an ouster clause is again a straightforward application of existing principles of the rule of law...Parliament cannot entrust a statutory decision-making process to a particular body, but then leave it free to disregard the essential requirements laid down by the rule of law for such a process to be effective.[147]
> ...the ultimate safeguard of judicial review remains essential if the rule of law is to be maintained. The special status of the IPT (like that of the Upper Tribunal) may be a reason for restricting the grant of permission for judicial review, but not for excluding it altogether.[148]

Nevertheless, this determination was made based on the balancing process rather than the approach of winner-takes-all. The clearest indication of the flexible legal mentality of English judicial review constitutionalism in this operation could be seen in the following paragraphs;

> ...the courts have not adopted a uniform approach, but have felt free to adapt or limit the scope and form of judicial review, so as to ensure respect on the one hand for the particular statutory context and the inferred intention of the legislature, and on the other for the fundamental principles of the rule of law, and to find an appropriate balance between the two...[149]
> That more flexible approach to the relationship between the legislature and the courts is in my view wholly consistent with the modern constitutional settlement...[150]

This pattern of doctrinal approaches and legal reasoning resembles in the judgment of Lord Sumption. On the one hand, it seeks to determine the extent to which Parliament is likely to confer the power to decide wider questions of law on the tribunal.[151] On the other hand, the court has to consider whether the decision-maker's statutory functions meet the requirements of the rule of law or not.[152] Lord Sumption clearly reached this conclusion based on the logic of legality by demonstrating that *'A right of access to a court or similar judicial body to review the lawfulness of administrative or executive acts is an essential part of the rule of law'*.[153] Although Lord Sumption reached a different conclusion from Lord Carnwath, namely that the rule of law is *'sufficiently vindicated by the judicial character of the Tribunal'*,[154] and *'there is nothing inconsistent with the rule of law about allocating a conclusive*

---

[146] ibid [122].
[147] ibid [123].
[148] ibid [126]; See also [127], [134].
[149] ibid [130].
[150] ibid [131].
[151] ibid [185].
[152] ibid [187].
[153] ibid [182].
[154] ibid [172].

jurisdiction by way of review to a judicial body other than the High Court',[155] it was the same process of balancing the twin concepts of parliamentary sovereignty and the rule of law under the framework of an unwritten constitution. In Lord Sumption's words,

> *The rule of law applies as much to the courts as it does to anyone else, and under our constitution, that requires that effect must be given to Parliamentary legislation. In the absence of a written constitution capable of serving as a higher source of law, the status of Parliamentary legislation as the ultimate source of law is the foundation of democracy in the United Kingdom. The alternative would be to treat the courts as being entitled on their own initiative to create a higher source of law than statute, namely their own decisions…*[156]
>
> *…The question is how to reconcile the limited character of its jurisdiction with the language of section 67(8).*[157]

Secondly, also parallel to *Cart*, although the judges correspondingly considered the statutory construction, they did so based on various doctrines. Specifically, Lord Carnwath determined that Section 67(8) *'adds nothing to the arguments'* and *'does nothing to weaken the case for ultimate control by the courts'*.[158] Also, the wording in parenthesis in Section 67(8) merely makes a difference to the ouster clause in *Anisminic* in a dispute that involves issues of fact, but not issues of law.[159] The approach that *'judicial review can only be excluded by "the most clear and explicit words"'* should remain applicable,[160] and it is not the role the court to *'stretch the words used beyond their natural meaning'*.[161] Additionally, Lord Carnwath applied the doctrine of isolation to reject the effect of the ouster clause on the issue of law, namely that the IPT *'…is not able to develop its own "local" law without scope for further review'*.[162] Instead, it would be consistent with the rule of law, if judicial review by the ordinary courts is developed.[163]

Meanwhile, Lord Lloyd-Jones reached the same conclusion as Lord Carnwath, namely that the court had the jurisdiction to conduct judicial review of the IPT's decision, but with a slightly different doctrinal approach. In brief, although the IPT was *'undoubtedly charged'* with a judicial function by the statute, the clearest and most explicit words was still required in excluding the supervisory jurisdiction of the High Court.[164] Also Section 67(8), which closely resembles to Section 4(4) of the Foreign Compensation Act 1950 disputed in *Anisminic*, did not achieve this requirement, even by adding the words in parenthesis.[165] For Lord Lloyd-Jones, the

---

[155] ibid [199].
[156] ibid [209].
[157] ibid [211].
[158] ibid [104], [107].
[159] ibid [108], [110].
[160] ibid [111].
[161] ibid.
[162] ibid [112].
[163] ibid [139]–[140].
[164] ibid [158]–[159], [163].
[165] ibid [163]–[165].

3.3 English Doctrinal Approaches

words in parenthesis affects issues of precedent fact, but had an inadequate effect on errors of law.[166]

Conversely, Lord Sumption considered the nature of the IPT acting on the same basis as the High Court as a decisive factor in determining that the jurisdiction of the High Court to review the IPT's decision should be excluded.[167] He considered the purposes of the RIPA and the functions of the IPT in detail,[168] and concluded that the material principle of the rule of law had already been satisfied for five reasons.[169] Firstly, the tribunal's permitted field in determining the question of law was extended by the word 'adjudicate'. This was a function that would otherwise be exercised by the High Court.[170] Secondly, it is indicated by the addition of the bracketed words to Section 67(8) that the draftsman intended the result to be different from that of *Anisminic*.[171] Thirdly, the right to apply for judicial review and an appeal is conceptually different, but amounts to the same thing in reality. It is then *'wrong in principle to construe the Act as allowing for judicial review on grounds indistinguishable from an appeal on the merits, when Parliament has so carefully circumscribed the conditions on which an appeal is available'*.[172] Fourthly, the main purpose of the RIPA to disclose secret intelligence contrary to the public interest indicates Parliament's intention to confine the examination to the IPT rather than the High Court.[173] Fifthly, to be consistent with the language of the RIPA, Section 67(8) should be read as excluding the scope of judicial review on the merits of the IPT's decision, but not on procedural fairness or incompetence.[174] Also, the disputed error was one *'within the permitted field of interpretative power which Parliament has conferred on the Tribunal'*.[175]

Alternatively, Lord Wilson reached a similar (dissenting) conclusion as Lord Sumption, but considered the interpretation of the words in parenthesis in Section 67(8) as a *'central specific question'*.[176] He determined the wording and context differently from Lord Carnwath and Lord Sumption, namely that it is *'totally clear in excluding judicial review of all the IPT's decisions'*.[177] This was reinforced by the consideration of the jurisdiction of the IPT, allocated by Parliament as an independent tribunal with the function of conducting *'judicial review of the lawfulness of*

---

[166] ibid [165]–[167].

[167] ibid [172], [187], [197], [206].

[168] For example, the IPT's function to ensure the confidentiality of secret material or its composition having a high judicial office as president (ibid [196]–[197]).

[169] Based on Laws LJ's approach in *Cart* 2009 (n 16) [198].

[170] Provided by Section 65(2) of RIPA (n 7 [200]).

[171] ibid [201].

[172] ibid [202].

[173] ibid [203].

[174] ibid [204]–[205].

[175] ibid [182], [206].

[176] ibid [222].

[177] ibid [224]–[232].

the actions of the intelligence services'.[178] In other words, legality can be fulfilled by the IPT, which is *'a judicial body of like standing and authority to that of the HC'*.[179]

It is evident from these unpacked doctrinal approaches and legal reasoning that the English courts have the flexibility to apply various justifications and doctrines in order to determine if the IPT's decision is covered by legality or not.[180] While Lord Wilson held that the court's role in protecting legality should not apply to all the IPT's decisions, Lord Sumption considered that it covered procedural fairness and incompetence, but not merits issues. On the other hand, Lord Carnwath determined that the role of the court and scope of judicial review cover issues of law, but not issues of fact.

It has been reflected on many occasions in the legal reasoning of judgments that these flexibilities are a product of the distinctive way the English courts understand their role in conducting judicial review based on their legal system's legal culture. Apart from quoting Professor Paul Craig's textbook that *'the scope of judicial review is not self-defining...not capable of being answered by linguistic or textual analysis of the statute alone'* and the answer *'must ultimately be based on a value judgment, the precise content of which will not necessarily be always the same'*,[181] Lord Carnwath made this clear by saying that

> The constitutional roles both of Parliament, as the maker of the law, and of the High Court, and ultimately of the appellate courts, as the guardians and interpreters of that law, are thus respected. The question in any case is "the level of scrutiny required by the rule of law" ...or... "what scope of judicial review ... is required to maintain the rule of law".[182]

As did Lord Sumption, who said that,

> The categorisation of errors of law as excesses of jurisdiction is the result of the unsystematic way in which English public law has developed over the past three centuries...the development since Anisminic of a legal principle which made excesses of jurisdiction of all errors of law has been accompanied by a recognition that the reasons for strictly construing ouster clauses may be more or less powerful, depending on the nature of the decision and the decision-maker...[183]
>
> I do not think that it would be either appropriate or wise for this court to answer it in wholly general terms, for the answer may vary according to the statutory context...[184]

More importantly, Lord Carnwath clearly expressed the need for a comparative study of the English and other common law approaches, particularly the Australian one. In his words, *'For completeness I should make clear that I have not overlooked*

---

[178] ibid [249].

[179] ibid [252].

[180] Lord Lloyd-Jones' reasoning that *'That provision...can at least be said to have squarely confronted what it sought to achieve as required by the principle of legality. To my mind, section 67(8) does not satisfy this requirement'* is clearly compatible with this book's proposed approach of deep-water legality (ibid [165]); See also [252] (Lord Wilson).

[181] Craig, Administrative Law (n 4) [16–016] in n 7 [83].

[182] n 7 [132] by citing Lady Hale, Lord Dyson and Lord Clarke in *Cart* 2011 (n 16).

[183] n 7 [182].

[184] ibid [207].

3.3 English Doctrinal Approaches

the many authorities to which we have been helpfully referred from other common law jurisdictions...'.[185] Also, the spirit of this book was recited in the judgment, namely that the English and Australian laws do not always apply the same doctrinal approaches to this similar kind of determination of the scope of judicial review.[186] According to the legal reasoning in *Kirk*, the English approach *'...is a step which this court [HCA] has not taken... there can be no automatic transposition of principles from one jurisdiction to the other because the constitutional context is too different'*.[187] Lord Carnwath also acknowledged that *'these decisions need to be read within the differing legal and constitutional arrangements of the jurisdictions concerned'*.[188] This statement will become more substantial in the next section by demonstrating a tangible contrast between the analysed flexibility of English judicial review and the relatively rigid pattern of doctrinal approaches and legal reasoning applied by the Australian courts in *Craig*, *Kirk* and *Hossain*.

3.3.4 Products of the English Legal Culture

As mentioned in Sect. 1.3 of Chap. 1, the English determination of the scope of judicial review of a tribunal and inferior court is usually regarded by the literature as pragmatic. Apart from Elliott and Thomas,[189] Wade and Forsyth also assert that

> The court makes a profoundly pragmatic case that permission to apply for judicial review of the UT should only be granted when the stringent "second tier appeal criteria" were met.[190]

The advantages and disadvantages of the different doctrinal approaches under the label of pragmatism have been discussed through various methodologies. For example, Craig takes certainty and flexibility as the criteria to compare the application of error of law in substituting the decisions between the English, US, Canadian and EU law.[191] Bell discusses, assesses and suggests the application of the second-appeals

---

[185] ibid [102].

[186] ibid.

[187] n 18 [64], [66] in n 7 [103]; Instead, the HCA did so through the concept of jurisdiction. This will be unpacked in detail later.

[188] n 7 [102].

[189] Mark Elliott and Robert Thomas, 'Tribunal Justice and Proportionate Dispute Resolution' (2012) 71 CLJ 297, 309.

[190] Wade and Forsyth (n 4) 222; See also Mark Elliott, 'From Heresy to Orthodoxy: Substantive Legitimate Expectations in English Public Law' in Matthew Groves and Greg Weeks (eds), *Legitimate Expectations in the Common Law World* (Hart Publishing 2016). Although the main analysis is related to substantive legitimate expectations (as will be discussed in Chap. 6), Elliott also mentioned the area of judicial review of tribunal's decision as example of the flexibility of approaches applied in English law.

[191] Paul Craig, 'Judicial Review of Questions of Law: A Comparative Perspective' in Susan R Ackerman and Peter L Lindseth (eds), *Comparative Administrative Law* (2nd edn, Edward Elgar 2017); See also Craig, *Administrative Law* (n 4) [16–040]–[16–044].

criteria in the post-*Cart* cases.[192] Meanwhile, Elliott and Thomas mainly comment on the second-tier appeal approach used by the UKSC in *Cart* as appropriate for determining the scope of judicial review in England.[193] On the other hand, Forsyth strongly criticises the pragmatic approach taken in *Racal*, *Page* and *Cart* on the grounds of judicial illegitimacy, uncertainty and conceptual confusion.[194] Otherwise, Robert Craig argues for more consideration of the separation of powers when determining the scope of judicial review, namely that a distinction should be drawn between the ouster clauses addressed to administrative and judicial bodies. On this basis, the clear parliamentary intention to reallocate judicial supervision to a new statutory body like the UT and IPT should be more respected. Therefore, the decision of the CA in *Privacy International* giving full effect to the ouster clause and barring the High Court's jurisdiction to conduct judicial review of the IPT's decision would be preferable.[195] In the same vein, Aronson argues that

> England needs its discretionary filter, if only to prevent its courts being flooded with challenges for any and every error of law, especially since their courts sometimes take a very relaxed view as to what might constitute such an error'[196]

The English approach is compared to the Australian law in some of the literature. For instance, although Boughey and Crawford accept that it was probably correct for the judgment in *Cart* not to draw back to the jurisdictional error approach, they also argue that this approach is significant and beneficial in defining the scope and relationship between the judiciary and parliament. Consequently, the English courts should consider the jurisdictional approach more by following the examples of Australian jurisprudence of adapting the approach into a form capable of serving the legal system's constitutional necessity.[197]

As mentioned by Lord Carnwath in *Privacy International*, the depth of analysis in these works is respectful.[198] However, it is essential to slightly withdraw to the deeper foundation whereby the determination of the scope of judicial review is understood under the particular constitutional setting of the legal system. Such an examination is offered in this chapter based on a framework of deep-water legality and legal culture. As Lord Wilson articulated in *Privacy International*, 'every legal

---

[192] Joanna Bell, 'The Relationship between Judicial Review and the Upper Tribunal: What have the Courts made of *Cart*?' (2018) PL 394.

[193] Elliott and Thomas (n 189).

[194] Christopher Forsyth, '"Blasphemy Against Basics': Doctrine, Conceptual Reasoning and Certain Decisions of the UK Supreme Court' in John Bell, Mark Elliott, Jason Varuhas and Philip Murray (eds), *Public Law Adjudication in Common Law Systems: Process and Substance* (Hart Publishing 2016).

[195] Robert Craig, 'Ouster Clauses, Separation of Powers and the Intention of Parliament: from *Anisminic* to *Privacy International*' (2018) PL 570.

[196] Aronson, 'Jurisdictional Error and Beyond' (n 8) 263.

[197] Boughey and Crawford, 'Reconsidering *R (on the Application of Cart) v Upper Tribunal* and the Rationale for Jurisdictional Error' (n 15).

[198] n 7 [102].

3.3 English Doctrinal Approaches

system has to identify some end-point beyond which there can be no challenge or further challenge to a judicial decision'.[199] This is indeed a question of what should be covered by legality and whether the issue in a disputed administrative action is one that the courts have a role in protecting or not. It is demonstrated in the above analysis that the English courts have a distinctly flexible pattern of doctrinal approaches and legal reasoning in determining the scope of judicial review of a quasi-judicial institution with legislative restrictions.

In short, despite staying with the distinction between jurisdictional error and non-jurisdictional error approach for a long time, the English approach was not rigid, since the courts could flexibly apply various justifications and doctrines in reaching different results of the balancing process between the twin concepts. Although the approach was moved to another form in *Anisminic*, the overall theme of flexibility was still shared. This was made explicit in the legal reasoning of *Cart* in three points. Firstly, the English courts can flexibly explain constitutional values like the twin concepts between the rule of law and parliamentary sovereignty and the common law theory in a way they consider appropriate to justify their scope of judicial review. Secondly, they can malleably adapt or engender new doctrines to determine their scope of judicial review in relation to the nature of the UT. Thirdly, the status of error of law has been not been fixed, but flexibly adapted. This pattern of various adaptable doctrines based on the balancing process between parliamentary sovereignty and the rule of law continued to be applied in *Privacy International*. The scope of judicial review in relation to the nature of the IPT and interpretation of the ouster clause was flexibly determined by the individual judges in this case. Importantly, these doctrinal approaches are connected to the flexible legal mentality of English judicial review constitutionalism.

This framework of legality and legal culture facilitates a more comprehensive understanding of the English cases and literature. For example, Lord Carnwath's statement in *Privacy International* that *'the Supreme Court in Cart does not turn on such sharp distinctions...'*,[200] becomes straightforward to understand because it is dictated by the flexible legal mentality of English judicial review constitutionalism. It also exemplifies what Bell describes as *'important seams of continuity with the past inherent in the Cart'*.[201] On the flip side, Robert Craig's argument to make a clearer distinction between courts and tribunals will be confronted by a certain degree of difficulty since the separation of powers in the UK is fluid in nature.[202] The connection between the flexibility of the English doctrinal approaches and its legal system's legal culture will become more obvious when

---

[199] ibid [238].

[200] ibid [84] (Lord Carnwath); Also various doctrinal approaches applied in other cases, namely *Anisminic*, *O'Reilly v Mackman*, *Boddington v British Transport Commission* [1999] 2 AC 143, *Lumba v Secretary of State for the Home Department* [2011] UKSC 12, *Racal* and *Cart* are all regarded as waves derived from the English legal culture.

[201] Joanna Bell, 'Rethinking the Story of *Cart v Upper Tribunal* and Its Implications for Administrative Law' (2019) 39 Oxford Journal of Legal Studies 74.

[202] See more in Sect. 2.3.3 of Chap. 2.

compared to the Australian law in the next section. Boughey and Crawford's description that '...*it* [the Australian approach] *could not simply be transplanted into Britain*',[203] will become tangible with an explanation of the the connection between the doctrinal approaches, deep understanding of legality and the legal culture in England and Australia.

3.4 Australian Doctrinal Approaches

Rather than moving flexibly, the Australian courts have continued to adhere to the distinction between jurisdictional error and non-jurisdictional error in determining the scope of judicial review relating to the nature of the institution and legislative restriction. This ground has become a central approach, covering all common law grounds of judicial review including jurisdictional fact. How this entrenched application of jurisdictional error is connected to the Australian legal culture will be demonstrated in this section by unpacking the legal reasoning of the courts in *Kirk* and surrounding cases. On the other hand, it will be demonstrated in the next chapter in the case of jurisdictional fact.

3.4.1 Prior to Kirk

The first step in discussing jurisdiction of the Australian court in conducting judicial review of tribunal and inferior court was presented in relation to the legislative restriction. In *R v Hickman, Ex parte Fox and Clinton*, not only that the inferior court was delegated the power to run public administration by the legislature, but the privative clause also gave restriction for its decision not to be reviewed by the court.[204] Justice Dixon proposed that, in general, a privative clause expanding the authority of the decision-maker was not constitutionally invalid.[205] However, it would exclude judicial review only when '*its face appears to be within power and is in fact a bona fide attempt to act in the course of its authority*'.[206]

This approach, known as the *Hickman* principle, has been applied as the main approach in dealing with privative clauses relating to matters of jurisdiction of the court in conducting judicial review of tribunals and inferior courts for many years.[207]

---

[203] Boughey and Crawford, 'Reconsidering *R (on the application of Cart) v Upper Tribunal* and the Rationale for Jurisdictional Error' (n 15) 607.
[204] (1945) 70 CLR 598.
[205] ibid.
[206] ibid.
[207] Aronson, Groves and Weeks (n 4) [18.20].

3.4 Australian Doctrinal Approaches

However, it was much criticised in the operation.[208] This section argues that this is because the doctrinal approach was not compatible with the Australian legal culture.[209] As analysed in the previous chapter, the understanding of the rule of law in Australia emphasises the rigid separation of powers for the purposes of maintaining the federal boundary of powers between court and executive. However, the *Hickman* principle excessively relied on judicial discretion. For example, while the privative clause was given to limit judicial review, the *Hickman* principle could not provide a clue, as to the extent that limitation affects. The judgment merely said that a privative clause is constitutional valid, but the courts could still claim their jurisdiction of judicial review by asserting that the decision breaches a fundamental jurisdictional requirement.[210] Therefore, it depended on the court deciding whether to intervene into the tribunal and inferior court's decisions or not. The boundary between court and executive was then not able to be set clearly.

Thus, the approach in determining the scope of judicial review of tribunals and inferior courts had been moved to the position giving more importance to the separation of powers between judicial review and non-judicial functions. The significant step was taken in *R v Kirby, Ex parte Boilermakers' Society of Australia*, involving the determination of the scope of judicial review of the Commonwealth Court of Conciliation and Arbitration ('CCCA').[211] The HCA asserted that *'the doctrine of the separation of powers forbids the amalgamation of judicial and non-judicial functions'*.[212] On this basis, the CCCA was considered as a non-judicial body. The conferral of the judicial power on it was thereby unlawful because it conflicted with the separation of powers. As described in the previous chapter, this separation of judicial power was the starting point in emphasising the premise of the rigid separation of powers when discussing the scope of judicial review. The doctrinal approaches in determining the scope of judicial review in cases have been operated with rigid mentality. This was done so through the ground of jurisdictional error. The significant cases, as they are the best in demonstrating influence of Australian legal culture on the approach, are those of *Craig* and *Kirk*.[213]

---

[208] ibid.

[209] As noted in Sect. 2.4.3 of Chap. 2, what profoundly influences the Australian courts' understanding of their constitutional role to conduct judicial review is a 'general implication' of Dixon's Legalism. Therefore, it is possible that sometimes, Dixon's particular judgments are in conflict with his proposed concept of legalism and the rigid legal mentality of Australian judicial review constitutionalism.

[210] Peter Cane and Leighton McDonald, *Principles of Administrative Law: Legal Regulation of Governance* (3rd edn, OUP 2018) 192–194.

[211] (1956) 94 CLR 254.

[212] ibid 257.

[213] Although Aronson argued that jurisdictional error firstly appeared in public law in 1905, its current understanding has been developed around 1980s–1990s. *Craig* was an important step in doing so (Aronson, 'Jurisdictional Error and Beyond' (n 8) 253).

In *Craig,* the claimant was charged with larceny and arson in the District Court of South Australia ('DCSA'), which held that the accused was without legal representation through no fault.[214] By relying on *Dietrich v The Queen,*[215] the judge considered that the trial should be postponed until further order. The claimant then argued with the HCA that the DCSA had committed a jurisdictional error because of the misunderstanding of the reasoning in *Dietrich.* Like the analysed English cases, it is questionable whether or not the court's role involves intervening in the proceedings of the DCSA, an institution with an adjudicative function. However, it is clear that the judgments in *Craig* applied different ways from *Cart* in claiming the court's jurisdiction to intervene into the DCSA's decision. There are two significant connections between legal reasoning of the judgments in *Craig* and the rigid legal mentality of Australian judicial review constitutionalism.

First, instead of being abandoned as was the case in *Anisminic,* the distinction between jurisdictional and non-jurisdictional error was applied in *Craig* to determine the scope of judicial review of the DCSA.[216] This was clearly expressed by Mr. Doyle, a barrister responding to the judges in an oral pleading of *Craig* that

> ...We certainly do not advance what is sometimes called "the wide Anisminic notion" that any error of law is jurisdictional...
> This Court has not accepted Lord Diplock's view that the distinction between jurisdictional and non-jurisdictional errors was for practical purposes abolished...[217]

The legal reasoning given in the judgment of *Craig* explained that, if an administrative decision contains a jurisdictional error, it exceeds its authority or power, and such an error will invalidate any order or decision of the executive.[218] This doctrine is directly compatible to the mentality of rigid separation of powers and concept of jurisdiction, analysed as an element in Australian legal culture. The legal reasoning of the judgment continues that '...*an administrative tribunal lacks authority either to authoritatively determine questions of law or to make an order or decision otherwise than in accordance with the law'.*[219] This means that the tribunal's decision is subject to judicial review by the court when it is not in accordance with legality. The framework of legality starts to operate in accordance with jurisdictional error.

Secondly, this jurisdictional error doctrine was applied to judicial review of both a tribunal and inferior court.[220] However, what is jurisdictional error for tribunal and for inferior court is different according to their nature under the framework of powers in the Australian constitution. The judgment asserted that '...*it is important to bear in mind a critical distinction which exists between administrative tribunals and*

---

[214] n 46 [5].

[215] (1992) 177 CLR 292.

[216] n 46 [9]. The court clearly denied that it had abandoned the distinction between jurisdictional error and non-jurisdictional error ([13]).

[217] n 3.

[218] n 46 [14].

[219] ibid.

[220] ibid [10].

3.4 Australian Doctrinal Approaches

courts of law'.[221] On the one hand, an inferior court is composed of persons with either formal legal qualifications or practical training, and it exercises jurisdiction as part of a hierarchical legal system entrusted with the administration of justice under the Constitutions. On the other hand, a tribunal is composed of persons without formal legal qualifications and it is not part of the hierarchical judicial structure.[222] Since the DCSA is undoubtedly a court, the primary focus of discussion was upon what constitutes jurisdictional error on the part of an inferior court. This legal reasoning also obviously demonstrates the logic of the rigid separation of powers in the courts' determinations of the scope of judicial review, which is considered from statutory construction in a particular case. The transcript of legal argument of *Craig* clearly expresses this as follow.

> *Justice Brennan: Do you wish to propound any criterion for determining whether an error is jurisdictional or not?*
> *Mr Peek: ...one can see things which do constitute it, such as a requirement to satisfy some definite condition precedent, often statutory, that an inquiry in relation to that will go to jurisdictional error...*[223]

Combining with the first point discussed above, an inferior court will fall into jurisdictional error for the purpose of the writ where it acts outside its scope of power. The judgment held that

> *Jurisdictional error is at its most obvious where the inferior court purports to act wholly or partly outside the general area of its jurisdiction in the sense of entertaining a matter or making a decision or order of a kind which wholly or partly lies outside the theoretical limits of its functions and power.'*[224]

The judgment then listed what can be regarded as jurisdictional error for inferior court. The categories are examples of the situations making the inferior court's decision excess its jurisdiction.[225] Although the list is not exhaustive,[226] it shows that what is regarded as jurisdictional error is rigidly considered from the nature of institution, according to the separation of powers prescribed in written document like constitution and statues.

---

[221] ibid [13].

[222] ibid [10].

[223] n 3.

[224] n 46 [12].

[225] For example, '*An inferior court would... act wholly outside the general area of its jurisdiction in that sense if, having jurisdiction strictly limited to civil matters, it purported to hear and determine a criminal charge*' (ibid).

[226] Legal reasoning in *Kirk*, which will be analysed below, confirms this point that '*Craig does not provide a rigid taxonomy of jurisdictional error*' (n 18 [73]).

3.4.2 Kirk

The legal reasoning in *Kirk* not only confirmed the doctrine of jurisdictional error, considered from the framework of separation of powers in *Craig*,[227] but it also entrenched how the doctrinal approach is linked to the rigid legal mentality of Australian judicial review constitutionalism.[228] Four main points are unpacked below.

Firstly, the court in *Kirk* clearly applied a distinctive understanding of Australian constitutional values and frameworks analysed in the legal system's legal culture in justifying and limiting its scope of judicial review. In addition to the entrenchment of jurisdiction of the HCA by section 75(v) and Chapter III of the constitution premised in *Plaintiff S157/2002 v Commonwealth of Australia*,[229] the judgment of *Kirk* extended that section 73 of the Constitution entrenched State Supreme Court's jurisdiction similarly to the Court of the Queen's Bench in England.[230] It leads to the consequence that the HCA can review decision of the Australian State Supreme Courts in the same way as the UKSC reviews the Queen's Bench. Additionally, state parliaments may not validly deprive the State Supreme Court's supervisory jurisdiction in conducting judicial review, which is the *'mechanism for the determination and the enforcement of the limits on the exercise of State executive and judicial power by persons and bodies other than the Supreme Court'*.[231] As Justice Spigelman reflected in extra-judiciary work, the process of convergence between State and Commonwealth judicial review was completed in *Kirk*.[232] It is clearly reflected in the judgment that these entrenchments of the courts' jurisdiction are products of the Australian legal culture, for example;

> The supervisory jurisdiction exercised by the State Supreme Courts by the grant of prerogative relief or orders in the nature of that relief is governed in fundamental respects by principles established as part of the common law of Australia.[233]

They are also regarded as the operation of the rule of law, securing *'a level of judicial enforcement of the legal limits on administrative decision-making at both levels of government'*.[234] In the transcript of legal argument of the case, Mr. Hatcher, a barrister tied this to the federal framework of separation of powers that *'In our respectful submission, the rule of law is assumed to operate under our Constitution*

---

[227] ibid [67]–[68].

[228] Aronson, Groves and Weeks ((n 4) [4.340]) argue *Kirk* as the most important HCA decision since *Craig*.

[229] (2003) 211 CLR 476 in *Kirk* (n 18) [66].

[230] n 18 [95]–[97].

[231] ibid [98].

[232] Spigelman (n 15).

[233] n 18 [99].

[234] Chris Finn, 'Constitutionalising Supervisory Review at State Level: The End of Hickman?' [2010] Public Law Review 92.

3.4 Australian Doctrinal Approaches

and binds New South Wales as much as any individual in the Commonwealth'.[235] Crawford and Goldsworthy also observe that *'The decision in Kirk has been widely applauded, for enhancing the rule of law and harmonising the principles of public law that apply at the State and Commonwealth levels.*[236]

Apart from that the scope of legislative power was also explained that it needs to follow the framework of separation of powers by not altering the authority of the court.[237] The judgment clearly demonstrated that Australian judicial review constitutionalism has influence on this.

> *The operation of a privative provision is…affected by constitutional considerations. More particularly although a privative provision demonstrates a legislative purpose favouring finality, the question arise about the extent to which the provision can be given an operation that immunises the decisions of an inferior court or tribunal from judicial review, yet remain consistent with the constitutional framework for the Australian judicial system.*[238]

This legal reasoning in operating privative clauses based on the framework of separation of powers and the written constitution has also been expressed in other sources, such as judges' speeches. For example, Chief Justice Gleeson stated that

> *… Parliament's capacity to empower administrative action is fettered by the limits imposed by the Constitution upon its powers. And, as the Constitution assumes the rule of law, a question may arise as to the consequences of that assumption in this context.*[239]

Secondly, the judgment stated clearly that the abandoning of jurisdictional error in *Anisminic*, which rendered the decision ultra vires, is not a step that this Court has taken.[240] Instead, the scope of judicial review in Australia is determined by the distinction between jurisdictional and non-jurisdictional error. This doctrine functions by marking the relevant limits of administrative power. If the decision of the inferior court is beyond its framework of power, it is regarded as containing a jurisdictional error, and therefore within the scope of judicial review by the State Supreme Court and HCA. The court will decide whether to intervene in actions, depending on whether or not the state executive or judicial power is excess to its jurisdiction. The judgment explicitly demonstrated that this doctrine is compatible with the analysed distinctive understanding of constitutional values in the Australian legal culture, particularly the rigid separation of powers. For example,

---

[235] n 12.

[236] Lisa Crawford and Jeffrey Goldsworthy, 'Constitutionalism' in Cheryl Saunders and Adrienne Stone (eds), *The Oxford Handbook of the Australian Constitution* (OUP 2018) 376.

[237] n 18 [96].

[238] ibid [93]. The judgment also explained this aspect at the federal level that *'In considering Commonwealth legislation, account must be taken of the two fundamental constitutional considerations pointed out in Plaintiff S157/2002 v The Commonwealth:…s 75(v) of the Constitution* [and]…*Ch III'* ([96]).

[239] Chief Justice Gleeson, 'Courts and the Rule of Law' (The Rule of Law Series, Melbourne University, 7 November 2001).

[240] n 18 [65].

> *Rather, the observations made about the constitutional significance of the supervisory jurisdiction of the State Supreme Courts point to the continued need for, and utility of, the distinction between jurisdictional and non-jurisdictional error in the Australian constitutional context.*[241]

Justice Spigelman also notes this connection in his secondary work that

> *The constitutional dimension of the distinction between jurisdictional and non-jurisdictional error places it at the centre of our administrative law jurisprudence. The distinction is necessitated in Australian law by our separation of powers doctrine which is, in many respects, more definitive, some would say more rigid, than that adopted by the constitutional law of other nations…*[242]

The High Court in *Kirk* extended this protection and affirmed the centrality of the concept of jurisdictional error in Australian administrative law.[243] Additionally, the conversation between Justice Hayne and Mr. Agius in the transcript of legal argument of *Kirk* also makes clear that jurisdictional error is a doctrine in complying the rule of law, requiring rigid separation of powers in Australia.

> *Justice Hayne: Now, yes, one matter of expressing that ground has been this notion of impossibility of compliance. It also had references to the rule of law too.*
> *Mr Agius: But the rule of law is brought in aid because it is said that the way in which the section is being interpreted renders it impossible with compliance therefore it is in breach of the rule of law, that therefore there is jurisdictional error. That is the structure of the argument. That is what is being put against us…*[244]

Leeming also concludes the meaning of jurisdictional error as an error made by a court or body exercising public power *'as to the limits of the authority'* it has to decide in some matters.[245] This is an expression of how the concept of jurisdiction dominates the Australian determination of the scope of judicial review through the application of jurisdictional error. As Leeming observed,

> *…the distinction* [between jurisdictional and non-jurisdictional error] *reflects the entrenched supervisory jurisdiction of the High Court and the Supreme Courts in relation to executive action, coupled with a fundamental conception that courts are different from persons and bodies exercising executive power in that they may and ordinarily will have some authority to decide question of law.*[246]

The compatibility of the jurisdictional error approach and the Australian legal culture can also be found in academic work. The most explicit one is those of Selway, who connects jurisdictional error to the particular understanding of many constitutional values, namely the separation of power, the concept of jurisdiction,

---

[241] ibid [100].

[242] Spigelman (n 15).

[243] ibid.

[244] n 12. See also Boughey and Crawford, 'Reconsidering *R (on the application of Cart) v Upper Tribunal* and the Rationale for Jurisdictional Error' (n 15) considering jurisdictional error as a doctrine for constitutional purpose in Australia.

[245] Leeming (n 11) 13.

[246] ibid 63.

3.4 Australian Doctrinal Approaches

the distinction between legality and merits, the distinction between the court and other governmental organs and the existence of the Australian written constitution, compared to the absence in the UK law;

> *This...explains why Australian courts must retain a distinction between jurisdictional errors and non-jurisdictional errors...Such a distinction is inherent in any analysis based upon separation of powers principles.*
>
> *... the constitutional context means that the courts cannot engage in merit review and are required to differentiate between jurisdictional errors and non-jurisdictional errors.*
>
> *When the role of the Commonwealth Constitution in identifying and limiting the role of the courts in judicial review is understood it is not surprising that countries with a written Constitution, such as Australia...have taken a more limited view of the proper role of judicial review than have countries with an uncontrolled Constitution, such as the UK...*[247]

Lastly, contrary to the complexity of the English one, Australian judicial review systematically ties the writ system to the approach of jurisdictional error. Cane and McDonald clarify this as follows;

> *The grounds of judicial review available under s75(v) are tightly linked to the available remedies. Substantively, 'jurisdictional error' has become the conceptual lodestar of judicial review under s 75(v)...as the constitutional writs are available only for excess or denial of jurisdiction.*[248]

In summary, rather than applying various doctrines, the Australian law is confined to the approach of jurisdictional error because it corresponds to the particular understanding of constitutional values in the Australian landscape. As Aronson, Groves and Weeks state, '*Kirk twice described the distinction between jurisdictional and non-jurisdictional error of law as useful. That was no accident*'.[249]

Thirdly, as shown above, while the various doctrines in *Cart* and *Privacy International* were determined by different applications, the consideration of jurisdictional error in Australian law has been applied in a relatively fixed way. Apart from legislative restrictions described above, the determination of the nature of institution was considered from the framework of separation of powers in the Constitution and particular statutory construction. According to the constitution, the ICNSW was regarded as '*a court of limited jurisdiction*', which should not '*be the final judge of its exercise of power; it should be subject to the control of the courts of more general jurisdiction*'.[250] Tribunals '*cannot be authoritatively determine questions of law, but that courts can*'.[251] The ICNSW cannot be turned into the

---

[247] Bradley Selway, 'The Principle behind Common Law Judicial Review of Administrative Action – The Search Continues' (2002) 30 Federal Law Review 217, 234–235.

[248] Cane and McDonald (n 210) 30–31; See also Aronson, Groves and Weeks (n 4) [1.100], [1.110]; for example that '*The language of jurisdictional error dominates Australia's judicial review in the HC's constitutional writ jurisdiction...*'.

[249] Aronson, Groves and Weeks (n 4) [4.350].

[250] n 18 [64].

[251] n 18 [69].

superior court of the record by legislative restriction. Mr. Hatcher clearly stated this mentality in transcript of legal argument of the case that

> ...It would still be an inferior court for the purposes of Craig. It is a court of limited jurisdiction. The distinction that is drawn in Craig between administrative tribunal and an inferior court is a distinction we would say predicated upon the fact that a Court sits in a hierarchy at the apex of which sits this Court so its decisions as to law and fact are subject to review...
> Yes. It is a statutory court and it is subject to prerogative relief in the court of general jurisdiction in the State.[252]

The courts are not required to engage in the balancing process of the rule of law and parliamentary sovereignty as the court in *Cart* and *Privacy International* did. Instead, they rigidly follow the framework of separation of powers prescribed in the written constitution in reaching the conclusion that the State Supreme Court has the jurisdiction to conduct judicial review of the ICNSW's decision.

Apart from the framework of the constitution, the nature of the institution can also be systematically considered through statutory construction. The judgment held that

> The most immediately relevant statutory context is found in the provisions that establish the inferior court, and regulate appeals from, or review of, its decisions. The decisions of many inferior courts are open to appeal or review for error of law...[253]

Justice Gummow also explicitly expresses this in the transcript of legal argument that

> What is the nature of the jurisdictional error? Is it a case where you say there has been – it is so difficult to work out what the body appears to have thought it was doing, but one says there is constructively a failure to apply themselves to the statutory tasks.[254]

Mr. Hatcher, a barrister responded that

> Yes, your Honour. They have come to a view of the legislation and so construed the legislation as to make it impossible of compliance and we say that that cannot accord with the implications arising under the Australian Constitution.[255]

This application of jurisdictional error considered from the constitution and statutory construction has also been recognised in judges' speeches and among scholars. For example, Chief Justice Gleeson stated that

> ...the statute in that case was construed to mean that the decision in question would not be invalidated on the ground of failure to conform to the limitations on power or authority, or the manner of its exercise, contained in the statute, provided that the decision was a bona fide attempt to exercise the power, that it related to the subject matter of the legislation, and that it was reasonably capable of reference to the power.[256]

---

[252] n 12.
[253] n 18 [87]–[88].
[254] n 12.
[255] ibid.
[256] Gleeson (n 239).

3.4 Australian Doctrinal Approaches

In the same vein, Boughey and Crawford concluded that *'Rather, Australian jurisprudence emphasises the importance of the statutory text, read in context and as a whole, in the light of established rules of construction'*.[257] Fisher makes it clear that

> Such a doctrine [jurisdictional error] *does indeed depend on the idea that statutes provide rigid frameworks that mark the boundaries of administrative power. Such boundaries can be policed through statutory construction*...[258]

This illustrates that the Australian courts are not relatively free to adapt a new doctrine and way of justification, but they determine the scope of judicial review according to the rigid framework of separation of powers prescribed in the written constitution and statutory construction. Jurisdictional error has become an entrenched ground in determining the scope of judicial review because it fulfils this requirement well.

This point becomes more explicit when compared to the English flexible pattern of doctrinal approaches and legal reasoning. It may seem that Lord Sumption in *Privacy International* also considered the purpose and jurisdiction of the IPT established by the RIPA in detail. However, English judges still have the comparative flexibility to choose a different pathway. As unpacked above, the other judges adapted various doctrines to determine the scope of judicial review in *Cart* and *Privacy International*. Prominently, Lord Brown of the UKSC clearly stated this mentality in an oral argument in *Cart*, saying that *'It is not the interpretation of the 2007 Act. It's rethinking the common law in this new context. What's a good idea? What's the necessary extended to the rule of law?'*.[259]

Fourthly, jurisdictional error is not only the doctrine in determining the scope of judicial review applied in *Craig* and *Kirk*, but also regarded as the central approach in the determination of the scope of judicial review in Australia. More cases will be unpacked in the following chapters in order to demonstrate this rigidity in applying jurisdictional error to determine the scope of judicial review based on the framework of separation of powers prescribed in the written constitution and statutory construction. As shown in the following transcript of the legal argument of *S20/2002*, rather than the distinction between error of law and fact as applied in England, the Australian courts apply jurisdictional error in determining all the common law grounds of judicial review;

> Justice Gummow: *That is right, but you do not need to talk about error of law and error of fact. It is just a jurisdictional error*...[260]

---

[257] Boughey and Crawford, 'Reconsidering *R (on the application of Cart) v Upper Tribunal* and the Rationale for Jurisdictional Error' (n 15) 607.

[258] Elizabeth Fisher, '"Jurisdictional" Facts and "Hot" Facts: Legal Formalism, Legal Pluralism, and the Nature of Australian Administrative Law' (2015) 38 Melbourne University Law Review 968, 972.

[259] n 1.

[260] The Transcript of legal argument in *Re Minister for Immigration and Multicultural Affairs, Ex parte Applicant S20/2002* (2003) 198 ALR 59.

3.4.3 After **Kirk**

It should be noted that, based on the above analysis, it is not claimed in this section that the rigidity of jurisdictional error is undisputable in Australia. For example, part of the legal reasoning in *Kirk* demonstrated a point of flexibility by referring to the concept of gravity of error when the court intervenes in a decision related to policy assessment.[261] This point was expanded in *Hossain v Minister for Immigration and Border Protection*, when Professor Jaffe's explanation that the language of jurisdiction is *'almost entirely functional…used to validate review when review is felt to be necessary'* and *'simply expresses the gravity of the error'* was mentioned.[262] Particularly, Edelman J argued for the requirement of materiality of jurisdictional error, saying that

> …exercise of construction is not dependent solely on the literal text. Rather, the statute is construed in light of the background principles and history of judicial review, as well as common law principles, including the principle that the consequences of an error that a legislature will be taken to intend will usually depend on the gravity of the error.[263]

This was reinforced by Kiefel CJ, Gageler J and Keane J, who explained that, by nature, the common law approach reflected

> …longstanding qualitative judgments about the appropriate limits of an exercise of administrative power to which a legislature can be taken to adhere in defining the bounds of such authority…Those common law principles are not derived by logic alone and cannot be treated as abstractions disconnected from the subject matter to which they are to be applied. They are not so delicate or refined in their operation that sight is lost of the fact that "decision-making is a function of the real world".[264]

This seems to be in conflict with the analysed rigidity of the Australian legal culture. Some scholars are greatly concerned that these approaches of gravity of error and threshold of materiality are pragmatic, excessively extend the established principles of the statutory context and, exceed the significant legality and merits distinction, thereby risking uncertainty and inconvenience.[265]

However, this concern is slightly excessive because, as noted in Chap. 1, the courts in any country, including England and Australia, can adapt their determination of the scope of judicial review according to the particular context. As Nettle J articulated, *'Much depends on the circumstances of the case'*.[266] This flexible adaptation can be described by various labels, including gravity of error and threshold of materiality. Nevertheless, what is found more interesting is the fact that the English

---

[261] n 18 [62]–[64].

[262] n 19 [18]–[19] (Kiefel CJ, Gageler J and Keane J) by citing Louis Leventhal Jaffe, 'Judicial Review: Constitutional and Jurisdictional Fact' (1957) 70 Harvard Law Review 953.

[263] n 19 [64].

[264] ibid [28].

[265] For example, Courtney Raad, *'Hossain v Minister for Immigration and Border Protection*: A Material Change to the Fabric of Jurisdictional Error?' (2019) 41(2) Sydney Law Review 265.

[266] n 19 [43].

3.4 Australian Doctrinal Approaches

and Australian courts apply different patterns of doctrinal approach and legal reasoning for this determination. While various doctrines and justifications are available in the English law, the Australian courts are relatively rigid in using the approach of jurisdictional error. For the Australian law, this shared theme, which was demonstrated in *Craig* and *Kirk*, appeared again in *Hossain*.[267] Two points can be demonstrated, as detailed below.

Firstly, the constitutional necessity in applying jurisdictional error in *Kirk* was duplicated in *Hossain*.[268] Explicitly, Kiefel CJ, Gageler J and Keane J pointed out that the concept of jurisdiction and the approach of jurisdictional error were necessary tools to express '*the constitutionally entrenched minimum content of the supervisory jurisdiction of a State Supreme Court to enforce the limits on the exercise of State executive*'.[269]

Secondly, although the doctrine of gravity of error and threshold of materiality have been mentioned, the operating approaches for determining the scope of judicial review remain the concept of jurisdiction and the consideration of statutory construction. The judgment of Kiefel CJ, Gageler J and Keane J reflected this at many junctures, for example,

> *In its* [jurisdiction's] *application to judicial review of administrative action the taking of which is authorised by statute, it refers to the scope of the authority which a statute confers on a decision-maker to make a decision of a kind to which the statute then attaches legal consequences…*[270]
>
> *The question of whether a particular failure to comply with an express or implied statutory condition in purporting to make a particular decision is of a magnitude which has resulted in taking the decision outside the jurisdiction conferred by the statute cannot be answered except by reference to the construction of the statute.*[271]

Also, jurisdictional error is applied as an approach that is compatible with the concept of jurisdiction and the application of statutory construction. Kiefel CJ, Gageler J and Keane J clarified this connection in their judgment, as follows;

> *Jurisdictional error…has come to be used to describe an error in a statutory decision-making process, correspondingly refers to a failure to comply with one or more statutory preconditions or conditions to an extent which results in a decision which has been made in fact lacking characteristics necessary for it to be given force and effect by the statute pursuant to which the decision-maker purported to make it.*[272]

Even Edelman J, who supported the concept of the threshold of materiality, also began to determine the scope of judicial review based on the considering the statutory construction, saying that,

---

[267] See also *Probuild Constructions (Aust) Pty Ltd v Shade Systems Pty Ltd* [2018] HCA 4 and *Maxcon Constructions Pty Ltd v Vadasz* [2018] HCA 5.
[268] n 19 [22].
[269] ibid [20].
[270] ibid [23].
[271] ibid [27].
[272] ibid [24].

The question is always one of construction of the legislation: which breaches of a provision does the legislation, either expressly or, more commonly, impliedly, treat as depriving the decision maker of power?[273]

Apart from this, the influence of the Australian legal culture was clearly illustrated in the legal reasoning of the judgment of Kiefel CJ, Gageler J and Keane J, who held that,

...the traditional distinction between jurisdictional and non-jurisdictional error cannot be avoided. The traditional distinction can be explained in more modern language. But an attempt to reframe the distinction in entirely new language is unlikely to be helpful.[274]

This well reflects that these approaches, namely the approach of jurisdictional error, the concept of jurisdiction and the application of statutory construction and legal reasoning, are not artificial, but rather products of the rigid legal mentality of Australian judicial review constitutionalism. This is the opposite of the English law, which gives individual judges the flexibility to adopt or avoid different approaches.

An additional point to examine is the academic discussion on this issue. It is evident that various aspects of the approach of jurisdictional error in the Australian law have been extensively debated. For example, Boughey and Crawford argue for the revision of some particular areas of law, such as the ambit of certiorari and injunction, in order to align it with the jurisdictional error approach and constitutional purpose.[275] Meanwhile, McDonald argues that jurisdictional error is pivotal, rather than central, because it is devoid of '*the variety of rules and principles those are enforced by judicial review*'.[276]

These debates are simplified by the analysis of the law through the lens of surface and deep-water legality and legal culture in this section. There is no doubt that, as Boughey and Crawford argue, '*In all three jurisdictions* [UK, Australia and Canada], ... *It is the role of Parliament to design and confer statutory executive power....and the courts must respect that choice*'.[277] This is the domain of the surface-water legality. The English and Australian courts similarly must respect Parliament's '*power to define the scope of statutory power as it thinks fit*' in the determination of the scope of judicial review.[278] Also, the establishment of quasi-judicial institutions as adjudicators for the specific area of public administration leads to calls to limit the role of the court in conducting judicial review.

However, at a deeper level, Boughey and Crawford continue to say that, '*The courts* [in the different countries]... *use different terms and labels and they do not all profess to identify the limits of statutory executive power in the same way*'.[279] It is demonstrated by the process of unpacking legal reasoning in the above cases that

---

[273] ibid [67].

[274] ibid [22].

[275] Crawford and Boughey, 'The Centrality of Jurisdictional Error: Rationale and Consequences' (n 8).

[276] McDonald (n 8).

[277] Boughey and Crawford, 'Jurisdictional Error: Do We Really Need It?' (n 8) 418.

[278] ibid 414.

[279] ibid 418.

3.4 Australian Doctrinal Approaches

the Australian courts apply a relatively rigid pattern of doctrinal approaches, namely the concept of jurisdiction, the approach of jurisdictional error and the consideration of statutory construction when making this determination.

More importantly, there is no disagreement in the literature that these approaches are connected to the Australian constitutional setting. For example, McDonald clearly states that jurisdictional error should be resisted because it marks the entrenchment of boundaries, especially those the courts have a duty to police by conducting judicial review.[280] In the same vein, Crawford and Boughey describe how the doctrine of jurisdictional error has become *'a device that coheres with the constitutional distribution of powers between Parliament and the courts'*.[281] Finally, according to Aronson;

> [Jurisdictional error] *used to apply only to judicial review of decisions of inferior courts, and that it used to have a very restricted meaning. From those early day, it now commands the whole field of common law judicial review in Australia.*[282]

This 'constitutional necessity' or 'constitutional requirement' of jurisdictional error has been extensively explored via the connotation of the Australian legal culture. Rather than referring to the twin concepts of parliamentary sovereignty and the rule of law, like the English law, the Australian courts understand their role as being to rigidly consider, refer to and follow the framework of separation of powers prescribed in the written constitution and statutory construction. This has become a simplified reason why Raad argues for the application of jurisdictional error in the way articulated by Mortimer J in his judgment in the Federal Court, rather than the requirement of materiality in *Hossain*,[283] or why McDonald argues for the application of the statutory approach, which can places Parliament and its statutes at the centre of the legal limits of administrative actions and, at the same time, redirects judicial creativity through an avowedly statutory channel.[284] Ultimately, this is because these scholars believe that these approaches flow well on the Australian river.

---

[280] McDonald (n 8).

[281] Crawford and Boughey, 'The Centrality of Jurisdictional Error: Rationale and Consequences' (n 8).

[282] Aronson, 'Jurisdictional Error and Beyond' (n 8) 249–250; See also Cheryl Saunders, 'Constitution as Catalyst: Different Paths within Australian Administrative Law' (2012) 10 NZJPIL; Simon Young and Sarah Murray, 'An Elegant Convergence? The Constitutional Entrenchment of 'Jurisdictional Error' Review in Australia' (2015) 11 Oxford University Commonwealth Law Journal 117.

[283] Raad (n 265).

[284] McDonald (n 8).

3.4.4 Products of the Australian Legal Culture

The aim of this section is to facilitate a more straightforward understanding of the laws in the light of their distinctive legal culture. Four points of the doctrinal approaches used to determine the scope of judicial review in *Craig*, *Kirk* and *Hossain* are unpacked and compared to the English law. Firstly, while the English courts can explain constitutional values in interpreting legislation restricting and justifying their jurisdiction of judicial review in various ways, the Australian courts do so in a relatively fixed way. For example, the rule of law is understood as emphasising the separation of powers, and being operated by a written constitution. Rigidly, legislative restrictions cannot operate in the way depriving the courts' jurisdiction according to the separation of powers. Secondly, rather than variation of doctrines, jurisdictional error has been applied as an entrenched doctrine in the determination of the scope of judicial review of tribunal and inferior court's decision. This is because it is compatible to the Australian judicial review geography. Thirdly, the application of jurisdictional error is considered from the framework of a written constitution and statutory construction. Fourthly, jurisdictional error becomes a central approach in deciding the scope of judicial review in Australia. Through the process of unpacking, all of these doctrinal approaches can be linked to the Australian legal culture in a clearer manner.

3.5 Conclusion

At the surface level, the scope of judicial review of decisions of quasi-judicial institutions is limited to a certain degree in both England and Australia. This can generally be explained by the fact that the courts have to respect the legislative power of parliament in granting authority to tribunals. On the other hand, it is the nature of common law that individual judges are able to adapt the determination of the scope of judicial review based on the particular context in order to fulfil their role in protecting the legality of administrative action. Therefore, there is also a degree of flexibility in both the English and Australian courts' determination of the scope of judicial review. The conclusory labels of pragmatism and formalism do not reveal very much in representing the English and Australian judicial review.

However, it is more interesting to learn that the English and Australian courts adhere to different modes of doctrinal approaches and legal reasoning in determining the scope of judicial review at the deeper level. In brief, for the English law, the courts have flexibility to consider the nature of the institution, interpret restrictive clauses and determine whether the tribunal's decision is covered by error of law or not based on the balance of parliamentary sovereignty and the rule of law. As for the Australian law, not only do the courts have to rigidly follow the framework of separation of powers prescribed in the written constitution and statutory construction in determining their jurisdiction, but the approach to do so is also confined to jurisdictional error. A snapshot of the examinations is provided in the table below.

3.5 Conclusion

Doctrinal approaches	English law	Australian law
Justifications	Directly influenced from elements in English judicial review constitutionalism	Directly influenced from elements in Australian judicial review constitutionalism
	But various ways by the individual judges in explaining them	Explained in relatively fixed way
Doctrines	Various between the individual judges namely	Entrenched at jurisdictional error (*Craig* and *Kirk*)
	Collateral fact theory/theory of limited review (pre-*Anisminic*)	
	Distinction between law and fact (*Anisminic*)	
	Jurisdictional error (*Cart*)	
	Judicial policy (*Cart*)	
	Second-tier appeal (*Cart*)	
	Doctrine of isolation (Lord Carnwath in *Privacy International*)	
	Detailed consideration of statutory construction (*Privacy International*)	
Applications	Varies and flexible depending on the doctrine	Rigidly considered from the framework of separation of powers, prescribed in the written constitution and statutory construction
Status of the ground	Error of law is adapted flexibly in the determination of the scope of judicial review including this area of judicial review of the decisions of tribunals and inferior courts	Jurisdictional error as entrenched and central approach in all areas of determination of the scope of judicial review
Nature of institution and legislative restriction	Considered in various ways by the individual judges	Answered in a relatively rigid way through the framework of separation of powers

Rather than argue whether the English approach is preferable to the Australian one or vice versa, the analysis in this chapter upholds a more inclusive understanding of the law by considering all the doctrinal approaches as being embedded in the English and Australian legal cultures. For the former, the various doctrinal approaches are the results of the nature of a balancing process between parliamentary sovereignty and the rule of law, the absence of an unwritten constitution and the fluid separation of powers. For the latter, the retention of jurisdictional error is influenced by the rigid legal mentality of the Australian legal culture.

As noted in Chap. 1, the fact that the English and Australian courts apply different doctrinal approaches and legal reasoning does not mean that the outcome in reality will also be different in parallel. To be specific, although jurisdictional error is entrenched and rigid in the Australian law, there are some situations in which remedies can be granted for non-jurisdictional errors,[285] as well as large areas where jurisdictional error is not restrictive, namely, the domain of the ADJR. However, it is still essential for academia to deeply explore the foundation of these different patterns of approaches and legal reasoning, particularly when they run in the same direction across the determination of all the common grounds of judicial review in England and Australia.

Other grounds of judicial review, namely jurisdictional fact, rationality, proportionality, substantive legitimate expectations will be examined in the next chapters. For example, various doctrinal approaches have been used flexibly to determine jurisdictional fact as an exceptional ground to review factual issues in the contemporary English cases. The relationship between jurisdictional fact and error of law is unclear and debatable; conversely, jurisdictional fact is an entrenched ground of judicial review and subset of jurisdictional error in Australia. All of these doctrinal approaches are also products of the English and Australian legal cultures. While this will strengthen the contrast between the flexibility of English judicial review and the relative rigidity of an Australian one, a comprehensive understanding cannot be complete without the process of unpacking and diving into deep-water.

---

[285] See *Project Blue Sky v Australian Broadcasting Authority* (1998) 194 CLR 355; *Wingfoot Australia Partners Pty Ltd v Kocak* (2013) 252 CLR 480.

Chapter 4
Influence of the Legal Cultures on Jurisdictional Fact

Abstract Although jurisdictional fact is a ground of judicial review in both England and Australia, its doctrinal approaches are different in these legal systems, as will be demonstrated in this chapter. In terms of the English law, the status and application of the ground are shown to fluctuate in the legal reasoning of cases such as *R v Secretary of State for the Home Department, Ex p Khawaja* [1984] AC 74 (HL), *E v Secretary of State for the Home Department* [2004] EWCA Civ 49, *R (A) v Croydon LBC* [2009] UKSC 8 and *R (Jones) v First-tier Tribunal* [2013] UKSC 19. The analysed distinctive elements of English legal culture were reflected in the pattern of flexible doctrinal approaches and legal reasoning applied in these cases. Conversely, the ground is far more entrenched with a relatively clear application in defining an issue as jurisdictional error in Australia. This is because the approach functions well within the Australian landscape. This was mainly demonstrated by the legal reasoning in *Timbarra Protection Coalition Inc. v Ross Mining NL & Ors* (1999) 46 NSW LR 55 and *Corporation of the City of Enfield v Development Assessment Commission* (2000) 199 CLR 135.

4.1 Introduction

> *Where the existence or non-existence of a fact is left to the judgment and discretion of a public body…, it is duty of the court to leave the decision of that fact to the public body to whom Parliament has entrusted the decision-making power…* (Lord Brightman, *Puhlhofer v Hillingdon London Borough Council*)[1]

> *The standard grounds of judicial review disclaim review on the merits, or review simply for factual error…Generally speaking, judicial review is not available to correct factual error…* (Justice Weinberg, *Cabal v Attorney-General of the Commonwealth*)[2]

The different doctrinal approaches applied by the English and Australian courts in determining the scope of judicial review of a quasi-judicial institution's decision on

---

[1] [1986] 1 AC 484, 518.
[2] [2001] FCA 583 [49].

© The Author(s), under exclusive license to Springer Nature Singapore Pte Ltd. 2021
V. Malsukhum, *Legal Culture, Legality and the Determination of the Grounds of Judicial Review of Administrative Action in England and Australia*,
https://doi.org/10.1007/978-981-16-1267-1_4

the grounds of error of law and jurisdictional error were examined in the previous chapter. It was found that the flexibility of English law and the entrenchment of Australian law were influenced by the English and Australian legal cultures respectively. Hence, the purpose of this chapter is to explore the influence of these legal cultures on another area with a similar root, namely, the scope of judicial review of a factual issue.

The above statements of Lord Brightman of the HL and Justice Weinberg of the Federal Court of Australia clearly describe the principles similarly applied by the English and Australian laws on a surface level. Generally, the courts do not conduct judicial review of the factual issues of an administrative action.[3] However, in some situations, they consider that some kinds of fact make an administrative action unlawful and claim the jurisdiction to conduct judicial review of them. Jurisdictional fact appears as such a ground of judicial review,[4] indicating unlawful and reviewable factual issues in both England and Australia. The courts determine the legality of factual determination by considering whether Parliament pre-conditionally requires it through the act to be reviewed and, if they consider that it does, they have the jurisdiction to conduct judicial review of the rejection or misinterpretation of the evidence related to that jurisdictional fact.[5]

However, the English and the Australian courts have different ways in determining jurisdictional fact as a ground of judicial review. On the one hand, Lord Hope stated in *R (Jones) v First-tier Tribunal* that *'a pragmatic approach should be taken to the dividing line between law and fact...'*.[6] As discussed in the previous chapters, although the label of 'pragmatic' or 'pragmatism' is conclusory and cannot represent the entire picture of English law, it can 'superficially' indicate flexibility of the English approach in determining the scope of judicial review. Jurisdictional fact has been determined by the various doctrinal approaches in different cases. On the other hand, the transcript seeking leave to appeal the case to the HCA in *Timbarra* below demonstrates that jurisdictional fact has been an entrenched ground of judicial review, under the central approach of jurisdictional error in Australia.

---

[3] The general principles supporting this position are described in Sect. 4.2 below.

[4] As discussed in Sect. 1.4 of Chap. 1, jurisdictional fact can be defined by various statuses, such as ground, doctrine or approach, all of which refer to the same thing, namely, the rule the courts apply to determine their jurisdiction of judicial review.

[5] See Mark Leeming, *Authority to Decide: the Law of Jurisdiction in Australia* (2nd edn, The Federation Press 2020) 13; Robin Creyke, John McMillan and Mark Smyth, *Control of Government Action; Text, Cases and Commentary* (5th edn, LexisNexis Butterworths 2019) [13.3.9]; Mark Aronson, Matthew Groves and Greg Weeks, *Judicial Review of Administrative Action and Government Liability* (6th edn, Thomson Reuters Australia 2017) [4.470]; Linda Pearson, 'Jurisdictional Fact: a Dilemma for the Courts' (2000) 17 Environmental and Planning Law Journal 453; Paul Craig, 'Judicial Review, Appeal and Factual Error' [2004] PL 788, 795; Peter Cane and Leighton McDonald, *Principles of Administrative Law: Legal Regulation of Governance* (3rd edn, OUP 2018) 182; William Wade and Christopher Forsyth, *Administrative Law* (11th edn, OUP 2014) 208, 234.

[6] [2013] UKSC 19 [16].

4.1 Introduction

Mr Flick: The consequence of this decision is that the fact in issue there... becomes a fact which is reviewable on the merits. It is a fact which becomes open to scrutiny by a superior court...

Justice Gummow: That depends on whether it is a jurisdictional fact....

The principles as to how one determines whether something is a jurisdictional fact are settled...[7]

The frameworks of legal culture and deep-water legality will be utilised in this chapter in an attempt to comprehensively understand these different approaches. The examination will be structured in the same way as the previous chapter. The reason for making jurisdictional fact the focus of this chapter will be explained in Sect. 4.2. After that, flexibility of the justifications and applications which the English courts apply to determine jurisdictional fact as a ground of judicial review will be unpacked in Sect. 4.3, from the legal reasoning in *R v Secretary of State for the Home Department, Ex parte Khawaja,*[8] *E v Secretary of State for the Home Department,*[9] *(R) A v Croydon LBC,*[10] until the described '*pragmatic distinction between law and fact*' in *Jones.*[11] In terms of comparison, the legal reasoning in *Timbarra Protection Coalition Inc v Ross Mining NL & Ors,*[12] *Corporation of the City of Enfield v Development Assessment Commission*[13] and later cases, namely *Anvil Hill Project Watch Association Inc v Minister for the Environment and Water Resources*[14] and *Plaintiff M 70/2011 v Minister for Immigration and Citizenship,*[15] will be unpacked in Sect. 4.4 to demonstrate that the Australian courts have relatively fixed justifications and applications in regarding jurisdictional fact as an entrenched ground of judicial review.[16]

Importantly, such flexibility and entrenchment will also be connected to the English and Australian legal cultures. In fact, this kind of connection between doctrinal approaches and the constitutional order of the legal systems has been mentioned by some judges and scholars. The prominent example is Justice Kirby of the HCA, who made the following statement in the transcript of legal argument of *Enfield;*

---

[7] The Transcript of legal argument in *Timbarra Protection Coalition Inc Ross Mining NL & Ors* (1999) 46 NSW LR 55.

[8] [1984] AC 74.

[9] [2004] EWCA Civ 49.

[10] [2009] UKSC 8.

[11] n 6. These cases are cited by judges and scholars as leading cases in this area, for example, Paul Craig, *Administrative Law* (8th edn, Sweet & Maxwell 2016) Chapter 17; Mark Elliott and Jason Varuhas, *Administrative Law: Text and Materials* (5th edn, OUP 2017) 65–81.

[12] (1999) 46 NSW LR 55.

[13] (2000) 199 CLR 135.

[14] [2007] FCA 1480.

[15] [2011] HCA 32.

[16] These cases are widely cited by scholars as leading cases in this area, for example, Creyke, McMillan and Smyth (n 5) [13.3.9]–[13.3.19]; Mark Aronson, 'The Resurgence of Jurisdictional Facts' (2001) 12 Public Law Review 17.

> ...they come from a different history and have a different purpose, and though there is a discretion at the end of each of them, they just have to proceed in a different way. That is not the first time that has happened in the inherited law from England.[17]

An in-depth examination of this statement will be made in this chapter by unpacking the different ways in which the English and Australian courts determine jurisdictional fact from the legal reasoning of leading cases, and connecting them to their 'different history and purpose' based on the concept of legal culture.

Finally, the general statement of the book that the legal cultures of England and Australia deeply influence their courts' determination of the grounds of judicial review will be affirmed in the last section. Additionally, jurisdictional fact is also connected to the analysis in the previous chapter. While the relationship between jurisdictional fact and error of law is non-fixed and debatable in English law, it is clear that jurisdictional fact is a subset of jurisdictional error in the Australian legal system. Furthermore, some of the associations between jurisdictional fact and the grounds related to the substantive exercise of discretion will be introduced in the final section of this chapter and analysed in the next.

4.2 Judicial Review of Factual Issues at Surface and Deep Levels

Parallel to the previous chapter, there is a tension between two sets of arguments related to the scope of judicial review of factual issues at the surface level of English and Australian law. On the one hand, the courts should not conduct judicial review because factual determinations are an area of administrative authority; on the other hand, the courts justify their jurisdiction to conduct judicial review of some factual issues by their role to protect the rule of law. They then need to elaborate lines to indicate the factual issues that need to be reviewed and these are different in the English and Australian law based on the different legal cultures. Through the deep-water perspective, the determination of jurisdictional fact as a ground of judicial review demonstrates this prominently.

4.2.1 Distinction Between Law and Fact

In addition to Lord Brightman's quote at the beginning of this chapter, the distinction between law and fact has been stated in a number of English cases. This approach is a continuation of the premise in *Anisminic*, which was analysed in the previous chapter. As Craig concludes, '*The effect of Anisminic, as interpreted in*

---

[17] The Transcript of legal argument in *Corporation of the City of Enfield v Development Assessment Commission* (2000) 199 CLR 135.

Racal, O'Reilly and *Page*, is that all errors of law became susceptible to review'.[18] However, the courts will leave factual and discretionary issues to the executive to decide. For example, Lord Hailsham made the following statement in *Chief Constable of the North Wales Police v Evans;*

> It is not intended to take away from those authorities the powers and discretions properly vested in them by law and to substitute the courts as the bodies making the decisions.[19]

This principle has also been recognised by scholars; for example, Cane stated that

> Traditionally, bodies exercising judicial review jurisdiction or hearing an appeal on a point of law have been reluctant to hold decisions and rules illegal on the basis of factual errors. In other words, they have given administrators more freedom in deciding issues of fact than in deciding issues of law.[20]

Likewise, apart from Justice Weinberg's statement at the start of this chapter, Chief Justice Mason of the HCA also made this assertion in *Australian Broadcasting Tribunal v Bond*[21] by citing Justice Brennan in *Waterford v The Commonwealth* stating that *'There is no error of law simply in making a wrong finding of fact'*,[22] and Justice Menzies, who made the following statement in *R v The District Court, Ex parte White;*

> Even if the reasoning whereby the Court reached its conclusion of fact were demonstrably unsound, this would not amount to an error of law on the face of record. To establish some faulty (e.g. illogical) inference of fact would not disclose an error of law.[23]

Australian scholars like Aronson, Groves and Weeks also mention this distinction, as follows;

> One of the most fundamental distinction in legal doctrine is that between law and fact.... Statutory mechanisms for seeking judicial correction of tribunals and other decision-makers are frequently restricted to correction for errors of law, not fact.[24]

Similarly, Creyke, McMillan and Smyth observe that *'Law/fact is now deeply rooted in public law'*.[25] However, this premise is usually presented in Australian literature in terms of the distinction between legality and merits rather than between law and fact.[26] Indeed, they have a 'similar implication at the surface level'. A factual evaluation can be considered as the merits part of an administrative decision, while a legal issue refers to the legality. As Creyke, McMillan and Smyth explain,

---

[18] Craig (n 11) [16–039]; See also Wade and Forsyth (n 5) 219–234; Timothy Endicott, *Administrative Law* (4th edn, OUP 2018) 319–330.

[19] [1982] 1 WLR 1155, 1160; See also *Piglowska v Piglowski* [1999] 1 WLR 1360, 1362.

[20] Peter Cane, *Administrative Law* (5th edn, OUP 2011) 182.

[21] (1990) 170 CLR 321 [88].

[22] (1987) 163 CLR 54, 77.

[23] (1966) 116 CLR 644, 654.

[24] Aronson, Groves and Weeks (n 5) [4.10].

[25] Creyke, McMillan and Smyth (n 5) [13.5.29].

[26] This starts moving into the territory of deep-water legality, which is fully discussed in Sect. 4.4 below.

The law/fact distinction permeates judicial review in two ways. First, judicial review is anchored in the legality/merits distinction, which is itself rooted in the difference between judicial and executive functions. The former is concerned with resolving disputed legal issues, often to do with the meaning of legislation. The latter is primarily concerned with applying legislation to the facts in the context of administrative decision-making, frequently involving the ascertainment and clarification of disputed or unclear facts.[27]

In short, whether presented in relation to law and fact or legality and merits, the English and Australian courts do not generally conduct judicial review of the factual determination in an administrative action. The reasons for this limitation have been widely discussed, but they can be conceptualised as two limbs, the first of which is simply related to democracy. Based on the separation of powers in general term, parliament entrusts and delegates the evaluation of facts to the administrative authority; therefore, it would be disrespectful of the legitimacy of parliament for the courts to assume the role of decision-makers.[28]

The second limb is related to the institutional competence of the executive. Because of their expertise and experience in specific fields of public administration, particularly technical ones, such as industrial law, trademarks and professional discipline,[29] administrative agents can better understand and interpret a factual reference in using a rule than judges.[30] In addition, if the court overturns the decision, it has to restart the entire process of gathering and analysing evidence relevant to the finding of facts. This is not only resource and time-consuming, but it also has an impact on correctly evaluating the facts.[31] Since facts are naturally complex and repeated by way of a historical narrative, no two-people perceive the same facts in precisely the same way.[32] When the decision-makers examine the facts before the courts, they find inevitable differences in the material placed before them. Although it is the same material, its meaning and evaluation differ based on the varied experience and backgrounds of the court and the decision-makers. Reverting back to the issue of the expertise of administrative agents, there is no reason to believe that the court can identify the facts more accurately through a judicial hearing than the decision-maker can through a fact-finding process.

It is evident that the democratic and institutional competences of the executive in determining factual issues are parallel to the reasons that limit the scope of judicial review of the decision of tribunals and inferior courts, which were analysed in the

---

[27] Creyke, McMillan and Smyth (n 5) [13.3.1].

[28] Jeffrey Jowell, 'Of Vires and Vacuums: The Constitutional Context of Judicial Review' in Christopher Forsyth (ed), *Judicial Review and the Constitution* (Hart Publishing 2000); Aronson, Groves and Weeks (n 5) [4.20].

[29] E.g. Fisher explains that an Environmental Impact Assessment is a process that involves the consideration of scientific fact, public participation and public administration (Elizabeth Fisher, '"Jurisdictional" Facts and "Hot" Facts: Legal Formalism, Legal Pluralism, and the Nature of Australian Administrative Law' (2015) 38 Melbourne University Law Review 968). See also Creyke, McMillan and Smyth (n 5) [7.5.13]–[7.5.16], [13.5.3].

[30] Aronson, Groves and Weeks (n 5) [4.20].

[31] Cane (n 20) 182–183.

[32] Endicott (n 18) 341–343.

4.2 Judicial Review of Factual Issues at Surface and Deep Levels   147

previous chapter. Likewise, these reasons are explained through the concept of deference in some of the literature.[33] As mentioned earlier, the language of deference is uncertain and fluctuates in different legal systems; therefore, it is not the focus of this chapter. However, judges' perception of deference can be an additional indicator of the influence of legal cultures. An obvious example will be shown in the sections below, while the concept of deference is debatable in English law, the HCA firmly rejected it in the determination of the jurisdictional fact in *Enfield*. These are also explainable through the English and Australian legal cultures.[34]

4.2.2 Courts' Reviews of Some Kinds of Fact

At this juncture, the general premise has been demonstrated that the English and Australian courts shall not conduct judicial review of the factual aspects of administrative action. However, this is not the only aspect at the surface level of the scope of judicial review of factual issues in England and Australia. In actual fact, the courts frequently claim their jurisdiction to re-gather facts or re-determine some factual issues based on the premise that *'The result can be as unjust when an administrative body gets the facts wrong as when it gets the law wrong'*.[35] Therefore, the courts have a role to conduct a judicial review of such factual issues in the name of protecting the rule of law.

This position has been generally described by English judges and scholars. For example, Wade and Forsyth cite a number of English cases in asserting that *'Certain mistakes of fact can carry an administrative authority or tribunal outside its jurisdiction'*.[36] Hence, the judicial control of a factual issue of administrative action *'promotes the rule of law'*.[37] In the same vein, Cane contends that *'In general, the law requires administrators to answer questions of fact consistently with relevant available evidence'*.[38] Likewise, in Australia, a judicial review of the determination of the fact is also justified by the rationale of the rule of law. For example, in *Bond*, Justice Mason stated that *'to expose all findings of fact, or the generality of them, to judicial review would expose the steps in administrative decision-making to*

---

[33] Matthew Lewans, *Administrative Law and Judicial Deference* (Hart Publishing 2016) 5; Aronson, Groves and Weeks (n 5) [4.40]–[4.60].

[34] In English law, the validity in debating the concept of deference is obvious in the area of judicial review of discretion, particularly on proportionality. This will be connected to the English legal culture in the next chapter.

[35] Endicott (n 18) 341.

[36] Wade and Forsyth (n 5) 208 by citing *Terry v Huntington* (1679) Hardr 480.

[37] Endicott (n 18) 356.

[38] Cane (n 20) 182.

comprehensive review by the courts...'.[39] Creyke, McMillan and Smyth also contend that *'A decision that is based on an incorrect fact can be an unfair decision...'*.[40]

4.2.3 Understanding Jurisdictional Fact by Means of Deep-Water Legality

The two sets of general principles in determining the scope of judicial review of factual issues have been described up to this point. While the courts are justified in conducting judicial review of factual issues based on the rule of law, the democratic reasons and institutional competences of the executives make them hesitate to do so. The implication is that the courts in most legal systems, including those of England and Australia, have to establish a line by which to determine whether or not the disputed factual issue needs to be reviewed, and they do so based on the logic of legality. As Cane stated, *'...not all errors of fact are errors of law* [in the sense that brings illegality to an administrative action]*'*.[41] The court will only conduct judicial review of a factual determination when it is 'unlawful'. Therefore, 'the scope of judicial review of a factual issue' is dependent upon 'the court's understanding of what legality shall cover'.

Among the grounds of judicial review of a factual issue, there are some which are 'not controversial' in terms of whether or not the court has jurisdiction to conduct judicial review. The prominent one is the *'No Evidence Rule'*, which is applicable when there is no evidence (at all) to satisfy the statutory element of the decision. The English and Australian courts similarly justify their scope of judicial review of this kind of factual issue.[42] The factual determination that lack of evidence is undoubtedly unlawful. This ground is commonly 'included in the courts' understanding of legality', and not the focus of the following sections, since the courts do not need deep-water, but merely surface-water legality to determine their scope of judicial review.

Instead, the focus of the next sections will be the grounds of judicial review of factual issues which are 'controversial' based on whether the court has the jurisdiction to conduct judicial review or not. Jurisdictional fact is specifically selected for a close examination in this chapter among various grounds in this middle area of the spectrum.[43] This is because its definition in general sense is similar in England and

---

[39] n 21 [44].

[40] Creyke, McMillan and Smyth (n 5) [13.1.2].

[41] Cane (n 20) 180.

[42] For English law, see *R v Criminal Injuries Compensation Board, Ex parte A* [1999] 2 AC 330. For Australian law, see *The Queen v Australian Stevedoring Industry Board, Ex parte Melbourne Stevedoring Co Pty Ltd* (1953) 88 CLR 100.

[43] The other grounds in this group relate to the ones of the substantive exercise of discretion. The different kinds of relationship between them and jurisdictional fact in England and Australia can also be tracked by the legal cultures. This will be discussed in detail in the next chapter.

Australia, relating to a review of the 'objective fact', whether the court considers that the statute requires the factual reference to be reviewed or not. However, as mentioned earlier, the English and Australian courts have different ways of determining jurisdictional fact as a ground of judicial review. The Australian courts are relatively entrenched in their determination, while the English courts adopt a more flexible approach.

Most scholars discuss the different approaches of the English and Australian law in terms of their advantages and disadvantages. For example, Williams argues that the line distinguishing jurisdictional from non-jurisdictional fact in England is unclear, and thus, needs to be restructured.[44] Elliott, Varuhas and Craig debate whether or not jurisdictional fact should be replaced by the four criteria established in *E*.[45] In Australia, although the validity of the ground has been entrenched, some scholars have also commented on its application. For example, Aronson points out that jurisdictional fact has been developed in a way that threatens the framework of the separation of powers by enabling the courts to expand their jurisdiction without considering the statutory construction.[46] The following sections do not contain this kind of functional analysis; instead, they slightly revert to the foundation exemplifying that these different doctrinal approaches are the result of the different English and Australian (deep-water) understanding of legality, as embedded in their different legal cultures.

4.3 English Doctrinal Approaches

It is demonstrated by the analysis in this section that the distinctive process in which the courts in *Khawaja*, *E*, *R (A) v Croydon* and *Jones* applied various malleable justifications and applications to determine the status of jurisdictional fact as a ground of judicial review is connected to the flexible English legal culture.

4.3.1 Prior to E

Before *Anisminic*, jurisdictional fact had been applied in the English law in parallel to the distinction between jurisdictional and non-jurisdictional error. If the court considered a factual reference as a pre-condition required by the statute and the administrative agencies failed to satisfy it, the court conducted a judicial review and

---

[44] Rebecca Williams, 'When is an Error not an Error? Reform of Jurisdictional Review of Error of Law and Fact' [2007] PL 793.

[45] This will be exemplified below.

[46] Aronson (n 16).

quashed the administrative action.[47] Afterwards, as discussed in the previous chapter, the judgments in *Anisminic* and *Page* abandoned the distinction between jurisdictional and non-jurisdictional error, and adopted the approach that all errors of law are jurisdictional errors. Therefore, whether or not jurisdictional fact remains a valid ground of judicial review is questionable.

Generally, jurisdictional fact has been categorised by scholars as a valid ground of judicial review by referring to *Khawaja*.[48] In this case, the appellant was an immigrant from India, who had been granted an entry certificate to the UK in 1974. However, he did not disclose the fact that he had been married in 1973 and this was only discovered later. At this point, an immigration order was made detaining the appellant as *'an illegal entrant'*, defined by Section 33(1) of the Immigration Act 1971 as *'a person unlawfully entering or seeking to enter in breach of a deportation order or of the immigration laws, and includes also a person who has so entered'*. Then, the appellant sought a judicial review from the court to quash this factual determination regarding him as an illegal entrant.[49]

It was clear from the judgments of this case that the scope of judicial review was determined through the ground of jurisdictional fact. When reviewing the phrase *'illegal entrant'*, the court considered whether its function had been delegated by parliament or not. For example, by referring to cases like *R v Secretary for the Home Department, Ex parte Zamir*, which Lord Fraser made the following statement;

> On this question,...an immigration officer is only entitled to order the detention and removal of a person who has entered to the country by virtue of an ex facie valid permission if the person is an illegal entrant. That is a "precedent fact" which has to be established.[50]

Lord Wilberforce also clarified this with the following assertion;

> The main argument on this part of the case [Zamir] was that cases where it was sought to remove an "illegal entrant" were part of a category of "precedent fact" cases – where an administrative discretion exists if, but only if, some precedent fact is established to exist, and the existence of which is independently triable by a court...The present, as other illegal entrant cases, does involve the making of a finding of fact by the administration as can be seen by an examination of the administrative process.[51]

In terms of justification, the two sets of arguments supporting and limiting the courts' jurisdiction in conducting judicial review were described in the judgments. For example, Lord Wilberforce mentioned the following;

> How far can, or should, the court find the facts for itself, how far should it accept, or consider itself bound to accept, or entitled to accept, the findings of the administrative authorities? On principle one would expect that, on the one hand, the court, exercising powers of review, would not act as a court of appeal or attempt to try or retry the issue. On the other

---

[47] E.g. *White and Collins v Minister of Health* [1939] 2 KB 838; *R v Fulham, Hammersmith and Kensington Rent Tribunal, Ex parte Zerek* [1951] 2 KB 1.
[48] Williams (n 44) 794–795.
[49] n 8, 95–98.
[50] [1980] AC 930 in ibid 97D-97F.
[51] ibid 99F-100B; See also 106E-109F (Lord Scarman).

4.3 English Doctrinal Approaches

hand, since the critical conclusion of fact is one reached by an administrative authority (as opposed to a judicial body) the court would think it proper to review it in order to see whether it was properly reached, not only as a matter of procedure, but also in substance and in law.[52]

It was emphasised in the conclusion of the judgment that

...whatever the theory may be, the courts have in general been willing and able to review for themselves the factual basis...They are dictated, on the other hand, by the fact that of necessity extensive fact-finding operations have to be carried out by the immigration authorities which cannot be repeated by the reviewing court....[53]

Likewise, Lord Scarman declared that

The principle formulated was that the courts will not intervene to quash the decision of a statutory authority unless it can be shown that authority erred in law, was guilty or a breach of natural justice or acted "unreasonably"[54]

On the other hand, the judge made the following assertion;

The court's duty is to examine into the truth of the facts set forth in the return... where the exercise of executive power depends upon the precedent establishment of an objective fact, the courts will decide whether the requirement has been satisfied.[55]

In terms of the application, Lord Wilberforce considered whether the factual determination in the present case was a jurisdictional fact or not by comparing it to the context in the other cases.[56] He concluded that '...*they* [the determinations in cases] *have not always consistently or correctly stated the basis on which such review should be made*'.[57] Lord Bridge supported this conclusion by stating that '...*all of these approaches rely upon the statutory juxtaposition of the immigration officer's power to refuse leave to enter and thereupon to order removal of the unsuccessful aspiring entrant...*'.[58]

In short, jurisdictional fact was implicitly accepted as a valid ground of judicial review in *Khawaja* and it was reasoned by two sets of values, namely the rule of law and the institutional competence of the decision-maker. However, the application how the judges identified the factual reference as a jurisdictional fact was not explained in detail, only that it depended on the situation.[59] Then, it was concluded that, in this case, the court had the jurisdiction to review the determination of the phrase *'illegal errant'*, since it was a precedent fact. Therefore, the court could

---

[52] ibid 101A-101D.

[53] ibid 104E-104G.

[54] ibid 109G-109H.

[55] ibid 110D-110F; See also 120E-120G (Lord Bridge).

[56] ibid 101D-104E.

[57] ibid 104G-104H.

[58] ibid 121H-122A.

[59] This particularly applies when compared with later English cases, as well as Australian cases, as will be revealed in the next sections.

require the submission or rejection of evidence related to the interpretation of this phrase.[60]

After *Khawaja*, there were a few cases in which the courts applied jurisdictional fact to indicate that the factual determination was reviewable.[61] However, the application of jurisdictional fact was still not certain in these cases. Subsequently, Lord Justice Carnwath established the criteria for the court to review certain factual issues in *E*. Since then, there has been a debate about whether this new approach in *E* replaces jurisdictional fact like the way *Anisminic* replaced jurisdictional error.

4.3.2 *E*

The appellants in *E* applied for asylum in the UK, but the application was declined by the Secretary of State for the Home Department. Afterward, new objective evidence related to the determination of the facts became available during the hearing and the date of promulgation in the process of appeal to the Immigration Appeal Tribunal ('IAT')[62] and the appellants presented it.[63] However, the IAT refused to consider this new evidence,[64] whereupon the case was taken to the CA on the ground that an important part of the IAT's decision was based on ignorance or mistaken facts.[65]

The issue in this case was that the IAA limits the right to appeal to the CA merely on a *'point of law'*.[66] Rather than applying jurisdictional fact like the judges in *Khawaja* did, Lord Justice Carnwath established a new approach to determine whether or not the re-submission of evidence related to the determination of the factual reference was included in his understanding of legality (regarded as a *'point of law'*). This demonstrates that the English courts can be relatively flexible in determining the scope of judicial review of factual issues. How this flexibility in the doctrinal approaches is connected to the English legal culture is discussed under three points below.

Firstly, Lord Justice Carnwath presented two sets of arguments in justifying and limiting the scope of judicial review, but he used terminologies that were different from those used in *Khawaja*. On the one hand, he mentioned *'the principle of finality'*, which meant that the court should respect the factual determination of the

---

[60] n 8, 97D-98E, 105B-106B, 113F-114D, 125H-126B, 128B-129C.

[61] For example, *Puhlhofer* (n 1) and *Dowty Boulton Paul Ltd v Wolverhampton Corporation (No 2)* [1976] Ch13.

[62] Under Part III of Schedule 4 of the Immigration and Asylum Act 1999 ('IAA').

[63] n 9 [6]–[9].

[64] ibid [11].

[65] ibid [1].

[66] Paragraph 23 of Schedule 4 of the IAA Act and paragraph 30 (2)(c) of the Immigration and Asylum Appeals (Procedure) Rules 2003.

4.3 English Doctrinal Approaches

decision-maker and the IAT, because their power was conferred on them by parliament.[67] On the other hand, the determination of the IAT needed to be supervised by the court because there was *'a risk of serious injustice, because...some important evidence which had been overlooked'*.[68] Furthermore, the balancing process was explicitly conducted in the judgment. For example, it held that the court's intervention in the administrative factual determination should be limited to law.[69] By this, the courts should only conduct judicial review of the serious factual determinations.[70] Although it was not as clearly expressed as it was in *Cart*, this legal reasoning reflected the twin concepts of parliamentary sovereignty and the rule of law. On the one hand, the rule of law justifies the court's conduct of a judicial review of some factual issues of administrative action; on the other hand, the jurisdiction is limited because the executives' authority to determine the facts, as delegated by Parliament, shall be final.

Secondly, Lord Justice Carnwath admitted that it was *'paradoxical'* for the court to find a fixed doctrine in dividing law and fact.[71] He described various doctrines that had been applied for this purpose; for example, the no evidence rule in *R v Criminal Injuries Compensation Board, Ex parte A*[72] and the misunderstanding or ignorance of an established and relevant fact in *Secretary of State for Education and Science v Tameside Metropolitan Borough Council*.[73] He also attempted to relate a breach of the rules of natural justice in factual determination to unfairness.[74] Importantly, Lord Justice Carnwath explained that the court can be flexible in applying these doctrines in particular cases, namely that *'...the application of these principles will vary according to the power or duty under review...'*.[75]

Apart from consolidating all the possible grounds for the court to determine whether or not a factual question is within the scope of judicial review, Lord Justice Carnwath also 'rearranged' four criteria in a new application that related factual determination to 'unfairness' as follows;

> First, there must have been a mistake as to an existing fact, including a mistake as to the availability of evidence on a particular matter.
> Secondly, the fact or evidence must have been "established", in the sense that it was uncontentious and objectively verifiable.
> Thirdly, the appellant must not been have responsible for the mistake.

---

[67] n 9 [29], [35].

[68] ibid [35].

[69] ibid [40], [42]–[43].

[70] ibid [38].

[71] ibid [44].

[72] [1999] 2 AC 330 in ibid [45].

[73] [1977] AC 1014 in n 9 [46].

[74] n 9 [48]–[49].

[75] ibid [43]. It is recognised that the quasi-judicial nature of a tribunal was also a factor in this consideration. This also demonstrates the flexibility of the English law, which will become more obvious in the discussion of *Jones* below.

Fourthly, the mistake must have played a material part in the tribunal's reasoning.[76]

Furthermore, Lord Justice Carnwath added a degree of flexibility to these criteria by saying that they are applied differently in different areas of public law.[77] He argued that *'the context was important'*;[78] therefore, this doctrine was an exception to the traditional one that was applied to a review of the submission of evidence in other cases.[79]

This variation of doctrines not only reveals the way in which legality can be flexibly understood by the English courts, but it also leads to a third point related to the validity of jurisdictional fact as a ground of judicial review. Although Lord Justice Carnwath did not specifically mention *'jurisdictional fact'* in the judgment, the second and fourth criteria, namely *'objective'* and *'play a material part in the tribunal's reasoning'*, are akin to identifying a reviewable precedent fact. This will be obvious in the next section, since they are parallel to the criteria of *'objectivity'* and *'essentiality'* in determining the jurisdictional fact in *Timbarra* and *Enfield* based on Australian law. These doctrinal approaches demonstrate the English courts' flexibility in determining the validity of the grounds of judicial review of factual issues. Rather than being fixed on jurisdictional fact, the criteria Lord Justice Carnwath applied in *E*, which looked like those used to review jurisdictional fact, were explained in terms of the doctrine of unfairness.

4.3.3 After E

After that, the application in *E* was applied in later cases,[80] apart from which, the relationship between jurisdictional fact and the criteria in *E* has been widely debated by scholars. For example, Wade and Forsyth categorise the criteria in *E* as a ground for reviewing factual issues apart from jurisdictional fact. The courts will conduct a judicial review when an erroneous and decisive fact is either jurisdictional, based on no evidence or unfair.[81] In the same vein, Elliott and Varuhas described the approach in *E* in the section of *'Supervision of the Fact-finding Process'*, apart from jurisdictional fact in the section of *'Applying Statutory Criteria to the Facts'*.[82] Craig also explains the existing law as follows;

> ...if the claimant can show that the error concerns a jurisdictional fact then the court will review the determination and will not require the claimant to prove the four criteria in the

---

[76] ibid [66].
[77] ibid [72].
[78] ibid [74].
[79] E.g. the *'Ladd v Marshall Principle'*, which is strictly applied in asylum cases (ibid [68]–[70]).
[80] E.g. *R (Tran) v Secretary of State for the Home Department* [2005] EWCA Civ 982.
[81] Wade and Forsyth (n 5) 234.
[82] Elliott and Varuhas (n 11) 65–76.

4.3 English Doctrinal Approaches

E case. In other instances the claimant must show that the four criteria in the E case have been met.[83]

However, in terms of functionality, Craig suggests that the criteria of unfairness in *E* should be *'the default position'* for the consideration of all kinds of errors of fact. This is mainly explained by the appropriateness of the judicial function in conducting judicial review.[84] Interestingly, Craig links this to legality in the following statement;

The reality is that the conception of "legality" within judicial review is used as a label to cover a variety of more specific grounds of challenge relating to the rule of law. The courts have on a number of previous occasions forged the link between factual mistake and error of law in order to facilitate judicial intervention.[85]

Instead of using the existing categorisation of the grounds of judicial review, Craig argues that *'...the reasoning in the E case was following a well-trodden path'*[86] based on its characteristic of balance;

It is important to be mindful of the respective roles of courts and initial decision-makers in deciding whether a factual error has occurred. There are...well-developed tests for maintaining judicial control over facts without the courts thereby assuming the role of primary fact-finder.[87]

In other words, Craig argues that the approach in *E* is 'advantageous' for searching for 'legality' in particular cases because it well balances the tension between judicial and executive functions in deciding factual issues.

Although corresponding with Craig's argument, this section has a different purpose. Rather than finding a solution to what the English approach should be like, it is emphasised that the flexibility between jurisdictional fact and the criteria in *E*, as well as all the academic debates, is embedded in the flexibility accorded to the English courts to understand legality. This 'deep understanding of legality' is rooted in the nature of English law, which will be clearly demonstrated in the next section with a comparison of Australian law, in which the validity of jurisdictional fact is much more entrenched based on the Australian legal culture. *R (A) v Croydon* is another case that demonstrates the fluctuation of English law in determining jurisdictional fact. Rather than following the approach in *E*, the judgments reintroduced jurisdictional fact in reviewing a precedent fact, but developed a clearer application than *Khawaja*.

---

[83] Craig (n 11) [17–019].
[84] ibid [17–014]-[17–035].
[85] ibid [17–018].
[86] ibid.
[87] ibid [17–036].

4.3.3.1 R (A) v Croydon

The appellants in *R (A) v Croydon* claimed that they were less than 18 years of age and were thus eligible for accommodation provided by the National Asylum Support Service under the Children's Act 1989. However, their claim was refused for the reason that they were not *'children in need within their area who appears to them to require accommodation'* according to Section 20 (1) of the Act. The appellants then sought a judicial review from the High Court.

Rather than taking the approach in *E*, the UKSC revived the jurisdictional fact doctrine from *Khawaja*, stating that there were two factual determinations in this case, namely, whether or not the child was *'in need'*, and whether that person was *'a child'* or not. Baroness Hale, Lord Hope and other judges went into a similar direction that parliament intended both questions to be decided on the authority of the decision-maker, but subjected to a review of the courts.[88] Parallel to the analysis of *E* above, there are three points of flexibility in determining jurisdictional fact in the case.

Firstly, in terms of justification, all the judges asserted that two sets of values were involved in determining the scope of judicial review of factual issues, but in a different way from *Khawaja* and *E*. Rather than the principle of finality and the interest of justice, Baroness Hale stated that *'It still requires us to decide which questions are to be regarded as setting the limits to the jurisdiction of the public authority and which questions simply relate to the exercise of that jurisdiction'*.[89] The decision would be unlawful if the decision-maker did not have this authority. This view was supported by Lord Hope, who explained that the intervention of the court was an appropriate process of judicialisation.[90] This reasoning further demonstrates flexibility accorded to the English courts in terms of providing various explanations of constitutional value in determining the scope of judicial review of the facts.

Secondly, similar to *E*, Baroness Hale discussed the various doctrines the court could apply when reviewing the factual determination.[91] However, in this case, the phrase *'child'* was applied to a question of *'jurisdictional or precedent fact of which the ultimate arbiters are the courts rather than the public authorities involved'*.[92] Baroness Hale clearly mentioned the precedent cases namely *Bunbury v Fuller*, *Zerek* and *Khawaja*.[93] This was the homecoming of the ground of jurisdictional fact. Lord Hope also supported the view by citing *Khawaja* that *'...where the exercise of executive power depends upon the precedent establishment of an objective fact, the*

---

[88] n 10 [26]–[29], [32]–[34], [50]–[51], [53], [66]–[68].
[89] ibid [31].
[90] ibid [48], [54].
[91] ibid [26].
[92] ibid [29].
[93] ibid [30] by citing *Bunbury v Fuller* (1853) 9 Ex 111; n 47; n 8.

4.3 English Doctrinal Approaches 157

courts will...decide whether the requirement has been satisfied'.[94] This legal reasoning illustrates that the status of jurisdictional fact as a ground of judicial review is not fixed, but flexible in England.

Thirdly, the judgments in *R (A) v Croydon* further clarified method for the application of jurisdictional fact that the court considers the proper function in conducting judicial review from construction of the relevant statues.[95] For example, Baroness Hale asserted that it was not appropriate to apply the definition of a child in Section 105(1), since the word needed to be read into Section 20(1).[96] Two main reasons were given for considering that this provision was a question of jurisdictional fact. The first related to legislative history in that Section 20(1), which succeeded Section 2 of the Child Care Act 1980, was consolidated from the Children Act 1948, which was established to assist children who needed help in the post-war welfare state.[97] Parliament delegates the duty to help children under the relevant age to the local authorities, but the courts are able to review their actions as the ultimate arbiter.[98] Baroness Hale asserted that there was no evidence that this purpose had changed in the process of drafting and considering the Review of Child Care Law, Report to Ministers of an Interdepartmental Working Party (1985) and the White Paper and the Law on Child Care and Family Services (1987).[99]

Another factor was the consideration of various duties related to the care of children established in the 1989 Act. Parliament leaves some of these to the authority of decision-makers, while others are intended to be controlled by the courts based on the principles of judicial review.[100] Many of the latter provisions relate to the determination of the age of the child.[101] For example, Section 46 gives the police the power to remove a child to suitable accommodation; however, the court can review this exercise of power when someone who is not a child is being removed.[102] Another example is Section 25, which is relatively akin to Section 20(1). Baroness Hale asserted that the court can intervene in the decision if a person who is not a child is locked up in this way.[103]

Based on these reasons, Baroness Hale concluded that the *'wording of the 1989 Act'*[104] gave the court the jurisdiction to conduct judicial review of the factual determination of the decision-maker in this case.[105] The word *'child'* was a jurisdictional

---

[94] ibid [52].
[95] ibid [31]–[33], [51]–[54].
[96] ibid [14].
[97] ibid [15].
[98] ibid [29].
[99] ibid [16].
[100] ibid [17].
[101] ibid.
[102] ibid [18].
[103] ibid [19].
[104] ibid [29].
[105] ibid [21], [32].

fact. Parliament intended the court to consider whether or not the pre-condition is satisfied in the exercise of statutory power.[106] In the same vein, Lord Hope also identified the scope of judicial review using statutory language and schemes.[107]

The flexibility of the English court to determine jurisdictional fact as a ground of judicial review has been demonstrated up to this point. The approach in *E* seemed to replace the doctrine of jurisdictional fact in *Khawaja,* but the doctrine was revived with a clearer application in *R (A) v Croydon*. The last step in emphasising this distinctively flexible process of English law is to unpack the judgments in *Jones*.

4.3.3.2 *Jones*

In *Jones*, a lorry crashed into the claimants' vehicle, as the driver attempted to avoid hitting a man who suddenly ran into the road. The claimants applied to the Criminal Injuries Compensation Scheme 2001 ('CICS') asking for compensation for the serious injuries they had sustained in the accident. However, the Social Entitlement Chamber rejected the application on the ground that it was not a *'crime of violence'* based on paragraph 8 of the scheme, because the primary aim of the man who ran into the road was to commit suicide, not to cause hardship to others or be deliberately reckless. Hence, he lacked the mens rea for the offence stipulated in Section 20. The case was appealed to the FTT and the UT, both of which dismissed it. Then, the claimants sought a judicial review by the CA, which held that the man would have foreseen that his action would possibly harm other road users; therefore, the FFT had erred in law, and its decision would be quashed. The case was then brought to the UKSC.

Although it was not labelled in the judgments, the determination of the scope of judicial review in this case was considered on the ground of jurisdictional fact. The court considered whether or not a factual reference, namely a *'crime of violence'*, was a pre-condition required by Parliament to be reviewed by court.[108] This consideration was made through the statutory construction. For example, Lord Hope pointed out that the aim of the CICS in compensating personal injury arose from a great variety of offences.[109] Although this kind of crime was defined in Section 20 of the Person Act 1861 as *'inflicting bodily injury, with or without weapon'*, this definition was not precise. It should be taken to mean either the actual intention to do harm or recklessness.[110] It was unnecessary for a person to have been able to foresee that his unlawful act might cause physical harm or the gravity of that harm

---

[106] ibid [24]–[25].
[107] ibid [53].
[108] n 6 [12]–[18].
[109] ibid [7]–[8].
[110] ibid [9]–[10].

4.3 English Doctrinal Approaches

described in the section.[111] Lord Hope supported that various definitions of the phrase *'a crime of violence'* had been applied in a variety of cases.[112]

Apart from the CICS and the Person Act 1861, the judgments also considered the court's jurisdiction through a new framework of a tribunal established under the TCEA.[113] The UT is a specialist institution appointed by Parliament to develop the structure and consistency of the decisions of different panels at the first-tier level. Parallel to the analysis of *Cart* in the previous chapter, the court shall not generally have the general authority to change the decisions of the UT.[114]

Having considered all the aforementioned factors, Lord Hope and Lord Carnwath held that whether or not a crime of violence had taken place was primarily a decision for the tribunal, not the courts. Since Parliament had entrusted the UT to develop a structured guidance on the use of the phrase. Lord Hope made the following statement;

> ...so that the expertise of tribunals at the first tier and that of the Upper Tribunal can be used to best effect. An appeal court should not venture too readily into this area by classifying issues as issues of law which are really best left for determination by the specialist appellate tribunals.[115]

This legal reasoning again demonstrates the flexibility accorded to the English courts in providing various justifications and applications to determine the jurisdictional fact. The nature of the institution has been brought into the consideration together with the statutory construction. This led Lord Hope to conclude, as quoted at the start of this chapter that *'A pragmatic approach should be taken to the dividing line between law and fact'*.

4.3.4 Products of the English Legal Culture

The above analysis has demonstrated flexibility and fluctuation of the English law in determining jurisdictional fact as a ground of judicial review through the process of unpacking various doctrinal approaches from the legal reasoning of leading cases. These are captured in a snapshot in the table below.

---

[111] ibid [11].
[112] ibid [12]–[14].
[113] ibid [16]–[20], [42]–[43].
[114] ibid [41].
[115] ibid [16].

English doctrinal approaches		
Status of jurisdictional fact	**Flexible and fluctuating**	
	Khawaja	Impliedly applied as a valid ground to review the precedent fact
	E	Debatable whether it should be replaced by the approach in E or not
	R (A) v Croydon	Clearly stated as a valid ground to review the precedent fact
	Jones	Similarly applied as in R (A) v Croydon, but not termed as jurisdictional fact
Justifications	**Flexible**	
	Khawaja	Duties of the courts in intervening or leaving the factual determination to the authority of decision-makers
	E	Interest of justice and the principle of finality
	R (A) v Croydon	Concept of limited jurisdiction and appropriate process of judicialisation
	Jones	Expertise and consistency of tribunal system and parliament trust
Application	**Flexible**	
	Khawaja	Not explained in detail, but regarded as dependent upon the particular case
	E	Four criteria lead the factual determination to unfairness. Some criteria, namely 'objectively verifiable' and 'play a material part of the reasoning' are compatible to those used to identify the precedent fact
	R (A) v Croydon	Considered from statutory construction
	Jones	Considered from statutory construction and nature of institution

Aside from the described jurisdictional fact, the factual issues are reviewed through other doctrines in some English cases, for example, 'the application of law to fact' in *R v Monopolies and Mergers Commission, Ex parte South Yorkshire Transport Ltd*.[116] These overlaps between the grounds of judicial review of factual issues lead English scholars to propose a solution by 'fixing certain flexibilities of the grounds'. Apart from Craig arguing that the approach in *E* was more comprehensive, Endicott suggests categorising the doctrines and adopting an analytical approach in reviewing errors of law and fact to relieve *'the uncertainty, variability and inconsistency'* of the cases.[117]

However, the above analysis demonstrates that these suggestions to 'fix certain flexibilities' of the grounds do not reflect what is really happening in the legal reasoning of the cases. The English courts will never establish a sharp view of the determination of jurisdictional fact. Therefore, the suggestion of one scholar is not

---

[116] [1993] 1 WLR 23.
[117] Timothy Endicott, 'Questions of Law' (1998) 114 LQR 292.

prioritised over the proposals of others in this section; rather, it is on digging deeply into the root of all the doctrinal approaches in the distinctively flexible process of the English law, since they are all products of the English legal culture. Two main elements are discussed below.

Firstly, there is no clear boundary of power between the executive and the courts due to the absence of a written constitution. Although the courts have considered their jurisdiction through statutory construction in some cases, they have still demonstrated flexibility by means of applying various justifications and factors that they have regarded as being the most appropriate for determining the jurisdictional fact in a particular case. This will become obvious when comparing the English law to its Australian counterpart in the next section. With a written constitution that prescribes a framework of the separation of powers, Australian courts have a more rigid legal mentality in determining jurisdictional fact. This results in them applying more fixed justifications and applications in their deliberations.

Secondly, the degree of malleability of the English approach is increased by the balance of the twin concepts of parliamentary sovereignty and rule of law, both of which need to be considered when the courts determine the scope of judicial review. On the one hand, they provide various justifications for claiming the jurisdiction of judicial review. On the other hand, they have to respect the delegation of the authority to determine factual issues from Parliament to the executive, defined in various terms. This nature of balancing process between the two sets of values also enables the English courts to flexibly adopt and rearrange various applications, ranging from the criteria in *E* to the statutory construction and institutional competence of the UT in *Jones* in their determination of jurisdictional fact. The different approaches in the Australian law, where there are no twin concepts for the courts to balance, will be demonstrated in the next section.

4.4 Australian Doctrinal Approaches

The Australian doctrinal approaches applied to determine jurisdictional fact as a ground of judicial review will be unpacked in this section based on the legal reasoning in *Timbarra*, *Enfield* and some later cases. It will be demonstrated that, in applying such approaches, the Australian courts do not fluctuate in their legal reasoning like their analysed English counterparts. However, they are confined to jurisdictional fact, which is regarded as an entrenched subset of jurisdictional error and determined through the rigid framework of separation of powers prescribed in the written constitution and statutory construction. Parallel to the jurisdictional error analysis in the previous chapter, the rigidity of jurisdictional fact is also embedded in the Australian legal culture.

4.4.1 Timbarra

Traditionally, jurisdictional fact was applied to define the jurisdiction of a court or tribunal by considering ascertainable facts, such as monetary value.[118] However, it was likely to be held in these cases that the factual determination was not jurisdictional,[119] until the late 1990s when the courts began to regard more objective facts as jurisdictional facts.[120] Nevertheless, the ground was not fully discussed until *Timbarra*, where the granting of development consent from Tenterfield Shire Council to Ross Mining NL & ORS was challenged by Timbarra Protection Coalition Inc. on the grounds that it would have a negative effect on the frogs, mammals, bats and owls in the area. Based on Section 77(3)(d1) of the Environmental Planning and Assessment Act 1979 (NSW) ('EPA'), Ross Mining had to submit a proposal, together with a Species Impact Statement ('SIS') because such a development was *'likely to significantly affect threatened species, populations or ecological communities, or their habitats'*. Since the consent to develop had been granted without the submission of a SIS, it was invalid.[121]

It can be seen that the main issue in this case was similar to those in the English cases analysed above, namely, considering whether a factual reference, *'likely to significantly affect threatened species'* in this case, should be reviewed by the court or not. However, while the English approach is flexible in this respect, it has been entrenched by the judgments of the NSW Court of Appeal that the scope of judicial review of this kind of factual determination must be considered on the ground of jurisdictional fact. The connection between the doctrinal approaches and the Australian legal culture can be discussed under three points.

Firstly, jurisdictional fact was clearly regarded as a ground of judicial review in *Timbarra,* as Chief Justice Spigelman declared that the issue in this case was whether or not the phrase in Section 77(3)(d1) was a jurisdictional fact.[122] Secondly, in terms of justification, it was explicitly held that the determination was based on the premise of the rule of law requiring rigid separation of powers. Chief Justice Spigelman held that it is important to consider whether Parliament intended the power to decide the factual reference to be given to the primary decision-maker or not, and if that was its intention, then it is not jurisdictional fact.[123] As he stated;

> *Where the process of construction leads to the conclusion that Parliament intends the primary decision maker to determine the existence or non-existence of the fact, the reason for*

---

[118] E Bullen, 'Legislative Limits on Environmental Decision-making: The Application of the Administrative Law Doctrines of Jurisdictional Fact and Ultra Vires' (2006) 23 EPLJ 265, 267.

[119] Nevertheless, the ground has been accepted as valid since then, for example, *Parisienne Basket Shoes Pty Ltd v Whyte* (1938) 59 CLR 369, 391.

[120] E.g. *Londish v Knox Grammar School* (1997) 97 LGERA 1; *Australian Heritage Commission v Mount Isa Mines Ltd* (1997) 187 CLR 297.

[121] n 12 [3]–[22].

[122] ibid [34].

[123] ibid [44].

4.4 Australian Doctrinal Approaches

the court not to intervene is either a rule of law of statutory interpretation as to the intent of Parliament, or the application of a rule of the common law to the exercise of a statutory interpretation...[124]

Conversely, if Parliament intended the factual determination to be subjected to the court, it would be a jurisdictional fact. According to Chief Justice Spigelman;

Where the process of construction leads to the conclusion that Parliament intended that the factual reference can only be satisfied by the actual existence (or non-existence) of the fact or facts, then the rule of law requires a court with a judicial review jurisdiction to give effect to that intention by inquiry into the existence of the fact or facts.[125]

Although the primary decision-maker has the expertise and experience to preliminarily decide the issue, the court has considerable experience of making ultimate judgments.[126]

This understanding of legality is clearly parallel to the distinctive Australian judicial review constitutionalism. If the factual determination is intended to be within the boundary of administrative authority, the court has no jurisdiction to conduct judicial review of it. However, if the factual reference is considered as to be a jurisdictional fact, the court has the jurisdiction to protect the decision-maker's boundary of power by ensuring that the intention of parliament is fulfilled.

Thirdly, Chief Justice Spigelman provided a clear application for the courts to identify a jurisdictional fact based on statutory construction.[127] Whether explicitly or implicitly,[128] the statutory formation and meaning of the words chosen by Parliament must be able to indicate the purpose and objective underlying the legislation.[129] Additionally, two criteria for considering statutory construction were proposed in the judgment. Firstly, the factual determination must *'objectively exist in fact'*, and secondly, the legislature must intend that *'the absence or presence of the fact is important so that to invalidate action under the statute'*.[130] These two criteria were defined as *'objectivity and essentiality'*,[131] and it was further explained that they were interrelated because the indicators of essentiality often suggest objectivity.[132] Apart from that, the judgment clarified that, in cases where a factual reference appears in a statutory formation that contains words that refer to the mental state of the primary decision-maker, such as 'opinion', 'belief' and 'satisfaction', although not necessarily, the construction is often against a conclusion of jurisdictional fact.

---

[124] ibid [41].
[125] ibid [40].
[126] ibid [90].
[127] ibid [28], [37].
[128] ibid [48],
[129] ibid [39].
[130] ibid [37].
[131] ibid [38].
[132] ibid

It is likely that Parliament leaves decision-makers the discretion to decide the factual reference.[133]

After that, Chief Justice Spigelman used these applications to consider whether or not the phrase *'likely to significantly affect threatened species'* was a jurisdictional fact. In doing so, he considered a number of factors of the provisions in the EPA. For example, he interpreted the legislative scheme in this case differently from the other cases because it was concerned with Section 77(3)(d1) of the Act, not Section 90(1)(c3).[134] Importantly, Chief Justice Spigelman held that Section 77 did not involve the exercise of statutory power by consent,[135] but established the requirements of an application culminating in Section 91(1).[136] Therefore, Section 77(3)(d1) did not confer a power on a decision-maker, but imposed a requirement on an applicant.[137] This was the key reason that the factual reference was more likely to be an objective fact.[138] Subsequently, Chief Justice Spigelman mentioned several cases to demonstrate that the court needed to distinguish a fact that had to be adjudicated upon during the course of the inquiry from one that was essentially preliminary to the decision-making process.[139]

The additional point was that there was no distinction between the phrases *'is critical habitat'* and *'is likely to significantly affect threatened species* in Section 77(3)(d1). Where the section referred to *'critical habitat'*, there was no issue of how this appeared to a consensual authority.[140] The consideration went further to other legislature that critical habitat in Section 4(1) of the EPA had the same meaning as in the Threatened Species Conservation Act 1995 (NSW), in which there was no issue of *'appearance'*, *'opinion'* or *'satisfaction'*. Whether or not a critical habitat is proposed to be developed is entirely a matter of objective fact[141]; therefore, it is unlikely that Parliament intended a significant difference in the statutory treatment of the two cases.[142]

Finally, Chief Justice Spigelman considered the purpose of the EPA in that a SIS enables the consensual authority's decision-making process to be better informed with the aim of enhancing the quality of the decision-making process by ensuring that detailed information is available to primary decision-makers in a systematic and well-ordered way.[143] This makes it more likely for the court to indicate that the

---

[133] ibid [42].

[134] E.g. *Londish* (n 120) in ibid [25]–[29], [31]–[33], [45]–[47].

[135] ibid [47]–[48].

[136] ibid [49]–[50].

[137] ibid [33].

[138] ibid [50]–[51].

[139] ibid [52]–[60] by citing cases like *Ex parte Hulin; Re Gillespie* (1965) 65 SR (NSW) 31, 33; *Parisienne Basket Shoes* (n 119).

[140] ibid [61].

[141] ibid [62].

[142] ibid [64].

[143] ibid [73].

EPA intended the requirement to prepare a SIS to be both objectively ascertained and essential.[144] The courts should be able to control this statutory requirement.[145]

Having considered all of these reasons, Chief Justice Spigelman held that the factual reference was a jurisdictional fact.[146] As demonstrated in the previous section, although the English courts also read into the relevant legislature in *R (A) v Croydon* and *Jones*, the application of statutory construction is more detailed in *Timbarra*. The Australian courts strictly focus on the wording of the legislature based on a clear framework of objectivity and essentiality. This is influenced by the importance given by the rigid legal mentality to the framework of separation of powers, which Chief Justice Gleeson and Justice Gummow also attach to this approach by repeatedly stating it in the transcript of legal argument of *Timbarra*, as follows;

> Mr Flick: ...the point of importance for this Court is what is the extent to which a court should project itself into the factual merits of a decision where - -
> Justice Gummow: That depends on the way Parliament has drawn its legislation when it creates these jurisdictions...
> Mr Flick:...But to answer your Honour, it is a question of statutory construction...
> Chief Justice Gleeson: This case turns upon the application of well-settled principles to the construction of the State statute in question...[147]

In short, the judgments in *Timbarra* applied clear justifications and applications in deciding whether or not the factual reference was a jurisdictional fact within the scope of judicial review. All of these doctrinal approaches are profoundly dictated by the Australian legal culture. This connection was determined was further entrenched in later cases, the most significant of which was *Enfield*.

4.4.2 Enfield

In this case, the Corporation of the City of Enfield challenged a decision of the Development Assessment Commission, which approved a provisional development plan proposed by Collex Waste Management Services Pty Ltd. to alter and add to an existing liquid waste treatment plant on its land on the grounds that the project belonged to *'a special industry'*, which was a non-complying development.[148] Based on Section 35(3)(a) of the Development Act (South Australia), the Commission had to refuse consent unless it concurred after notifying the public.[149] This case was brought to the Supreme Court of South Australia, and thereby the HCA, to decide

---

[144] ibid [76].
[145] ibid [77].
[146] ibid [81], [94].
[147] n 7.
[148] n 13 [2], [9].
[149] ibid [3]–[8], [10]

whether or not the factual reference, namely *'special industry'* was a jurisdictional fact.[150] Entrenched from *Timbarra*, there were three points of connection between the doctrinal approaches to determine the jurisdictional fact in *Enfield* and the Australian legal culture, as explained below.

Firstly, the judgments affirmed the justification for judicial review relating to the Australian judicial review constitutionalism. On the one hand, it was explained that the court had no jurisdiction to conduct judicial review if the issue was not a jurisdictional fact because there were grey areas of uncertainty to the practical judgment.[151] The judgment of Justice Brennan in *Quin* was described to support this point that

> *The merits of administrative action, to the extent that they can be distinguished from legality, are for the repository of the relevant power and, subject to political control, for the repository alone.*[152]

On the other hand, the judgment reserved the right for the court *'to inquire into the relevant facts to decide jurisdictional fact'*.[153] This perspective was shown by referring to the US case namely, *Marbury v Madison*, he stated that *'...an essential characteristic of the judicature is that it declares and enforces the law which determines the limits of the power conferred by statute upon administrative decision-makers'*.[154] Apart from Section 75(v) of the Constitution, Justice Gaudron also linked the justification to the concept of jurisdiction that administrative bodies are compelled to operate within the relevant limitations of their powers,[155] and the courts should ensure that they only exercise their administrative powers within the limits of their jurisdiction and in accordance with the laws that govern their exercise.[156] She stated that *'To do less is to abdicate judicial responsibility'*.[157]

Interestingly, while the concept of deference allowing various intensities of judicial review is debatable in English law, it was completely rejected in *Enfield*, when the judge made the following statement;

> *However, in Australia this situation is the product not of any doctrine of "deference", but of basic principles of administrative law respecting the exercise of discretionary powers.*[158]

> *Commentary upon Chevron* [applying the doctrine of deference] *has seen it as indicative of a "delegalisation" of the administrative process...*[159]

---

[150] ibid [12].
[151] ibid [38].
[152] ibid [44] by citing *Attorney-General (NSW) v Quin* (1990) 170 CLR 1, 36.
[153] ibid [38].
[154] ibid [43].
[155] ibid [54]–[55].
[156] ibid [56].
[157] ibid [60].
[158] ibid [44].
[159] ibid [42].

4.4 Australian Doctrinal Approaches

Whether or not the courts should intervene in the factual determination depends on the rule of law, the separation of powers and the concept of jurisdiction.[160] The mentality that influenced their approaches was also clearly expressed in the transcript of legal argument of the case; for example,

> *Justice Kirby: It may reserve that in the name of the rule of law to the courts themselves.*
> *Justice Gummow: It* [Deference] *is a means of curbing ...It built on another foundation – ...that is how it seems to me – no immediate analogy here.*
> *Justice Kirby: It* [Deference] *is a very nebulous word that can cover a whole multitude of attitudes...*
> *But I just do not quite see how it works as a legal proposition, as distinct from maybe some sociological explanation of why courts come to a particular conclusion in a particular case.*[161]

This illustrates the distinctive mentality of the Australian courts that, rather than attempting a balance, the scope of judicial review is rigidly determined based on the framework of the separation of powers. If parliament intends the court to review the factual determination of the executive, its constitutional role is to protect the rule of law and the jurisdiction of the executive. However, if the court considers the factual determination to be within the scope of the executive, it has no jurisdiction to conduct judicial review.[162] The courts do not determine the approach of their intervention flexibly based on their full creativity.

Secondly, in considering the statutory construction, the application of the jurisdictional fact in *Timbarra,* namely the criteria of objectivity and essentiality, were emphasised in *Enfield.* The judgment considered the construction of the Development Act when addressing the phrase *'special industry'* as a jurisdictional fact in three main points. Firstly, Section 35 of the Act had a different statutory scheme from Section 33. The planning merits were not involved in the satisfactory conditions for lifting the prohibition imposed by Section 32.[163] Secondly, the text of Section 35 did not suggest that the determination of whether the responsible authority is obliged to consent rests upon its own classification of the relevant circumstances. Therefore, the legislation did not define the criteria of operation as being the opinion of the relevant authority of the classification of the development.[164] Section 25 is not an opinion or satisfaction reasonably formed based on the material put before the decision-maker. However, it is stipulated in direct terms as a precondition, which obliges refusal or a grant of consent.[165] Thirdly, the judgment determined that the construction related to regulation 16(2) of the development regulations, made by the Governor under the power conferred by Section 108 of the Development Act, did not turn the imperative element in regulation 16(1) into the expression of an opin-

---

[160] ibid [40], [59]–[60].

[161] n 17.

[162] This is endorsed by Gageler that *'the better label is "respect" for an agency's interpretation rather than deference'* (Stephen Gageler, 'Deference' (2015) 22 Australian Journal of Administrative Law 151).

[163] n 13 [32].

[164] ibid [33].

[165] ibid [34].

ion. The nature of the determination under regulation 16(1) was correctly interpreted in the present case, since it is consistent with the character of the prohibition upon the granting of consent imposed in Section 35(3) without a concurrence.[166]

This application of jurisdictional fact was consistent with the approach in *Timbarra*, where the scope of judicial review was considered based on a framework of the separation of powers. The reason given was adherent to the statutory construction. Justice Hayne implicitly regarded these doctrinal approaches as being based on the logic of legality in the transcript of legal argument of *Enfield* that *'We have to begin, do we not, with the statute and the regulation, identify what the issue was and what is the alleged illegality or unlawfulness…'*.[167]

Thirdly, the status of jurisdictional fact as a valid ground of judicial review in Australia became even more entrenched in *Enfield*. For example, the legal reasoning clearly connoted *'jurisdictional fact'* as the term used to identify *'criterion, satisfaction of which enlivens the power of the decision-maker to exercise a discretion'*.[168] Importantly, while the English courts are flexible and unclear in regarding a jurisdictional fact as covered by an error of law, the ground has been included as a subset of jurisdictional error in Australian law, as demonstrated in the previous chapter. This clear and systematic categorisation of the grounds of judicial review is also a product of the Australian legal culture, as will be exemplified in Chaps. 5 and 6.

4.4.3 *After* Timbarra *and* Enfield

Up to this point, the analysis of *Timbarra* and *Enfield* has demonstrated that the Australian courts have been relatively fixed in their approach to intervene in factual issues. Some of the cases after *Timbarra* and *Enfield* will be explored in this section in order to demonstrate the continuity of jurisdictional fact in the light of the Australian legal culture. The prominent ones are *Anvil Hill* and *M70/2011*.

In *Anvil Hill*, it was questioned whether the proposed action of the construction and operation of an open-cut coal mine and ancillary facilities was a controlled action, which would have or be likely to have a significant impact on a matter protected by the Environment Protection and Biodiversity Conservation Act 1999 (Cth).[169] It was clear from the legal reasoning of the judgment that this question was considered based on the jurisdictional fact approach.[170] Apart from affirming the validity of the ground, its application was also rigid in terms of the consideration of statutory construction. As the judgment of Stone J stated,

---

[166] ibid [36]–[37].

[167] n 17.

[168] n 13 [28].

[169] n 14 [1]–[2]. Although jurisdictional fact was applied in this case as a ground under the ADJR, the entrenchment of jurisdictional fact is also demonstrated well as a product of the Australian legal culture. Therefore, it is included in this section.

[170] *Timbarra* was directly cited (ibid [59]–[61] (Stone J)).

4.4 Australian Doctrinal Approaches

Ultimately the question whether a particular finding of fact is jurisdictional depends on the proper construction of the relevant statute. The consequence of characterising a fact as jurisdictional is that the finding of fact can be reviewed on the merits and the court's opinion may be substituted for that of the administrative decision-maker.[171]

Additionally, the criteria for determining the jurisdictional fact setup in *Timbarra* and *Enfield*, namely objectivity and essentiality and the recognition of a reference to the mental state by the use of words such as 'opinion', 'belief' or 'satisfaction', were also applied in *Anvil Hill*.[172] The judgment then concluded that the court's role did not involve intervening in the case because the factual reference was not a jurisdictional fact.[173] There were no various doctrinal approaches moving flexibly between cases, like the analysed English law.

Notably, the legal reasoning in the judgment was explicit in that the entrenched status and application of jurisdictional fact were products of the Australian legal culture, particularly how the rule of law and separation of powers are distinctively understood. For example, *Timbarra* was cited in the judgment of Justice Stone that,

…Where the process of construction leads to the conclusion that parliament intended that the factual reference can only be satisfied by the actual existence (or non-existence) of the fact or facts, then the rule of law requires a court with a judicial review jurisdiction to give effect to that intention by inquiry into the existence of the fact or facts.[174]

Another case that demonstrates the continuous adherence to jurisdictional fact in Australia is *Plaintiff M70/2011*. The fact of this case was that the minister wanted to transfer the applicant, an asylum seeker, from detention on Christmas Island to Malaysia. However, it was disputed as to whether or not Malaysia was a 'specified country' to which minister had the lawful discretionary power to transfer 'offshore entry' people.[175] Entrenched from *Timbarra* and *Enfield*, Chief Justice French applied jurisdictional fact to determine whether the factual reference was a jurisdictional fact or not by adopting the clear definition that it was a ground *'applied to the exercise of a statutory power is often used to designate a factual criterion, satisfaction of which is necessary to enliven the power of a decision-maker to exercise a discretion'*.[176] Similarly, the ground was determined through the framework of separation of powers prescribed in the written constitution and statutory construction. As French CJ held,

The question is one of statutory construction…
…Absent clear words, the subsection should not be construed as conferring upon courts the power to substitute their judgment for that of the Minister by characterising the matters…as jurisdictional facts[177]

---

[171] ibid [60].
[172] ibid [63].
[173] ibid [70]–[71].
[174] ibid [61].
[175] n 15 [5]–[18].
[176] ibid [57].
[177] ibid [58].

[On the other hand,] ...*If the Minister were to proceed to make a declaration on the basis of a misconstrued criterion, he would be making a declaration not authorised by the Parliament. The misconstruction of the criterion would be a jurisdictional error.*[178]

The doctrine that *'Where a power is expressly conditioned upon the formation of a state of mind by the decision-maker, be it an opinion, belief, state of satisfaction or suspicion, the existence of the state of mind itself will constitute a jurisdictional fact'* was applied once again.[179] Chief Justice French reached the conclusion from these doctrinal approaches that the factual reference was not a jurisdictional fact.[180] The justifications given were evidently compatible to the analysed particular understanding of constitutional values in Australia. For example, it was not the role of the court to conduct judicial review because the framework of powers perceived from the wording of s 198A(3)(a) of the Migration Act indicates that the determination should be *'the subject of the Minister's assessment'* in order to *'support the continuance of the matters'*.[181]

Interestingly, while French CJ considered that the factual reference in *M70/2011* meant that the court could not intervene, the majority of judges namely Gummow, Hayne, Crennan and Bell JJ, held that it was a jurisdictional fact.[182] Despite these different outcomes, the majority applied the same doctrinal approaches as French CJ. The application of the ground also remained on the detail attention of the proper construction, text, context and purpose of Section 198A of the Act.[183] The justification for claiming the factual reference as jurisdictional fact was consistently compatible with the Australian legal culture. For example, the access and protections of such references to Section 198A *'must be provided* [by courts] *as a matter of legal obligation'*.[184] It was held that *'the Minister's declaration was made beyond power... s 198A(1) cannot be engaged to take either plaintiff from Australia to Malaysia'*.[185]

This point needs some clarification. Although the Australian approach is confined to jurisdictional fact, it does not mean that the outcome of the case must always be fixed among judges in the same way as the scope of judicial review of a factual issue is limited. As Fisher points out, the courts, particularly the ones at state level, can still respond flexibly to a *'hot situation'* and the complexity of day-to-day public administration in different subject matters, namely planning law and environment law.[186] In other words, the Australian courts also have to assess the particular statutory scheme in their determination of the scope of judicial review.[187] The operation of legal formalism (on jurisdictional fact) *'is not blind to the importance of*

---

[178] ibid [59].

[179] ibid [57].

[180] ibid [60]–[67].

[181] ibid [61].

[182] ibid [136].

[183] ibid [109]–[119].

[184] ibid [116].

[185] ibid [136].

[186] Elizabeth Fisher, 'Environmental Law as "Hot Law"' (2013) 25 Journal of Environmental Law 347.

[187] For example, see the consideration in *Timbarra* (n 12) [44]–[94].

4.4 Australian Doctrinal Approaches

context'.[188] This aspect of flexibility was also mentioned by Chief Justice Spigelman, as follows;

> *Determining whether a fact or event, or combination of such, has the requisite quality of essentiality to be classified as jurisdictional, always requires a multiplicity of factors to be considered. Different judges may reach divergent conclusions.*[189]

Parallel to the analysis in the previous chapter, at the surface level, both the English and Australian courts have to respect the legislative power of parliament to authorise decision-makers to decide factual issues, and base their determination of the scope of judicial review upon that ground.

However, at the deeper level, it is demonstrated by the process of unpacking the legal reasoning of the above-mentioned leading cases that different modes of doctrinal approaches are adopted to determine the scope of judicial review in England and Australia. To be specific, the Australian courts have to determine the scope of judicial review by adhering to the rigid framework of separation of powers prescribed in the written constitution and statutory construction. It is demonstrated in this section that this operation can be fulfilled based on the concept of jurisdictional error and its derivatives, such as jurisdictional fact, which Fisher regards as representing the idea *'that public administration is capable of operating within clearly identifiable legal boundaries'.*[190]

Apart from *Anvil Hill* and *M70/2011*, there are a number of cases at both at the federal and state levels that demonstrated plenty of opportunity for the courts to abandon their adherence to the application of jurisdictional fact; however, they did not do so, but stayed with jurisdictional fact and the fixed doctrinal approaches in determining them. Importantly, the legal mentality of the Australian courts that rigidly relies on the separation of powers can be found on many occasions. For example, Judge Basten stated in *Barrick Australian v Williams* that

> *Where a power is said to depend upon, not the existence of a contingency, the satisfaction of the decision-maker as to the contingency, the jurisdictional fact will be the relevant state of satisfaction… if the matter is one requiring evaluative judgment, it is more likely that the legislature intended that the officer form an opinion as to the contingency, rather than that the power be engaged only where the objective facts are established…*[191]

As an additional indicator, while various debates on jurisdictional fact in English academic circles were described in the previous section, the smaller room accorded to Australian scholars to comment on the validity of the ground is demonstrated in this section. At the bottom line, jurisdictional fact is *'firmly established in the*

---

[188] Elizabeth Fisher, '"Jurisdictional" Facts and "Hot" Facts: Legal Formalism, Legal Pluralism, and the Nature of Australian Administrative Law' (n 29) 975–976.

[189] James Spigelman, 'The Centrality of Jurisdictional Error' 21 Public Law Review 77, 86.

[190] Elizabeth Fisher, '"Jurisdictional" Facts and "Hot" Facts: Legal Formalism, Legal Pluralism, and the Nature of Australian Administrative Law' (n 29) 976.

[191] (2009) 74 NSWLR 733 [26]; See also *Woolworths v Pallas Newco* (2004) 61 NSWLR 707; *Anor and Gedeon v Commissioner of the New South Wales Crime Commission* (2008) 236 CLR 120; *Caterpillar of Australian Pty Ltd v Industrial Court of New South Wales* (2009) 78 NSWLR 43.

Australian legal system.[192] Meanwhile, the understanding of the law based on the framework of legal culture and deep-water legality offered in this book makes the comments on the doctrinal development of the jurisdictional fact in the literature more straightforward. For example, Keane argues for rigid application of jurisdictional fact according to the distinction between legality and merits.[193] In the same way, Justice Mason asserted in a secondary work that *'the parameters within which administrative power may be exercised cannot exceed the constitutional limits of Parliament's legislative power'*.[194] This is similar to Aronson's suggestion that the ground of jurisdictional fact should not be expanded in a way that enables the court to intervene in any factual issue, because it would result in blurring the distinction between legality and merits.[195] Hence, Chief Justice Spigelman issued a conclusory statement that jurisdictional fact is not a *'blank cheque to the judiciary to intervene whenever a judge believes the outcome to be undesirable'*.[196] These authors are all arguing for the same thing, namely, to develop the doctrinal approaches in a way that is compatible to the Australian legal culture.

4.4.4 Products of the Australian Legal Culture

In this section, the relatively rigid doctrinal approaches applied to determine jurisdictional fact as a ground of judicial review have been unpacked from the legal reasoning in *Timbarra, Enfield, Anvil Hill, M70/2011*. Rather than being flexible, the Australian courts have relatively clear and fixed justifications and applications to determine jurisdictional fact as a ground of judicial review in the cases. These are captured in the snapshot below.

Australian doctrinal approaches in *Timbarra* and *Enfield* and later cases		
Status of jurisdictional fact	Entrenched as valid ground of judicial review and a subset of jurisdictional error	
Justifications	Relatively fixed	
	To intervene	Not to intervene
	The rule of law The rigid separation of powers The concept of jurisdiction The principle of legality Rejection of deference	The rule of law The separation of powers Distinction between legality and merits
Applications	Strictly considered from statutory construction With the criteria of objectivity and essentiality	

---

[192] Leeming (n 5) 65; See also Aronson, Groves and Weeks (n 5) [4.470]–[4.480].

[193] P A Keane, Legality and Merits in Administrative Law: An Historical Perspective (2009) 1 Northern Territory Law Journal 117, 136.

[194] Brian Mason, 'Jurisdictional Facts after Plaintiff M70' (2013) 24 PLR 37, 39.

[195] For example, Aronson (n 16).

[196] Spigelman (n 189), 87.

Importantly, these doctrinal approaches and legal reasoning are influenced by the rigid legal mentality of Australian judicial review constitutionalism, namely that the scope of judicial review must be strictly considered by following the framework of the separation of powers prescribed in the written constitution and the construction of the relevant statutes. Jurisdictional fact becomes an entrenched ground of judicial review, and systematically fits as a subset of jurisdictional error. The concept of deference, which appears in England and facilitates flexibility in considering the scope of judicial review, is firmly rejected in Australia. Unlike the English law, there is only room for scholars to debate the development of the ground, rather than its validity. All of these analyses clarify the following statement made by Justice Gageler in a speech;

> *The distinction between fact and law has application not merely in the context of general questions of statutory construction, but more broadly, such as in circumstances where an error of law establishes a statutory ground of appeal. In Australia, it also has a constitutional dimension, underpinning the principles of the separation of judicial power and strong form judicial review of administrative action.*[197]

While the English courts are flexible when determining jurisdictional fact, this does not fit the Australian courts' understanding of legality based on the Australian legal culture. Chief Justice Mason verified this statement by referring to the approach in *Enfield* as *'the Australianisation of our law'*.[198]

4.5 Conclusion

It was demonstrated in the previous chapter that the English and Australian courts have a 'different way' to reach a 'similar conclusion' in determining the scope of judicial review of the decisions of tribunals and inferior courts. This assertion goes further in this chapter by revealing 'the different doctrinal approaches and conclusions' in the English and Australian determinations of jurisdictional fact as a ground of judicial review. On the one hand, the jurisdictional fact doctrine was implicitly abandoned in *Anisminic*, and replaced with the distinction between law and fact; however, it waved back as an exception for the court to intervene in factual issue. The modern law then becomes flexible in applying various justifications and applications in the determination; in fact, it has been debated whether jurisdictional fact should be a valid ground of judicial review or not. On the other hand, the Australian courts' approaches in determining jurisdictional fact as an entrenched ground of judicial review. Connecting this to the previous chapter, while jurisdictional fact

---

[197] Justice Gageler, 'What is a Question of Law?' (The National Conference of Tax Institute Justice Hill Memorial Lecture, March 2014).

[198] Anthony Mason, 'The Evolving Role and Function of the High Court' in Brian Opeskin and Fiona Wheeler (eds), *The Australian Federal Judicial System* (Melbourne University Press 2000) 116.

systematically fits into jurisdictional error in Australian law, how jurisdictional fact relates to an error of law in English law is left open.

Importantly, these differences are not randomed; rather, they are the products of the understanding of the English and Australian courts of the deep-water legality embedded in their different legal cultures. The pragmatic approach in *Jones* would definitely not be adopted by Australian judges; likewise, English lawyers would be doubtful when hearing that Australian judges absolutely reject the concept of deference.

The way in which this theme runs through the determination of the grounds of judicial review related to the substantive exercise of discretion will be demonstrated in the following chapters. For example, while the status, justification and application of the English courts in determining proportionality as a ground of judicial review have been widely debated, they have been firmly excluded by the Australian courts. Furthermore, since jurisdictional fact is a ground of judicial review of factual issues, it inevitably overlaps with the grounds relating to the substantive exercise of discretion. The differences in the relationship between these grounds of judicial review in England and Australia will be discussed in the next chapter. For example, in English law, not only has it been debated whether jurisdictional fact is replaced by a factual evaluation against unfairness, but the grounds are also mixed with rationality and proportionality. Conversely, the grounds, namely jurisdictional fact, illogicality and irrationality and *Wednesbury*, are systemically categorised under jurisdictional error in Australia. Indeed, Spigelman CJ has stated this since *Timbarra* that when factual determination is not jurisdictional fact, the court may inquire into when there is an unreasonableness of the decision.[199] This is similar to Justice Gaudron, who held in *Enfield* that when it is not jurisdictional fact, the question is only whether the decision is reasonable or not. However, if it is a jurisdictional fact, it has nothing to do with the grounds related to the substantive exercise of discretion.[200] All of these points will be analysed as the further products of the legal cultures in the next chapter.

---

[199] n 12 [41].
[200] n 13 [59].

Chapter 5
Influence of the Legal Cultures on the Grounds Relating to Substantive Exercise of Discretion

Abstract The English and Australian legal systems initially adopted a similar approach in reviewing the substantive exercise of discretion, namely, *Wednesbury* Unreasonableness; however, the doctrinal approaches have been developed differently in both countries. The legal reasoning in *Kennedy v Charity Commission* [2014] UKSC 20 and *Pham v Secretary of State for the Home Department* [2015] UKSC 19 demonstrates the flexibility the English courts have in developing new doctrinal approaches like anxious scrutiny and modified rationality and in adopting grounds from European Union law and the European Court of Human Rights like proportionality to determine the scope of judicial review. Conversely, the Australian legal culture has reduced the speed of development in this area. New ground of illogicality and irrationality has not been flexibly accepted and proportionality has been rejected in Australia. This is evident from cases like *Re Minister for Immigration and Multicultural Affairs; Ex p Applicant S20/2002* (2003) 198 ALR 59, *Re Minister for Immigration and Citizenship v SZMDs* [2010] HCA 16 and *Re Minister for Immigration and Citizenship v Li* [2013] HCA 18. These differences are unpacked and deeply understood through the framework of deep-water legality and legal culture in this chapter.

5.1 Introduction

> *They* [The courts] *can only interfere with an act of executive authority if it be shown that the authority has contravened the law… When an executive discretion is entrusted by Parliament to a body such as the local authority in this case, what appears to be an exercise of that discretion can only be challenged in the courts in a strictly limited class of case* (Associated Provincial Pictures Houses Ltd v Wednesbury Corporation)[1]

The above judgment of Lord Greene premises one of the most 'confusing' grounds of judicial review in England and Australia,[2] called *'Wednesbury Unreasonableness'*

---

[1] [1948] 1 KB 223, 228.

[2] Regarded by scholars and judges, for example, Geoff Airo-Farulla, 'Reasonableness, Rationality and Proportionality' in Matthews Groves and H P Lee (eds), *Australian Administrative Law* (CUP

or 'Irrationality'.[3] Both the English and Australian courts similarly began with this approach when deciding the scope of judicial review of the substantive exercise of administrative discretion. However, this area of the law has evolved differently in different legal systems with the passage of time.

On the one hand, the determination of judicial review of administrative discretion is flexible in the English courts. They are able to apply various concepts and grounds, such as irrationality and anxious scrutiny, and include the influence of interrelated legal cultures, such as proportionality, in their consideration.[4] The degree of intensity in reviewing administrative discretion varies among these approaches. For example, according to Lord Justice Laws in *R v Secretary of State for Education and Employment, Ex parte Begbie;* '*the Wednesbury principle itself constitutes a sliding scale of review more or less intrusive according to the nature and gravity of what is at stake…*'.[5]

On the other hand, rather than being flexible, the Australian courts' determination of judicial review of the substantive exercise of discretion is confined to the legal system's constitutional guidelines. This was recognised in the transcript of the legal argument of *Re Minister for Immigration and Multicultural Affairs, Ex parte Applicant S20/2002*, when Chief Justice Gleeson asked whether the court should undertake the English approach of '*treating unreasonableness under the rubric of abuse of power*',[6] and Mr. Gageler, a barrister in the case, gave the following response;

> The English position, though, appears to have departed from the fundamental point to which jurisprudence in this Court has adhered, that is, that judicial review is concerned with policing legal limits on a decision-maker's power, that is, judicial review is at heart concerned with jurisdictional error. That fundamental point appears to have been departed from in some of the more recent cases in the House of Lords [of England].[7]

In addition, in *Murrumbidgee Groundwater Preservation Association Inc v Minister for Natural Resources,* Chief Justice Spigelman explained that,

> A challenge to the exercise of a statutory power on the basis of irrationality or unreasonableness requires the Court to be conscious of the permissible scope of judicial review. The legality and merits dichotomy is at the heart of Australian administrative law and the

---

2007); Mark Aronson, 'The Growth of Substantive Review' in John Bell, Mark Elliott, Jason Varuhas and Philip Murray (eds), *Public Law Adjudication in Common Law Systems: Process and Substance* (Hart Publishing 2016); Rebecca Williams, 'Structuring Substantive Review' [2017] PL 99; William Wade and Christopher Forsyth, *Administrative Law* (11th edn, OUP 2014) 302–305. The relationship between these studies and the focus of this chapter is explained below.

[3] Lord Diplock's terminology in *Council of Civil Service Unions v Minister for the Civil Service* [1985] AC 374, 410–411.

[4] This will be unpacked in Sect. 5.3 below.

[5] [2000] 1 WLR 1115, 1130B-1130D.

[6] The Transcript of legal argument in *Re Minister for Immigration and Multicultural Affairs, Ex parte Applicant S20/2002* (2003) 198 ALR 59.

[7] ibid.

boundary between the two is policed more rigorously in this country than appears to have become the case in recent years in other common law jurisdictions...[8]

This mentality results in the firm rejection of proportionality in Australia, and emerging grounds like illogicality and irrationality are slowly being developed.[9] As Creyke, McMillan and Smyth conclude, *'English courts, by contrast, have long shown greater readiness than Australian courts to develop "unreasonableness", "irrationality" and "proportionality" as pivotal criteria in administrative law'*.[10]

This area of judicial review of administrative discretion is commonly recognised as one of the hardest to understand and map-out in administrative law. The aim is to simplify it in this chapter by unpacking the different doctrinal approaches from the legal reasoning in leading English and Australian cases, comparing and demonstrating them as products of the differences between English and Australian legal cultures. After this introduction, Sect. 5.2 will move the focus of this chapter to the issues and debates in the area. Next, flexibility accorded to the English courts in *Kennedy v Charity Commission*[11] and *Pham v Secretary of State for the Home Department*[12] in terms of justifications, doctrines and applications, as well as their ability to adopt interrelated legal cultures into their determination of the scope of judicial review will be unpacked in Sect. 5.3. Conversely, the relatively fixed justifications, doctrines, applications and systematic categorisation between the grounds applied in *Re Minister for Immigration and Multicultural Affairs, Ex parte Applicant S20/2002*,[13] *Minister for Immigration and Citizenship v SZMDs*[14] and *Minister for Immigration and Citizenship v Li*[15] will be demonstrated in Sect. 5.4. In the final section, the analysis in this chapter will be concluded, and pave the way for the study of substantive legitimate expectations in the next chapter.

5.2 Judicial Review of Administrative Discretion at Surface and Deep Levels

As discussed above, while some concepts are recognised and applied in the determination of judicial review of administrative discretion in the same way in England and Australia, others are treated differently. The classification of these points is explained as being located at surface and deep-water levels. It begins with two sides

---

[8] (2005) 138 LGERA 11, 127.
[9] This will be unpacked in Sect. 5.4 below.
[10] Robin Creyke, John McMillan and Mark Smyth, *Control of Government Action; Text, Cases and Commentary* (5th edn, LexisNexis Butterworths 2019) [15.2.11].
[11] [2014] UKSC 20.
[12] [2015] UKSC 19.
[13] (2003) 198 ALR 59.
[14] [2010] HCA 16.
[15] [2013] HCA 18.

of the concept floating on the surface-water level of the two countries. On the one hand, the courts generally avoid interfering with administrative discretion, since this is a power granted to administrative agents so that they can consider the merits of a particular situation during the course of public administration. On the other hand, the courts claim jurisdiction to conduct judicial review of some administrative discretion, particularly when it *'contravenes the law'*.[16] According to the framework of this book, the courts play a role in protecting surface-water legality. Nevertheless, from a deep-water perspective, the English and Australian courts have different doctrinal approaches in deciding the extent to which they should intervene in administrative discretion. The comparison of these differences and their connection to the English and Australian 'deep-water' understanding of legality and legal cultures will be exemplified as the focus of this chapter.

5.2.1 Discretion: Power to Choose

Discretion is an unavoidable feature of administrative law, being the *'power for the administrator to choose how to act'* during the course of public administration.[17] Similar to factual determination described in the previous chapter,[18] it is necessary and indeed beneficial, to give administrative agents the authority for two main reasons. Firstly, not only can a rule not be applied itself, but discretion also allows the merits of particular cases to be considered, which leads to flexibility, consistency and responsiveness in implementing the rule.[19] Furthermore, granting discretion to public administrators, who have experience and expertise in particular administrative activities, generates an efficient public administration.[20] Secondly, it is more democratic to allow public administrators to exercise their discretion rather than a non-elected organ like the court because they are the persons assigned the task by the legislature.[21]

These reasons form the basis of the first part of the court's understanding of its role when conducting judicial review, namely, that it should avoid interfering with public administrators' substantive exercise of their discretion.[22] As conceptualised

---

[16] Lord Greene's words in *Wednesbury* (n 1).

[17] Mark Elliott and Jason Varuhas, *Administrative Law: Text and Materials* (5th edn, OUP 2017) 235; See also Peter Cane, *Administrative Law* (5th edn, OUP 2011) 140–143; Wade and Forsyth (n 2) 286.

[18] However, the relationship between the grounds of judicial review of factual determinations and one of the substantive exercise of discretion is the point at the deep-water level, which is argued as being influenced by the legal culture in Sects. 5.3 and 5.4 below.

[19] Wade and Forsyth (n 2) 286; Peter Cane and Leighton McDonald, *Principles of Administrative Law: Legal Regulation of Governance* (3rd edn, OUP 2018) 196.

[20] Cane (n 17) 140–141.

[21] Paul Craig, *Administrative Law* (8th edn, Sweet & Maxwell 2016) [21-002].

[22] Elliott and Varuhas (n 17) 262.

5.2 Judicial Review of Administrative Discretion at Surface and Deep Levels

by Craig, *'it is not for the courts to substitute their choice as to how the discretion ought to have been exercised for that of the administrative authority'*.[23] This mentality similarly floats on the surface level of both the English and Australian law. In terms of the former, Lord Greene continued the quotation shown at the beginning of this chapter with the following statement;

> *When discretion of this kind is granted the law recognises certain principles upon which that discretion must be exercised, but within the four corners of those principles the discretion, in my opinion, is an absolute one and cannot be questioned in any court of law.*[24]

This premise has been frequently cited as the starting point of the English courts' determination of the scope of judicial review in later cases.[25]

The necessity of discretion has also been explained in Australia, in the Kerr Report 1971, which read as follows;

> *In recent times in Australia… there has been a considerable expansion in the range of activities regulated, and in the volume and range of services provided, by government and statutory authorities.… This expansion has been accompanied, as it must be, by a substantial increase in the powers and discretions conferred by statute on Ministers of the Crown, officers of the administration and statutory authorities…*[26]

This was followed by the position that the Australian courts should generally not intervene in the exercise of administrative discretion. For example, Justice Mason of the HCA directly cited *Wednesbury* in *Minister for Aboriginal Affairs v Peko-Wallsend Ltd*;

> *The limited role of a court reviewing the exercise of an administrative discretion must constantly be borne in mind. It is not the function of the court to substitute its own decision for that of the administrator by exercising a discretion which the legislator has vested in the administrator.*[27]

Then, it became explicit in the judgment of Justice Brennan in *Attorney-General (NSW) v Quin*,[28] when he made the following statement; *'The duty and jurisdiction of the court to review administrative action do not go beyond the declaration and enforcing of the law which determines the limits and governs the exercise of the repository's power'*.[29] Consequently, the courts' jurisdiction to conduct judicial review is limited, as the administrative discretion does not go beyond the law. In the

---

[23] Craig (n 21) [21–002].
[24] n 1.
[25] E.g. *R v Cambridge Health Authority, Ex parte B* [1995] 2 All ER 129 and *R (Rogers) v Swindon NHS Primary Care Trust* [2006] 1 WLR 2649.
[26] Australian Commonwealth Administrative Review Committee, *Kerr Report* (Parliamentary Paper no 144/1972, August 1971) [15].
[27] (1986) 162 CLR 24 [15](d).
[28] (1990) 170 CLR 1. The main discussion in *Quin* is on the grounds of legitimate expectations. Therefore, its legal reasoning will be unpacked in the next chapter.
[29] ibid [17].

same vein as the English law, this judgment has been cited in a number of Australian cases.[30]

5.2.2 Courts Review Some Exercises of Discretion

While the courts accept their limitation to intervene in the substantive exercise of administrative discretion, the second part of their understanding is that they still have a role to conduct judicial review if an exercise of discretion is *'unreasonable, arbitrary, capricious or inconsistent'*.[31] In this situation, the court needs to observe *'what the law says about how administrative discretion should be exercised'*[32] or review whether *'the exercise of discretion is in a proper and lawful way in accordance with the presumed intentions of the legislature that conferred it'*.[33] Either way leads to protecting the surface-water legality, which is similarly recognised in England and Australia.

In terms of English law, this premise was explained by Lord Russell in *Kruse v Johnson* that if a local authority is unjust, *'the court might well say "Parliament never intended to give authority to make such rules; they are unreasonable and ultra vires"'*.[34] It was then referred to in a number of English cases; for example, *R v Board of Education*[35] and *Williams v Giddy*,[36] until *Wednesbury*, when Lord Greene held that

> The power of the court to interfere in each case is is not as an appellate authority to override a decision of the local authority, but as a judicial authority which is concerned, and concerned only, to see whether the local authority have contravened the law by acting in excess of the powers which Parliament has confided in them.[37]

Most scholars refer this protection of surface-water legality to the rule of law; for example, Elliott and Varuhas state that *'the existence of unlimited or unregulated discretion is considered anathema to the rule of law'*.[38] In the same vein, Cane explains that *'It is a basic tenet of the rule of law, as expounded by AV Dicey, that discretionary power should be controlled: uncontrolled…discretion is undesirable in most contexts'*.[39] Also, Wade and Forsyth assert that *'What the rule of law*

---

[30] E.g. *NAIS v Minister for Immigration and Multicultural Affairs* (2005) 228 CLR 470.
[31] Wade and Forsyth (n 2) 259, 286–288, 291; Elliott and Varuhas (n 17), 222–223, 235, 239, 247; Farulla (n 2) 212–213.
[32] Cane (n 17) 140; Wade and Forsyth (n 2) 286.
[33] Wade and Forsyth (n 2) 259.
[34] [1898] 2 QB 91, 100.
[35] [1910] 2 KB 165.
[36] [1911] AC 381 (See n 8 of Chapter 11 of Wade and Forsyth (n 2)).
[37] n 1, 234.
[38] Elliott and Varuhas (n 17) 235.
[39] Cane (n 17) 171.

demands is not that wide discretionary power should be eliminate, but that the law should control its exercise'.[40]

As for Australian law, the basis on which the courts conduct judicial review of some substantive exercise of discretion has also been accepted and stipulated in the 1971 Kerr Report that *'In the case of administrative decisions the judicial correction of which on the merits is possible because they raise justiciable issues...'*.[41] Evidence can also be found in the judgments of cases; for example, in *House v The King*, Justice Starke asserted that *'...it* [discretion] *must be exercised judicially, according to rules of reason and justice, and not arbitrary or capriciously or according to private opinion'*.[42] Subsequently, Chief Justice Brennan made the following observation in *Kruger v Commonwealth*;

> ...when a discretionary power is statutorily conferred on a repository, the power must be exercised reasonably, for the legislature is taken to intend that the discretion be so exercised.[43]

This has also been described by Australian scholars, for example, Aronson, Groves and Weeks clearly assert that *'An act or decision can be judicially reviewed on the ground of its unreasonableness'*.[44]

5.2.3 Extent of Judicial Review of Administrative Discretion

Up to this point, two parts of the courts' understanding of their role in conducting judicial review of administrative discretion have been described. On the one hand, administrative agents are allowed to use their discretion with the aim of enhancing the efficiency and effectiveness of public administration. Therefore, the courts should not usurp this power by quashing administrative decisions based on the discretion of administrators. On the other hand, the courts have to conduct judicial review to ensure that the exercise of discretion is in accordance with the law, for instance, it is not misused or unreasonable. These bases are recognised at the surface level of the law in both England and Australia.

However, the turning point is the question of 'how the court would determine a discretion as unreasonable'. As discussed in Chap. 1, there are some kinds of substantive exercises of discretion that are controversial and the courts need to consider whether or not they lead to the unlawfulness of an administrative action. This has become a decisive point in the determination of the scope of judicial review in both

---

[40] Wade and Forsyth (n 2) 286.
[41] Kerr (n 26) [390].
[42] (1936) 55 CLR 499, 503.
[43] (1997) 190 CLR 1, 36. See also *Minister for Immigration and Border Protection v Singh* (2014) 139 ALD 50 [43].
[44] Mark Aronson, Matthew Groves and Greg Weeks, *Judicial Review of Administrative Action and Government Liability* (6th edn, Thomson Reuters Australia 2017) [6.390].

England and Australia. For example, according to Wade and Forsyth, *the next requirement …is that the courts should draw those limits in a way which strikes the most suitable balance between executive efficiency and legal protection of the citizen'*.[45] In Australia, Chief Justice French also held in *Li* that *'Lawfulness, fairness and rationality… lie at the heart of administrative justice'*.[46] The most prominent statement is that made by Justice Brennan in *Quin,* as follows;

> If it be right to say that the court's jurisdiction in judicial review goes no further than declaring and enforcing the law prescribing the limits and governing the exercise of power, the next question immediately arises: what is the law? And that question, of course, must be answered by the court itself.[47]

The extent to which the court in a legal system considers administrative discretion as unreasonable is characterised in this section as a product of its deep understanding of what law is, which is embedded in the legal system's legal cultures. Comparative methodology illustrates that English and Australian courts use different doctrinal approaches to determine the grounds of judicial review related to the substantive exercise of discretion based on their diverse legal cultures.

As explained in the introduction, various grounds of judicial review and their application have considerably evolved in English law from the traditional *Wednesbury* unreasonableness to the adaptation of a variety of intensity and the adoption of proportionality from EU law and the ECHR into the courts' consideration of the scope of judicial review. The cases that best demonstrate the flexibility of doctrinal approaches and the mentality of the English courts, and are thereby selected for the analysis in the next section, are *Kennedy* and *Pham*.

The law in Australia also began with *Wednesbury,* but its development has been relatively different. In brief, the HCA accepted a new ground called *'irrationality and illogicality'* to challenge a decision made by the Refugee Review Tribunal ('RRT') in *S20/2002*. However, these grounds were relatively rigid considered because manifest reasoning had to be demonstrated for an administrative action to be regarded as unlawful.[48] They were later categorised with the other grounds like *Wednesbury* and jurisdictional fact under the central approach of jurisdictional error in *SZMDS* and *Li*. Also, proportionality was completely rejected in these cases.

These different approaches between the English and Australian law have been described and analysed in some literature, but mainly in respect of their functionality. For example, there has been a widespread debate among English scholars about the preference in applying the grounds of judicial review, particularly between rationality and proportionality. Some argue that proportionality or the concept of anxious scrutiny has a better framework for reviewing administrative discretion,[49] while

---

[45] Wade and Forsyth (n 2) 286.
[46] n 15 [14].
[47] n 28 [20].
[48] n 13 [61].
[49] E.g. Craig (n 21) [21–007]-[21–014]; Paul Craig, 'Proportionality, Rationality and Review' [2010] NZLR 265; Julian Rivers, 'Proportionality and Variable Intensity of Review' (2006) 65 CLJ

5.2 Judicial Review of Administrative Discretion at Surface and Deep Levels

others contend that proportionality intrudes excessively on the merits of administrative action, and therefore *Wednesbury* remains the appropriate approach in reviewing administrative discretion,[50] or support the concept of deference in reducing the degree of intensity of a review of the grounds.[51] At the same time, some scholars conclude that all the grounds of judicial review of substantive administrative discretion have a similar basis,[52] or that it is unnecessary to choose between them[53]; otherwise, the grounds are said to merge into a kind of scale or spectrum.[54] Australian scholars have analysed the advantages and disadvantages of adopting these various English doctrines and grounds into the Australian legal system.[55] Interestingly, rather than debating on this issue, the traditional models like *Wednesbury* are adopted in most of the literature. Meanwhile, proportionality is firmly rejected in Australia.[56]

Instead of giving a solution for these debates, a dive will be made into deep water in the next sections in order to understand the determination of the grounds of judicial review of the substantive exercise of administrative discretion from the perspective of the legal culture. This connection has been recognised by scholars, particularly in Australia; for example, by Cane and McDonald in the following statements;

> *Nonetheless, it is important to acknowledge that the strict separation of powers in Australia plays a substantial role in heightening judicial sensibilities to the importance of leaving some latitude for administrators to get things "wrong"*[57]

In terms of English law, Lord Reed stated in *Bank Mellatt v HM Treasury (No 2)* that

> *...the degree of restraint practised by courts in applying the principle of proportionality, and the extent to which they will respect the judgment of the primary decision maker, will*

---

174. Otherwise, this camp argues that unreasonableness should be improved by giving the review structure and intensity by the consideration of weight and balance (See Paul Craig, 'The Nature of Reasonableness Review' (2013) 66 Current Legal Problems 131).

[50] Tom Hickman, 'Problems for Proportionality' [2010] New Zealand Law Review 303; *R v Secretary of State for the Home Department, Ex parte Brind* [1991] 1 AC 696 (Lord Lowry).

[51] Murray Hunt, 'Sovereignty's Blight: Why Contemporary Public Law needs the Concept of 'Due Deference"' in Nick Bamforth and Peter Leyland (eds), *Public Law in a Multi-layered Constitution* (Hart Publishing 2003).

[52] Williams (n 2).

[53] Jowell Jeffrey, 'Proportionality and Unreasonableness: Neither Merger nor Takeover' in Hanna Wilberg and Mark Elliott (eds), *The Scope and Intensity of Substantive Review: Traversing Taggart's Rainbow* (Hart Publishing 2015).

[54] E.g. Taggart's Rainbow Review (see Michael Taggart, 'Proportionality, Deference, Wednesbury' [2008] NZL Rev 423) and Laws' Sliding Scale (n 5).

[55] Matthew Groves and Greg Weeks, 'Modern Extensions of Substantive Review: A Survey of Themes in Taggart's Work and in the Wider Literature' in Hanna Wilberg and Mark Elliott (eds), *The Scope and Intensity of Substantive Review: Traversing Taggart's Rainbow* (Hart Publishing 2015); Farulla (n 2); Aronson (n 2).

[56] Michael Taggart, 'Australian Exceptionalism in Judicial Review' (2008) 36 Federal Law Review 1; Cane and McDonald (n 19) 169.

[57] Cane and McDonald (n 19) 24.

depend upon the context and will in part reflect national traditions and institutional culture.[58]

The next sections are the detailed examinations of these statements. The doctrinal approaches, namely justifications, doctrines, applications, influence of international treaties and the validity and categorisation of the grounds of judicial review will be unpacked from legal reasoning of the aforementioned leading cases, and demonstrated as products of the English and Australian legal cultures. Furthermore, these analyses will facilitate a better understanding of the academic concepts and debates mentioned above. In essence, a framework of deep-water legality and legal culture will draw all the elements of the English and Australian determination of judicial review of administrative discretion into one holistic picture.

5.3 English Doctrinal Approaches

Rather than the particular grounds of judicial review, like jurisdictional fact and substantive legitimate expectations referred to in the previous and subsequent chapters, the overarching grounds of judicial review related to unreasonableness, applied by the English and Australian courts in conducting judicial review of the substantive exercise of administrative discretion are the subject of the analysis in this chapter. However, this and the next sections do not contain descriptions of all the cases in this area, but are focused instead on particularly connecting the overarching doctrinal approaches of leading English and Australian cases with a framework of deep-water legality and legal culture. For the English law, this section starts with a summary of the 'choices' the courts have in determining the scope of judicial review of substantive administrative discretion, namely, *Wednesbury*, modified rationality, the concept of anxious scrutiny, proportionality and deference.[59] These approaches have existed in English case law for some time. However, *Kennedy* and *Pham* illustrate them as ways in which '(deep-water) legality can be flexibly operated in England' based on the legal mentality of English judicial review constitutionalism.

---

[58] [2013] UKSC 38 [71].

[59] I have analysed this area of the law in Voraphol Malsukhum, 'Is Anything Lost by not Having Proportionality as a General Head of Judicial Review of Administrative Action' (2020) 49(2) Thammasat Law Journal 363. However, this was done to compare the functionality of the grounds of judicial review between the EU, English and French laws, which is different from the aim of this section.

5.3.1 Choices in English Law

The first approach for the English court in conducting judicial review of administrative discretion is the aforementioned W*ednesbury* unreasonableness. Although it has been applied in a few cases,[60] this ground has been widely criticised by English scholars and judges as being *'unreasonably rigid'* and therefore, *'undesirable'*.[61] This is because of its application that administrative discretion will be *'unlawful'* if it is *'so unreasonable that no reasonable authority could ever come to it'*.[62] Lord Greene cited an example of this situation in *Short v Poole Corporation*, in which the decision to dismiss a school teacher because of her red hair was deemed to be unreasonable.[63] This approach is so stringent that it is unlikely to be applicable to a real-life situation and it would be difficult for the claimant to win the case. The initial comment of *Wednesbury* came from no lesser a person than Lord Diplock, who stated that the ground is *'so outrageous in its defiance of logic or of accepted moral standards that no sensible person who had applied his mind to the question to be decided could have arrived at it'*.[64]

According to the methodology of this book, *Wednesbury* is 'an operation of legality in the narrowest sense'. Only administrative discretion that is *'so unreasonable'* can make an administrative action unlawful. This causes courts and scholars to attempt to move to other approaches by asserting that *'Wednesbury is not a monolithic ground of judicial review'* over administrative discretion in England.[65] The first to mention is that the courts apply the ground of rationality with variable standards of review for cases with different subject matters; for instance, the court raises the intensity of a review in cases that involve human rights.[66] The most-cited of these cases is *R v Ministry of Defence, Ex parte Smith*, in which Lord Bingham made the following statement in the Court of Appeal;

> *But in judging whether the decision-maker has exceeded this margin of appreciation the human rights context is important. The more substantial the interference with human rights, the more the court will require by way of justification before it is satisfied that the decision is reasonable...*[67]

This kind of broader application than the position in *Wednesbury* is commented by scholars in various ways. For example, some consider it positively as the modification of rationality (so-called *'Modified Rationality'* or *'Super-Wednesbury'*), or

---

[60] Cane (n 17) 186–188.
[61] Craig, *Administrative Law* (n 21) [21–001], [21–007]; Wade and Forsyth (n 2) 303.
[62] n 1, 230.
[63] [1926] Ch 66.
[64] n 3, 410.
[65] See Cane (n 17) 189–192; Wade and Forsyth (n 2) 304–305.
[66] See Cane (n 17) 186–188; Craig (n 21) [21–010]-[21–011].
[67] [1996] QB 517, 554.

as making a contribution under the concept of anxious scrutiny, not only applied to rights-based cases,[68] but expanded to apply to cases that are non-rights-based.[69]

Another option for the English courts to determine the scope of judicial review of administrative discretion is the use of proportionality as a ground of judicial review. Indeed, this door has been open since Lord Diplock stated in *CCSU* that the courts could adopt proportionality, *'which is recognised in the administrative law of several of our fellow members of the European Economic Community'* into their consideration.[70] As briefly described in Chap. 2, proportionality enters English law by two main routes in practice.[71] Firstly, as a member state of the EU, proportionality is directly applied in England when decision-makers are acting within the scope of EU law. Secondly, proportionality was introduced into the English law by Article 2 of the HRA, in relation to Sect. 6 of the HRA. Since it is clear from the jurisprudence of the ECHR that proportionality is a general principle of law[72]; therefore, the English courts can review and quash a breach of the qualified Convention rights by proportionality.[73]

The application of proportionality in EU law and the ECHR, namely its methodology and intensity of review, has been adopted in these areas. In terms of the former, there is a series of questions to consider regarding proportionality. The first is whether it is necessary for the public administration to take a measure (known as the 'Necessity Question'). The second is whether the measure is sufficient to achieve an aim (the 'Sufficiency Question'). The third is the question of finding a balance between burdening an individual and fulfilling public administration (known as a 'Narrow Sense of Proportionality').[74] As for the latter, the level of intensity in undertaking a judicial review of administrative discretion can vary; for instance, the courts will review cases that involve fundamental rights more intensively than others.[75] Additionally, they will apply a different level of intensity when reviewing these same rights-based cases in different circumstances. The classic example is that the court in *R (Animal Defenders International) v Secretary of State for Culture, Media and Sport* reviewed the limitation of political speech at election time more

---

[68] E.g. *Bugdaycay v Secretary of State for the Home Department* [1987] 1 AC 514; Lord Carnwath, 'From Judicial Outrage to Sliding Scales: Where Next for Wednesbury' (the ALBA Annual Lecture, 12 November 2013); Lord Sumption, 'Anxious Scrutiny' (Bar Association Annual Lecture, 4 November 2014).

[69] Paul Craig, 'Judicial Review and Anxious Scrutiny: Foundations, Evolution and Application' [2015] PL 60.

[70] n 3.

[71] Proportionality is also applied on the grounds of substantive legitimate expectations, which will be discussed in the next chapter.

[72] Craig, *Administrative Law* (n 21) [20–042]-[20–044].

[73] Recognised in a number of cases such as *Alconbury Developments Ltd v Secretary of State for the Environment* [2001] 2 WLR 1389 and *R v Secretary of State for the Home Department, Ex parte Daly* [2001] 2 AC 532.

[74] Paul Craig, *EU Administrative Law* (3rd edn, OUP 2018) 642–643.

[75] E.g. *R (Quila) v Secretary of State for the Home Department* [2011] UKSC 45.

5.3 English Doctrinal Approaches

intrusively than the freedom of speech in the context of private interest in *Belfast City Council v Miss Behavin' Ltd*.[76]

As discussed above, on the one hand, this application of proportionality is regarded as being positive, for example, it has a '*more structured analysis*', which requires the administration to '*justify its policy choice*' and the courts to '*strike down a decision*' in more specific detail than *Wednesbury*.[77] Thereby, it is argued that proportionality should become a general head of judicial review in the UK, even without referring to the ECHR.[78] Lord Sumption connected this with the concept of anxious scrutiny that '*Anxious scrutiny was originally designed to broaden the test for substantive review at common law by importing some element of the doctrine of proportionality from the case-law of the ECHR*'.[79]

On the other hand, some scholars regard the variable intensity of review as a dangerous element of the proportionality test, leading the court to substitute the discretion of decision-makers with its own. This has led to an increasing debate about the concept of deference to render the use of proportionality approach. In the same vein, a number of scholars question the extent to which the courts should defer to the institutional and democratic competences of the decision-makers.[80] For example, it is argued that the degree of deference should be based on the subject of the case.[81]

The status of the HRA in the domestic law is more complex; for example, the different answers to the question, 'what is the role of the courts according to the HRA?', can lead to different determinations of the common law grounds of judicial review. For instance, in *Miss Behavin,* Baroness Hale asserts that the role of the court in adjudicating cases involving human rights (under the HRA) is quite different from its role in an ordinary judicial review.[82] This can support the argument that proportionality should be applied in cases that directly involve human rights, but *Wednesbury* reasonableness applied in cases that do not directly involve such rights, which may be compatible with Taggart's rainbow concept.[83] Alternatively, the idea that the role of the HRA is to introduce a substantive approach from the ECHR to domestic law[84] can support Craig's argument that proportionality should be a general head of judicial review in the UK.[85]

---

[76] [2008] 1 AC 1312.

[77] Paul Craig, 'Unreasonableness and Proportionality in UK Law' in Evelyn Elllis (ed), *The Principle of Proportionality in the Laws of Europe* (Hart Publishing 1999) 91–100.

[78] ibid.

[79] Sumption (n 68).

[80] Elliot and Varuhas (n 17) 284–302.

[81] Alison Young, 'In Defence of Due Deference' (2009) 72 MLR 554.

[82] n 76.

[83] n 54.

[84] *R v Denbigh High School HL, Ex parte Begum* [2006] UKHL 15.

[85] *Alconbury* (n 73) (Lord Slynn).

Rather than preferring or criticising these approaches, this section regards them as 'choices', which the English courts can 'flexibly' apply in their determination of the scope of judicial review. Lord Justice Laws also made the following statement, which is compatible with the methodology of this book;

> On the surface at least the test of unreasonableness or irrationality which the rule propounds is monolithic; it leaves no scope for a variable standard or review according to the subject-matter of the case...
> But in fact the courts, while broadly adhering to the monolithic language of Wednesbury, have to a considerable extent in recent years adopted variable standards of review...[86]

While Laws only noted the variable standards prior to the HRA, it is pointed out in this section that all the aforementioned doctrinal approaches, namely, modified rationality, anxious scrutiny, proportionality and deference are 'the widened-up operations of legality', reflecting 'how legality is understood at the deep-water level in England'. All these choices available to the English courts are the background for understanding how the doctrinal approaches in *Kennedy* and *Pham* are connected to the English legal culture.

5.3.2 Kennedy

The claimant in *Kennedy* was a journalist, who had asked the Charity Commission to disclose information related to the affairs of a specific charity. However, the decision-maker refused the request according to Sections 2(2) and 32(2) of the Freedom of Information Act 2000 ('FOIA'), on the grounds that it had absolute exemption from the duty to disclose *'any document placed in its custody or created by it, for the purposes of an inquiry which it has in the public interest conducted in the exercise of its function'*.[87] The applicant then respectively appealed to the Information Commission, Information Tribunal, High Court, CA and finally, the UKSC.

The focus of this case is not the consideration of the FOIA, since all the judgments of the UKSC agreed that the applicant's claim could not succeed by referring to Section 32.[88] After examining the wording and construction of the sections[89] and comparing it to the Inquiries Act 2005,[90] Lord Mance held as follows;

> ...the construction is clear: section 32 was intended to provide an absolute exemption which would not cease abruptly at the end of the court, arbitration or inquiry proceedings,

---

[86] John Laws, '*Wednesbury*' in Christopher Forsyth and Ivan Hare (eds), *The Golden Metwand and the Crooked Cord: Essays in Honour of Sir William Wade QC* (Hart Publishing 1998) 186–187.
[87] n 11 [2]–[23], [160]–[171].
[88] ibid [101].
[89] ibid [28].
[90] ibid [31]–[33].

5.3 English Doctrinal Approaches

but would continue until the relevant documents became historical records... [According to Section 63(1) of the FIOA].[91]

Also, since a document becomes a historical record in 30 years after the year of its creation based on Section 62(2) of the FOIA, it is not likely that the aim of the provision is that an inquiry should run for more than 30 years.[92]

Instead, the point is Lord Mance's legal reasoning after examining Section 32, which was as follows;

> ...however [it] *does not mean that the information held by the Charity Commission as a result of its inquiries may not be required to be disclosed outside section 32 under other statutory and/or common law powers preserved by section 78 of the FOIA*[93]

This means that the protection of the legality of administrative discretion does not only rely on Section 32 of the FOIA, but also other laws. Apart from the Charities Act 1993 ('CRA'), the point was raised in the case to what extent domestic laws should be read under the protection of freedom of expression in Article 10 of the ECHR.[94]

The conclusion of the case was split into two camps. Firstly, although the majority, namely, Lord Neuberger, Lord Mance, Lord Clarke, Lord Sumption and Lord Toulson considered that the CRA had a higher standard of not disclosing information when reviewing administrative discretion than the ECHR jurisprudence, they accepted the presumption of openness in common law. Therefore, the CRA could be compared to Article 10 of the ECHR.[95] Conversely, Lord Wilson and Lord Carnwath held that there was no basis in reading down Article 10 of the ECHR in determining the FOIA and CRA.

More important than this conclusion was the legal reasoning of the extent to which the courts should adopt norms from interrelated legal cultures like the ECHR (through the HRA) into in their common law determination of legality. Although the distinctive elements of English legal culture, namely an unwritten constitution and the twin concepts of parliamentary sovereignty and the rule of law, were not directly defined in the judgments of *Kennedy* as they were in *Cart*, some connections between the English legal culture and the doctrinal approaches can be drawn under three points.

Firstly, apart from the phrase that the disclosure of information may be required by *'other statutory and/or common law powers',* Lord Mance also set the determination of the scope of judicial review in this case as part of the operation of legality by emphasising that *'the scheme regarding disclosure of court documents ought to be regarded with the principle that any such scheme must be "in accordance with*

---

[91] ibid [34] (Lord Mance), agreed by [102]–[104] (Lord Toulson), [171]–[172], [200] (Lord Wilson), [221] (Lord Carnwath).

[92] ibid [104] (Lord Toulson).

[93] ibid [34].

[94] ibid [34], [102].

[95] ibid [43]–[56] (Lord Mance), [109]–[132] (Lord Toulson), [136] (Lord Clarke), [157] (Lord Sumption).

law".[96] Next, he demonstrated his (deep) understanding of (English) legality as not ending with the domestic law, but being open to the influence of interrelated legal cultures, like the provisions in the ECHR. He explicitly called for *'the general principle of open justice'* and argued that the court must act *'in accordance with any applicable Convention rights'.*[97] This was claimed to be a *'fruitful feature'* in the UK.[98] Legality does not *'need to be protected by any particular statute or route'.*[99] This flexible operation of legality can be termed *'a common law presumption in favour of openness in a context',*[100] which was supported by Lords Toulson and Sumption, as follows;

> What we now term human rights law and public law has developed through our common law over a long period of time...This has always been the way of the common law and it has not ceased on the enactment of the Human Rights Act 1998...[101]

While the adoption of the norms from interrelated legal cultures into the determination of the scope of judicial review is accepted, the relationship between the ECHR and domestic law is a different point. Lord Mance explains that, although it is flexible, the determination should still begin with the domestic law, as follows;

> In some areas, the common law may go further than the Convention, and in some contexts it may also be inspired by the Convention rights and jurisprudence...And in time, of course, a synthesis may emerge. But the natural starting point in any dispute is to start with domestic law, and it is certainly not to focus exclusively on the Convention rights, without surveying the wider common law scene.[102]

Therefore, in the current case, the court shall *'regard to first the Charities Act and then article 10'.*[103] Based on this approach, Lord Mance found that the objectives of the CRA of maintaining public trust, accountability, proportionality and transparency by disclosing information to the public,[104] were *'comparable to any that might arise under article 10'.*[105] Hence, the CRA was *'no less favourable'* in imposing a general duty to disclose information on the public authorities than the ECHR.[106]

---

[96] ibid [37].

[97] ibid [37].

[98] ibid [38].

[99] ibid [39].

[100] ibid [45], [47]. Lord Justice Toulson's reasoning in *R (Guardian News and Media Ltd) v City of Westminster Magistrates' Court* [2013] QB 618 [88] that *'The development of the common law did not come to an end on the passing of the Human Rights Act 1998. It is in vigorous health and flourishing in many parts of the world which share a common legal tradition'* has been quoted (ibid [46]).

[101] ibid [133].

[102] ibid [46].

[103] ibid [42].

[104] ibid [43].

[105] ibid [45]. The analysis of the jurisprudence of Article 10 of the ECHR was done in [58]–[100] (Lord Mance) and [142]–[146] (Lord Toulson).

[106] ibid [101]. The other majority judgments also followed the same direction (e.g. [135], [147], [149] (Lord Toulson), [154] (Lord Sumption)).

5.3 English Doctrinal Approaches

Indeed, the core character of the English operation of deep-water legality is not that it is 'always open' to influences from interrelated legal cultures, but that it is based on 'flexible lines whether to open or not'. This was demonstrated when the dissenting judgments did not agree with the approach of openness. For example, Lord Wilson explained the court's role in conducting a judicial review as *'a social watchdog'* to consider whether the administrative discretion was *'in accordance with an elaborate statutory scheme, drawn by Parliament'*.[107] Lord Carnwath also perceived the role of the court in protecting legality as depending *'on the statutory or other legal framework within which the particular inquiry is established'*.[108]

Instead of arguing for or against either judgment, the focus of this section is the flexibility how the individual judges in *Kennedy* can provide different understandings of whether their determination of the scope of judicial review of administrative discretion was influenced by interrelated legal cultures. This process was described by Lord Neuberger in an extra judicial speech, as follows;

> *Initially at least, the attitude of many lawyers and judges in the UK to the Convention was not unlike that of a child to a new toy. As we became fascinated with the new toy, the old toy, the common law, was left in the cupboard. Recently, the judges have tried to bring the common law back to centre stage. The most dramatic example of this is the UK Supreme Court's decision earlier this year in Kennedy v Charity Commissioners*[109]

This metaphorical description of common law, the ECHR (through the HRA) and the relationship between them as toys, either or both of which the courts feel free to pick up or leave during their play times, demonstrates clearly that the doctrinal approach to determine the scope of judicial review in *Kennedy* is a product of the flexible mentality of English judicial review constitutionalism.

As described in Sect. 5.3.1 above, the flexibility of the relationship between the HRA and common law is usually related to the doctrines the courts apply in determining the scope of judicial review. This is the second point of a doctrinal approach to be unpacked from the legal reasoning of *Kennedy*. Similar to the methodology of Lord Diplock in *CCSU* and Lord Woolf in *Coughlan*,[110] Lord Mance in *Kennedy* listed a range of doctrines the English courts can apply to determine the scope of judicial review of the substantive exercise of discretion, from the rigid *Wednesbury*,[111] the modification of *Wednesbury* and the concept of anxious scrutiny,[112] the principles of fair procedure,[113] to proportionality. Apart from that the application of the grounds was also described referencing to Craig's work that *'both reasonableness*

---

[107] ibid [189].

[108] ibid [241].

[109] Lord Neuberger, 'The Role of Judges in Human Rights Jurisprudence: A Comparison of the Australian and UK experience' (Conference at the Supreme Court of Victoria, Melbourne, 8 August 2014).

[110] This will be exemplified in the next chapter.

[111] n 11 [51].

[112] ibid [52]–[54] by citing *Bugdaycay* (n 68); *Smith* (n 67).

[113] ibid [53].

192   5 Influence of the Legal Cultures on the Grounds Relating to Substantive Exercise…

review and proportionality involve considerations of weight and balance, with the intensity of the scrutiny and the weight to be given to any primary decision maker's view depending on the context'.[114] Moreover, the overlap and preference between them are accepted, as shown in the following statement;

> The advantage of the terminology of proportionality is that it introduces an element of structure into the exercise, by directing attention to factors such as suitability or appropriateness, necessity and the balance or imbalance of benefits and disadvantages. There seems no reason why such factors should not be relevant in judicial review even outside the scope of Convention and EU law.[115]

This part of legal reasoning demonstrates that the English courts are able to apply various doctrines and applications in their determination of the scope of judicial review. It was followed by the statement that these approaches '*enable them* [the courts] *to perform their constitutional function in an increasingly complex polity'*.[116] This means that the flexibility of the court's determination of the substantive exercise of discretion is a product of its constitutional function. While the judgment stopped here, it is continued in this section that the 'constitutional function' has a deep perspective based on the English legal culture.

Unlike some of the cases analysed in the previous chapters, the elements of English judicial review constitutionalism were not directly prescribed in the legal reasoning of *Kennedy*. However, some scholars have noted the connection between the doctrinal approaches and the courts' deep understanding of their role in conducting judicial review embedded in the English constitutional settings. A prominent one was Elliott and Varuhas, who made the following assertion;

> …the law in this area has long been a barometer signifying the courts' perception of how fundamental constitutional principles shape their own role relative to that of executive government. As the law continues to evolve in this area, as it surely will, much will therefore turn upon the UKSC's understanding of where the constitutional parameters of judicial review lies; in an unwritten constitutional order such as that of the UK.[117]

It is proposed in this book that the way to make this assertion more concrete is to compare this position to the different doctrinal approaches of the Australian law, which are based on the existence of a written constitution. Hence, making this connection and comparison explicit is a co-function of this section and the next one.

Another distinctive element of the English legal culture, argued in *Kennedy* as influencing the described flexibility of doctrines and the adoption of interrelated legal cultures, is the twin concept of parliamentary sovereignty and the rule of law. Likewise, this was not mentioned directly in the legal reasoning of the judgments. However, this section points out that it was operational in the legal reasoning of *Kennedy*. All the judgments, whether they accepted or rejected the reading down of

---

[114] ibid [54] by citing Craig, 'The Nature of Reasonableness Review' (n 49).
[115] ibid [54].
[116] ibid [52] by citing *R (Q) v Secretary of State for the Home Department* [2004] QB 36 [112] (Lord Phillips).
[117] Elliott and Varuhas (n 17) 314–315.

5.3 English Doctrinal Approaches 193

domestic law by Article 10 of the ECHR, described two sides of value the courts are required to consider in determining the scope of judicial review. For example, Lord Mance argues that the disclosure of information underpins democracy and accountability, legitimate interest and openness when taking administrative action,[118] particularly in cases that involve charities, like this one.[119] For this reason, the court should review administrative discretion not the disclosure of information. On the other hand, public administration requires information to be *'genuinely private, confidential or sensitive'*[120] in some situations, particularly those that relate to national security or international affairs. This supports the position that the court should not force public administrators to disclose the information by means of a judicial review because they are *'not equipped by training or experience, or furnished with the requisite knowledge or advice'*.[121]

These are explained by the individual judges in various terms. For example, Lord Toulson referred to the values of *'open justice'*, *'democracy'*, *'the rule of law'*, *'public confidence'*, *'checks and balances'* and *'transparency of the legal process'*[122] to be considered along with *'public interest'* and *'discretion granted by parliament in running public administration'*.[123] These are all regarded as part of the *'constitutional landscape'*.[124] Importantly, all the judgments point out that they need to be *'balanced by the court'* on the case-by-case basis. For example, Lord Mance asserted that

> *These competing considerations, and the balance between them, lie behind the issues on this appeal*[125]

> *All such considerations can and would need to be taken into account,...they are no reason why the balancing exercise should not be undertaken.*[126]

In the same vein, Lord Toulson prescribed that

> *...in the case of a statutory inquiry Parliament decided to leave it to the public body to rule on what should be disclosed, balancing the public interest in its decision being open to proper public scrutiny against any countervailing factors, but the exercise of such power must be amenable to review by the court.*[127]

---

[118] n 11 [1].
[119] ibid [49].
[120] ibid [1].
[121] ibid [53] by citing *IBA Healthcare Ltd v Office of Fair Trading* [2004] ICR 1364 (Carnwath LJ) and *Brind* (n 50) 767 (Lord Lowry).
[122] ibid [110], [112], [115], [118].
[123] ibid [107], [114], [121], [123], [130].
[124] ibid [108].
[125] ibid [1].
[126] ibid [50].
[127] ibid [123].

There is no standard formula for determining how strong the countervailing factor or factors must be. The court has to carry out a balancing exercise which will be fact-specific.[128]

It is argued in this section that the balancing process between these values in determining the scope of judicial review of administrative discretion is an 'implication' of the balancing process between the twin concepts of parliamentary sovereignty and the rule of law. On the one hand, the explanation of *'democracy and accountability, legitimate interest and openness'* and *'open justice'* in administrative action endorse the necessity for the courts to conduct judicial review in order to protect the rule of law of administrative action. On the other hand, parliamentary sovereignty guides the court not to change the legal framework, where parliament grants the administrative agent the role to exercise discretion regarding the confidentiality of public administration. These two sides of mentality were resolved through the process of balancing by the court, which facilitated the malleability in their determination of the scope judicial review, as described above. This application of flexible doctrinal approaches based on the flexible mentality of English legal culture is continuously illustrated in *Pham,* as detailed below.

5.3.3 *Pham*

The claimant in *Pham* was born in Vietnam, migrated to the UK, and acquired British nationality. Later, the Home Secretary made an order under Section 40(2) of the British Nationality Act 1981 ('BNA'), which deprived him of his British nationality and announced that he was to be deported to Vietnam on the grounds of national security, since he had received terrorist training in Yemen. However, the Vietnamese government declined the claimant's Vietnamese nationality and he pleaded that his Vietnamese citizenship had been lost when he was granted the British one. Therefore, the order of the decision-maker was unlawful, since he was going to be stateless based on the meaning of Article 1(1) of the Convention related to the Status of Stateless Persons, as he was *'not considered as a national by any state under the operation of its law'*. The case was brought to the Special Immigration Appeals Commission, the CA and eventually, the UKSC.[129]

Again, the judges reached an agreement on the conclusion of the case, namely that there was no evidence that the Vietnamese Government treated the claimant as a non-national by the operation of its law, so the decision was not unlawful based on Section 40(4) of the BNA.[130] Instead, this section is focused on the legal reasoning and doctrinal approaches applied by the court in determining the scope of judicial review of administrative discretion, especially when it relates to an interrelated legal

---

[128] ibid [113]. See also [125], [140], [153] (Lord Toulson), [175] (Lord Wilson).
[129] n 12 [1]–[30].
[130] ibid [35]–[38] (Lord Carnwath), [63], [66]–[67] (Lord Mance), [101]–[102] (Lord Sumption), [112] (Lord Sumption).

culture like EU law. Lord Carnwath addressed two points in this respect, the first of which was whether the order was lawful, since the deprivation of the claimant's British nationality would also cause him to lose his citizenship of the EU.[131] The second was whether or not consideration must be given to the question of proportionality if such consideration fell within the ambit of EU law.[132] Similar to *Kennedy*, these were the questions on which the courts determined their scope of judicial review based on their understanding of legality. Three points of the doctrinal approaches unpacked from the legal reasoning of *Pham* can demonstrate the courts' flexibility in operating legality.

Firstly, the flexibility in adopting interrelated legal cultures into the operation of legality was confirmed in *Kennedy,* particularly since Lord Mance argued that it is open for the courts to consider EU law if *'it offers advantages over the relevant domestic law'*.[133] However, the *'starting point'* remains identifying *'the ultimate legislative authority'* in the domestic law.[134] Parliamentary sovereignty was emphasised as being significant; therefore, *'...we must view the UK as independent, Parliament as sovereign and European law as part of domestic law because Parliament has so willed'*.[135] Importantly, Lord Mance obviously included EU law as a part of the *'domestic constitutional arrangements'* when he made the following statement;

> *...a domestic court must ultimately decide for itself what is consistent with its own domestic constitutional arrangements, including in the case of the 1972 Act what jurisdictional limits exist under the European Treaties...*[136]

This part of legal reasoning in *Pham* is a prominent output of this aspect of English legal culture. It is possible and flexible for the English courts to adopt an interrelated legal culture as the source of an understanding of their role in the conducting of judicial review. By way of comparison, it will be demonstrated in the next section that this kind of adoption of international treaty as part of legality is almost impossible in Australia because of the country's legal culture.

The second point that demonstrates flexibility of doctrinal approaches in the determination of the scope of judicial review in *Pham* is the validity of proportionality as a doctrine adopted from EU law. It will be clarified that the conclusion of all judgments was similar because this point had to be a preliminary issue remitted by the SIAC, according to the availability of the facts. When it was not, the court did not deal with it.[137] However, the focus of this section is the legal reasoning for the

---

[131] This was also pointed out by other judges, namely ibid [31], [39] (Lord Carnwath), [68]–[69] (Lord Mance).

[132] ibid [39] (Lord Carnwath).

[133] ibid [72].

[134] ibid [80].

[135] ibid [80].

[136] ibid [90].

[137] ibid [56]–[62] (Lord Carnwath), [102] (Lord Sumption), [110] (Lord Sumption), [121] (Lord Reed).

application of proportionality, as if this has been pointed out to the SIAC. It is clear that the judgments accepted the advantages of proportionality and argued for its status to be a general head of judicial review in common law. For example, by referring to *Kennedy* and Craig's work, Lord Carnwath argued that these approaches were in greater force in the present case.[138] Proportionality would *'ensure that any future consideration by the higher courts will be informed by a clear understanding of the practical differences...'*.[139] This was similar to Lord Mance, who regarded proportionality as *'a tool directing attention to different aspects of what is implied in any rational assessment of the reasonableness of a restriction'*.[140] This is even clear in Lord Reed's judgment, as follows;

> It may be helpful to distinguish between proportionality as a general ground of review of administrative action, confining the exercise of power to means which are proportionate to the ends pursued, from proportionality as a basis for scrutinising justifications put forward for interferences with legal rights.[141]

Although the conclusions were similar, there was a small difference in the opinions of the relationship between proportionality and rationality. Lord Sumption doubted that '*...if the withdrawal of Mr Pham's British nationality was within the ambit of EU law it will be necessary to apply to the decision the principle of proportionality*'.[142] He pointed out that this could mislead people to perceive that '*...the principle of proportionality as it applies in EU law is liable to produce a different result in a case like this by comparison with ordinary principles of English public law*',[143] instead, he expressed the following belief;

> ...although English law has not adopted the principle of proportionality generally, it has for many years stumbled towards a concept which is in significant respects similar, and over the last three decades has been influenced by European jurisprudence even in areas of law lying beyond the domains of EU and international human rights law.[144]

Therefore, what should be done is to *'expand the scope of rationality review so as to incorporate at common law significant elements of the principle of proportionality'*.[145] However, Lord Reed contended that it did not mean that *'...the Wednesbury test, even when applied with "heightened" or "anxious" scrutiny, is identical to the principle of proportionality as understood in EU law'*.[146]

Rather than giving a certain solution to how the relationship between rationality and proportionality, and between the ECHR or EU law and common law should be,

---

[138] ibid [60]; See also [94]–[95] (Lord Mance).

[139] ibid [62].

[140] ibid [96], [98] by citing Lübbe-Wolff, 'The Principle of Proportionality in the Case Law of the German Federal Constitutional Court' (2014) 34 HRLJ 12, 16–17.

[141] ibid [113].

[142] ibid [103].

[143] ibid [104].

[144] Ibid [105].

[145] ibid.

[146] ibid [115].

it is pointed out in this section that the norms from interrelated legal culture, like Convention rights and proportionality, could be adopted as part of the court's understanding of legality in *Pham* 'in a flexible manner'. Similar to *Kennedy*, the implication of the balancing process between the twin concepts appeared in *Pham*. For example, Lord Sumption regarded the *'individual's right to nationality'* and *'national security'* as being located on *'the* [different] *weightiest ends of the sliding scale'*, whereby the courts have to determine *'the approach they court takes to draw a balance'*.[147]

5.3.4 Other Elements in the English Picture

Arguments that supported the application of proportionality, either as a model for developing common law rationality or as a general head of judicial review, continued after *Kennedy* and *Pham*. For example, in *Keyu v Secretary of State for Foreign and Commonwealth Affairs,* Lord Neuberger argued that *'the four-stage* [proportionality] *test…should now be applied in place of rationality in all domestic judicial review cases'*.[148] However, this is not a conclusion of the scope of judicial review of administrative discretion in England. For example, when Lord Mance ended his judgment in *Kennedy,* he clearly stated that *'The nature of judicial review in every case depends on the context'*.[149] In the same vein, Lord Reed stated in *Pham* that *'proportionality is not a monolithic principle, expressed and applied in a uniform way in different legal systems and in different contexts'*.[150] This has also been recognised by some scholars; for example, Elliott and Varuhas conclude their chapter by saying that *'the general tenor of these cases is that the law in this area is evolving'*[151] and Craig also made the following similar statement that *'Judicial deliberation in this area, whether under the guise of reasonableness or proportionality, is never going to be uncontroversial'*.[152]

Apart from this, there is also room to debate the relationship between the grounds of judicial review; for example, whether or not a factual determination can be argued as being unreasonable using the *Wednesbury* approach.[153] In the same vein, the criteria set by Lord Justice Carnwath in *E* demonstrates an attempt to merge the doctrine of jurisdictional fact and unfairness into a general test to review the facts. These efforts by scholars to categorise or rearrange the grounds also result in a variety of terminologies being applied in the English literature, for instance,

---

[147] ibid [108].
[148] [2015] UKSC 69 [131].
[149] n 11 [51].
[150] n 12 [117] by citing *Bank Mellatt* (n 58) [69]–[72] (Lord Slynn).
[151] Elliott and Varuhas (n 17) 309.
[152] Craig, 'The Nature of Reasonableness Review' (n 49) 167.
[153] E.g. *Secretary of State for Education and Science v Tameside MBC* [1977] AC 1014.

unreasonableness,[154] the rule of reason and law[155] and the abuse of power.[156] At the bottom line, it could be concluded that the grounds for administrative discretion and those for factual issues described in the previous chapter usually merge and overlap in the English law.

5.3.5 Products of the English Legal Culture

Rather than concluding the English determination of the scope of judicial review of administrative discretion under the label of pragmatism, the underlying complexities of legal reasoning have been unpacked in detail under the systematic points of doctrinal approaches and are encapsulated in the snapshot below.

Doctrinal Approaches	English Law
Choice of grounds and concepts the courts can apply in conducting judicial review	Wednesbury unreasonableness Modified rationality Anxious scrutiny Proportionality in cases related to Convention rights (with Deference) Proportionality in common law without reference to the HRA

Application	Varied depending on the grounds, for example;
	    Stringent and rigid (Traditional *Wednesbury*)
	    Variable intensities of review (Modified rationality)
	    Methodology of structured analysis and variable intensities of review (Proportionality)
	    Various degrees depending on the case (Deference)

Influence of international treaties	Flexible to be included in the scope of legality However, the extent depends on particular cases and individual judges
Relationship between the grounds	Overlap between ones of administrative discretion and ones of factual determination

Academic debates	Various as room is opened up, for example;
	    Development in applying particular concepts
	    Preferences between the grounds
	    Relationship between the HRA and common law
	    Whether and should proportionality become a general head of judicial review

---

[154] Craig, *Administrative Law* (n 21) [19–002].
[155] Wade and Forsyth (n 2) 293–305.
[156] Farulla (n 2) 214–215.

5.4 Australian Doctrinal Approaches

Doctrinal Approaches	English Law	
Justifications	Various and flexible, but containing a similar kind of balancing process	
	To intervene (Implication of the rule of law)	Not to intervene (Parliamentary Sovereignty)
	Open justice, Democracy, Rule of law, Public confidence, Checks and balances and Transparency of the legal process (*Kennedy*) Right to nationality (*Pham*)	Public interest and Discretion granted by parliament in running the public administration (*Kennedy*) National security (*Pham*)

Importantly, all the doctrinal approaches and legal reasoning in the prior cases of *Kennedy* and *Pham*, as well as the secondary elements, namely, a variety of academic debates, terminologies and overlaps between the grounds, are connected to English legal culture. Two connections are explicit, the first of which is that the flexibility in taking the ECHR and EU law into the consideration of the scope of judicial review of administrative discretion in *Kennedy* and *Pham* are products of the flexible legal mentality of the English courts, particularly in the aspect of accepting an interrelated legal culture as part of their constitutional arrangement. The second is that the legal reasoning in *Kennedy* and *Pham* demonstrate the implications of a balancing process between the twin concepts of parliamentary sovereignty and the rule of law. This uncertain consideration of interrelated legal culture as the source of mentality on the role of the court in conducting judicial review and the nature of the balancing process led to the flexibility of the doctrinal approaches applied in the cases. Additionally, the absence of a written constitution is believed to be another factor that influences this flexibility. This will be clarified in the next section when it is compared with the different story of Australian law. The scope of judicial review of administrative discretion in Australia is determined by relatively fixed doctrinal approaches. The relationship between the grounds of judicial review are systematically categorised in the judgments. The influence of interrelated legal cultures, like proportionality, are firmly rejected. All of these approaches are connected to the written constitution and rigid framework of the separation of powers.

5.4 Australian Doctrinal Approaches

In contrast to the English law, the grounds of judicial review of administrative discretion have not changed much in Australia. Rather than being flexible, *Wednesbury* Unreasonableness is described as the '*perennial feature of the* [Australian] *common law*'.[157] Correspondingly, the reason for this rigid position does not hide under swirling water, but is tangible based on the premise of the distinction between legality and merits. The courts have a role to ensure that discretionary power complies

---

[157] Creyke, McMillan and Smyth (n 10) [15.2.2].

with the legal limits. A judicial review will only be conducted when administrative discretion becomes ultra vires and the ground that leads to such a case is that discretion is so unreasonable that *'no reasonable person could ever come to it'* or goes *'beyond anything that could have been intended by the conferring of the discretionary power'*.[158] Traditional *Wednesbury* unreasonableness has been applied in a number of cases; for example, the judgments in *Peko* held that

> The preferred ground on which this is done...[is] that the decision is "manifestly unreasonable". This ground of review was considered by Lord Greene in Wednesbury, in which his Lordship said that it would only be made out if it were shown that the decision was so unreasonable that no reasonable person could have come to it.[159]

Subsequently, in *Griffiths v Rose,* Justice Perram further increased the degree of rigidity in applying the ground of unreasonableness by holding that a review on this basis will only succeed *'...when a level of unreasonableness is reached which, in essence, permits of no contrary view'*.[160]

Different from the English law, the channel of 'other choices' the courts can use to step away from *Wednesbury* has not been opened much. As described in Chap. 2, Australia is not a member of the EU and has not ratified the ECHR; therefore, there is no aspect of this interrelated legal culture that can influence the adoption of proportionality into the domestic law, as well as an act to imply it, like the HRA.[161] Although the ADJR operates in tandem with the common law, the application in determining the scope of judicial review through unreasonableness is similarly settled at the standard of *Wednesbury*.[162] Therefore, the relationship and preference between the common law and the ADJR on this point have not been debated in the same way as those between the ECHR and the common law in the UK. Similarly, the concept of deference limiting the intensity of the review has not been widely discussed; indeed, it was firmly rejected since *Enfield,* as demonstrated in the last chapter.[163]

However, this does not mean that there are no 'moves' in this area of Australian law at all. The prominent one is the introduction of new ground of judicial review of administrative discretion in *S20/2002* called *'illogicality and irrationality'*. This is because Section 476(2)(b) of the Migration Act 1958 (Cth) ('MA') at that time provided that a decision of the RRT could not be challenged on the ground *'that the decision involved an exercise of a power that is so unreasonable that no reasonable person could have so exercised the power [Wednesbury]'*. Therefore, the applicant had to argue instead that the RRT's decision was *'irrational, illogical and not based upon findings or inferences supported by logical grounds'*. Completely different

---

[158] Kerr (n 26) 11–12 (vi).

[159] n 27 [15].

[160] (2011) 192 FCR 130 [50].

[161] Administrative Review Council Federal Judicial Review in Australia, *Report No 50* (2012) [7.44].

[162] ADJR, s 5(2)(g), 6(2)(g).

[163] The rule of restraint may be argued to be an alternative for deference. This will be exemplified in the analysis of *S20/2002* and *SZMDs* below.

5.4 Australian Doctrinal Approaches

from the flexibility of English law, the consideration of illogicality and irrationality as a ground of judicial review requires serious manifestation of unreasonableness in order to treat the administrative discretion as unlawful.[164] Its validity, application and relationship with other grounds were further considered later in *SZMDs* and *Li*. Additionally, the proposal to apply proportionality as a general ground of judicial review has been firmly rejected.[165]

Because of the described slow development, it is not necessity to describe other prior Australian cases as background material as in the previous section. Instead, this section will be directly focused on unpacking the legal reasoning of *S20/2002*, *SZMD* and *Li*, and connecting them as products of the Australian legal culture. Although this has been recognised in some literature, the navigating approach of unpacking and comparing it to the English law will make the connection become clearer for both English and Australian law.

5.4.1 S20/2002

The applicant in *S20/2002* was refused the protection of a visa, since the Minister for Immigration and Multicultural Affairs was not satisfied that the applicant was a person Australia was obliged to protect based on the criterion in Section 36(2) of the MA.[166] This decision was subsequently approved by the RRT, which has the power to affirm, vary or set aside the delegate's decision based on Sections 65 and 415 of the MA. As explained above, the applicant challenged the decision for being illogical, irrational, or not based on findings or inferences of fact supported by logical grounds.[167] Despite some different details in the decisions of individual judges,[168] they all agreed that illogicality and irrationality was a valid ground of judicial review. Three points that demonstrate the connection between the determination of these grounds and Australian legal culture are unpacked below.

Firstly, similar to the English law, the determination of illogicality and irrationality as ground of judicial review was explicitly described as an operation of legality by Chief Justice Gleeson in the following statement;

> ...where there is a duty to act judicially, a power must be exercised "according to law...", and irrationality of the kind ... may involve non-compliance with the duty....In a context

---

[164] Aronson, Groves and Weeks (n 44) [6.420].

[165] The rejection is also expressed in the determination of substantive legitimate expectations in *Re Minister for Immigration and Multicultural Affairs, Ex parte Lam* (2003) 214 CLR 1. This will be unpacked in the next chapter.

[166] n 13 [2].

[167] ibid [1]–[4] (Gleeson CJ) and [82]–[109] (Kirby J). Indeed, the decision was also challenged on the grounds that it was affected by either actual or apprehended bias. However, this issue is not the focus of this section.

[168] For example, Justice Kirby was the only judge who endorsed heightened scrutiny in conducting judicial review of administrative discretion, which imperils life or liberty (ibid [158]–[159]).

such as the present, it is necessary to identify and characterise the suggested error, and relate it to the legal rubric under which a decision is challenged.[169]

The logic of legality was applied so that the court would only be able to conduct judicial review when the administrative discretion was regarded as being unlawful. However, the determination of judges in *S20/2002* as to whether the disputed administrative discretion was unlawful or not was clearly different from the English law. Rather than being flexible the extent to which an interrelated legal culture influences the domestic law, the court in *S20/2002* connected the determination of the scope of judicial review to the centrality of jurisdictional error.[170] Justice Kirby made this point clear in the following statement;

> *Where the reasons of a tribunal established by the Parliament to make decisions and exercise powers of the kind in question, disclose an irrational, illogical or perverse process of reasoning, it may sometimes be concluded that the "decision" thereby made does not conform to the requirements of the Act. It may involve jurisdictional error...More importantly, it will authorise relief from this Court under its constitutional mandate to hold all officers of the Commonwealth answerable to the Constitution and to the other laws pursuant (or subject) to which they exercise their powers.*[171]

This is systematic and parallel to the area of judicial review of quasi-judicial institutions and jurisdictional fact analysed in Chaps. 3 and 4.

Next, it was shown in the previous section that various grounds of judicial review overlap in England, and the courts leave these open to decide in later cases and for scholars to discuss whether or not they are covered by legality. In Australia, although the grounds of judicial review like *Wednesbury,* illogicality and irrationality are corresponding in nature, an attempt was made to categorise their application in the judgments of *S20/2002*. For example, Chief Justice Gleeson described the overlap as follows;

> *As with illogicality and irrationality, unreasonableness is a protean concept, and may require closer definition where it is said to be relevant to judicial review of an administrative decision...*[172]

Similarly, while the relationship between the grounds of judicial review of administrative discretion and those of factual determination is flexible in England, the judgment in *S20/2002* attempted to clarify their validity, since Justices McHugh and Gummow held that

> *The jurisdictional fact which supplies the hinge upon which a particular statutory regime turns may be so identified in the relevant law as to be purely factual in content. It was to prevent litigation directly on such questions of fact that legislatures stipulated the opinion of the decision-maker as to specified matters. That in turn led the courts to treat the formation of the statutory state of satisfaction as "reasonable" and thus to posit some criterion*

---

[169] ibid [9] by citing *Australian Broadcasting Tribunal v Bond* (1990) 170 CLR 321, 367.
[170] ibid [59].
[171] ibid [81]; See also [34] (McHugh and Gummow JJ).
[172] ibid [20].

5.4 Australian Doctrinal Approaches

for the assessment of the factual elements which went to supply that state of satisfaction...[173]

This means that illogicality and irrationality, claimed as a ground in *S20/2002*, can apply when reviewing an administrative decision that encompasses subjectively unreasonable factual findings. Read with *Enfield* and *Timbarra*, the formation becomes that jurisdictional fact is applied to review objective factual determination, while illogicality and irrationality can apply for reviewing the subjective unreasonableness of both factual determination and administrative discretion. This formation was added and considered in *SZMDs* and *Li*, which will shortly be unpacked below.

Next, the judgment in *S20/2002* emphasised *'the limitation placed by legislatures upon statutory "appeals" from specialist tribunals and decision-makers, and the scope of judicial review procedures created by statutes'*.[174] This leads to the second point that, instead of the different applications to determine the scope of judicial review being dependent upon the doctrine, illogicality and irrationality were strictly determined based on the statutory construction of the relevant legislature. This application was repeatedly described by all the judges in the relatively same manner. For example, Chief Justice Gleeson stated, *'We are concerned with the statutory provisions that operate upon the state of satisfaction, or lack of satisfaction, of an administrative decision-maker'*.[175] The words *'we are concerned'* demonstrate well how the framework of the separation of powers prescribed in the relevant legislation is important to the mentality of the Australian courts. Justice Kirby also explained that

The nature and source of the official's power will usually be deduced from the enactment pursuant to which he or she has acted. By contrast, the review can be conducted pursuant to the statute that confers the power on the official, or the Constitution.[176]

The legislative provision that confers the jurisdiction on the administrative decision-maker and the nature of the decision for which it provides, construed in its statutory and constitutional context, will also supply the limits of that jurisdiction and indicate the circumstances that will establish whether the decision-maker has trespassed beyond, or otherwise misconceived, his or her authority to act.[177]

The legal reasoning in *S20/2002* that has been unpacked up to this point demonstrates that illogicality and irrationality were accepted as a valid ground of judicial review of the subjective exercise of discretion and the factual determination of administrative action. This was formulated apart from jurisdictional fact, but they are all systematically categorised as a subset of jurisdictional error. Parallel to the previous chapters, the application in determining the grounds was relatively fixed in the consideration of statutory construction. Compared to the English law, all of these doctrinal approaches demonstrate a relatively clear answer to 'the question of

---

[173] ibid [54]. See also [125] (Kirby J).
[174] ibid [58].
[175] ibid [8].
[176] ibid [113].
[177] ibid [123]; See also [116].

what is law?'. Using similar logic to the English law analysis, this different operation of legality and determination of the scope of judicial review are products of the Australian legal culture. As shown above, it was difficult to demonstrate the connection between the scope of judicial review and legal culture in the case of English law, but this was a comparatively simple process in terms of the Australian law, because the distinctive elements of Australian legal culture were directly referred to as the justification for determining the scope of judicial review in *S20/2002*. These are the rule of law, the distinction between legality and merits, the entrenchment of the jurisdiction of the HCA by Section 75(v) of the written constitution, and the centrality of jurisdictional error. For example, Justices McHugh and Gummow explained that

> In Re Minister for Immigration and Multicultural Affairs, Ex parte Lam, we emphasised that the distinction between jurisdictional and non-jurisdictional error which informs s 75(v) manifests the separation between the judicial power and the legislative function of translating policy into statutory form and the executive function of administration of those laws.[178]

The legal reasoning given by Justice Kirby was also explicit. For example, he stated that

> According to the present doctrine of this Court interpreting s 75(v), a person seeking relief under that provision must establish jurisdictional error in order to secure the issue of the writs of Mandamus or prohibition. Therefore, if the appellant can establish jurisdictional error, he may obtain relief from this Court.[179]

Unlike *Kennedy*, the judgments in *S20/2002* did not describe two sides of values, transformed from the twin concepts between parliamentary sovereignty and the rule of law, as well as the process of balancing them. Instead, the distinctive elements of the Australian legal culture were directly explained to support the courts' fixed and clear approaches in determining the scope of judicial review. Justice Kirby defined this set of related elements as '*this country's peculiar constitutional arrangements*'.[180]

5.4.2 SZMDs

The situation in *SZMDs* was relatively similar to that in *S20/2002*. The applicants requested the protection of a visa under Section 36(2) of the MA, claiming that they feared they would be prosecuted in Pakistan because of their homosexuality. The decision-maker rejected the application and the RRT approved the rejection on the ground that it was not satisfied with the obligation to protect. The difference from *S20/2002* in terms of fact was that unreasonableness was no longer prohibited from

---

[178] ibid [58]–[59].
[179] ibid [119], [122], [154]; See also [112]–[114] (Kirby J), [173] (Callinan J).
[180] ibid [168].

5.4 Australian Doctrinal Approaches

being argued against the RRT because of the amendment of the legislation.[181] Therefore, the applicant in *SZMDs* appealed the case to the Federal Court and the HCA on the grounds that the decision was *'unreasonable, illogical and irrational'*, and thereby consisted of a jurisdictional error.[182] The legal reasoning given by the judgments in *SZMDs*, following *S20/2002*, demonstrates how the doctrinal approaches to determine the scope of judicial review became relatively fixed in the light of the Australian legal culture. Three points can be unpacked, as detailed below.

Firstly, even though the conclusion of the case was divided into two sides,[183] all the judgments clearly regarded the determination of illogicality and irrationality as an operation of legality. For example, Justices Crennan and Bell stated that *'...satisfaction of the existence of facts must amount in point of law to what an empowering provision prescribes or specifies'*.[184] This is also parallel to the judgment in *S20/2002*; rather than possessing the features of flexibility as in the English law, jurisdictional error is the central approach in the operation of Australian deep-water legality. This was clarified by Justices Gummow and Kiefel at the very front of their judgments, when they declared that *'...the only avenue of judicial review in the present case was that rooted in s 75(v) of the Constitution itself and that required jurisdictional error to quash the administrative decision in question'*.[185] Justices Crennan and Bell also clearly stated that *'The main question arising on the appeal is whether "illogicality", "irrationality", or "lack of articulation" in a finding of jurisdictional fact can amount to jurisdictional error'*.[186]

Furthermore, rather than being debatable like the relationship between common law and the ECHR in English law, the judgments of Justices Gummow and Kiefel illustrated that the present case '[does] *not arise under one of the systems of review of administrative decisions which are established by laws of the Commonwealth and under which the grounds of review are not limited to those involving jurisdictional error...in particular, the ADJR'*,[187] but *'the application of the doctrine of jurisdictional error'*.[188] They clarified the fact that the English approaches, namely, the rubric of abuse of power and the consideration of whether to import proportionality from EU law into the domestic law, were not required in the present case.[189]

Next, the categorisation between common law grounds of judicial review were described in additions to *S20/2002*. Justices Gummow and Kiefel began by

---

[181] By introducing the privative clause in Section 474 of the MA in the light of *Plaintiff S157/2002 v Commonwealth* (2003) 211 CLR 476.

[182] n 14 [1]–[4], [8]–[15], [56]–[72], [90]–[120].

[183] While the majority, which consisted of Justices Heydon, Crennan and Bell, held that the RRT's decision was not illogical and irrational (ibid [56]–[137]), Justices Gummow and Kiefel held a dissenting opinion that it was (ibid [1]–[55]).

[184] ibid [122].

[185] ibid [7] then emphasised in [36].

[186] ibid [94], [123], [130]–[131].

[187] ibid [5], then emphasised in [28].

[188] ibid [29].

[189] ibid [27].

explaining the different application of jurisdictional fact in the English and Australian laws. For instance, the ground is generally covered in the English court's understanding of legality, but the extent of the understanding is flexible and debatable. In their words,

> In the English system the "jurisdictional fact" was an appropriate marker for the enforcement of legality; how much further the field for judicial review of administrative action extended remained a matter of debate.[190]

This is different from the Australian deep-water legality, which involves determining jurisdictional fact by rigidly considering the statutory construction.[191] Factual determination becomes unlawful when it fails to exercise jurisdiction.[192] This application of jurisdictional fact was claimed to have *'added significance where the law in question is made by a legislature'*.[193]

Not only is this application of jurisdictional fact parallel with those in *Timbarra* and *Enfield* analysed in the previous chapter, but Justices Gummow and Kiefel also clarified that jurisdictional fact can be confused with unreasonableness,[194] and rather than leaving this room open, Justices Crennan and Bell attempted to establish a categorisation between them. Firstly, they asserted that the *Wednesbury* standard should be retained in applying unreasonableness.[195] The court conducts judicial review of discretion through *Wednesbury 'in circumstances where no reasons are required'*.[196] Secondly, jurisdictional fact is based on the ground that *'...fact-finding must be based on probative material, one correlative of which is that a decision based on no evidence displays jurisdictional error'*.[197] Thirdly, the judgment affirmed that illogicality and irrationality could be applied as a way to review the state of satisfaction[198] in the reasoning process of administrative discretion, similar to *S20/2002*.[199]

This legal reasoning clarified the formation of the categorisation between the grounds of judicial review from *S20/2002*. While *Wednesbury* could be applied as *'a safety net'* for reviewing administrative discretion, when no reasons were required,[200] illogicality and irrationality could be applied to review the subjective legal reasoning of factual determination and administrative discretion and jurisdictional fact could be applied for reviewing objective fact related to the submission of evidence. However, all of these grounds are covered under the approach of

---

[190] ibid [18], [20]–[22].
[191] ibid [23].
[192] ibid [24].
[193] ibid [25].
[194] ibid [39].
[195] ibid [124].
[196] ibid [128].
[197] ibid [124].
[198] ibid [124].
[199] ibid [131].
[200] A term applied by Creyke, McMillan and Smyth (n 10) [15.2.2].

5.4 Australian Doctrinal Approaches

jurisdictional error, regarded as Australian deep-water legality.[201] The judgment went further than *S20/2002* by demonstrating that these approaches are clearly different from the English law, where proportionality has been adopted from EU law and merged into the common law.[202] This was also clear from the transcript of legal argument of the case, in which Justice Kiefel stated that

> *The word "proportionality" can have many colours to it. Sometimes when it is waved around in English decisions it does not entirely mean quite the same thing as the system from which it is derived…*[203]

Apart from the categorisation, the determination of the aforementioned grounds of judicial review of administrative discretion is relatively fixed on the consideration of statutory construction. For example, Justices Gummow and Kiefel stated that *'Many of the leading authorities in this court in which administrative decisions were challenged concerned legislative regimes…'*.[204] Similarly, Justices Crennan and Bell asserted that *'This Court has observed with reference to s 75(v) of the Constitution and jurisdictional error that where a statutory power is conferred the legislature is taken to intend that the discretion is to be exercised reasonably and justly'*.[205] Subsequently, although the conclusions of the judges in *SZMDs* were different, they similarly considered the statutory construction of the MA in a very detailed manner, and this was explicitly done without the interference of an interrelated legal culture.[206]

In terms of justification, similar to *S20/2002*, the legal reasoning in *SZMDs* demonstrates direct references to the distinctive elements of Australian legal culture, namely, the written constitution. For example, Justices Gummow and Kiefel asserted that the judicial review in this case *'was that rooted in section 75(v) of the Constitution'*.[207] Additionally, Justices Gummow and Kiefel further explained that the privative clause in Section 474 of the MA ousting the judicial review of the RRT's decision was ineffective based on the premise in *Plaintiff S157/2002*.[208] This determination of the scope of judicial review related to the status of the privative clause was systematic to the analysis of *Kirk* in Chap. 3. Eventually, they stated that the distinction between jurisdictional error and non-jurisdictional error was connected to the *'setting of the Australian Constitution'*.[209] Indeed, not only jurisdictional error, but all the relatively fixed doctrinal approaches the courts applied to

---

[201] n 14 [132].

[202] ibid [127].

[203] The Transcript of legal argument in *Minister for Immigration and Citizenship v SZMDs* [2010] HCA 16.

[204] n 14 [34].

[205] ibid [123].

[206] ibid [41]–[54] (Gummow and Kiefel JJ), [131]–[136] (Crennan and Kiefel JJ).

[207] ibid [7].

[208] ibid [7].

[209] ibid [16].

determine the scope of judicial review in *SZMDs* were products of the rigid mentality of Australian judicial review constitutionalism.

5.4.3 Li

Following on from *S20/2002* and *SZMDs*, the situation in *Li* was also based on the same statutory regime of the MA. The applicant requested that the process of reviewing her visa be postponed until the outcome of her skills assessment was finalised. The application was refused by the Minister for Immigration and Citizenship and the refusal was approved by the Migration Review Tribunal ('MRT') under Section 363(1)(b) of the MA. The case was appealed to both the Federal Court and the HCA on the grounds that the MRT's decision was one that no reasonable tribunal could have made.[210] It is comprehensively shown in this section how the doctrinal approaches from *S20/2002* and *SZMDs* were further entrenched in *Li* in the light of the Australian legal culture in the three points.

Firstly, the judgments in *Li* affirmed that the scope of judicial review was determined by the logic of legality. For example, Chief Justice French held that *'Every statutory discretion, however broad, is constrained by law'*.[211] He also cited *R v Anderson, Ex parte Ipec-Air Pty Ltd*[212] and *Sharp v Wakefield*[213] to explain that *'a discretion allowed by statute to the holder of an office is intended to be exercised according to the rules of reason and justice, not according to private opinion; according to law'*.[214] The rationality ground required by the rules of reason is *'an essential element of lawfulness in decision-making'*.[215] Justices Hayne, Kiefel and Bell also asserted that *'…when something is to be done within the discretion of an authority, it is to be done according to the rules of reason and justice. That is what is meant by "according to law"'*.[216] They emphasised that

> Whether a decision-maker be regarded, by reference to the scope and purpose of the statute…the final conclusion will in each case be that the decision-maker has been unreasonable in a legal sense.[217]

Next, although the grounds on which to review administrative discretion were categorised in a slightly different way from *SZMDs*, the relationship between them has been defined, rather than left open. For example, Chief Justice French accepted

---

[210] n 15 [1]–[16] (French CJ), [33]–[45] (Hayne, Kiefel and Bell JJ).
[211] ibid [23] by citing *Shrimpton v The Commonwealth* (1945) 69 CLR 613, 629–630.
[212] [1965] HCA 27.
[213] [1891] AC 173.
[214] n 15 [24].
[215] ibid [26].
[216] ibid [65] by citing *Sharp v Wakefield* [1891] AC 173, 179.
[217] ibid [72].

5.4 Australian Doctrinal Approaches

the overlap between the traditional *Wednesbury* unreasonableness[218] and illogicality and irrationality, as ground for reviewing the process of giving reasoning in administrative discretion.[219] However, he clarified that

> A distinction may arguably be drawn between rationality and reasonableness on the basis that not every rational decision is reasonable. It is not necessary for present purposes to undertake a general consideration of that distinction which might be thought to invite a kind of proportionality analysis to bridge a propounded gap between the two concepts.[220]

Rather than being debatable, this legal reasoning was designed to re-check that the door for incorporating proportionality into the Australian common law had been properly locked. Justices Hayne, Kiefel and Bell also considered that, although *Wednesbury* is not the endpoint in controlling discretion,[221] its development should not be flexible as it was in the English law; instead, the determination was subjected to *'the scope and purpose of the statute'*.[222] In the same vein, Justice Gageler also held that *Wednesbury* should remain in the Australian law rather than being modified.[223]

In short, the judgments in *Li* did not attempt to distinguish the grounds rigidly as they did in *SZMDs*. However, they emphasised that the courts must determine the unlawfulness of administrative discretion through the approach of jurisdictional error and the consideration of the relevant statutory construction, as opposed to being varied and influenced by an interrelated legal culture like the English law. This is the second point in considering the relatively rigidity of the doctrinal approaches in the Australian law. For example, Chief Justice French cited Justice Dixon in *Shrimpton v The Commonwealth,* as follows;

> Every statutory discretion is confined by the subject matter, scope and purpose of the legislation under which it is conferred. Where the discretion is conferred on a judicial or administrative officer without definition of the grounds upon which it is to be exercised then.[224]

Justices Hayne, Kiefel and Bell also held that *'The legal standard of reasonableness must be the standard indicated by the true construction of the statute'*.[225] Similarly, Justice Gageler stated that

> Implication of reasonableness...is a manifestation of the general and deeply rooted common law principle of construction that such decision-making authority as is conferred by

---

[218] ibid [26]–[27].
[219] ibid [28].
[220] ibid [30].
[221] ibid [64], [68].
[222] ibid [72].
[223] ibid [113].
[224] ibid [23] by citing [1945] HCA 4; See also the reference to *FAI Insurances Ltd v Winneke* (1982) 151 CLR 342 [24] that *'discretionary power is to be ascertained by reference to the scope and purpose of the statutory enactment'*.
[225] ibid [67], [74], [88]–[89].

statute must be exercised according to law and to reason within limits set by the subject-matter, scope and purposes of the statute.[226]

In the aspect of justification, a similar set of elements of the Australian legal culture as that applied in *S20/2002* and *SZMDs* was referred to in *Li*. The most prominent were Chief Justice French citing Justice Dixon in *Shrimpton v The Commonwealth* that *'Complete freedom from legal control, is a quality which cannot ... be given under our Constitution to a discretion...'*,[227] and Justice Gageler's assertion that the court can order relief to compel the performance by the MRT under Section 75(v) of the Constitution.[228]

5.4.4 Other Elements in the Australian Picture

Up to this point, the relatively fixed doctrinal approaches applied to review administrative discretion in *S20/2002*, *SZMDs* and *Li* have been shown in this section. In essence, the emerging ground of illogicality and irrationality was accepted, but applied rigidly, namely, through the consideration of the relevant statutory construction. Different from the merger of judicial review of the factual issues and the evaluation of unfairness in *E*, the relationship between the grounds, namely illogicality and irrationality, *Wednesbury* and jurisdictional fact, has been categorised in Australia. Unlike the unclear boundary between the ECHR and the English common law, these grounds for an Australian common law judicial review do not interrelate with the ADJR. Rather than various choices of domestic law and interrelated legal cultures, proportionality was firmly rejected in the cases. In the same vein, the approaches in the Australian cases did not come with various ways of justification like those in *Kennedy* and *Pham*; instead, they were steadily backed up by a set of distinctive elements of the Australian legal culture, namely the written constitution, the distinction between legality and merits and the separation of powers.

These doctrinal approaches based on the Australian legal culture continued after *Li*. For example, the judgment in *Minister for Immigration and Border Protection v Singh* was as follows;

> There is...a presumption of law that Parliament intends an exercise of power to be reasonable...Subject to any impinging Constitutional consideration, the presence of a clear statutory qualification or contrary intention may be capable of modifying or excluding either implication.[229]

Subsequently, in *Fiorentino v Companies Auditors and Liquidators Disciplinary Board*, Justice Wigney further summarised and entrenched the principles in *Li* and *Singh*, for example;

---

[226] ibid [90]–[92].
[227] ibid [23].
[228] ibid [104].
[229] n 43 [43].

5.4 Australian Doctrinal Approaches

Legal unreasonableness can be a conclusion reached by a supervising Court after the identification of an underlying jurisdictional error in the decision-making process...

The legal standard of reasonableness and the indicia of legal unreasonableness will need to be found in the scope, subject and purpose of the particular statutory provisions in issue in any given case.[230]

In terms of proportionality, although there are some arguments for its advantages based on functionality,[231] it is still not a separate ground of judicial review in Australia and this is clearly because of the Australian legal culture. Apart from Taggart regarding proportionality in Australia as *'a bridge too far'*, it was compared to the English law in a Report of the Law Council of Australia with the following comment;

The reason for the UK expansion of judicial review is due to peculiar factors – UK's geopolitical positioning in the EU, the HRA and the absence of a written Constitution which incorporates a strict separation of powers. Due to the nature of Australia's written Constitution it might not be desirable (or even possible) to create rights of review that use a principle such as proportionality.[232]

This clarifies the connection between the approach and legal culture, not only for Australian law, but also English law. The rejection of proportionality in Australia is also parallel to the area of judicial review based on the grounds of substantive legitimate expectations. This is the subject of an analysis in the next chapter.

All the doctrinal approaches in the cases result in that the room for scholars to debate the determination of the scope of judicial review of administrative discretion in Australia is relatively smaller than in England. Significantly, almost all the literature emphasises the connection between the approaches and the Australian constitutional orders. Examples of the prominent ones are as follows;[233]

Because there is a constitutional separation of powers, the High Court has a strongly arguable basis for its conclusion that the making of executive (including administrative discretionary) decisions is not a matter for the judicial arm of government. (Sir Anthony Mason)[234]

...the Australian courts... slowly but surely turn up the intensity of review of factual findings. The effect of this, in my view, has clearly been to enhance the integrity of administrative decision-making in this country. (Farulla)[235]

---

[230] [2014] FCA 641 [76](a)(b)(f).

[231] n 55.

[232] n 161.

[233] See also Brian Preston, 'Judicial Review of Illegality and Irrationality of Administrative Decisions in Australia' (2006) 18 Australian Bar Review 17; Aronson, Groves and Weeks (n 44) [5.10], [6.390], [6.450].

[234] Mason A, 'Mike Taggart and Australian Exceptionalism' in David Dyzenhaus, Murray Hunt and Grant Huscroft (eds), *A Simple Common Lawyer: Essays in Honour of Michael Taggart* (Hart Publishing 2009) 182.

[235] Farulla (n 2) 232.

5.4.5 Products of the Australian Legal Culture

Parallel to the previous chapters, the discussion of the flexible aspects of the Australian law is explicit in the legal reasoning of some cases. For example, in *S20/2002*, Justice Kirby proposed an increase of intensity of review in the way that the courts should not *'be confined to the rigidities and technical limitations of a bygone age'*.[236] From his perspective, a *'more rigorous examination'* through judicial review can be taken in some cases related to human rights.[237] He asserted that this was not an *'endorsement of an unrestrained judicial review'*.[238] Therefore, it is not concluded in this section that the Australian cases will necessarily result in limiting the courts' jurisdiction to conduct judicial review of the substantive exercise of discretion. As demonstrated in *Li*, the court can still refer to unreasonableness as a basis to invalidate an unjust administrative decision when no specific legal error can be identified.

Instead, the focus of this section is the rigid pattern of doctrinal approaches and legal reasoning distinctively applied by the Australian courts in determining the scope of judicial review. This was examined based on the legal reasoning in *S20/2002*, *SZMDs* and *Li*. A snapshot of the analysis is captured in the table below.

Doctrinal Approaches	Australian Law
Grounds of Judicial Review	*Wednesbury* unreasonableness Illogicality and irrationality Jurisdictional fact All are covered under jurisdictional error, which does not include proportionality
Relationship between them	Overlapping in nature, but the courts try to clarify the validity and categorisation between them
Application	Fixed Considered from the relevant statutory construction
Influence of interrelated legal cultures	None
Relationship to the ADJR	Clear separation between common law and an ADJR judicial review
Academic debates	Some argue for the advantages of the variety of intensities of review, but there are much fewer debates than those in the English law Firm rejection of the concept of deference
Justification	Fixed at the separation of powers, the rule of law, concept of jurisdiction, Section 75(v) of the constitution

---

[236] n 13 [159].

[237] ibid [150] by citing *R v Secretary of State for the Home Department, Ex parte Bugdaycay* [1987] AC 514, 531 and 537 (Lord Bridge and Lord Tempelman).

[238] ibid [148].

Unlike the English law, the influence of the Australian constitutional setting on these distinctive doctrinal approaches is not hidden, but recognised in a volume of literature. There is a distinctive understanding of the rule of law, giving importance to the rigid distinction between legality and merits, based on the framework of the separation of powers prescribed in the written constitution. In short, the conclusory label of formalism in relation to the determination of the grounds of judicial review related to the substantive exercise of discretion has been turned into a concrete examination in this section. Although the concept of *'the rule of restraint'* has been raised,[239] its application in practice is relatively strict based on the framework of the separation of powers. This is parallel to the way in which the doctrines of gravity of errors and threshold of materiality were regarded in *Hossain*.[240] If it amounts to a jurisdictional error considered from the relevant statutory context, the courts will neither defer nor restrain it.[241] Mr. Gageler's statement in the transcript of the legal argument of *SZMDs* was clear on the difference from the English law in that *'it is hard to think of illogicality as a question of degree'*.[242]

5.5 Conclusion

> *The legality and merits distinction will also continue in Australia to be a strong constraint on the development of unreasonableness.*
> *…the divergence in English law is to be explained also by a greater readiness in some English decisions to escape the construction of the legality and merits distinction and to declare administrative action to be invalid.*[243]

These commonly-recognised differences between the English and Australian courts' determination of the scope of judicial review of administrative discretion were unpacked in this chapter through the framework of deep-water legality and legal culture. In summary, the English courts have choices in the determination, ranging from the domestic one like *Wednesbury*, modified rationality, anxious scrutiny, to those adopted from interrelated legal cultures, like proportionality and deference. The applications, justifications and relationship between common law and the ECHR or EU law have been given flexibly by individual judges. These approaches influence other elements in the English picture like various debates among scholars, the relationship between the grounds of judicial review and the various terminologies applied in this area.

On the other hand, the Australian courts apply three main grounds, namely, *Wednesbury*, illogicality and irrationality and jurisdictional fact in determining the scope of judicial review of administrative discretion in common law, which are

---

[239] n 13 [147]–[150].
[240] See Sect. 3.4.3 of Chap. 3.
[241] ibid [149].
[242] n 203.
[243] Creyke, McMillan and Smyth (n 10) [15.2.9]–[15.2.11].

clearly distinctive from the ADJR. The attempts to categorise the application between them are taken under the central approach of jurisdictional error. The applications of the grounds are relatively fixed at the consideration of the relevant statutory construction without being influenced by an interrelated legal culture.

These different doctrinal approaches have been analysed as products of the differences between English and Australian legal culture. While the fixed approaches in Australia are the result of the rigid framework of the separation of powers prescribed in the written constitution, the flexibility in English law is a product of the balance between the twin concepts of parliamentary sovereignty and the rule of law and the absence of a written constitution. The next chapter will contain a further applicability of the framework of deep-water legality and legal culture to better understand of the determination of an emerging ground of judicial review related to the exercise of discretion, which is substantive legitimate expectations.

Chapter 6
Influence of the Legal Cultures on Legitimate Expectations

Abstract This chapter contains a comparative analysis of English cases in the area of legitimate expectations, namely, *Richmond-Upon-Thames* [1994] 1 WLR 74, *Hamble Fisheries Ltd* [1995] 2 All E R 714 and *R v North and East Devon Health Authority; Ex parte Coughlan* [2000] 3 All ER 850 and Australian cases namely, *Kioa v West* (1985) 159 CLR 550, *Attorney-General (NSW) v Quin* (1990) 170 CLR 1, *Minister of State for Immigration & Ethnic Affairs v Ah Hin Teoh* [1995] HCA 20 and *Re Minister for Immigration and Multicultural Affairs; Ex parte Lam* (2003) 214 CLR 1. While the English courts flexibly regard substantive legitimate expectations as a valid ground of judicial review, the Australian courts firmly reject it. It is pointed out that these different doctrinal approaches and legal reasoning are products of the English and Australian legal cultures.

6.1 Introduction

> [The] *review of Coughlan…and the later cases reveals a striking contrast between, on the one hand, the relatively narrow scope of the actual decision in that case and, on the other, the wide ranging and open-ended nature of the legal discussion.* (Lord Carnwath, *United Policyholders Group v Attorney General of Trinidad and Tobago*)[1]

> *Australian courts have not accepted that the concept of legitimate expectations can underpin substantive entitlements as distinct from informing the content of procedural fairness. Indeed, there are those who…call the legitimate expectation in our public law a zombie principle.* (Chief Justice French)[2]

There is no better way to start this chapter than with the above statements, displaying 'completely' different approaches of the determination of substantive

---

[1] [2016] UKPC 17 [110].
[2] Chief Justice Robert French, 'The Globalisation of Public Law: A Quilting of Legalities' (Public Law Conference, Cambridge, 12 September 2016).

legitimate expectations, as an 'emerging' ground of judicial review in English and Australian administrative law.[3]

Legitimate expectations denotes a claim by individuals that he or she has a legitimate expectation to be treated in a certain way based on public administrator's promise, general policy, representation or past practice. When the public administrator changes its decision against such representation, the individual then seeks judicial review to protect his or her expectation.[4] Two main types of legitimate expectations can be categorised from two kinds of benefit claimed by the individuals. While procedural legitimate expectations is where an individual claims an existence of process right,[5] substantive legitimate expectations is applied in claiming a particular benefit due to a representation.[6]

On the one hand, the first quotation of Lord Carnwath in the judgment of *United Policyholders Group*[7] above discusses *Coughlan*[8] and other cases[9] as evolving substantive legitimate expectations as a ground of judicial review in England. The courts strike a balance between narrowing and widening the application of the ground. The determination stands on a spectrum allowing the courts to adopt *'a more or less intrusive quality of review'*.[10] For example, the judgment recommended *'caution'* when applying the ground in a kind of case involving policy issues.[11] In such cases, Lord Woolf's approach in *Coughlan*, particularly the third category relying on the abuse of power doctrine,[12] is narrowly interpreted.[13] On the other hand, the second quotation by Chief Justice French of the HCA reveals that substan-

---

[3] When compared to a ground like rationality, substantive legitimate expectations was not developed in English law until the 1990s by cases like *R v Home Secretary, Ex parte Khan* [1984] 1 WLR 1337. Besides, it was not fully accepted until *R v North and East Devon Health Authority, Ex parte Coughlan* [2000] 3 All ER 850 in 2000. In Australian law, although rejected, the ground has not been fully discussed until *Re Minister for Immigration and Multicultural Affairs, Ex parte Lam* (2003) 214 CLR 1 in 2003.

[4] Peter Cane, *Administrative Law* (5th edn, OUP 2011) 161; Timothy Endicott, *Administrative Law* (4th edn, OUP 2018) 302.

[5] For example, an opportunity to make a representation before being detained (*Attorney General of Hong Kong v Ng Yuen Shiu* [1983] 2 AC 629). See others in Paul Craig, *Administrative Law* (8th edn, Sweet & Maxwell 2016) [22-001].

[6] For example, a fishing licence for a bigger vessel (*R v Ministry of Agriculture, Fisheries and Food, Ex parte Hamble Fisheries Ltd* [1995] 2 All E R 714).

[7] This case was held in the Privy Council, not the UKSC. However, these facts do not detract from its significance in demonstrating influences of English legal culture.

[8] n 3.

[9] Discussing the judgments of Lord Justice Laws in *R v Secretary of State for Education and Employment, Ex parte Begbie* [2000] ELR 445 and *Nadarajah Abdi v The Secretary of State for the Home Department* [2005] EWCA Civ 1363 as opportunities taken to develop the details of the ground (n 1 [87]).

[10] *United Policyholders Group* (n 1) [100] discussing *Begbie* (n 9) (Laws LJ).

[11] n 1 [100].

[12] n 3 [57], [70]. This will be analysed in Sect. 6.3 below. In short, abuse of power is applied as a doctrine to expand the application of the ground.

[13] n 1 [121].

6.1 Introduction

tive legitimate expectations is not a valid ground of judicial review in Australia. The individual cannot base on the ground in claiming substantive benefit promised by the public administrator.

Indeed, English and Australian judges and scholars recognise the influence of constitutional orders on this difference between the determination of legitimate expectations. For example, Lord Justice Sedley states that *'The development of the law of legitimate expectations has done much to conclude the argument about the moral and jurisprudential foundations of judicial review'*.[14] At its heart, this chapter aims to complete comprehensive understanding on these recognitions through the methodologies of deep-water legality and legal culture. It will unpack legal reasoning of these different doctrinal approaches from the judgments of leading English and Australian cases, and connect them to the English and Australian legal cultures.

The examination will be simply structured. Section 6.2 will exemplify to what extent legitimate expectations is a focus of this chapter. Section 6.3 will unpack the legal reasoning in *Coughlan*[15] and a line of English cases before and after it,[16] to reflect the distinctive process that the courts applied flexible justifications and doctrines in determining substantive legitimate expectations as a ground of judicial review. This will be analysed as a product of how legality is deeply understood in the light of the English legal culture. Next, Sect. 6.4 will unpack legal reasoning in *Lam* and a line of Australian cases,[17] to demonstrate that the Australian courts have been fixed in rejecting substantive legitimate expectations. Apart from that, it will be demonstrated that the courts' justifications and applications in determining procedural legitimate expectations are not flexible, but relatively fixed. The courts do not adopt influences from interrelated legal cultures in the determination. These doctrinal approaches will be connected to Australian legal culture. The final section concludes this, and points out some connections to the previous chapters, for example, how substantive legitimate expectations are complicated with the other grounds

---

[14] Stephen Sedley, *Lions Under the Throne: Essays on the History of English Public Law* (CUP 2015) 156; See also Mark Elliott, 'From Heresy to Orthodoxy: Substantive Legitimate Expectations in English Public Law' in Matthew Groves and Greg Weeks (eds), *Legitimate Expectations in the Common Law World* (Hart Publishing 2016).

[15] Considered as a leading case in this area. For example, Hughes asserts that *'Coughlan is undeniably significant because it was the first time that a court required a public authority to abide by a substantive promise…Thus the case… is the pinnacle of the enforcement of substantive legitimate expectations'*. Importantly, it relates to *'the broader development of the scope and boundaries of Administrative Law'* (Kirsty Hughes, 'R v North and East Devon Health Authority [2001]: Coughlan and the Development of Public Law' in Satvinder Juss and Maurice Sunkin (eds), *Landmark Cases in Public Law* (Hart Publishing 2017) 181).

[16] They are *R v Secretary of State for Transport, Ex parte Richmond-Upon-Thames London Borough Council* [1994] 1 WLR 74; *Hamble Fisheries* (n 6); *R v Secretary for the Home Department, Ex parte Hargreaves* [1997] 1 WLR 906; *Begbie* (n 9); *R (Bibi) v Newham London Borough Council* [2002] 1 WLR 237; *Nadarajah* (n 9); *United Policyholders Group* (n 1).

[17] They are *Kioa v West* (1985) 159 CLR 550; *Attorney-General (NSW) v Quin* (1990) 170 CLR 1; *Minister of State for Immigration & Ethnic Affairs v Ah Hin Teoh* [1995] HCA 20; *Kaur v Minister for Immigration and Citizenship* (2012) 290 ALR 616.

like *Wednesbury* and proportionality in England, while the categorisation is continuously systematic in Australia.

6.2 Legitimate Expectations at Surface and Deep Levels

Parallel to the previous chapters, legitimate expectations is supported as a ground of judicial review by administrative law values namely the individual's autonomy to plan their lives, as a part of the rule of law. However, it is also limited by the values of freedom of administrative autonomy, in the light of the separation of powers. These two sides of values 'generally' appear at the 'surface' level of both English and Australian law. Thereby, the determination of legitimate expectations as a ground of judicial review, particularly the substantive legitimate expectations, becomes controversial and requires legal culture to be explored through the methodology of deep-water legality in clarifying understanding. This section exemplifies this outline and points it out as the focus of analysis.

6.2.1 General Concepts Supporting and Rejecting the Ground

As discussed in the previous chapters, according to the separation of powers, when public administrators exercise discretions within their boundaries of power given by Parliament,[18] the courts should not see themselves as having role to conduct judicial review. This value of administrative autonomy is also explainable in the case of legitimate expectations. Although the public agent gives promise to the individual, the discretionary power of the executive delegated from Parliament should not be fettered.[19] Additionally, it is still the executive's area of expertise to adopt the most appropriate decision for public administration or the individual, especially with the need to quickly respond to changing circumstances.[20] The courts' intervention giving the individual what the agent has promised can ossify the development of public administration. These reasons, therefore, limit scope of judicial review on the ground of legitimate expectations because it is the executive's authority rather than the court's.[21]

On the other hand, the rule of law supports the courts in conducting judicial review of this kind of circumstance. This is described in various explanations, for

---

[18] The analysis in this chapter is located merely in the case of intra vires legitimate expectations, not the case of ultra vires legitimate expectations (See Craig (n 5) [22-032]).

[19] ibid [22-009]; William Wade and Christopher Forsyth, *Administrative Law* (11th edn, OUP 2014) 460.

[20] Craig (n 5) [22-009]-[22-010]; Philip Sales and Karen Steyn, 'Legitimate Expectations in English Public law: An Analysis' [2004] PL 564, 567–568.

[21] Again, these reasons could be discussed by the concept of deference.

example, decision-makers shall not infringe individuals' ability to plan their lives by changing the decision from what he or she has legitimately expected by representation.[22] Raz asserts that individuals should be able to know and expect the legal consequences of the public authorities' actions.[23] Changing the decision from what the decision-maker has been promised is unfair to the individuals.[24] Indeed, this not only means protecting individuals' interests,[25] but also the administration itself because the ground enhances administrative efficacy, predictability, formal equality and consistency, legal certainty and reliance and trust in public administration.[26] Therefore, the courts should have the role as *'the guardians of longer-term tradition'* in conducting judicial review by this ground in order to protect legitimate expectation of the individuals.[27]

6.2.2 Understanding Legitimate Expectations Through Legal Culture

These two sides of values are generally explainable at surface level in England and Australia. The tension between them leads to controversy in determining the scope of judicial review of administrative action through the ground of legitimate expectations. As introduced, there are two kinds of legitimate expectations namely procedural and substantive. It shall be clarified that the tension is more directed to substantive legitimate expectations than procedural legitimate expectations. This is because procedural legitimate expectations has natural justice or procedural fairness as a rationale.[28] As discussed in Chap. 1, judges generally feel more comfortable to tell public bodies what procedures administrative agents should follow.[29] They do

---

[22] Craig (n 5) [22-002].

[23] Joseph Raz, *The Authority of Law* (Clarendon Press 1979) Chapter 11; Alternatively, the ground is justified in terms of people security and human rights (see Dawn Oliver, *Common Values and the Public-Private Divide* (Butterworths 1999) 67–69, 99–102; Jeffrey Jowell, 'Beyond the Rule of Law: Towards Constitutional Judicial Review' [2000] PL 671, 677–678).

[24] This is the basis of how substantive legitimate expectations overlap with the grounds relating to substantive exercise of discretion, analysed in the previous chapter. It will be exemplified in Sects. 6.3 and 6.4 below.

[25] Sales and Steyn (n 22) 569–571.

[26] Soren Schonberg, *Legitimate Expectations in Administrative Law* (OUP 2000) Chapter 1; Craig (n 5) [22-005]-[22-008]. There is variation in explaining these values, for example, Jowell categorises equality, access to justice and legal certainty outside the rule of law (Jeffrey Jowell, 'Of Vires and Vacuums: The Constitutional Context of Judicial Review' in Christopher Forsyth (ed), *Judicial Review and the Constitution* (Hart Publishing 2000) 335).

[27] Craig (n 5) [22-008].

[28] Jowell (n 26) 331–332.

[29] ibid 329.

not need to be evaluated by elected agents in a democracy.[30] According to the methodology of this book, they are generally covered by the surface-water legality. The English and Australian courts have similar understanding that they have a role in conducting judicial review on the ground.[31]

This is different from substantive legitimate expectations, which two values are generally more in competition. On the one hand, the courts are limited to intervene into administrative discretion. Although being promised, the administrative agent still has authority given by Parliament to change the decision. On the other hand, the courts are required by the rule of law to protect the individuals who have legitimate expectation from the administrative agent's promise. As demonstrated above, the English and Australian courts have different ways in determining substantive legitimate expectations as a ground of judicial review. While the English courts' determinations have been flexible, the ground has been firmly rejected by the Australian courts.

This difference has been widely studied in English and Australian literature.[32] However, most of the papers are based on a comparative analysis of the advantages and disadvantages of the application of the ground in the two countries. On the one hand, the Australian articles consider whether to adopt the ground into the legal system. For example, Aronson, Groves and Weeks assert that the English doctrinal approach of substantive legitimate expectations in *Coughlan* is dangerous to the distinction between legality and merits and could distort legal certainty.[33] On the other hand, the English works consider the extent of the application and development of the ground. For example, Sales and Steyn point out the real risk in expanding the ground through the concept of abuse of power as it would damage the distinction between appeal and review.[34] It can be seen that these works are mainly focused on the conclusions of the English legal system's acceptance of the ground and the Australian legal system's rejection of it.

Instead, it will be pointed out in the following sections that the different doctrinal approaches applied to determine the substantive legitimate expectations in England and Australia are products of the courts' deep understanding of legality. This will be

---

[30] Iain Steele, 'Substantive Legitimate Expectations: Striking the Right Balance?' (2005) 121 LQR 300.

[31] See Jowell (n 26) 332; Cane (n 4) 160–164; Mark Elliott and Jason Varuhas, *Administrative Law: Text and Materials* (5th edn, OUP 2017) 193–198; Wade and Forsyth (n 19) 450.

[32] E.g. Sales and Steyn (n 20) and Mark Elliott, 'From Heresy to Orthodoxy: Substantive Legitimate Expectations in English Public Law' (n 14) for English law and Cameron Stewart, 'The Doctrine of Substantive Unfairness and the Review of Substantive Legitimate Expectations' in Matthew Groves and H P Lee (eds), *Australian Administrative Law: Fundamentals, Principles and Doctrines* (CUP 2007); Matthew Groves, 'Substantive Legitimate Expectations in Australian Administrative Law' (2008) 32 Melb UL Rev 470; Greg Weeks, 'Holding Government to its Word: Legitimate Expectations and Estoppels in Administrative Law' in Matthew Groves (ed), *Modern Administrative Law in Australia: Concepts and Context* (CUP 2014) for Australian law.

[33] Mark Aronson, Matthew Groves and Greg Weeks, *Judicial Review of Administrative Action and Government Liability* (6th edn, Thomson Reuters Australia 2017) [7.150].

[34] Sales and Steyn (n 20) 589–591; See also Steele (n 30).

examined by unpacking the different legal reasoning of leading English and Australian cases and connecting them to the English and Australian legal cultures. Additionally, in the Australian section, procedural legitimate expectations will also be examined. This is because there are some aspects requiring deep-water legality in deciding the ground. For example, parallel to the previous chapters, the courts' applications relying on statutory construction is obviously demonstrate the influence of the Australian legal culture.

6.3 English Doctrinal Approaches

Different from the previous chapters, since elements of the English legal culture are not directly expressed in the legal reasoning of the aforementioned leading cases, it will firstly be demonstrated in this section that the English determination entails a distinctive process, in which the courts strike a balance between the two sides of justification, supporting and rejecting substantive legitimate expectations as a ground of judicial review in the particular case based on various doctrines. This process was established by Lord Justice Laws' judgment in *Richmond-Upon-Thames* and further developed by later cases before being fully recognised in *Coughlan*, and continued thereafter. This process will then be pointed out as the distinctive operation of English deep-water legality, influenced by the flexible English mentality.[35]

6.3.1 Prior to Coughlan

Procedural legitimate expectations came to English law in the early 1970s in the form of an extension of the rules of natural justice.[36] Since then, there has been a long line of cases in which the courts granted the benefit in terms of procedural right to the claimants.[37] As mentioned, both the validity and rationale of this ground have been firmly accepted in these English cases. It is not a focus of this section.

---

[35] Some of the authors in the literature apply this in terms of the courts' feeling. For example, Steele states that '*The courts are gradually feeling their way towards an acceptable balance the conflicting interests at stake in substantive legitimate expectation cases*' (Steele (n 23) 300). However, the approach of legal mentality is used in this book.

[36] *Schmidt v Secretary of State for Home Affairs* [1969] 2 WLR 337 (Lord Denning).

[37] E.g. *R v Liverpool Corporation, Ex parte Liverpool Taxi Fleet Operators' Association* [1972] 2 QB 299; *Attorney General of Hong Kong v Ng Yuen Shiu* (n 5).

6.3.1.1 Richmond-Upon-Thames

The situation has been different in the case of substantive legitimate expectations. The acceptance of which as a ground of judicial review has been controversial since it was discussed early in *Richmond-Upon-Thames*.[38] In this case, the Secretary of State for Transport announced a policy to restrict night flying based on the noise produced by the aircraft, but later cancelled it. The claimant argued that this policy generated a legitimate expectation that the restriction would be applied for at least five years.[39] The claimant then sought judicial review claiming the benefit it would gain from the announced policy.[40] Lord Justice Laws clearly recognised that this case was different from other cases as the claimant requested for *'merits'*, not procedural.[41] Although the conclusion of the case was that the decision was not unlawful on the ground of substantive legitimate expectations,[42] it is pointed out in this section that substantive legitimate expectations 'was not fully rejected' in this case. Based on the big picture methodology, Lord Justice Laws set up a process deciding whether or not the court had a role to play in conducting judicial review or not and there was a step in this process, in which support of substantive legitimate expectations was recognised. However, in a later step, it was overridden by the value rejecting the ground. This process is parallel to the points of doctrinal approaches namely justifications and doctrines the courts apply in determining status of the ground as follows.

Firstly, Lord Justice Laws established justifications for both accepting and rejecting substantive legitimate expectations as a ground of judicial review. On the one hand, he argued that whether legitimate expectations was procedural or substantive, *'the discipline of fairness'* is needed to be considered, because it prevents decision-makers from breaking their promises.[43] On the other hand, he observed that substantive legitimate expectations could obstruct the duty and fetter public administrators from using their discretion choosing the most appropriate decision in particular circumstances to fulfil their responsibility.[44] The analysis of later cases below will clarify that these sides of value are the implication of the twin concepts of parliamentary sovereignty and the rule of law, which are provided in various ways, depending upon individual judges.

Secondly, Lord Justice Laws held that these justifications in supporting and rejecting the ground have to be balanced depending on the particular situation. It was stated that *'...the doctrine of legitimate expectation may or should in some*

---

[38] Indeed, there were some cases on substantive legitimate expectations before *Richmond-Upon-Thames*, for example, *R v Inland Revenue Commission, Ex parte Preston* [1985] AC 835 and *re Findlay* [1985] AC 318. However, the validity of substantive legitimate expectations has not been explicitly discussed in them, but in *Richmond-Upon-Thames*.

[39] n 16, 76D-77C.

[40] ibid 92A-D.

[41] ibid 92C-93B.

[42] ibid 94B-94F.

[43] ibid 93A-93B.

[44] ibid 93B-F.

6.3 English Doctrinal Approaches

circumstances be deployed so as to protect a substantive legitimate expectation of a favourable result in the particular case'.[45] The condition to be fulfilled is that the change must be justified by *'the overriding public interest'*.[46] This legal reasoning demonstrated that although the court decided that the conclusion of this case should be rejecting the ground, another side of argument accepting the ground was not absolutely abandoned. It actually depends on the context whether the claim of substantive legitimate expectations is included in the meaning of English legality.

Additionally, Lord Justice Laws argued that this process of balancing fairness with public administrator autonomy is an initial duty of the decision-maker,[47] because public interest will be better served by the change.[48] However, the change also has to be *'reasonable'*.[49] Although the decision in this case was not unreasonable,[50] his judgment implicitly justified the role of the court to conduct judicial review if the change had been unreasonable.

The third step in Lord Justice Laws' process is that the court defines and applies a doctrine to determine whether the change of decision is reasonable or not, and in this case, it was the *Wednesbury* doctrine.[51] It will be demonstrated in the later cases that this does not stop at *Wednesbury*, but can be applied flexibly by the individual judges.

In short, Lord Justice Laws' characteristic process for the determination of substantive legitimate expectations in *Richmond-Upon-Thames*, describes two sides of justifications supporting and rejecting the ground, followed by the public administrator's duty to counter-balance and the court's duty to review the process. The *Wednesbury* doctrine was applied in this case for the court to determine its scope of judicial review. The case was concluded that the decision of the Secretary of State for Transport was not unreasonable.[52] Thus, the argument of the claimants was not found to be valid. When considering the big picture, this process did not fully reject the validity of substantive legitimate expectations as part of the protection of (deep-water) legality. It will be shown below that this is completely different from the Australian law, where substantive legitimate expectations were denied at the point at which it began.[53] In the later cases, the English courts restarted the consideration with two sides of justifications accepting and rejecting the ground before entering the balancing process again. This was demonstrated in *Hamble Fisheries*, where a similar process was adopted but the conclusion was different. Substantive legitimate expectations was accepted as a ground of judicial review.

---

[45] ibid 94D-E by citing Christopher Forsyth, 'The Provenance and Protection of Legitimate Expectations' [1988] CLJ 238.
[46] ibid 94A-B.
[47] ibid 94B-C.
[48] ibid.
[49] ibid 94C-D.
[50] ibid 94F-H.
[51] ibid 94C-D.
[52] ibid 94 F-H.
[53] Particularly in *Quin* (n 17).

6.3.1.2 Hamble Fisheries

The applicants in *Hamble Fisheries* sought judicial review for a license to fish by beam trawler for pressure stock in the North Sea on the basis of several grounds, namely failure to exercise discretion and the breach of legitimate expectation.[54] On the latter, the claimant clearly expressed that his claim was supported by the value of legal certainty that the new policy would retrospectively strike at his accrued interests.[55] Lord Justice Sedley began with a clarification that the claim fell under substantive legitimate expectations, not procedural.[56] There were three points of the legal reasoning in his judgment discussing the distinctive process established by Lord Justice Laws in *Richmond-Upon-Thames*.

Firstly, Lord Justice Sedley added further details in the justifications supporting and rejecting the ground. Apart from the tension between the argument against *'fettering a public body'*[57] and the upholding of *'fairness in public administration'*,[58] Lord Justice Sedley also described that *'the interest of good administration'* is legal alchemy, which gives an expectation sufficient legitimacy to secure enforcement in public law.[59] These values were recognised as *'the constitutional importance of ministerial freedom to formulate and to reformulate policy'* and *'the interests of those individuals'*.[60] It was also referred to *'the line between individual consideration and inconsistency'*.[61] Lord Justice Sedley reinforces this in an extra judicial work that *'It is in the development of the law of legitimate expectation that sensitivity both to policy needs and to individuals' interests is arguably seen at its best'*.[62] This demonstrates a variety of justifications individual English judges can turn the twin concepts into and apply to determine substantive legitimate expectations.

Additionally, Lord Justice Sedley further explained the balancing process between the two sides of value of this case in his extra-judiciary work that *'There is no set scale; indeed the two* [the policy imperative and the individual's expectation] *cannot usually be quantified in the same manner'*.[63] He clarifies this co-function between the decision-maker and the court in balancing the values that

> The balance must in the first instance be for the policy-maker to strike; but if the outcome is challenged by way of judicial review.... While policy is for the policy-maker alone, the

---

[54] n 6 [1]-[23].
[55] ibid [14].
[56] ibid [23].
[57] ibid [25].
[58] ibid.
[59] ibid [42] by citing *Attorney General of Hong Kong v Ng Yuen Shiu* (n 5) (Lord Fraser).
[60] ibid [47].
[61] ibid [19].
[62] Stephen Sedley, *Ashes and Sparks: Essays on Law and Justice* (CUP 2011) 260.
[63] ibid 261.

6.3 English Doctrinal Approaches

fairness of his or her decision not to accommodate reasonable expectations which the policy will thwart remains the court's concern (as of course does the lawfulness of the policy).[64]

This part of his legal reasoning clearly connects the consideration of the ground to legality. It means that the claim of substantive legitimate expectations could be considered as part of legality. This logic is implicitly supported by some scholars. For example, Craig argues that proportionality should be used as a test to determine *'the legality of action'* that purports to resile from the substantive legitimate expectations.[65]

Secondly, the doctrine Lord Justice Sedley applied in determining the balance was not limited to *Wednesbury*, but expanded to broad concepts like *'rationality, legality and fairness'*.[66] If the decision is unlawful in any way that obliterates good government, the court is justified in conducting judicial review of it. There is no fixed answer to this; rather, it depends upon individual cases.[67] In the same way as in the previous chapter, this was a gateway for the courts to expand the application of the ground to other doctrines rather than merely *Wednesbury*. The expansion will be more explicit in *Coughlan*, which will be analysed below.

Thirdly, Lord Justice Sedley left room for the ground to be developed according to the influences of interrelated legal culture. He explained that substantive legitimate expectations originated from EU law under the concept of legal certainty.[68] However, there is no *'exhaustive formulation'* in its application,[69] but a great *'variety of approaches and applications'*.[70] The way Lord Justice Sedley considered a number of EU cases in addressing the present case was the first step of welcoming and allowing interrelated legal cultures to be adapted into the English consideration of the ground. This point will become clearer in the analysis of *Coughlan* and *United Policyholders Group* below.

Up to this point, it has been demonstrated that the conclusions of *Richmond-Upon-Thames* and *Hamble Fisheries* were different. While the claim of the ground was not valid in the former, it was in the latter. Some scholars regard this as that Sedley and Laws *'sought to push or oppose the development of legitimate expectations'*.[71] However, this difference is regarded in this section to be the result of flexibility the courts can apply when determining the status of substantive legitimate expectations as a ground of judicial review. This is further demonstrated in *Hargreaves*, when the *Wednesbury* doctrine was brought back.[72]

---

[64] n 6 [47].

[65] Craig (n 5) [22–020]. The adoption of proportionality as a doctrine for the determination of the ground will be exemplified below.

[66] n 6 [49]–[50].

[67] ibid [50].

[68] ibid [26], [31], [33].

[69] ibid [39].

[70] ibid [33]–[39].

[71] Hughes (n 15) 182–183, 188–189.

[72] n 16, 920F-921F, 923F-G (Hirst LJ), 924H-925B, 925D-E (Pill LJ).

6.3.1.3 *Hargreaves*

In *Hargreaves*, the Home Secretary announced a policy whereby prisoners would be entitled to home leave when they had served one-third of their sentence. Later, such policy was changed and restricted to prisoners who had served at least one-half of their sentence. The applicants then sought judicial review of the Home Secretary's decision claiming the benefit of home leave as their legitimate expectation. The judgments, particularly by Lord Justice Hirst, clearly regarded Lord Justice Sedley's approach in *Hamble Fisheries* as *'Heresy'*.[73]

However, the bigger picture reveals that it was not a complete heresy, but merely that rejecting substantive legitimate expectations as a ground of judicial review was concluded in this particular case. *Hargreaves* applied *Wednesbury* as a doctrine to determine the ground due to nature of subject matter in the case, involving penal policy related to national security.[74] As Jowell argues, the court usually applies *Wednesbury* as a way to deny its scope of judicial review.[75] This can be seen from the legal reasoning in the case itself that '...*the court must bear in mind the context of the respondent's decision, a decision which was of importance in an area where he bears grave responsibilities and which is a matter of great public concern, namely penal policy'*.[76]

This demonstrates that the English courts have flexibility in determining whether the claim on substantive legitimate expectations in the particular case shall be covered by (deep-water) legality. Rather than rejecting substantive legitimate protection, *'slow, incremental steps'* were made in most English cases.[77] The core case confirming this flexible mentality is *Coughlan*, where Lord Woolf categorised all possible doctrines in determining substantive legitimate expectations as a ground of judicial review.

6.3.2 *Coughlan*

The claimant in *Coughlan* requested a benefit that she could live in a supported living house for life on the ground of substantive legitimate expectations as it was promised by the local health authority.[78] Like the previous cases, the court undertook the distinctive process of balancing two conflicting values. As Lord Woolf stated,

> The court's task in all these cases is not to impede executive activity but to reconcile its continuing need to initiate or respond to change with the legitimate interests or expectations

---

[73] ibid 921D-F (Hirst LJ).
[74] ibid 909C-F.
[75] Jowell (n 26) 334.
[76] n 16, 925A-B (Pill LJ).
[77] Weeks (n 32) 233–234.
[78] n 3 [3], [50], [53].

6.3 English Doctrinal Approaches

of citizens or strangers who have relied, and have been justified in relying, on a current policy or an extant promise.[79]

Added from the previous cases, Lord Woolf divided the available doctrines the court could apply in determining the scope of judicial review into three categories;

(a) The court may decide that the public authority is only required to bear in mind its previous policy or other representation, giving it the weight it thinks right but no more, before deciding whether to change course. Here the court is confined to reviewing the decision on Wednesbury grounds...

(b) On the other hand the court may decide that the promise or practice induces a legitimate expectation of, for example, being consulted before a particular decision is taken. Here it is uncontentious that the court itself will require the opportunity for consultation to be given unless there is an overriding reason to resile from it in which case the court will itself judge the adequacy of the reason advanced for the change of policy, taking into account what fairness requires...

(c) Where the court considers that a lawful promise or practice has induced a legitimate expectation of a benefit which is substantive, not simply procedural, authority now establishes that here too the court will in a proper case decide whether to frustrate the expectation is so unfair that to take a new and different course will amount to an abuse of power. Here, once the legitimacy of the expectation is established, the court will have the task of weighing the requirements of fairness against any overriding interest relied upon for the change of policy[80]

Lord Woolf significantly explained that the court will play a different role in these categories.[81] While the second category related to procedural legitimate expectations, the first and third categories related to substantive legitimate expectations.[82] Lord Woolf used *Hargreaves* and *Findlay* as cases in which the court applied *Wednesbury* in determining the ground of substantive legitimate expectations.[83] These categorises clearly demonstrate flexibility of the English courts in perceiving their role when determining the scope of judicial review.

Importantly, the third category further enabled the court to consider the validity of the ground through the doctrine of abuse of power.[84] Lord Woolf asserted that *'...the court is there to ensure that the power to make and alter policy has not been abused by unfairly frustrating legitimate individual expectations'*.[85] This doctrine was a key device allowing the court to be flexible in determining substantive legitimate expectations. The explanation of the abuse of power could be fashioned in whatever way the court would like the conclusion to be. In other words, the courts

---

[79] ibid [65].
[80] ibid [57].
[81] ibid [58].
[82] ibid.
[83] ibid [57].
[84] ibid.
[85] ibid [66].

have flexibility in perceiving whether the claim in the particular case is covered by legality or not.

Despite that, Lord Woolf also cautioned that *'Abuses of power may take many forms'*.[86] *'The court's power of supervision'* should be limited to the aspect of the decision, *'which is equally the concern of the law'*.[87] Additionally, the court should limit its role to cases *'...where the expectation is confined to one person or a few people, giving the promise or representation the character of a contract'*.[88] This part of the legal reasoning has two functions. Firstly, it confirmed that the process of the English court, which was holding the two sides of justifications before balancing them dependent on the particular situation, has been continuously applied. On the one hand, Lord Woolf supported the position of the court as the final arbiter to consider whether the decision amounted to an abuse of power.[89] On the other hand, Lord Woolf reminded that its adjudicative role was limited to ensuring fairness to the individuals.[90] He further asserted that *'The limits to its (legitimate expectation) role have yet to be finally determined by the courts. Its application is still being developed on a case by case basis'*.[91]

Secondly, it was the affirmation that the consideration of the ground was an operation of legality. Lord Woolf explicitly pointed out that whether the administrative agent chose to follow the promise or change the decision, these were *'two lawful exercises of power'*.[92] Both *'the promise'* and *'the policy change'* are flexibly included in the English courts' understanding of legality. It will be seen below that this is completely different from the Australian law, in which the courts have a relatively fixed way in understanding and determining substantive legitimate expectations as not part of their role in protecting legality.

Also noteworthy is that the judgment of Lord Woolf in *Coughlan* demonstrated that it is possible for the court to adopt influences from interrelated legal culture in determining substantive legitimate expectations. To justify that the respondent's decision was an abuse of power,[93] Lord Woolf considered that the public authority was obliged by article 8(1) and not justified by article 8(2) of the ECHR.[94] Although the HRA had not come into force at the time of the case, Lord Woolf made the following assertion;

---

[86] ibid [69].
[87] ibid [65].
[88] ibid [59].
[89] ibid [69].
[90] ibid [82].
[91] ibid [71].
[92] ibid [66].
[93] ibid [89], Conclusion (c).
[94] ibid [90], Conclusion (c).

6.3 English Doctrinal Approaches   229

> *Once the Human Rights Act 1998 is in force it will be the obligation of the court as a public authority to give effect to this value, except to the extent that statutory provision makes this impossible.*[95]

As will be seen below, influence of interrelated legal cultures is difficult to be adopted in Australian law because the courts have to be aware that they may not fit the rigid framework of separation of powers prescribed in the written constitution.

In summary, Lord Woolf's judgment in *Coughlan* demonstrates that various justifications and doctrines can be applied by different judges in determining substantive legitimate expectations in the particular case. It was found in *Coughlan* that the administrative decision was an abuse of power, contrary to its existence in law; therefore, the court had the role to conduct judicial review.[96] This was different to the courts in *Hargreaves* applying *Wednesbury* as the first category because the contexts of the cases were different.[97]

6.3.3 After Coughlan

After *Coughlan*, the flexibility of justifications and doctrines in considering the status of substantive legitimate expectations as a ground of judicial review has continued.[98] A few of the most important cases are illustrated as follow.[99] The first example was *Begbie*, where Lord Justice Laws described the first and third categories in *Coughlan* as '*not hermetically sealed*'.[100] In fact, all the grounds of judicial review, i.e. illegality, *Wednesbury* and proportionality, come from the same root, which is the concept of the abuse of power appearing in various forms.[101] The consideration of scope of judicial review constitutes '*a sliding scale of review, more or less intrusive according to the nature and gravity of what is at stake*'.[102] The nature of the case was an important part of the consideration. For example, in the case of a general policy that affected the public at large, called a macro-political field, judges shall have '*no position*' to adjudicate.[103] There will be less opportunity for the court to supervise the administrative decision. Therefore, the *Wednesbury* principle should be applied to control the administrator's action.[104] The courts perceive themselves as

---

[95] ibid.
[96] ibid [81], [89], Conclusion (c).
[97] ibid [76].
[98] Hughes (n 15) 200.
[99] ibid 193–197.
[100] n 9, 1130F-1130G.
[101] ibid 1129F-1130F.
[102] ibid 1130B-1130D.
[103] ibid 1130G-1130H.
[104] ibid.

having no ability to wear *'the garb of a policy-maker'*.[105] On the other hand, in the case of fewer and certainly identifiable players like *Coughlan*, the court can be more intrusive in reviewing the administrative action.[106] In contrast to Lord Justice Laws, even though Lord Justice Sedley greatly supported the ground in *Hamble Fisheries*, the conclusion of his judgment in *Begbie* was limited.[107]

The flexibility of English doctrinal approaches in determining substantive legitimate expectations was also confirmed in *Bibi*, when Lord Justice Schiemann discussed that *'The categories of unfairness (in Coughlan) are not closed, and precedent should act as a guide and not as a cage'*.[108] This opened up possibilities for the courts to search for the scope of legality in a flexible manner for the particular case. In this case, a traditional ground like relevant consideration was applied to conclude that the claimant had a legitimate expectation.[109]

Another noteworthy case is *Nadarajah*, in which Lord Justice Laws explained the concept of good administration as justification in determining the court's jurisdiction.[110] The flexibility in terms of doctrine was confirmed in that

> The three categories of case there described by Lord Woolf represent, I would respectfully suggest, varying scenarios in which the question whether denial of the expectation was proportionate to the public interest aim in view may call for different answers.[111]

Following *Begbie*, Lord Justice Laws held that *'All these considerations...are pointer not rules'*.[112] The process of balancing is not precisely calculable and its measurement is not exact.[113] Parallel to the analysis in the previous chapter, Lord Justice Laws flexibly applied proportionality, as a doctrine adopted from an interrelated legal culture to decide the scope of judicial review in this case.[114]

It can also draw back to the judgment of Lord Carnwath in *United Policyholders Group* at the beginning of this chapter entailing discussions on flexibility in *Begbie* and *Nadarajah*. The first notable point in the legal reasoning of the judgment is that Lord Carnwath's statement connects *'Laws LJ's search for a constitutional foundation for the principle of legitimate expectation'* with the *'the rule of law principle of legal certainty'*.[115] Originally a European concept,[116] legal certainty has been used in

---

[105] ibid.

[106] ibid 1131A-1131C.

[107] See Hughes (n 15) 199.

[108] n 16 [27] by citing *R v Inland Revenue Comrs, Ex parte Unilever plc* [1996] STC 681, 690F.

[109] ibid [49].

[110] n 9 [52], [68]–[70].

[111] ibid [70].

[112] ibid [69].

[113] ibid.

[114] ibid [69].

[115] Through the discussion in Mark Elliott, 'From Heresy to Orthodoxy: Substantive Legitimate Expectations in English Public Law' (n 14) (see *United Policyholders Group* (n 1) [118]).

[116] It is mostly explained along with the rule of law. See Paul Craig, *EU Administrative Law* (3rd edn, OUP 2018) Chapter 18; J Schwarze, *European Administrative Law* (Sweet & Maxwell 1992) Chapter 6.

6.3 English Doctrinal Approaches   231

shaping the administrative laws of many countries in Europe, including England, since the 1970s.[117] As shown above, it was argued in *Hamble Fisheries* that *'the effect of the new policy is to strike retrospectively at accrued interests of the applicants, offending against the principle of legal certainty which is closely bound up (at least in European law) with the doctrine of legitimate expectation'*.[118] Therefore, the legal reasoning in *United Policyholders Group* was a reintroduction of the concept of legal certainty to justify the court's determination of substantive legitimate expectations as a ground of judicial review. This demonstrates another product of the English legal culture whereby the English courts can flexibly integrate or reintroduce interrelated legal culture to their determination of the scope of judicial review. There is no kind flexibility in Australia, as will be seen in the next section.

Secondly, the approach of Lord Carnwath in *United Policyholders Group* reflects a variety of doctrines the courts can flexibly apply to operate the balancing process between the rule of law and parliamentary sovereignty. On the one hand, the court conducts judicial review to uphold legal certainty when a government has reneged on its promise.[119] On the other hand, the court should be cautious when intervening in a government policy in the macro-political field, which is regarded as a matter for the executive to decide.[120] The approach in *Coughlan* should be narrowly interpreted and only applied in cases *'involving a clear promise by the authority, made to a defined group in return for specific action by them within a defined time scale, and designed to further the authority's own purposes'* such as *Coughlan* an *Paponette*.[121] This balancing process can be achieved based on the proportionality doctrine, whereby the court can take any conflict with wider policy into account in determining whether the government had good reasons for reneging on its promise or not.[122]

6.3.4 Products of the English Legal Culture

This section has demonstrated flexibility of the doctrinal approaches the English courts apply in determining substantive legitimate expectations as a ground of judicial review. As mentioned, English scholars willingly recognise this flexibility, for

---

[117] Craig, *Administrative Law* (n 5) [22–003]; See also P Reynolds, 'Legitimate Expectations and the Protection of Trust in Public Officials' [2011] Public Law 330 and Elliott and Varuhas (n 31) 187–189.

[118] n 6 [14].

[119] n 1 [118].

[120] ibid [112]–[117].

[121] ibid [120]. Lord Carnwath further clarified this in *Finucane* [2019] UKSC 7 [157] that *'the Coughlan principle was directed to the particular case of a promise made to an identifiable person or group relating to a substantive benefit,…distinguished from other categories of legitimate expectation in the wider sense…'*, namely one of *'policy statements made to the public in general'*.

[122] n 1 [120]-[121].

example, Williams observes different types of cases in the area of legitimate expectations.[123] Parallel to the previous chapters, this flexibility can be explained as an example of the idea of pragmatism. For example, Joe Tomlinson supports the narrow interpretation in *Coughlan* and regards it as *'both pragmatic and justified'*.[124] The flexibility also leads to debates on the application of the ground, as well as the choice of doctrine. For instance, Joanna Bell's comments on Lord Carnwath's approach in *United Policyholder Group* on the grounds of ambiguity in the language that *'policy must be consistently applied'* and the difficulty in determining an *'identifiable defined group'*.[125]

Instead of assessing the doctrine or providing a solution for the variation in this, the section, it is connected to the English legal culture. This makes Lord Carnwath's conclusory notion in *United Policyholders Group* of why and how *'the intense judicial and academic controversy ... remains unresolved more than 15 years later'* tangible.[126] In the same way, Elliott's argument that the orthodoxy of the English law is distinctive as the courts calibrate the nature and intensity of a substantive review,[127] has been exemplified through the framework of deep-water legality and legal culture. The various doctrinal approaches flexibly applied by the English courts to determine substantive legitimate expectations have been unpacked from the legal reasoning of leading cases. Four connecting points can be drawn, as detailed below.

Firstly, different judges can provide various justifications for accepting or rejecting the ground. The next section will demonstrate that the Australian courts do not have this variety of justifications, but the relatively fixed according to the analysed elements of Australian legal culture. Additionally, it is recognised that the English courts need to justify themselves clearly in claiming or rejecting its jurisdiction. This is because of a lack of documented provisions, so that the courts have to avoid being accused of infringing either of the two values. If they refuse to conduct judicial review, they could be accused of not protecting the rule of law. Conversely, if they intervene in an executive's decision, they could be accused of lacking respect for the sovereignty of parliament. Therefore, the English courts have to hold two sides of justifications at the start of each case. While accepting the ground, they caution limitation in intervening in administrative actions and, while rejecting the ground, they state the values supporting the ground.

Secondly, the two mentioned features of unwritten constitution and the balancing process between parliamentary sovereignty and the rule of law enable the courts to flexibly apply various doctrines in determining the ground. Parallel to the previous chapter, the discrepancy ranges from *Wednesbury*, relevant and irrelevant

---

[123] Rebecca Williams, 'The Multiple Doctrines of Legitimate Expectations' (2016) 132 LQR 639.

[124] Joe Tomlinson, 'The Narrow Approach to Substantive Legitimate Expectations and the Trend of Modern Authority' (2017) 17 Oxford University Commonwealth Law Journal 75.

[125] Joanna Bell, 'The Privy Council and the Doctrine of Legitimate Expectation Meet Again' (2016) 75 CLJ 449; See also the discussion on proportionality in Hughes (n 15).

[126] n 1 [110].

[127] Mark Elliott, 'From Heresy to Orthodoxy: Substantive Legitimate Expectations in English Public Law' (n 14) 234–243.

6.3 English Doctrinal Approaches

considerations, abuse of power to proportionality. This is clearly different from Australian law, where the courts firmly reject abuse of power, and apply jurisdictional error as the central approach in determining the scope of judicial review in all grounds, including procedural and substantive legitimate expectations. Thirdly, the English courts can integrate factors from interrelated legal cultures into their consideration of the ground. This is clearly different from Australian law, where it is difficult to import interrelated legal cultures into the courts' consideration of the ground, because clear frameworks are prescribed in a document. According to these three points, the status of substantive legitimate expectations as a ground of judicial review (the fourth point) therefore has been flexible and has fluctuated. The table below contains a snapshot of this.

English doctrinal approaches		
Justifications	**Various**	
	To intervene	Not to intervene
	Discipline of fairness (*Richmond-Upon-Thames*) Individual consideration (*Hamble Fisheries*) Legality (*Coughlan*) Concept of good administration (*Nadarajah*)	Fettering a public body (*Richmond-Upon-Thames*) Inconsistency and legal certainty (*Hamble Fisheries*) Legality (*Coughlan*)
Doctrines	**Various and flexible**	
	Wednesbury (*Richmond-Upon-Thames*) Rationality, legality and fairness (*Hamble Fisheries*) 3 categories; *Wednesbury*, procedural fairness and abuse of power (*Coughlan*) The categories are '*not hermetically sealed*' and '*not closed*'. A traditional ground like relevant and irrelevant considerations can be included (*Begbie* and *Bibi*) Proportionality (*Nadarajah*)	
Influences from interrelated legal culture	**Possible for the court to adopt**	
	Legitimate expectations comes from EU law, but is not '*exhaustive formulation*' (*Hamble Fisheries*) The court could adopt the ECHR through the HRA into the determination (*Coughlan*) Adopting proportionality as a doctrine in determining the ground (*Nadarajah*) Flexibility to apply the concept of legal certainty (originally the European concept) as justification for the court to conduct judicial review (*United Policyholders Group*)	
Status as the grounds of judicial review	**Procedural legitimate expectations**	**Substantive legitimate expectations**
	Accepted	Flexible and fluctuated whether to accept (*Hamble Fisheries*, *Coughlan* and the later cases) or reject (*Richmond-Upon-Thames* and *Hargreaves*)

Importantly, this section demonstrates that this flexibility is inevitable because they are products of the flexible English legal culture. Parallel to Chaps. 4 and 5, these are in relation to two main elements. Firstly, the balancing process between the two sides of justifications in accepting and rejecting the ground reflects the balance between the twin concepts of parliamentary sovereignty and the rule of law. Although have not been explicitly expressed,[128] the above analysis demonstrates that they permeate in all the analysed judgments. On the one hand, in the light of the rule of law, the courts have a role to protect the lawfulness of administrative decisions. This side of justification in accepting the ground represents situation in which the rule of law overrides the parliamentary sovereignty. Hence, the courts have role to conduct judicial review on this ground. On the other hand, the side of limitation rejecting the ground prefers to characterise the conclusion of balancing parliamentary sovereignty over the rule of law. In these cases, the courts have no role to conduct judicial review because the claims are not considered as a part of legality.

Secondly, the framework of the unwritten Constitution in English law also has an impact on flexibility. As Jowell argues that;

> *It is an inescapable feature of an unwritten constitution that its dimensions emerge in the course of concrete decisions raising questions about the appropriate balance of power between instruments of government...*[129]

These two significant elements of English legal culture, namely, the nature of balancing conflicting values and the absence of a documentary prescription of the court's jurisdiction make the determinations to be flexible. Similar to the approach applied in the previous chapters, this will be obvious when compared to Australian law, where the ground has been firmly rejected, as embedded in the legal system's legal culture that has a written Constitution to prescribe and entrench the jurisdiction of the courts when conducting judicial review.

6.4 Australian Doctrinal Approaches

Completely different from English law, this section reveals that the Australian courts regard themselves clearly as not having a role to conduct judicial review through substantive legitimate expectations. In other words, the ground is not included in their (deep) understanding of legality.[130] Additionally, the determination of procedural legitimate expectations is fixed with a clear set of rules, limiting the courts to adopt influences from interrelated legal culture into the consideration. These doctrinal approaches will be unpacked from legal reasoning of *Kioa v West*, *Quin*, *Teoh* and *Lam*. Importantly, it will be demonstrated that the distinctive ele-

---

[128] Only Lord Justice Laws's judgment in *Nadarajah* (n 9) [67] stated the rule of law.

[129] Jowell (n 26) 339.

[130] The status of the ground has to be repeated for multiple times in this section in order to illustrate the stability of the Australian doctrinal approaches.

6.4.1 Prior to Lam

The first case discussed here is *Kioa v West*, an immigration case where the applicants were deported by the Minister for Immigration and Ethnic Affairs' decision under the MA. In seeking judicial review, the applicants claimed that they had legitimate expectation that their daughter was entitled to be heard before the decision was made.[131] In the HCA's judgments, there are two main points demonstrating the connections between the determination of legitimate expectations and Australian legal culture.

6.4.1.1 *Kioa v West*

Firstly, in terms of justification, the court relied on the logic of legality in accepting procedural legitimate expectations as a ground of judicial review. All the judgments asserted that the courts shall generally protect the requirements of natural justice or procedural fairness, regarded as a matter of law.[132] For example, Justice Mason viewed the protection of procedural legitimate expectations as *'a fundamental rule of the common law doctrine of natural justice'*,[133] which has been associated with procedures followed by *'courts of law'*.[134] Justice Deane also stated that *'…the standards of procedural fairness…are recognised as fundamental by the common law'*.[135] Justice Brennan explained this in terms of the supremacy of Parliament in the Australian constitution encouraging the courts to declare the validity or invalidity of executive action by judicial review.[136] All of these justifications are part of the surface-water legality. As described above, procedural legitimate expectations mainly requires general administrative law values in support.

However, the influence of deep-water legality was more obvious in terms of application on how the Australian courts determine procedural legitimate expectations. A set of rules directing the determination of the scope of judicial review to the separation of powers was established. The scope of judicial review in a particular case is considered according to the nature of the power exercised and the statutory

---

[131] n 17 [9].
[132] ibid [16], [19] (Gibb J) [28], [30]-[31] (Mason J), [21] (Wilson J), [9] (Brennan J), [2] (Deane J).
[133] ibid [28].
[134] ibid [30].
[135] ibid [2]; See also [9] (Brennan J).
[136] ibid [12].

provisions governing its exercise.[137] Justice Brennan explained that the court has jurisdiction to declare a supposed exercise of statutory power invalid for its failure to comply with the procedural requirements prescribed by the statute.[138] This is the duty of the court based on the *'judicial construction of the statute'*.[139] The courts can only intervene if there is a clear manifestation of an intention that is contrary to the statute.[140] In a situation in which the legislative intent is unclear, the court must consider the claim based on the concept of procedural fairness and reasonableness.[141] Justice Brennan mentioned that this concept of fairness may lead the court *'to place itself in the shoes of the repository of the power to determine whether the procedure adopted was reasonable and fair'*.[142] However, this action has to be limited to a narrow scope due to the rigid distinction between legality and merits. The merits were for the executive to consider and the courts were ill-suited to trespass into this field.[143]

These applications demonstrate that the Australian courts have a relatively fixed way of operating (deep-water) legality. They determine the ground of procedural legitimate expectations based on the statutory construction. They will be able to intervene when there is clear manifestation of an intention that is contrary to the statute. If it is not clear, prima facie is that it is in the area of merits, not legality. The scope of the judicial review becomes narrow only when the decision is unfair. Parallel to the previous chapters, this application is compatible to the rigid legal mentality of Australian judicial review constitutionalism namely the rigid framework of separation of powers. In comparison, these rules are not much mentioned in the determination of procedural legitimate expectations in the English law.[144] Without the framework of separation of powers prescribed in a written constitution, the English courts have relatively more flexibility to search for the scope of judicial review.

6.4.1.2 *Quin*

The Australian court's distinctive approach in determining procedural legitimate expectations in the light of Australian legal culture was confirmed in *Quin*. In that case, the applicants were magistrates in NSW under the Justices Act 1902 (NSW). Thereafter, they were invited by the Attorney-General to make an application for appointment under the (new) Local Courts Act 1982 (NSW). The applicants claimed

---

[137] ibid [12] (Gibbs J), [32] (Mason J), [7] (Deane J).
[138] ibid [12].
[139] ibid [9].
[140] ibid [31], [34] (Mason J).
[141] ibid [34].
[142] ibid [35].
[143] ibid [27].
[144] See n 37.

6.4 Australian Doctrinal Approaches

that these proceedings had been denied procedural fairness as they had a legitimate expectation that they would be given an opportunity to answer the allegations in the consideration of their applications for appointment.[145] Three points of doctrinal approaches influenced by the rigid Australian mentality can be discussed as follows.

Firstly, in terms of justification, Justice Brennan clearly connected the determination of the scope of judicial review to the premise of legality by asserting that *'At common law judicial review does not consist in assessing the legal effect of the steps taken preliminary to the exercise of a power but in a determination of the legality of the exercise or purported exercise of the power'*.[146] He further added that *'This case raises in an acute form the question whether the remedies of judicial review are available to protect a legitimate expectation against the exercise of an executive or administrative power which otherwise accords with law'*.[147] Again, procedural legitimate expectations is simply justified by the surface water legality.

Secondly, more directed to the deep-water legality, the judgments in *Quin* confirmed that the Australian courts' application in determining legitimate expectations was influenced by the Australian legal culture. For example, Justice Mason directly gave importance to the separation of powers, which delegates the executive the discretion to change a new policy.[148] It cannot *'by representation or promise disable itself from performing a statutory duty'*.[149] This was reinforced by the fact that the executive is an expert in a particular field of public administration.[150] Therefore, judicial review will be available only when *'the purported exercise of power is excessive or otherwise unlawful'*.[151] The court has a role to declare and enforce the law affecting the extent and exercise of power.[152] He stated that

> The duty and jurisdiction of the court to review administrative action do not go beyond the declaration and enforcing of the law which determines the limits and governs the exercise of the repository's power.[153]

Despite the courts having jurisdiction to conduct judicial review in some situations based on the statutory construction, Justice Brennan stated that they must be wary of trespassing into the merits of the decision.[154]

Thirdly, the Australian law cannot flexibly use various doctrines in determining procedural legitimate expectations as a ground of judicial review, like the ways in

---

[145] n 17 [11] (Mason CJ).

[146] ibid [3].

[147] ibid [16].

[148] ibid [23].

[149] ibid.

[150] ibid [26].

[151] ibid [17] (Brennan J).

[152] ibid [20].

[153] ibid [17]. This statement has been widely cited in the determination of other grounds of judicial review. This demonstrates that the law is systematic and mature.

[154] ibid [20].

which it is done in England. The courts have no sliding scale for the court to be more or less intrusive. Justice Brennan clearly contended that

> ...the court needs to remember that the judicature is but one of the three co-ordinate branches of government and that the authority of the judicature is not derived from a superior capacity to balance the interests of the community against the interests of an individual. The repository of administrative power must often balance the interests of the public at large and the interests of minority groups or individuals. The courts are not equipped to evaluate the policy considerations which properly bear on such decisions, nor is the adversary system ideally suited to the doing of administrative justice: interests which are not represented as well as interests which are represented must often be considered[155]

The scope of judicial review was determined by relying on the 'concrete' statutory construction. The prima facie is that this is an area of merits. Thus, it is the duty of the executive to decide.[156] The court is allowed to intervene in the narrowest manner.[157]

All these doctrinal approaches were clearly connected to the distinctive elements of Australian legal culture, such as the rigid separation of powers, statutory construction and the distinction between legality and merits. Apart from the ground of procedural legitimate expectations, *Quin* triggered a discussion on substantive legitimate expectations. This was not raised directly by the claimant, but from the judgment.[158] For example, Justice Mason mentioned that a claim of legitimate expectations may take the form of *'a substantive right, privilege or benefit or of a procedural right, advantage or opportunity'*.[159] Furthermore, he argued that, although procedural legitimate expectations was claimed in this case, it had the characteristics of substantive legitimate expectations.[160] This was mentioned in comparison to the English cases[161] debating whether the scope of legality should be expanded for substantive benefit or not.[162]

However, all the judgments in *Quin* rejected substantive legitimate expectations as part of (deep-water) legality in Australian law. The legal reasoning demonstrates this straightforwardly by explaining elements of the Australian legal culture such as the separation of powers and the distinction between legality and merits. For example, Justice Mason explained that substantive legitimate expectations will entail curial interference with administrative decisions on the merits. This would preclude decision-makers from making a decision they considered to be the most appropriate in the circumstances.[163] It was discussed as *'Some advocates of judicial intervention*

---

[155] ibid.

[156] ibid.

[157] *Wednesbury* doctrine was applied in this case (ibid [19] (Brennan J)).

[158] ibid [34] (Mason J).

[159] ibid [32] (Mason J).

[160] ibid [33].

[161] *Khan* (n 3); *R v Secretary of State for the Home Department; Ex parte Ruddock* (1987) 1 WLR 1482.

[162] n 17 [35].

[163] ibid [37].

6.4 Australian Doctrinal Approaches

which encourages the courts to expand the scope and purpose of judicial review...'.[164] Justice Brennan firmly asserted that this advocacy was misplaced and that the courts have to protect legality by considering the separation of powers. Although the courts *'have a duty to uphold and apply the law which recognises the autonomy of the three branches of government within their respective spheres of competence'*,[165] they would not be following the separation of powers and their own legitimacy if they trespassed on the merits.[166]

Interestingly, Justice Brennan mentioned clearly that this exclusion of substantive legitimate expectations in Australian (deep) understandings of legality is a product of how the rule of law is understood. In his words, *'The authority of the courts and their salutary capacity judicially to review the exercise of administrative power depend in the last analysis on their fidelity to the rule of law, exhibited by the articulation of general principles'*.[167] The gate through which the court can step to review the merits has not been unlocked.[168] The notion of legitimate expectation would *'become a stalking horse for excesses of judicial power'*.[169] Additionally, Justice Brennan tied the determination to the idea of pragmatism and formalism in that, if the courts were given flexibility in conducting judicial review on the ground of substantive legitimate expectations, they would be *'adrift on a featureless sea of pragmatism'*.[170] He further explained that *'...the notion of a legitimate expectation is too nebulous to form a basis for invalidating the exercise of a power when its exercise otherwise accords with law'*.[171]

6.4.1.3 *Teoh*

These fixed approaches in determining the ground as influenced by Australian legal culture will be affirmed in *Lam* in the next section. Before that, *Teoh* will be discussed as another case demonstrating further influence of the Australian legal culture on the courts' approach to procedural legitimate expectations.[172] In *Teoh*, the applicant was a foreign national applying for a permanent entry permit into Australia. The application was refused on the ground that he was convicted of drug offences and sentenced to imprisonment, therefore he did not meet the policy requirement for residential status be of good character. However, the applicant claimed that the rejection of the resident status would lead the applicant's wife and

---

[164] ibid [21] (Brennan J).
[165] ibid.
[166] ibid [22].
[167] ibid.
[168] ibid [26].
[169] ibid [24].
[170] ibid [22].
[171] ibid.
[172] n 17.

young children, who were in Australia, to face a bleak future. This was not in compliance with article 3(1) of the ratified United Nations Convention on the Rights of the Child. It gave rise to a legitimate expectation that the Minister would act in conformity with it and treat the best interest of the applicant's children as a primary consideration.

While the analysis of *Coughlan* above showed that a factor from an interrelated legal culture, namely the provision of an international treaty, could possibly be flexibly integrated into the English court's consideration of the ground, the judgments in *Teoh* demonstrate it is not the case in Australian law. It is difficult to claim that the provision gives rise to procedural legitimate expectations in Australian law. The treaty cannot operate as a direct source of individuals' rights and obligations in the country,[173] unless it is stipulated in a statute.[174] The reason was clear from the way the separation of powers is particularly understood in Australian legal culture.

With that said, the courts could recognise the significance of an international treaty. The majority of judgments accept that a ratified provision is capable of giving rise to the legitimate expectations of the claimant. Justices Mason and Deane held that the courts should favour the construction of a ratified treaty.[175] The reasoning was that *'it is because Parliament, prima facie, intends to give effect to Australia's obligations under international law'*.[176] Therefore, international treaties can play a part in the courts' development of the common law.[177]

Nonetheless, this importation of a norm from interrelated legal cultures into the consideration of the court has two main limitations, the first of which is that the courts can do this *'with due circumspection'*.[178] The logic of the separation of powers considers that the *'Judicial development of the common law must not be seen as a backdoor means to create the law'*.[179] It is the main duty of parliament, not the court, to incorporate conventions into the domestic law. The court was reminded that legitimate expectation is not a binding rule of law.[180] Secondly, the judgments emphasised that the importation of international treaties to consider legitimate expectation is only valid in the aspect of procedural fairness.[181] Unlike the English law, the courts cannot take a factor into account when considering the ground of substantive legitimate expectations.

On the other hand, Justice McHugh gave a dissenting opinion that the ratification of a convention can be part of the consideration of the court, but by no means, did

---

[173] ibid [25] (Mason and Deane JJ), [20] (Toohey J), [35] (McHugh J).

[174] ibid [25] (Mason and Deane JJ).

[175] ibid [26].

[176] ibid.

[177] ibid [27]-[28] (Mason and Deane JJ), [22]-[23], [32] (McHugh J).

[178] ibid [28] (Mason and Deane JJ).

[179] ibid.

[180] ibid [36] (Mason and Deane JJ).

[181] ibid [37] (Mason and Deane JJ), [26] (Toohey J).

not give any rise to legitimate expectation, whether procedural or substantive.[182] This was a different conclusion from the majority, but it was based on a similar kind of reasoning. It was justified by the separation of powers in that the executive does not have a duty to make the effect of the treaty a domestic law. Justice McHugh asserted that;

> If the result of ratifying an international convention was to give rise to a legitimate expectation that that convention would be applied in Australia, the Executive government of the Commonwealth would have effectively amended the law of this country.... If the expectation were held to apply to decisions made by State officials, it would mean that the Executive government's action in ratifying a convention had also altered the duties of State government officials.[183]

This legal reasoning in *Teoh* demonstrated that the court had limited access to interrelated legal culture in the determination of legitimate expectations as a ground of judicial review. Although the possibility was accepted by the majority, it came with limitations. This approach was clearly determined through the premise of the rigid separation of powers, which is distinctively understood in Australian legal culture. Justice McHugh relied on a similar kind of reasoning, but reached a different conclusion that the interrelated legal culture could never give rise to legitimate expectation.

6.4.2 Lam

So far, an attempt has been made to point out that there are relatively fixed ways in considering whether the category of legitimate expectations is covered by the Australian deep-water legality or not. While procedural legitimate expectations is included on the condition of clear manifestation of a contrary statutory intention, substantive legitimate expectations is completely excluded. The legal reasoning of *Kioa v West*, *Quin* and *Teoh* demonstrate that these are influenced by the Australian legal culture. It was affirmed and further discussed in *Lam*.

In the case, the claimant's visa application was cancelled because he failed to pass the character test. The decision-maker had informed the claimant that it would seek information from a third party (the children's carer) before the cancellation. However, the decision-maker did not do so. In seeking judicial review, the claimant argued that the decision-maker failed to apply procedural fairness to the case.[184] In the judgments of the HCA, the notion that substantive legitimate expectations should be protected in Australia, was firmly rejected for the foreseeable future.[185]

---

[182] ibid [3] (McHugh J).
[183] ibid [38].
[184] n 3 [2]-[3], [23]-[24], [40], [109]-[111], [125]-[128].
[185] Weeks (n 32) 243–244.

The legal reasoning of this argument in the light of the Australian legal culture is examined below.

Beginning with the judgment of Chief Justice Gleeson, Australian law generally accepts procedural legitimate expectations as a ground for judicial review.[186] He used English cases like *Attorney General of Hong Kong v Ng Yuen Shiu* to illustrate that the meaning of legality includes procedural fairness.[187] In relation to the application, while the judgment in English law is flexibly applied to various categories like abuse of power, Chief Justice Gleeson considered whether or not the court had jurisdiction from the perspective of the statutory framework and separation of powers,[188] and applied the doctrine of jurisdictional error as the central approach for this consideration. If the administrative action contains a jurisdictional error, the court has the jurisdiction to conduct judicial review. However, he held that the applicant in this case had not lost any opportunity to advance his case. Hence, there was no procedural unfairness.[189] The court then did not have the jurisdiction to conduct judicial review because there was no jurisdictional error occurring. This usage of the jurisdictional error doctrine is another indicator of the distinctive rigidity of the Australian legal culture.

In terms of substantive legitimate expectations, Chief Justice Gleeson admitted that there was no clear-cut distinction between a substantive and procedural expectation. The applicant's claim could convert a procedural expectation into something substantive.[190] However, he affirmed that the ground was applied far too broadly.[191] The claim required the concept of legitimate expectations to carry more weight than it could bear.[192] It could have a negative effect by raising judicial review of an administrative action to *'a level of high and arid technicality'*.[193] The Australian understanding of deep-water legality does not include the expansion of legitimate expectation to protect substance.

This was entrenched by the judgments of Justices McHugh and Gummow. The important issue for procedural legitimate expectations is the prohibition of adopting an interrelated legal culture in the consideration of the court. The judges describe a dissenting opinion in *Teoh* that the ratification of international treaties did not impose liability on the executive.[194] Such an obligation is not a relevant mandatory consideration.[195] Significantly, the separation of powers was the reason for this approach. The executive is granted discretionary powers to fulfil its task of

---

[186] n 3 [33].
[187] ibid [31].
[188] ibid [27].
[189] ibid.
[190] ibid [28].
[191] ibid [25].
[192] ibid.
[193] ibid.
[194] ibid [81].
[195] ibid [99]-[101].

6.4 Australian Doctrinal Approaches

executing and maintaining the statutory law; therefore, the judicial branch has no jurisdiction to add or vary the content of those powers based on a particular view of the executive's handling of an international affair.[196] Compared to English law, doctrine influenced from interrelated legal culture will not be applied by the Australian courts because it conflicts with the landscape of their legal culture.

As for substantive legitimate expectations, Justices McHugh and Gummow began by questioning whether the rejection of substantive legitimate expectations gives rise to a jurisdictional error or not.[197] They explained the status in English law whereby the ground was accepted,[198] but held the position in *Quin* that the ground shall be rejected and retained in this case.[199] It was clear from their legal reasoning that this rejection is influenced by Australian legal culture. For example, Justices McHugh and Gummow made the following assertion;

> *In Australia, the existence of a basic law which is a written federal constitution, with separation of the judicial power, necessarily presents a frame of reference which differs from both the English and other European systems referred to above. Considerations of the nature and scope of judicial review, whether by this Court under s 75 of the Constitution or otherwise, inevitably involves attention to the text and structure of the document in which s 75 appears. An aspect of the rule of law under the Constitution is that the role or function of Ch III courts does not extend to the performance of the legislative function of translating policy into statutory form or the executive function of administration.*[200]

This means that the courts have to consider the structure and framework of the separation of powers and the federal system when deciding the scope of judicial review.[201] The approach in *Coughlan,* where the ground was determined based on the concept of abuse of power, or the principle of proportionality, was therefore rejected because it would have given the court the authority to decide the merits, which would have infringed the separation of powers.[202]

Similar to the other grounds relating to substantive exercise of discretion analysed in the previous chapter, Justices McHugh and Gummow linked the determination of legitimate expectation to the doctrine of jurisdictional error. They contended that whether the court should conduct judicial review or not *'is manifested in the distinction between jurisdictional and non-jurisdictional error which informs s75(v)'*.[203] The courts have a duty to conduct judicial review if a jurisdictional error occurs, but they have no jurisdiction to do so in the absence of such an error. If they trespass into the merits, this will infringe the separation of powers.

Other judges apart from Justices Gleeson and McHugh and Gummow have taken a similar approach. For example, Justice Hayne argued that the abuse of power is in

---

[196] ibid [102].
[197] ibid [65].
[198] ibid [66].
[199] ibid [67].
[200] ibid [76].
[201] ibid [72]-[73].
[202] ibid [73].
[203] ibid [77].

danger of being used without the carefully articulation of its content.[204] In addition, Justice Callinan stated that *'legitimate expectation is an unfortunate one and apt to mislead'*.[205] In short, all the judgments in *Lam* affirmed the approaches of the Australian law in accepting procedural legitimate expectations as a matter of law, but with clear applications and limitations. However, they rejected substantive legitimate expectations as a valid ground of judicial review. All of these factors demonstrate that the elements of Australian legal culture play a role in all the court's processes to determine the scope of judicial review.

6.4.3 After Lam

After *Lam*, the approaches remained relatively stable. There were cases in which procedural legitimate expectations was accepted as part of legality; for example, *NAFF of 2002 v Minister for Immigration and Multicultural and Indigenous Affairs*,[206] and cases in which the claimant attempted to rely on *Coughlan*'s approach in terms of expanding the scope of judicial review to protect substantive legitimate expectations; for example, *McWilliam v Civil Aviation Safety Authority*.[207] However, they all failed.[208]

Not only being entrenched in judgments, these doctrinal approaches in determining legitimate expectations as ground of judicial review are less debated in Australia. Two arguments have been firmly admitted. Firstly, legitimate expectations is adopted in cases of alleged procedural unfairness with limitations.[209] The approach in *Teoh* to give greater effect to international treaties was rejected.[210] Secondly, whether with the doctrine of proportionality or not, substantive legitimate expectations is firmly rejected.[211] These are clearly embedded in the Australian legal culture.[212] The ground has not been developed on the substance of the decision as it has in English law.[213]

---

[204] ibid [119].

[205] ibid [140].

[206] (2004) 221 CLR 1 (see more in Alison Duxbury, 'The Impact and Significance of Teoh and Lam' in Matthew Groves and H P Lee (eds), *Australian Administrative Law: Fundamentals, Principles and Doctrines* (CUP 2007) 312–315).

[207] [2004] FCA 1701.

[208] Stewart (n 32) 295–297; See also *Kaur* (n 17) [65].

[209] Groves (n 32); Anthony Mason, 'Procedural Fairness: Its Development and Continuing Role of Legitimate Expectation' (2005) 12 Australian Journal of Administrative Law 103.

[210] Michael Taggart, 'Australian Exceptionalism in Judicial Review' (2008) 36 Federal Law Review 1, 14–15; Duxbury (n 206) 307–310.

[211] Taggart (n 210) 24–25.

[212] Groves (n 32); Weeks (n 32) 226–229, 241–246.

[213] Aronson, Groves and Weeks (n 33) [7.150].

6.4.4 Products of the Australian Legal Culture

In the same vein as the discussion of formalism in the previous chapters, the entrenchment in the determination of legitimate expectations embedded in the Australian constitutional setting was drawn into a kind of conclusory statement. For example, Groves asserts that '*…many judges and commentators reject the doctrine* [of substantive legitimate expectations] *on the simple basis that it is incompatible with the Australian doctrine of separation of powers.*'[214] This section dives deeply by unpacking the legal reasoning in leading cases to demonstrate the entrenchment of the doctrinal approaches applied by the Australian courts in determining procedural and substantive legitimate expectations as grounds of judicial review, as shown in the snapshot in the table below.

Australian doctrinal approaches		
Justifications	Entrenched and systematic	
	Procedural legitimate expectations	Substantive legitimate expectations
	Mainly justified by surface-water legality (*Kioa v West, Quin*)	Rejected by the rule of law, separation of powers and distinction between legality and merit (*Quin, Lam*)
Applications	Clear rules based on the separation of powers and statutory construction (*Kioa v West, Quin*) Considered as practical matter (*Lam*)	Rejected '*adrift on a featureless sea of pragmatism*' (*Quin, Lam*)
Doctrines	Limited to the narrow scope of judicial review without balancing process in the similar way with *Wednesbury* (*Quin*) Linked with jurisdictional error (*Lam*)	Not part of jurisdictional error (*Lam*)
Influences from interrelated legal cultures	Limited access to interrelated legal culture in the determination of procedural legitimate expectations (*Teoh*)	Prohibited to be adopted into the consideration of the court (*Teoh, Lam*)
The status of the grounds	Limitedly accepted as a valid ground of judicial review	Completely rejected

Importantly, these doctrinal approaches are connected to the rigid legal mentality of Australian judicial review constitutionalism. Firstly, procedural legitimate expectations is accepted as a ground of judicial review. The court considers the scope of legality in the particular case based on statutory construction under the framework of the separation of powers. The distinction between legality and merits is cautionary. Access to an interrelated legal culture to consider the ground is limited because

---

[214] Groves (n 32) 516.

this could infringe the framework between legislative and judiciary. The ground is determined based on the doctrine of jurisdictional error. If the executive does not exceed its boundary of power, there is no jurisdictional error; therefore, the court has no jurisdiction to conduct judicial review.

Substantive legitimate expectations has been rejected as part of (deep-water) legality in the Australian law based on a similar mentality concerning constitutional structures. It is perceived as being in the area of merits, which is for the executive to decide rather than the courts. This approach can be understood by the separation of powers framed in the written Constitution. Since the courts regard the ground as not making a jurisdictional error, they have no jurisdiction to conduct judicial review. The Australian law does not give the courts the same kind of flexibility as the English law gives to their counterparts. Instead, they have to consider and follow the constitutional structure when determining the scope of review.

6.5 Conclusion

As recognised by some scholars, although substantive legitimate expectations is valid in England, claim for judicial review on this ground will not always be successful. For example, while Lord Justice Sedley accepted substantive legitimate expectations as a valid ground of judicial review in *Hamble Fisheries*, he held that the claimant's expectation was not legitimate.[215] Also, as Thomas points out, there were only a few cases in which the English courts had considered the disputed administrative action as unlawful on the ground of substantive legitimate expectations.[216] On the other hand, although substantive legitimate expectations is not valid in Australia, the courts can still conduct judicial review of the administrative action alleged to be unfair in the same manner as substantive legitimate expectations through other grounds, such as *Wednesbury* unreasonableness or illogicality and irrationality.

However, what is emphasised in this chapter is the different modes of doctrinal approaches and legal reasoning applied for such determination in England and Australia. It is undisputable that the Australian courts also have flexibility in the determination of procedural legitimate expectations as a ground of judicial review, namely, to decide the particular requirement of procedural fairness based on the circumstance of the case. However, it is a different kind of flexibility from that of the English law. As Justice Mason of the HCA noted, '*It would require a revolution in Australian judicial thinking to bring about an adoption of the English approach to substantive protection of legitimate expectations*'.[217] This has been exemplified in

---

[215] n 6 [59]–[60].

[216] Robert Thomas, 'Legitimate Expectations and the Separation of Powers in English and Welsh Administrative Law' in Matthew Groves and Greg Weeks (eds), *Legitimate Expectations in the Common Law World* (Hart Publishing 2017).

[217] Mason (n 209) 108.

6.5 Conclusion

this chapter by the unpacking process of legal reasoning of leading cases and the framework of deep-water legality and legal culture.

On the one hand, as a product of the flexible legal mentality of English judicial review constitutionalism, the English courts have flexibility in applying various doctrinal approaches in considering the ground. On the other hand, the Australian courts apply a relatively fixed doctrinal approach in firmly rejecting the validity of substantive legitimate expectations as a ground of judicial review. Parallel to Chaps. 3, 4 and 5, these differences are two ways in operating deep-water legality. Rather than arguing for or against one over the other, this area of legitimate expectations confirms the general statement of this book that the determination of the grounds of judicial review can be more comprehensively understood in the light of legal culture.

Apart from that, the analysis above can also be connected to the previous chapter. On the one hand, apart from the overlaps between the grounds over factual issues and the grounds relating to substantive exercise of discretion, *Wednesbury* and proportionality were adopted as a doctrine in the determination of substantive legitimate expectations in England. Scholars thereby discuss the relationships between these grounds. On the other hand, the categorisation of grounds remains clear in Australian law. While objective fact is reviewed through jurisdictional fact, subjective discretion is reviewed through illogicality and irrationality and *Wednesbury* is regarded as a safety net in determining the scope of judicial review. They are all included in jurisdictional error. Conversely, proportionality and substantive legitimate expectations are not the part of jurisdictional error. These flexible and fixed relationships between the grounds in England and Australia also demonstrate influences of the English and Australian legal culture respectively.

Chapter 7
Conclusion

Abstract Some of the notions derived from the comparison of English and Australian judicial review in this book are articulated in this chapter. The book's place in the administrative law scholarship is also examined with an emphasis on its contribution, namely its provision of concrete examples of the connection between the doctrinal analysis and the legal system's constitutional setting. Not only are the constitutional orders embedded in English and Australian legal culture and the determination of the grounds of judicial review dived deeper and broader, but they are also systematised by the framework of deep-water legality. Further implications of deep-water legality and legal culture as a useful framework for navigating other administrative law doctrines and the determination of the grounds of judicial review in other legal systems apart from England and Australia are also briefly discussed.

7.1 Mapping the Book in Administrative Law Scholarship

The Latin quotation, *'Ubi societas, ibi ius'*, which is translated as *'wherever there is society, there is law'*,[1] is one of the very first things learned in studying law. It reflects 'hermetical sealing' in that the law must change to meet the needs of society. It also forms the basis of a comparative legal study of the way in which the law is particularly conditioned by social facts in the different legal systems of the world.[2] It is generally recognised that different legal systems have diverse ways of interpreting and applying their laws and administrative law is no exception. For instance, Bell asserts that

> ...it is not possible for administrative lawyers to assume that there is a single, universal function that the law serves in most countries. Administrative law is closely bound up with

---

[1] Aaron Fellmeth and Maurice Horwitz, *Guide to Latin in International Law* (OUP 2009).
[2] Konrad Zweigert and Hein Kötz, *An Introduction to Comparative Law* (3rd edn, OUP 1998) 2, 4, 15, 21; Mathias Reimann, 'Comparative Law and Neighbouring Disciplines' in Mark Elliott and David Feldman (eds), *The Cambridge Companion to Public Law* (CUP 2015) 13–14.

© The Author(s), under exclusive license to Springer Nature Singapore Pte Ltd. 2021
V. Malsukhum, *Legal Culture, Legality and the Determination of the Grounds of Judicial Review of Administrative Action in England and Australia*,
https://doi.org/10.1007/978-981-16-1267-1_7

national institutions and traditions, as well as national constitutional values and ways of operating.[3]

Ackerman and Lindseth also observe that '*it* [administrative law] *frames the interaction between law and politics; it provides the conceptual vocabulary for their transformation over time in response to social change*'.[4] Specifically, it is commonly acknowledged that the courts in different legal systems determine the scope of judicial review in diverse ways based on their different constitutional orders. Apart from Craig's statement quoted at the very beginning of this book, Aronson also asserts the following;

> ...*whilst every country therefore accepts the need for lines* [to be drawn to determine the scope of judicial review], *each uses different terminology and techniques to express how they will set these margins.*[5]

This has generated a range of comparative studies of the different ways the scope of judicial review is determined between legal systems, especially those of England and Australia, which have a similar root, but have been developed differently. Aronson referred to this when he made the following statement;

> *Everyone in fact agrees that it would be dysfunctional to allow judicial review of all legal errors, but different legal systems have different ways of filtering out unwanted or unnecessary challenges. England's filtration system is different from ours* [Australian law][6]

It has been shown throughout this book that the existing works in the field are mainly focused on comparing the advantages and disadvantages of the different doctrinal approaches applied in determining the grounds of judicial review within and between the English and Australian law. Knight's book, in which he assesses the strengths of the different approaches applied by the courts in England, Australia, New Zealand and Canada to determine the line between judicial vigilance and restraint in the schemata of the scope of review, grounds of review, intensity of review and contextual review,[7] is a good example of the kind of work that aimed to have a functional purpose.[8]

---

[3] John Bell, 'Comparative Administrative Law' in Mathias Reimann and Reinhard Zimmermann (eds), *The Oxford Handbook of Comparative Law* (2nd edn, OUP 2019) 1251.

[4] Susan R Ackerman and Peter L Lindseth, 'Comparative Administrative Law: An Introduction' in Susan R Ackerman and Peter L Lindseth (eds), *Comparative Administrative Law* (Edward Elgar 2010) 18.

[5] Mark Aronson, 'Jurisdictional Error and Beyond' in Matthew Groves (ed), *Modern Administrative Law in Australia* (CUP 2014) 262. See similar kind of recognitions in William Wade and Christopher Forsyth, *Administrative Law* (11th edn, OUP 2014) 212–213; Robin Creyke, John McMillan and Mark Smyth, *Control of Government Action; Text, Cases and Commentary* (5th edn, LexisNexis Butterworths 2019) [2.3.2].

[6] Aronson (n 5) 263.

[7] Dean Knight, *Vigilance and Restraint in the Common Law of Judicial Review* (CUP 2018).

[8] See more in Ralf Michaels, 'Functional Method' in Mathias Reimann and Reinhard Zimmermann (eds), *The Oxford Handbook of Comparative Law* (2nd edn, OUP 2019).

7.1 Mapping the Book in Administrative Law Scholarship

Meanwhile, some authors connect particular doctrinal aspects to the legal systems' constitutional orders; for example, in the case of legitimate expectations, Groves and Weeks state that,

...the differences in approach between Australia and the UK are significant...There are compelling constitutional reasons for courts in reach jurisdiction to decide matters regarding legitimate expectations as they do...[9]

This kind of connection is also explored by Daly, who connects *'the core values revealed by the practice of administrative law'*, namely the rule of law, good administration, democracy and the separation of powers with *'the courts' doctrinal choices'* in the areas of process, substance and remedial discretion.[10]

The connection between a doctrinal analysis and the legal system's constitutional setting becomes more concrete in this book. Not only are the constitutional orders embedded in legal culture and the determination of the grounds of judicial review dived into deeper and more broadly, but they are also systematised based on the framework of deep-water legality.[11] In summary, the differences between English and Australian judicial review have been unpacked based on a particular form of legal culture, namely 'legal mentality of judicial review constitutionalism', which refers to the shared legal thinking of the individual judges in understanding their role in conducting judicial review according to distinctive constitutional orders. On the one hand, the nature of the balancing process between the twin concepts of parliamentary sovereignty and the rule of law and the absence of a written constitution to clearly prescribe the court's jurisdiction, lead the English courts to understand that their role in conducting judicial review in a flexible way. On the other hand, the Australian courts understand their role as being relatively rigid by following the constitutional guidelines, namely the federal framework of the separation of powers prescribed in the written constitution. These means of legal thinking were extracted from the judgments, secondary works and speeches of individual English and

---

[9] Matthew Groves and Greg Weeks, 'The Legitimacy of Expectations About Fairness: Can Process and Substance be Untangled?' in John Bell, Mark Elliott, Jason Varuhas and Philip Murray (eds), *Public Law Adjudication in Common Law Systems: Process and Substance* (Hart Publishing 2016) 187.

[10] Paul Daly, 'Administrative Law: A Values-based Approach' in John Bell, Mark Elliott, Jason Varuhas and Philip Murray (eds), *Public Law Adjudication in Common Law Systems: Process and Substance* (Hart Publishing 2016).

[11] Authors in this field who also apply this kind of methodological approach, but to different subject matter, are worth noting here. The prominent one is Boughey, who examines the constitutional and statutory frameworks of judicial review in Canada and Australia and applies them as a driving seat to understand the doctrinal approaches in the two legal systems. Indeed, it is interesting to note that, although Boughey's work is focused on the effect of the framework on judicial reasoning and approaches in enforcing human rights, it shares some similar conclusions with this book in the part about Australian law. For example, *'the use of strict, formalist principles to define the boundaries between judicial and administrative functions'* and *'refusal to follow various overseas developments and maintenance of a traditional approach to judicial review'* are pointed out as the Australian courts' main methods (Janina Boughey, *Human Rights and Judicial Review in Australia and Canada: The Newest Despotism?* (Hart Publishing 2017) 14, 59).

Australian judges in Chap. 2. Most prominently, while Lord Mance of the UKSC stated that the role of the English court is *'best left unanswered'*, in other words, flexible and open,[12] Chief Justice Gleeson of the HCA made the following statement;

> *The Constitution, the legislation governing judicial review, and the relevant principles of the common law, define the limits of the authority of courts to override administrative decisions.*[13]

These diverse legal cultures produce a different substantive understanding of the English and Australian courts of the 'law' or 'legal question', regarded as 'deep-water legality'. However, in practice, barristers cannot appear in court and argue that the administrative action does not comply with the principle of legality; hence, it needs to be brought through ground of judicial review. The influence of these two legal systems' deep-water legality on the determination of the controversial grounds of judicial review was examined and compared in Chaps. 3, 4, 5, and 6. The different doctrinal approaches were unpacked in these chapters, namely the status of the grounds, justifications, applications, doctrines, as well as the integration of the interrelated legal culture in the courts' determination of the grounds of judicial review, from the legal reasoning of leading English and Australian cases.

The demonstration began in Chap. 3 with central and traditional grounds, such as error of law and jurisdictional error before proceeding to the grounds of factual issues in Chap. 4, particularly jurisdictional fact. The most controversial area, namely the grounds relating to the substantive exercise of discretion was discussed in Chap. 5, before addressing emerging ground like substantive legitimate expectations in Chap. 6. The described three themes, namely, legal culture, deep-water legality and the determination of the grounds of judicial review, have been connected and become a framework of this book. Apart from demonstrating the different dimensions of the English and Australian judicial review, some overall themes concerning the English and Australian determination of the scope of judicial review can also be identified.

7.2 English Law Standing on the Edge of Two Boats

On the one hand, the English courts have the flexibility to apply various doctrinal approaches in their determination of the grounds of judicial review. They can provide malleable explanations in justifying or limiting their jurisdictions, from the direct reference to parliamentary sovereignty, the rule of law and the common law theory in *R (Cart) v Upper Tribunal* and *R (Privacy International) v Investigatory Powers Tribunal* to the interest of justice and the principle of finality in *E v Secretary*

---

[12] Lord Mance, 'The Rule of Law - Common Traditions and Common Issues' (175th Anniversary of Founding of Hoge Raad, the Netherlands, 1 October 2013).

[13] Chief Justice Gleeson, 'Judicial Legitimacy' (Australian Bar Association Conference, New York, 2 July 2000).

7.2 English Law Standing on the Edge of Two Boats

of State for the Home Department, the concept of limited jurisdiction and the appropriate process of judicialisation in *R (A) v Croydon LBC*, the expertise and consistency of the tribunal system in *R (Jones) v First-tier Tribunal*, fairness in *R v Secretary of State for Transport, Ex parte Richmond-Upon-Thames London Borough Council*, individual consideration, inconsistency and legal certainty in *R v Ministry of Agriculture, Fisheries and Food, Ex parte Hamble Fisheries Ltd* and the concept of good administration in *Nadarajah Abdi v The Secretary of State for the Home Department*. In the same vein, various doctrines, namely, jurisdictional error, judicial policy and second-tier appeal in *Cart*, four criteria leading factual determination to unfairness in *E*, *Wednesbury* in *Richmond-Upon-Thames* and *R v Secretary for the Home Department, Ex parte Hargreaves*, abuse of power in *R v North and East Devon Health Authority, Ex parte Coughlan* and proportionality in *Kennedy v Charity Commission, Pham v Secretary of State for the Home Department* and *Nadarajah*, have been flexibly elaborated, applied and adapted by individual judges in their determination of the scope of judicial review. Additionally, it is possible for the courts to adopt norms from interrelated legal cultures in their consideration, for example, the ECHR through the HRA.[14]

This variety of doctrinal approaches leads to the grounds of judicial review having a fluctuating status in English law. Error of law has been flexibly adapted, particularly in the judicial review of the decisions of tribunals and inferior courts. The jurisdictional fact doctrine was implicitly abandoned in *Anisminic Ltd v Foreign Compensation Commission*, but recurred as a valid ground for the court to review the precedent fact in *R v Secretary of State for the Home Department, Ex parte Khawaja*, and then being debated as to whether it should be replaced by the approach in *E*. However, it was clearly applied as a valid ground in *R (A) v Croydon* and *Jones*. The grounds relating to the substantive exercise of discretion, namely, *Wednesbury* unreasonableness, modified rationality and proportionality overlap. Also, whether and to what extent to accept substantive legitimate expectations as a ground of judicial review was fluctuating.

Apart from the legal reasoning and doctrinal approaches of the determination of the grounds of judicial review in these cases, the English deep-water understanding of legality has also led to an extensive academic discussion. As shown throughout the previous chapters, scholars have attempted to find descriptors of the flexibility of the courts' determination of grounds; for example, the conclusory labels of pragmatic reasoning and pragmatism, the concept of deference, as well as Gelborn and Robinson's seedless grape of the scope of judicial review.[15]

Rather than preferring or arguing with one of these doctrinal approaches and academic concepts, it is pointed out in this book that they are all rooted in the flexible nature of the English legal culture. Based on the metaphor of sailing boats, the approaches of the English courts when determining the grounds of judicial review

---

[14] The citations of these cases in this paragraph were reiterated throughout the previous chapters. In the interests of saving space, they will not be repeated here.

[15] E Gellhorn and G Robinson, 'Perspectives on Administrative Law' (1975) 75 Columbia Law Review 771, 780–781.

are reminiscent of the traditional Thai idiom saying, *'having one's legs on the edge of two (separate) boats'*. This implies a situation in which it is difficult to clearly decide which way to go between two possible choices that are very different and cannot function together.[16] It is equivalent to standing with a leg on each of two boats that are drifting apart. The English courts have the flexibility to choose (and sail) whichever of the two boats they consider to be the most appropriate, which will expand or narrow the grounds of judicial review. On a surface level, it seems that the choice of these two boats is inconsistent because the lines between reviewable and non-reviewable are swirling. However, this inconsistency is not necessarily problematic from a deep-water perspective; in fact, it is merely the result of the geographical features of an English river.

7.3 Australian Law's Choice of One Boat for a Journey

On the other hand, it has been demonstrated by the examination that the Australian doctrinal approaches are relatively confined, since the courts determine their jurisdiction based on the rigid framework of the separation of powers, prescribed in the written constitution and statutory construction. It is difficult for the Australian courts to consider factors from interrelated legal cultures because they are aware that those factors may infringe this rigid framework of the constitutional setting.

These doctrinal approaches lead the grounds of judicial review to have a relatively clear and systematic status. In *Craig v The State of South Australia* and *Kirk v Industrial Court (NSW)*, jurisdictional error was regarded as a central approach in all common law grounds of judicial review. It was also firmly held in *Timbarra Protection Coalition Inc v Ross Mining NL & Ors*, *Corporation of the City of Enfield v Development Assessment Commission*, *Anvil Hill Project Watch Association Inc v Minister for the Environment and Water Resources* and *Plaintiff M 70/2011 v Minister for Immigration and Citizenship* that jurisdictional fact was an entrenched subset of jurisdictional error. While illogicality and irrationality was used for the subjective exercise of discretion in *Minister for Immigration and Citizenship v SZMDs*, *Re Minister for Immigration and Multicultural Affairs, Ex parte Applicant S20/2002* and *Re Minister for Immigration and Citizenship v Li*, *Wednesbury* was considered as a safety net for the courts' review of administrative discretion. Procedural legitimate expectations is accepted with limitations in *Kioa v West* and *Minister of State for Immigration & Ethnic Affairs v Ah Hin Teoh*, while proportionality was firmly rejected, either as a ground for reviewing discretion or as a doctrine for substantive legitimate expectations in *Attorney-General (NSW) v Quin* and *Re Minister for Immigration and Multicultural Affairs, Ex parte Lam*.

---

[16] *Thai Dictionary (Royal Society Version) B E 2554* <http://www.royin.go.th/dictionary/> accessed 3 March 2018.

Apart from Taggart's Australian Exceptionalism, this unpacking and exploration of the doctrinal approaches in the courts' determination of the grounds of judicial review is a full detailed picture of the conclusory labels of formalistic reasoning, formalism and the firm rejection of deference. They are all demonstrated to be products of the Australian courts' perception of their role as relatively rigid based on their legal culture.

In contrast to the English law, it seems that the Australian courts choose to jump into a boat for the journey, whether to accept or reject, expand or narrow the grounds of judicial review and they steer the boat by adopting clear sailing protocols. It is difficult for the Australian courts to borrow a sailing technique or tool from a neighbour (interrelated legal culture), since they are aware that those techniques or tools may not accommodate the natural features under their rivers. The lines between reviewable and non-reviewable are relatively consistent, seen through clear water.

7.4 Standing and Further Implications of Deep-Water Legality and Legal Culture

It may seem that the main areas of research in this book are apparent to administrative law scholarship and, in reality, both the English and Australian courts can flexibly define the situations in which judicial review is appropriate. Also, the ability of the judiciary to choose interpretation and argumentation is a common feature of the common law system. Furthermore, the English and Australian laws share some of the initial grounds of judicial review and legal features. However, what has been articulated in depth in this book is that the legal mentality, doctrinal approaches and legal reasoning in determining the scope of judicial review are different in these two common law countries. Importantly, these differences are deeply dominated by their legal systems' legal culture.

Rather than the conclusory labels of pragmatism and formalism, this framework of legality and legal culture better reveals the underlying complexity of why the English and Australian courts adhere to different modes of doctrinal approaches and legal reasoning. This makes any kind of statement that the law should be understood within its particular constitutional setting tangible. Additionally, the unpacking process of legal reasoning given in the judgments of the leading cases is argued to be the best way to express the influence of legal culture on the determination of the grounds of judicial review. Furthermore, this argument cannot be synthesised from an independent analysis of the English or Australian law, but from a comparative study in which the distinctive patterns of doctrinal approaches and legal reasoning shared across the common law grounds of judicial review in the two legal systems are found. In short, what *'Ubi societas, ibi ius'* means in detail for the scope of judicial review doctrines in England and Australia is demonstrated in this book. The differences between the laws of England and Australia, namely between the fluctuation and entrenchment of jurisdictional error and jurisdictional fact and between the variation and firm rejection of proportionality and deference, have been systematically untangled based on the approaches of deep-water legality and legal culture. This kind of exercise has never been undertaken in this depth and detail before, despite its obvious importance.

Not only does this framework facilitates a more comprehensive understanding of these laws, but it also becomes a necessary block for any analysis of the development of the grounds of judicial review. For example, the courts in both legal systems are similarly confronted with the issue of inconsistency when they shift to a different doctrinal approach to determine the scope of judicial review. However, this point is addressed more seriously in the Australian literature than the English. The understanding of these laws through deep-water legality and legal culture simplifies the reason for this, namely that inconsistency caused by a variety of doctrinal approaches is more problematic in Australia because it is more incompatible with the Australian landscape. On the other hand, it has been shown through a number of statements made by English judges and scholars that inconsistency is probably part of the identity of the English judicial review. Therefore, the English and Australian laws cannot be measured on the exact same meter, since they are embedded in different legal cultures. Although they started from the same (English) foundation, the English/Australian legal cultures shaped the development of the common law principles of judicial review in different directions.

Finally, it is also essential to note that this book is a starting point rather than a complete exploration. There are a number of points to be further expanded in order to entrench the argument that legal culture plays an indispensable role in the doctrinal development of judicial review. For example, as clearly stated in Chap. 2, the particular focus of this book is the legal mentality of judges in perceiving their role to conduct judicial review based on the distinctive constitutional settings of the legal system. This is because the court plays the leading role in determining the scope of judicial review in each case. However, there are also other cultural aspects worth considering, for example, the wider developments of administrative law in relation to political attitudes, or the mentality of other actors in the legal system, such as particular judicial office-holders. In addition, a doctrinal analysis can be conducted on other cases, apart from the leading ones selected here. Also, the grounds of judicial review with less room for controversy than the selected ones in the book, such as improper purpose or fettering of discretion, can also be navigated by deep-water legality and legal culture.

Apart from that, the additional aim of this book is to argue that the framework of deep-water legality and legal culture can be applied to understand the determination of the grounds of judicial review in other legal systems, apart from those of England and Australia. For example, the French system does not have proportionality as a general head of judicial review,[17] but has an equivalent approach called 'Maximum Control', which entails the Conseil d'État extensively reviewing the merits of a

---

[17] Neville Brown and John Bell, *French Administrative Law* (5th edn, Clarendon Press 1998) 239–267.

7.4 Standing and Further Implications of Deep-Water Legality and Legal Culture

decision by providing suggestions and frameworks to the administration.[18] Besides, the Conseil d'État is able to intervene in administrative action under the broad scope of legality.[19] As Bell and Brown that *'The general principles of law… have been imported into the principle of legality through a broadening of the notion of loi, a breach of which is a ground of judicial review'*.[20] This approach may be problematic because of the separation of powers, if considered in the context of English and Australian law. However, the consideration of French legal culture lessens this problem,[21] because the judges are former administrative civil servants, who have knowledge and experience and are trained as experts in the field of public administration.[22] Having spent time within the administration, they are less likely to be swayed by arguments of relative expertise.[23] In short, there must be a distinct connection between legal culture, legality and the determination of the grounds of judicial review in French law.

Besides the scope of judicial review, the influence of legal culture on other administrative law doctrines in England and Australia was momentarily revealed in the earlier chapters. For example, as shown in Chap. 2 and 3, while the flexibility on the distinction between tribunals and the courts is distinguished in English law, there is a relatively rigid framework in Australian law based on the provisions in the written constitution, particularly Chapter III and Section 72. This also results in different kinds of restrictive clause systems in England and Australia. In Chap. 5, while the relationship between a judicial review in the HRA and the common law in England is flexible and debatable, the relationship between judicial review in the ADJR and common law in Australia is clearer and systematic.

Since all of these extensions require a considerable amount of space for a detailed examination, they must be the subject of future research, rather than included in this book, which shall end by emphasising its spirit and proclaiming the necessity to dive deeply into the legal mentality of the legal system in order to fully understand any legal doctrine.

---

[18] John Bell, Sophie Boyron and Simon Whittaker, *Principles of French Law* (2nd edn, OUP 2008) 186–188.

[19] The only exception in which the court will not substitute an administrative decision is on the ground of assessment of the facts. When it comes to the area of discretionary power, the courts would only substitute judgment if it is a manifest error (ibid).

[20] ibid 216.

[21] I addressed this point in Voraphol Malsukhum, 'Is Anything Lost by not Having Proportionality as a General Head of Judicial Review of Administrative Action' (2020) 49(2) Thammasat Law Journal 363, but for a purpose other than the one in this book.

[22] John Bell, *French Legal Cultures* (2nd edn, CUP 2008) 157–159, 196–198.

[23] ibid 191–195.

7.5 Concluding Remarks

The administrative law of many legal systems has continually been criticised based on the grounds that the courts excessively extend their power to intervene in any administrative action of their choosing, which leads to the indeterminable and improper scope of judicial review and judicial legitimacy.[24] Most scholars simply connect this situation to some constitutional orders of the legal system, for example, the written constitution is accredited with influencing Australian law, English flexible approach is chastised as disadvantageous. Rather than focusing on these final outcomes, this book illuminates that the connection between the determination of the scope of judicial review, deep-water legality and the legal system's legal culture can be explored at a more detail and in-depth level. Although, at the end of the day, the courts still determine the grounds of judicial review using their own volition, their approaches are not just random. The principle of legality is not just a fig-leaf, but is deeply embedded in the legal system's legal culture, and thereby, dictates the way courts empower, justify, constrain or limit their scope of judicial review. It is anticipated that this framework of legal culture and legality will be a useful tool to navigate the process of determining the scope of judicial review in the English and Australian legal systems, and by extension, other legal systems. The entire process can be compared to one who sails a boat with a compass, showing the direction relative to the geography. After all,

> *He who loves practice without theory is like the sailor who boards ship without a rudder and compass and never knows where he may cast*
> (Leonardo da Vinci, 1453–1519)

---

[24] See various publications in 'Judicial Power Project' <http://judicialpowerproject.org.uk/> accessed 3 March 2018.

Bibliography

Textbooks

Appleby G, Reilly A and Grenfell L, *Australian Public Law* (3rd edn, OUP 2019)
Aronson M, Groves M and Weeks G, *Judicial Review of Administrative Action and Government Liability* (6th edn, Thomson Reuters Australia 2017)
Arthurs HW, *Without the Law; Administrative Justice and Legal Pluralism in Nineteenth-Century England* (University of Toronto Press 1985)
Atiyah PS and Summers RS, *Form and Substance in Anglo-Amercian Law: A Comparative Study of Legal Reasoning, Legal Theory, and Legal Institutions* (Clarendon Press 1996)
Bagehot W, *The Collected Works of Walter Bagehot*, vol 5 (St John-Stevas N ed, The Economist 1974)
Barendt E, *An Introduction to Constitutional Law* (OUP 1998)
Bauman Z, *Culture as Praxis* (Sage 1999)
Bell J, *French Legal Cultures* (2nd edn, CUP 2008)
Bell J, Boyron S and Whittaker S, *Principles of French Law* (2nd edn, OUP 2008)
Blackstone W, *An Analysis of the Laws of England*, vol 1 (The Clarendon Press 1771)
Blankenburg E and Bruinsma F, *Dutch Legal Culture* (2nd edn, Kluwer Law International 1995)
Boughey J, *Human Rights and Judicial Review in Australia and Canada: The Newest Despotism?* (Hart Publishing 2017)
Brandy A, *Proportionality and Deference under the UK Human Rights Act: An Institutionally Sensitive Approach* (CUP 2012)
Brown N and Bell J, *French Administrative Law* (5th edn, Clarendon Press 1998)
Cane P, *Administrative Tribunals and Adjudication* (Hart Publishing 2010)
———, *Administrative Law* (5th edn, OUP 2011)
———, *Controlling Administrative Power: An Historical Comparison* (CUP 2016)
Cane P and McDonald L, *Principles of Administrative Law: Legal Regulation of Governance* (3rd edn, OUP 2018)
Connolly AJ, *The Foundations of Australian Public Law: State, Power, Accountability* (CUP 2017)
Cotterell R, *Law's Community: Legal Theory in Sociological Perspective* (OUP 1995)
Craig P, *Public Law and Democracy in the United Kingdom and the United States of America* (Clarendon Press 1990)
———, *EU Administrative Law* (3rd edn, OUP 2018)
———, *The Hamlyn Lectures: UK, EU and Global Administrative Law* (CUP 2015)
———, *Administrative Law* (8th edn, Sweet & Maxwell 2016)

Crawford L, *The Rule of Law and the Australian Constitution* (The Federation Press 2017)
Creyke R, McMillan J and Smyth M, *Control of Government Action; Text, Cases and Commentary* (5th edn, LexisNexis Butterworths 2019)
Daly P, *A Theory of Deference in Administrative Law: Basis, Application and Scope* (CUP 2012)
De Smith, *Judicial Review of Administrative Action* (1st edn, Stevens & Sons Limited 1958)
Derry Irvine, *Human Rights, Constitutional Law and the Development of the English Legal System* (Hart Publishing 2003)
Dicey AV, *Introduction to the Study of the Law of the Constitution* (7th edn, Macmillan 1908)
———, *Introduction to the Study of the Law of the Constitution* (10th edn, Macmillan 1959)
Dworkin R, *Taking Rights Seriously* (Bloomsbury Academic 2013)
Dyzenhaus D, *Legality and Legitimacy: Carl Schmitt, Hans Kelsen, and Hermann Heller in Weimar* (Clarendon Press 1997)
Elliott M and Varuhas J, *Administrative Law: Text and Materials* (5th edn, OUP 2017)
Endicott T, *Administrative Law* (4th edn, OUP 2018)
Fellmeth A and Horwitz M, *Guide to Latin in International Law* (OUP 2009)
Fisher E, *Risk Regulation and Administrative Constitutionalism* (Hart Publishing 2007)
Fordham M, *Judicial Review Handbook* (6th edn, Hart Publishing 2012)
Friedman L, *The Legal System: A Social Science Perspective* (Russell Sage Foundation 1975)
———, *The Republic of Choice: Law, Authority and Culture* (Harvard University Press 1990)
Geertz C, *The Interpretation of Cultures: Selected Essays* (Basic Books 1973)
———, *The Interpretation of Cultures: Selected Essays* (2nd edn, Basic Books 1993)
Gleeson M, *The Rule of Law and the Constitution* (ABC Books 2000)
Goldsworthy J, *Australia: Devotion to Legalism in Interpreting Constitutions: A Comparative Study* (Oxford Constitutions of the World 2007)
Harlow C and Rawlings R, *Law and Administration* (3rd edn, CUP 2009)
Henderson E G, *Foundations of English Administrative Law: Certiorari and Mandamus in the Seventeenth Century* (Harvard University Press 1963)
Hewart, *The New Despotism* (London Ernest Benn Ltd 1928)
Irving H, *To Constitute a Nation: A Cultural History of Australia's Constitution* (CUP 1997)
Jaffe LL, *Judicial Control of Administrative Action* (Little, Brown 1965)
Johnson D, *The Japanese Way of Justice: Prosecuting Crime in Japan* (OUP 2002)
Josev T, *The Campaign against the Courts: A History of the Judicial Activism Debate* (The Federation Press 2017)
Juss S and Sunkin M, *Landmark Cases in Public Law* (Hart Publishing 2017)
Knight D, *Vigilance and Restraint in the Common Law of Judicial Review* (CUP 2018)
Lazarus L, *Contrasting Prisoners' Rights: A Comparative Examination of Germany and England* (OUP 2004)
Leeming M, *Authority to Decide: the Law of Jurisdiction in Australia* (2nd edn, The Federation Press 2020)
Lewans M, *Administrative Law and Judicial Deference* (Hart Publishing 2016)
Leyland P, *The Constitution of the United Kingdom: A Contextual Analysis* (3rd edn, Hart Publishing 2016)
Lloyd GER, *Demystifying Mentalities* (CUP 1990)
Loughlin M, *Foundations of Public Law* (OUP 2012)
McLean J, *Searching for the State in British Legal Thought: Competing Conceptions of the Public Sphere* (CUP 2012)
Nason S, *Reconstructing Judicial Review* (Hart Publishing 2015)
Oliver D, *Common Values and the Public-Private Divide* (Butterworths 1999)
Parkinson P, *Tradition and Change in Australian Law* (5th edn, Thomson Reuters 2013)
Raz J, *The Authority of Law* (Clarendon Press 1979)
Robson WA, *Justice and Administrative law: A Study of the British Constitution* (3rd edn, Stevens & Amp 1951)
Saunders C, *The Constitution of Australia: A Contextual Analysis* (Hart Publishing 2011)

Schonberg S, *Legitimate Expectations in Administrative Law* (OUP 2000)
Schwarze J, *European Administrative Law* (Sweet & Maxwell 1992)
Searle JR, *The Social Construction of Reality* (London 1995)
Sedley S, *Ashes and Sparks: Essays on Law and Justice* (CUP 2011)
———, *Lions Under the Throne: Essays on the History of English Public Law* (CUP 2015)
Shapiro S, *Legality* (Belknap Press of Harvard University Press 2011)
Stebbings C, *Legal Foundations of Tribunals in Nineteenth Century England* (CUP 2006)
Stellios J, *The Federal Judicature* (LexisNexis 2010)
Turpin C and Tomkins A, *British Government and the Constitution* (7th edn, CUP 2012)
Tushnet M, *The New Constitutional Order* (Princeton University Press 2009)
Wade H, *Towards Administrative Justice* (University of Michigan Press 1963)
Wade W and Forsyth C, *Administrative Law* (11th edn, OUP 2014)
———, *Administrative Law* (10th edn, OUP 2009)
Zweigert K and Kötz H, *An Introduction to Comparative Law* (3rd edn, OUP 1998)

Contribution to Edited Books

Ackerman SR and Lindseth PL, 'Comparative Administrative Law: An Intoduction' in Ackerman SR and Lindseth PL (eds), *Comparative Administrative Law* (Edward Elgar 2010)
Airo-Farulla G, 'Reasonableness, Rationality and Proportionality' in Groves M and Lee HP (eds), *Australian Administrative Law* (CUP 2007)
Allan T, 'The Rule of Law as the Foundation of Judicial Review' in Christopher Forsyth (ed), *Judicial Review and the Constitution* (Hart Publishing 2000).
Aroney N, 'The Justification of Judicial Review: Text, Structure, History and Principle', in Rosalind Dixon (ed) *Australian Constitutional Values* (Hart Publishing 2018)
Aronson M, 'Jurisdictional Error without the tears' in Groves M and Lee HP (eds), *Australian Administrative Law: Fundamentals, Principles and Doctrines* (CUP 2007)
———, 'Jurisdictional Error and Beyond' in Groves M (ed), *Modern Administrative Law in Australia* (CUP 2014)
———, 'The Growth of Substantive Review' in Bell J, Elliott M, Varuhas J and Murray P (eds), *Public Law Adjudication in Common Law Systems: Process and Substance* (Hart Publishing 2016)
Bell J, 'Comparative Administrative Law' in Reimann M and Zimmermann R (eds), *The Oxford Handbook of Comparative Law* (2nd edn, OUP 2019)
———, 'Administrative Law in a Comparative Perspective' in Örücü E and Nelken D (eds), *Comparative Law: A Handbook* (Hart Publishing 2007)
Bignami F, 'Comparative Administrative Law' in Elliott M and Feldman D (eds), *The Cambridge Companion to Public Law* (CUP 2015)
Boughey J and Crawford L, 'Jurisdictional Error: Do We Really Need It?' in Elliott M, Varuhas J and Stark S (eds), *The Unity of Public Law?: Doctrinal, Theoretical and Comparative Perspectives* (Hart Publishing 2018)
Cane P, 'Understanding Administrative Adjudication' in Pearson L, Harlow C and Taggart M (eds), *Administrative Law in a Changing State: Essays in Honour of Mark Aronson* (Hart Publishing 2008)
Carnwath R, 'No Need for a Single Foundation' in Forsyth C (ed), *Judicial Review and the Constitution* (Hart Publishing 2000)
Cotterrell R, 'The Concept of Legal Culture' in Nelken D (ed), *Comparing Legal Cultures* (Dartmouth 1997)
———, 'Comparative Law and Legal Culture' in Reimann M and Zimmermann R (eds), *The Oxford Handbook of Comparative Law* (2nd edn, OUP 2019)

Craig P, 'Jurisdiction, Judicial Control and Agency Autonomy, A Special Relationship' in Loveland I (ed), *American Influences on Public Law in the UK* (OUP 1995)

——, 'Unreasonableness and Proportionality in UK Law' in Elllis E (ed), *The Principle of Proportionality in the Laws of Europe* (Hart Publishing 1999)

——, 'Judicial Review of Questions of Law: A Comparative Perspective' in Rose-Ackerman SR and Lindseth PL (eds), *Comparative Administrative Law* (2nd edn, Edward Elgar 2017)

Crawford L and Goldsworthy J, 'Constitutionalism' in Saunders C and Stone A (eds), *The Oxford Handbook of the Australian Constitution* (OUP 2018)

Daly P, 'Administrative Law: A Values-based Approach' in Bell J, Elliott M, Varuhas J and Murray P (eds), *Public Law Adjudication in Common Law Systems: Process and Substance* (Hart Publishing 2016)

Dannemann G, 'Comparative Law: Study of Similarities or Differences?' in Reimann M and Zimmermann R (eds), *The Oxford Handbook of Comparative Law* (2nd edn, OUP 2019)

Duxbury A, 'The Impact and Significance of *Teoh* and *Lam*' in Groves M and Lee HP (eds), *Australian Administrative Law: Fundamentals, Principles and Doctrines* (CUP 2007)

Elias DS, 'The Unity of Public Law?', in Elliott M, Varuhas J and Stark S (eds), *The Unity of Public Law?: Doctrinal, Theoretical and Comparative Perspectives* (Hart Publishing 2018)

Elliott M, 'From Heresy to Orthodoxy: Substantive Legitimate Expectations in English Public Law' in Groves M and Weeks G (eds), *Legitimate Expectations in the Common Law World* (Hart Publishing 2016)

Feldman D, '*Anisminic Ltd v Foreign Compensation Commission* [1968]: In Perspective' in Juss S and Sunkin M (eds), *Landmark Cases in Public Law* (Hart Publishing 2017)

Forsyth C, "Blasphemy Against Basics': Doctrine, Conceptual Reasoning and Certain Decisions of the UK Supreme Court' in Bell J, Elliott M, Varuhas J and Murray P (eds), *Public Law Adjudication in Common Law Systems: Process and Substance* (Hart Publishing 2016)

Foster M, 'The Separation of Judicial Power' in Saunders C and Stone A (eds), *The Oxford Handbook of the Australian Constitution* (OUP 2018)

French R, 'Administrative Law in Australia: Themes and Values Revisited' in Groves M (ed), *Modern Administrative Law in Australia: Concepts and Context* (CUP 2014)

Friedman L, 'The Concept of Legal Culture: A Reply' in Nelken D (ed), *Comparing Legal Cultures* (Dartmouth 1997)

——, 'The Place of Legal Culture in the Sociology of Law' in Freeman M (ed), *Law and Sociology* (OUP 2006)

Gageler S, 'Legalism' in Blackshield T, Coper M and Williams G (eds), *The Oxford Companion to the High Court of Australian* (OUP 2001)

——, 'The Constitutional Dimension' in Groves M (ed), *Modern Administrative Law in Australia: Concepts and Context* (CUP 2014)

Groves M and Boughey J, 'Administrative Law in the Australian Environment' in Groves M (ed), *Modern Administrative Law in Australia: Concepts and Context* (CUP 2014)

Groves M and Lee HP, 'Australian Administrative Law: The Constitutional and Legal Matrix' in Groves M and Lee HP (eds), *Australian Administrative Law: Fundamentals, Principles and Doctrines* (CUP 2007)

Groves M and Weeks G, 'Modern Extensions of Substantive Review: A Survey of Themes in Taggart's Work and in the Wider Literature' in Wilberg H and Elliott M (eds), *The Scope and Intensity of Substantive Review: Traversing Taggart's Rainbow* (Hart Publishing 2015)

——, 'The Legitimacy of Expectations About Fairness: Can Process and Substance be Untangled?' in Bell J, Elliott M, Varuhas J and Murray P (eds), *Public Law Adjudication in Common Law Systems: Process and Substance* (Hart Publishing 2016)

Gummow W, 'Common Law' in Saunders C and Stone A (eds), *The Oxford Handbook of the Australian Constitution* (2018 OUP)

Hayne K, 'Rule of Law' in Saunders C and Stone A (eds), *The Oxford Handbook of the Australian Constitution* (2018 OUP)

Hirst J, 'Nation Building, 1901–14' in Bashford A and Macintyre S (eds), *The Cambridge History of Australia Volume2: The Commonwealth of Australia* (CUP 2013)
Hughes K, '*R v North and East Devon Health Authority* [2001]: *Coughlan* and the Development of Public Law' in Juss S and Sunkin M (eds), *Landmark Cases in Public Law* (Hart Publishing 2017)
Hunt M, 'Sovereignty's Blight: Why Contemporary Public Law needs the Concept of 'Due Deference'' in Bamforth N and Leyland P (eds), *Public Law in a Multi-layered Constitution* (Hart Publishing 2003)
Jackson V, 'Comparative Constitutional Law: Methodologies' in Rosenfeld M and Shaïo A (eds), *The Oxford Handbook of Comparative Constitutional Law* (OUP 2012)
Jowell J, 'Proportionality and Unreasonableness: Neither Merger nor Takeover' in Wilberg H and Elliott M (eds), *The Scope and Intensity of Substantive Review: Traversing Taggart's Rainbow* (Hart Publishing 2015)
——, 'Of Vires and Vacuums: The Constitutional Context of Judicial Review' in Forsyth C (ed), *Judicial Review and the Constitution* (Hart Publishing 2000)
——, 'Administrative Law' in Bogdanor V (ed), *The British Constitution in the Twentieth Century* (OUP 2003)
——, 'The Rule of Law' in Jowell J and O'Cinneide C (eds), *The Changing Constitution* (9th edn, OUP 2019)
King M, 'Comparing Legal Cultures in the Quest for Law's Identity' in Nelken D (ed), *Comparing Legal Cultures* (Dartmouth 1997)
Krygier M, 'The Hart-Fuller Debate: Transitional Societies and the Rule of Law' in Cane P (ed), *The Hart-Fuller Debate in the Twenty-first Century* (Hart Publishing 2010)
Laws J, '*Wednesbury*' in Forsyth C and Hare I (eds), *The Golden Metwand and the Crooked Cord: Essays in Honour of Sir William Wade QC* (Hart Publishing 1998)
——, 'Illegality: The Problem of Jurisdiction' in Forsyth C (ed), *Judicial Review and the Constitution* (Hart Publishing 2000)
Lee HP, 'Improper Purpose' in Groves M and Lee HP (eds), *Australian Administrative Law: Fundamentals, Principles and Doctrines* (CUP 2007)
Legrand P, 'What "Legal Transplants"?' in Nelken D and Feets J (eds), *Adapting Legal Cultures* (Hart Publishing 2001)
Loughlin M, 'Why the History of English Administrative Law is not Written' in Dyzenhaus D, Hunt M and Huscroft G (eds), *A Simple Common Lawyer: Essays in Honour of Michael Taggart* (Hart Publishing 2009)
Maitland W, 'The Shallows and Silences of Real Life' in HAL Fisher (ed), *Collected Papers* (CUP 1911)
Mason A, 'The Evolving Role and Function of the High Court' in Opeskin B and Wheeler F (eds), *The Australian Federal Judicial System* (Melbourne University Press 2000)
——, 'Mike Taggart and Australian Exceptionalism' in Dyzenhaus D, Hunt M and Huscroft G (eds), *A Simple Common Lawyer: Essays in Honour of Michael Taggart* (Hart Publishing 2009)
Merry SE, 'What is Legal Culture' in Nelken D (ed), *Using of Legal Culture* (Wildy, Simmonds & Hill Publishing 2012)
Michaels R, 'Functional Method' in Reimann M and Zimmermann R (eds), *The Oxford Handbook of Comparative Law* (2nd edn, OUP 2019)
Mortimer D, 'The Constitutionalisation of Administrative Law', in Saunders C and Stone A (eds) *The Oxford Handbook of the Australian Constitution* (OUP 2018)
Nelken D, 'Towards a Sociology of Legal Adaption' in Nelken D and Feest J (eds), *Adapting Legal Cultures* (Hart Publishing 2001)
——, 'Comparative Sociology of Law' in Benakar R and Travers M (eds), *Introduction to Law and Social Theory* (Hart Publishing 2002)
——, 'Comparative Law and Comparative Legal Studies' in Esin Ö and Nelken D (eds), *Comparative Law: A Handbook* (Hart Publishing 2007)

——, 'Defining and Using the Concept of Legal Culture' in Esin Ö and Nelken D (eds), *Comparative Law: A Handbook* (Hart Publishing 2007)
Owens N, 'The Judicature', in Saunders C and Stone A (eds) *The Oxford Handbook of the Australian Constitution* (OUP 2018)
Pennisi C, 'Sociological Uses of the Concept of Legal Culture' in Nelken D (ed), *Comparing Legal Cultures* (Dartmouth 1997)
Poole T, 'Between the Devil and the Deep Blue Sea' in Pearson L, Taggart M and Harlow C (eds), *Administrative Law in A Changing State: Essays in Honour of Mark Aronson* (Hart Publishing 2008)
Reimann M, 'Comparative Law and Neighbouring Disciplines' in Elliott M and Feldman D (eds), *The Cambridge Companion to Public Law* (CUP 2015)
Sidebotham N, 'Relevant and Irrelevant Considerations' in Groves M and Lee HP (eds), *Australian Administrative Law: Fundamentals, Principles and Doctrines* (CUP 2007)
Stewart C, 'The Doctrine of Substantive Unfairness and the Review of Substantive Legitimate Expectations' in Groves M and Lee HP (eds), *Australian Administrative Law: Fundamentals, Principles and Doctrines* (CUP 2007)
Taggart M, 'Reinventing Administrative Law' in Bamforth N and Leyland P (eds), *Public Law in a Multi-Layered Constitution* (Hart Publishing 2003)
Thomas R, 'Legitimate Expectations and the Separation of Powers in English and Welsh Administrative Law' in Groves M and Weeks G (eds), *Legitimate Expectations in the Common Law World* (Hart Publishing 2017)
Weeks G, 'Holding Government to its Word: Legitimate Expectations and Estoppels in Administrative Law' in Groves M (ed), *Modern Administrative Law in Australia: Concepts and Context* (CUP 2014)
Young S, 'Privative Clauses: Politics, Legality and the Constitutional Dimension' in Groves M (ed), *Modern Administrative Law in Australia: Concepts and Context* (CUP 2014)

Journal Articles

Airo-Farulla G, 'Rationality and Judicial Review of Administrative Action' (2000) 24 Melbourne University Law Review 543
Allan T, 'Legislative Intent and Legislative Supremacy: A Reply to Professor Craig' (2004) 24 OJLS 563
——, 'The Constitutional Foundations of Judicial Review: Conceptual Conundrum or Interpretative Inquiry?' (2002) 61 CLJ 87
——, 'Constitutional Dialogue and the Justification of Judicial review' (2003) 23 OJLS 563
——, 'Questions of Legality and Legitimacy: Form and Substance in British Constitutionalism' (2011) 9 International Journal of Constitutional Law 155
Aronson M, 'The Resurgence of Jurisdictional Facts' (2001) 12 Public Law Review 17
Arthurs HW, 'Rethinking Administrative Law: A Slightly Dicey Business' (1979) 17 Osgoode Hall LJ 1
Bell J, 'Rethinking the Story of *Cart v Upper Tribunal* and Its Implications for Administrative Law' (2019) 39 Oxford Journal of Legal Studies 74
——, 'The Privy Council and the Doctrine of Legitimate Expectation Meet Again' (2016) 75 CLJ 449
——, 'The Relationship between Judicial Review and the Upper Tribunal: What have the Courts made of *Cart*?' (2018) PL 394
Biehler H, 'Legitimate Expectation – An Odyssey' (2013) 50 Irish Jurist N S 40
Boughey J and Crawford L, 'Reconsidering *R (on the application of Cart) v Upper Tribunal* and the Rationale for Jurisdictional Error' (2017) PL 592

Brennan G, 'Courts, Democracy and the Law' (1991) 17 Commonwealth Law Bulletin 696
Brian P, 'The Enduring Importance of the Rule of Law in Times of Change' (2012) 86 Australian Law Journal 175
Bullen E, 'Legislative Limits on Environmental Decision-making: The Application of the Administrative Law Doctrines of Jurisdictional Fact and Ultra Vires' (2006) 23 EPLJ 265
Buxbaum HL, 'German Legal Culture and the Globalisation of Competition Law: A Historical Perspective on the Expansion of Private Antitrust Enforcement' (2005) 23 Berkeley Journal of International Law 474
Cane P, 'The Making of Australian Administrative Law' (2003) 24 Australian Bar Review 114
———, 'Judicial Review in the Age of Tribunals' [2009] PL 479
Challenor B, 'The Balancing Act: A Case for Structured Proportionality under the Second Limb of the Lange Test' (2015) 40 UW Austl L Rev 267
Craig P, 'Legislative Intent and Legislative Supremacy: A Reply to Professor Allan' (2004) 24 OJLS 585
———, 'Formal and Substantive Conceptions of the Rule of Law: An Analytical Framework' [1997] PL 467
———, 'Ultra Vires and the Foundations of Judicial Review' (1998) 57 CLJ 63
———, 'The Common Law, Shared Power and Judicial Review' (2004) 24 OJLS 237
———, 'Judicial Review, Appeal and Factual Error' [2004] PL 788
———, 'Proportionality, Rationality and Review' [2010] NZLR 265
———, 'The Nature of Reasonableness Review' (2013) 66 Current Legal Problems 131
———, 'Judicial Review and Anxious Scrutiny: Foundations, Evolution and Application' [2015] PL 60
Craig R, 'Ouster Clauses, Separation of Powers and the Intention of Parliament: from *Anisminic* to *Privacy International*' (2018) PL 570
Crawford L and Boughey J, 'The Centrality of Jurisdictional Error: Rationale and Consequences' (2019) 30 PLR 18
Dixon O, 'The Law and the Constitution' (1935) 51 LQR 590
———, 'Aspects of Australian Federalism' (1944) 5 The University of Toronto Law Journal 241
———, 'Judicial Method' [1956] 29 ALJ 468
Dworkin R, 'Hart's Postscript and the Character of Political Philosophical' (2004) 24 OJLS 23
Elliott M, 'The Ultra Vires Doctrine in a Constitutional Setting: Still the Central Principle of Administrative Law' (1999) 58 CLJ 129
Elliott M and Thomas R, 'Tribunal Justice and Proportionate Dispute Resolution' (2012) 71 CLJ 297
Endicott T, 'Questions of Law' (1998) 114 LQR 292
Fallon R, 'The Rule of Law as a Concept in Constitutional Discourse' (1997) 97 Columbia Law Review 1
Feldman D, 'The Nature of Legal Scholarship' (1989) 52 MLR 498
Finn C, 'Constitutionalising Supervisory Review at State Level: The End of Hickman?' [2010] Public Law Review 92
Fisher E, 'Food Safety Crises as Crises in Administrative Constitutionalism' (2010) 20 Health Matrix 55
———, '"Jurisdictional" Facts and "Hot" Facts: Legal Formalism, Legal Pluralism, and the Nature of Australian Administrative Law' (2015) 38 Melbourne University Law Review 968
———, 'Environmental Law as "Hot Law"' (2013) 25 Journal of Environmental Law 347
Forsyth C, 'The Provenance and Protection of Legitimate Expectations' [1988] CLJ 238
———, 'Of Fig Leaves and Fairy Tales: the Ultra Vires Doctrine, the Sovereignty of Parliament and Judicial Review' (1996) 55 CLJ 122
Friedman L, 'Is there a Modern Legal Culture?' (1994) 7 Ratio Juris 117
Fuller L, 'The Forms and Limits of Adjudication' (1978) 92 Harvard Law Review 353
Gageler S, 'The Underpinnings of Judicial Review of Administrative Action' (2000) 28 Federal Law Review 303

Galligan D, 'Judicial Review and the Textbook Writers' (1982) 2 OJLS 257
Gellhorn E and Robinson G, 'Perspectives on Administrative Law' (1975) 75 Columbia Law Review 771
Gordon S, 'The Relation of Facts to Jurisdiction' (1929) 45 QLR 458
Gould B, '*Anisminic* and Jurisdictional Review' [1970] PL 358
Groves M, 'Substantive Legitimate Expectations in Australian Administrative Law' (2008) 32 Melb UL Rev 470
Hammond, 'The Judiciary and the Executive' (1991) 1 Journal of Judicial Administration 81
Harlow C, 'Changing the Mindset: The Place of Theory in English Administrative Law' (1994) 14 OJLS 419
Hayne K, 'Deference: An Australian Perspective' [2010] PL 75
Heydon D, 'Judicial Activism and the Death of the Rule of Law' 10 Otago L Rev 493
Hickman T, 'Problems for Proportionality' [2010] New Zealand Law Review 303
Jaffe LL, 'Judicial Review: Constitutional and Jurisdictional Fact' (1957) 70 Harvard Law Review 953
Jaffe LL and Henderson E, 'Judicial Review and the Rule of Law: Historical Origins' (1956) 72 Quarterly Review
Josev T, 'The Late Arrival of the "Judicial Activism" Debate in Australian Public Discourse' (2013) 24 Public Law Review 17
Jowell J, 'Beyond the Rule of Law: Towards Constitutional Judicial Review' [2000] PL 671
Kirby M, 'Judicial Activism: Power without Responsibility-No, Appropriate Activism Conforming to Duty' (2006) 30 Melb UL Rev 576
Knight Chistopher, 'The Rule of law, Parliamentary Sovereignty and the Ministerial Veto' (2015) 131 The Law Quarterly Review 547
Krygier M, 'Law as Tradition' (1986) 5 Law and Philosophy
Laborde C, 'The Concept of the State in British and French Political Thought' (2000) 48 Political Studies 540
Lindell G, 'Why is Australia's Constitution Binding?' (1986) 16 Federal Law Review 29
Lübbe-Wolff, 'The Principle of Proportionality in the Case Law of the German Federal Constitutional Court' (2014) 34 HRLJ 12
Malsukhum V, 'Is Anything Lost by not Having Proportionality as a General Head of Judicial Review of Administrative Action' (2020) 49(2) Thammasat Law Journal 363
Mason A, 'Administrative Review – The Experience of the First Twelve Years' (1989) 18 Federal Law Review 122
——, 'Procedural Fairness: Its Development and Continuing Role of Legitimate Expectation' (2005) 12 Australian Journal of Administrative Law 103
Mason B, 'Jurisdictional Facts after *Plaintiff M70*' (2013) 24 PLR 37
McDonald L, 'Jurisdictional Error as Conceptual Totem' (2019) 42 UNSW Law Journal 1019
Metzger G, 'Administrative Law as the New Federalism' [2008] Duke Law Journal 2023
——, 'Administrative Constitutionalism' (2012) 91 Texas Law Review 1897
Nelken D, 'Disclosing/Invoking Legal Culture: An Introduction' (1995) 4 Social & Legal Studies 435
——, 'Using the Concept of Legal Culture' (2004) 29 Austl J Leg Phil 1
Oliver D, 'Is the 'Ultra Vires' Rule the Basis of Judicial Review?' [1987] PL 543
Pearson L, 'Jurisdictional Fact: a Dilemma for the Courts' (2000) 17 Environmental and Planning Law Journal 453
Preston B, 'Judicial Review of Illegality and Irrationality of Administrative Decisions in Australia' (2006) 18 Australian Bar Review 17
Raad C, '*Hossain v Minister for Immigration and Border Protection*: A Material Change to the Fabric of Jurisdictional Error?' (2019) 41(2) Sydney Law Review 265
Raz J, 'The Rule of Law and its Viture' (1977) 93 LQR 195
Reynolds P, 'Legitimate Expectations and the Protection of Trust in Public Officials' [2011] Public Law 330
Rivers J, 'Proportionality and Variable Intensity of Review' (2006) 65 CLJ 174

Sackville R, 'The Limits of Judicial Review of Executive Action – Some Compensations between Australia and the US' (2000) 28 Federal Law Review 331
Sales P and Steyn K, 'Legitimate Expectations in English Public law: An Analysis' [2004] PL 564
Samuel G, 'Can Legal Reasoning Demystified?' (2009) 29 Legal Studies 181
Saunders C, 'Constitution as Catalyst: Different Paths within Australian Administrative Law' (2012) 10 NZJPIL 154
Sawer G, 'Error of Law on the Face of an Administrative Record' (1956) 3 University of Western Australia Annual Law Review 24
Scott L, 'Evolution of Public Law' 14 J Comp Legis & Int'l L 163
Sedley S, 'Human Rights: a Twenty-First Century Agenda' [1995] PL 386
Selway B, 'The Principle behind Common Law Judicial Review of Administrative Action – The Search Continues' (2002) 30 Federal Law Review
Shapiro S, Fisher E and Wagner W, 'The Enlightenment of Administrative Law: Looking inside the Agency for Legitimacy' (2012) 47 Wake Forest Law Review 463
Spencer T, 'An Australian Rule of Law' (2014) 21 Australian Journal of Administrative Law 98
Spigelman J, 'The Integrity Branch of Government' 78 Australian Law Journal 724
——, 'The Centrality of Jurisdictional Error' 21 Public Law Review 77
Steele I, 'Substantive Legitimate Expectations: Striking the Right Balance?' (2005) 121 Law Quarterly Review 300
Stellios J, 'Concepts of Judicial Review: Commentary on Dixon' (2015) 43 Federal Law Review 511
Stone A, 'The Limits of Constitutional Text and Structure: Standards of Review and the Freedom of Political Communication' (1999) 23 Melb U L Rev 668
Sunstein CR and Vermeule A, 'The New Coke: On the Plural Aims of Administrative Law' (2016) 2015.1 The Supreme Court Review 41
Taggart M, 'Australian Exceptionalism in Judicial Review' (2008) 36 Federal Law Review 1
——, 'Proportionality, Deference, *Wednesbury*' [2008] NZL Rev 423
Tomlinson J, 'The Narrow Approach to Substantive Legitimate Expectations and the Trend of Modern Authority' (2017) 17 Oxford University Commonwealth Law Journal 75
Wait M, 'The Slumbering Sovereign: Sir Owen Dixon's Common Law Constitution Revisited' (2001) 29 Federal Law Review 57
Webber J, 'Culture, Legal Culture, and Legal Reasoning: A Comment on Nelken' (2004) 29 Austl J Leg Phil 27
Williams R, 'When is an Error not an Error? Reform of Jurisdictional Review of Error of Law and Fact' [2007] PL 793
——, 'The Multiple Doctrines of Legitimate Expectations' (2016) 132 LQR 639
——, 'Structuring Substantive Review' [2017] PL 99
Woolf L, 'Droit Public- English Style' [1995] PL 57
——, 'Judicial Review- The Tensions Between the Executive and the Judiciary' (1998) 114 LQR 579
Young S and Murray S, 'An Elegant Convergence? The Constitutional Entrenchment of 'Jurisdictional Error' Review in Australia' (2015) 11 Oxford University Commonwealth Law Journal 117
Young A, 'In Defence of Due Deference' (2009) 72 MLR 554

Speeches

Chief Justice French, 'Australia's Constitutional Evolution' (John Fordham Law School Constitutional Law Master Class, 20 January 2010)
——, 'Courts in a Representative Democracy' (University of Southern Queensland, Toowoomba, 25 June 2010)

——, 'The Courts and the Parliament' (Queensland Supreme Court Seminar, Brisbane, 4 August 2012)

——, 'The Rule of Law as a Many Coloured Dream Coat' (20th Annual Lecture Singapore Academy of Law, Singapore, 18 September 2013)

——, 'Common Law Constitutionalism' (Robin Cooke Lecture, Wellington, New Zealand, 27 November 2014)

——, 'Statutory Interpretation and Rationality in Administrative Law' (National Administrative Law Lecture, Canberra, 23 July 2015)

——, 'The Globalisation of Public Law: A Quilting of Legalities' (Public Law Conference, Cambridge, 12 September 2016)

Chief Justice Gleeson, 'Legality: Spirit and Principle' (The Second Magna Carta Lecture, New South Wales Parliament House, Sydney, 20 November 2003)

——, 'Judicial Legitimacy' (Australian Bar Association Conference, New York, 2 July 2000)

——, 'Courts and the Rule of Law' (The Rule of Law Series, Melbourne University, 7 November 2001)

——, 'The Role of a Judge in a Representative Democracy' (Judiciary of the Commonwealth of the Bahamas, 4 January 2008)

Justice Gageler, 'What is a Question of Law?' (The National Conference of Tax Institute Justice Hill Memorial Lecture, March 2014)

Justice Hayne, '"Concerning Judicial Method"- Fifty Years on' (The Fourteenth Lucinda Lecture, Monash University, 17 October 2006)

Justice Kirby, 'Judicial Activism' (The Bar Association of India Lecture, New Delhi, 6 January 1997)

Justice McHugh, 'Tensions between the Executive and the Judiciary' (Australian Bar Association Conference, Paris, 10 July 2002)

——, 'Judicial Method' (Democracy and the Law, the Australian Bar Association Conference, London, 5 July 1998)

Lady Hale, 'The Supreme Court in the United Kingdom Constitution' (The Bryce Lecture 2015, Oxford, 5 February 2015)

——, 'UK Constitutionalism on the March?' (The Constitutional and Administrative Law Bar Association Conference, 12 July 2014)

——, 'Who Guards the Guardians?' (Public Law Project Conference, 14 October 2013)

Lord Carnwath, 'From Judicial Outrage to Sliding Scales: Where Next for *Wednesbury*' (the ALBA Annual Lecture, 12 November 2013)

Lord Hope, 'The Role of the Supreme Court in Protecting the Rights of the Individual in a Jurisdiction with no Written Constitution' (Remarks made to introduce the Glasgow Bar Association Seminar, 9 December 2011)

Lord Mance, 'The Rule of Law – Common Traditions and Common Issues' (175th Anniversary of Founding of Hoge Raad, the Netherlands, 1 October 2013)

Lord Neuberger, 'The Role of Judges in Human Rights Jurisprudence: A Comparison of the Australian and UK experience' (Conference at the Supreme Court of Victoria, Melbourne, 8 August 2014)

——, 'The Supreme Court and the Rule of Law' (The Conkerton Lecture, 9 October 2014)

——, 'The UK Constitutional Settlement and the Role of the UK Supreme Court' (The Legal Wales Conference, 10 October 2014)

Lord Phillips, 'Judicial Independence and Accountability: A View from the Supreme Court' (The Politics of Judicial Independence, 8 February 2011)

Lord Sumption, 'Anxious Scrutiny' (Bar Association Annual Lecture, 4 November 2014)

Murray P, 'Process, Substance and the History of Error of Law Review' (Cambridge Public Law Conference, September 2014)

Sir Brennan, 'The Parliament, the Executive and the Courts: Roles and Immunities' (School of Law, Bond University, 21 February 1998)
Justice Spigelman, 'Jurisdictional Integrity' (2nd Lecture National Lecture Series for the Australian Institute of Administrative Law, 5 August 2004)

Conference Papers and Websites

Drewry G, 'The Judicialisation of "Administrative" Tribunals in the UK: From Hewart to Leggatt' (2009) 28 TRAS http://rtsa.ro/tras/index.php/tras/article/view/27
Fisher L, 'Challenging Land Use Decisions in the UK and Australia: Three Overlapping Narratives' (Cityscapes: A Conference on Comparative Land Use Law, Yale Law School, 1–2 April 2016)
Gardner J, 'Can there be a Written Constitution?' http://papers.ssrn.com/sol3/papers.cfm?abstract_id=1401244
Waluchow W, 'Constitutionalism' The Stanford Encyclopedia of Philosophy https://plato.stanford.edu/archives/spr2014/entries/constitutionalism/

Policy Documents

Australian Commonwealth Administrative Review Committee Report, *Kerr Report* (Parliamentary Paper no 144/1972, August 1971)
Administrative Review Council Federal Judicial Review in Australia, *Report No 50* (2012)
Committee on Administrative Tribunals and Enquiries, *Report 1957*
Committee on Ministers' Powers, *Report 1932*
Review of Administrative Law in the United Kingdom, *Discussion Paper April 1981*
Review of Tribunals by Sir Andrew Leggatt, *Tribunals for users: One system, One service 2001*
The Law Commission, *A Consultation Paper No. 180 on Housing: Proportionate Dispute Resolution – The Role of Tribunals*
Judicial Review: Proposals for further reform, 2013, Cm 8703

Others

Thai Dictionary (Royal Society Version) B.E. 2554
Oxford Advance Learner's Dictionary (9th edn, OUP 2015)